FUNDAMENTALS *of* PSYCHOLOGY

Applications for Life and Work

M.

Fundamentals of

PSYCHOLOGY

Applications for Life & Work

Joseph Culkin, Ph.D.
Professor
Department of Social Science
Queensborough Community College
of the City University of New York

Richard S. Perrotto, Ph. D.
Professor
Department of Social Science
Queensborough Community College
of the City University of New York

South-Western Educational Publishing

I(T)P

International Thomson Publishing

South-Western Educational Publishing is a division of International Thomson Publishing Inc. The ITP trademark is used under license.

Library of Congress Cataloging-in Publication Data

Culkin, Joseph
    Fundamentals of psychology : applications for life and work /
Joseph Culkin, Richard S. Perrotto.
        p. 408   cm.
    Includes bibliographical references and index.
    ISBN 0-538-65048-6
    1. Psychology.   I. Perrotto, Richard S.   II. Title.
    BF121.C79   1996   94-6813
    150—dc20   CIP

               Editor in Chief: *Peter McBride*
            Project Manager: *Laurie Wendell*
    Production Coordinator: *Tricia Boies*
                      Editor: *Alan Biondi*
            Senior Designer: *Elaine St. John-Lagenaur*
               Photo Editor: *Kathryn Russell/Pix Inc.*
        Electronic Prepress: *A. W. Kingston Publishing, Inc.*
          Marketing Manager: *Carolyn Love*

1 2 3 4 5 6 7 8 9 VH 03 02 01 00 99 98 97 96 95

Printed in the United States of America

Contents

1   Introduction to Psychology

2

The Biological Roots of Behavior

3

Sensation and Perception

4

States of Consciousness

5

Learning

6

Memory

7

Thinking, Language, and Intelligence

8 — Human Growth and Development

9 — Motivation and Emotion

10

Personality

11

Psychology and Health

12

Abnormal Psychology and Therapy

13

Psychology of Social Behavior

14   Applied Psychology

Preface

Anyone who has taught courses in introductory psychology as long as we have surely has discovered that many students find the topic difficult to grasp. We believe that part of the reason lies in the nature of the material. Psychology is a discipline based on scientific methodology and often relies on complex research designs to gather data. Also, beginning students are struck immediately by the large vocabulary and often abstract concepts that psychologists use to explain behavior and mental processes. As a result, the typical student struggles to understand psychology and find much relevance to his or her own life. What should be an enlightening experience can quickly become a "turnoff."

Textbooks often reinforce students' feelings of being overwhelmed. Most provide too much material to be covered in a single course, contain too many "key terms," and they are not always explained succinctly. Furthermore, many texts emphasize research methodology at the expense of making the material relevant to students lives. These considerations motivated us to write an introductory psychology text that would be most accessible to students of psychology.

About This Text

We firmly believe that an introductory psychology textbook should cover the most fundamental topics in psychology in a concise manner. To this end, we have developed *Fundamentals of Psychology: Applications for Life and Work*. All the major topics found in other textbooks are included herein, but our book is briefer because we use straightforward language and have avoided unnecessary detail. Descriptions of research methodology, a necessary component of an introductory psychology text, are kept to a minimum and are balanced by applications from everyday life applications to make the material more relevant and enjoyable to students.

Features of This Text

The pedagogical elements of *Fundamentals of Psychology: Applications for Life and Work* were developed to help students understand psychology's basic principles and terminology and discover its relevance to their lives.

1. **Outline:** Each chapter begins with an outline of A- and B-level heads which provides just enough information to acquaint the reader with the main topics of the chapter.

2. **Learning Objectives:** The chapter outline is followed by a list of learning objectives that focus on the chapter's main topic areas. Generally, each learning objective corresponds to topics listed in the chapter outline and forms the basis of the end-of-chapter summary.

3. **Chapter Opener:** Each chapter opens with a hypothetical situation or brief, real-life vignette which bears on an important topic from the chapter. Where pertinent, we draw upon the chapter opener in the narrative to illustrate aspects of the chapter material.

4. **Boldfaced Terms:** The most important terms in each chapter appear in boldfaced print and are clearly explained. Important terms have been limited to around 25 per chapter. Boldfaced terms are also included in a marginal and end-of-text glossary.

5. **Marginal Glossary:** All boldfaced terms in the narrative are presented in the margins as abbreviated definitions to enhance the reader's learning experience. Phonetic spellings of difficult-to-pronounce terms are included in the marginal glossary.

6. **Issues and Applications:** To show the relevance of psychology to everyday life and work, we have included a special boxed feature called "Issues and Applications." Each chapter has two installments of this feature. One focuses on an important issue in psychology applied to everyday life such as "Improving Your Study Skills," in Chapter 6, "Memory." The second deals with an application of psychology to work situations like "Sexual Harassment in the Workplace" in Chapter 14, "Applied Psychology."

7. **Biography:** Each chapter features a brief biographical sketch of an important figure in psychology. The biography focuses on each individual's important contributions to psychology and, wherever possible, interesting aspects of the individual's personal life.

8. **Lists and Tables:** To simplify, summarize, and organize the material and to create visual appeal, each chapter contains bulleted lists and tables.

9. **Illustrations and Photographs:** The explanation of concepts and research findings is enhanced by illustrations—diagrams, graphs, and drawings. Each chapter also contains photographs, including those of important psychologists, to further enhance visual appeal.

10. **Summary:** Each chapter narrative concludes with a summary, presented in numbered paragraph form corresponding to like-numbered learning objective at the beginning of the chapter.

11. **Questions for Review and Discussion:** To complete the wraparound effect of the chapter and reinforce what students have learned, we provide one question to review each learning objective posed at the beginning of the chapter and summarized at the end of the chapter narrative.

12. **Applying Psychology:** Each chapter concludes with an activity which allows students to apply a principle or research finding learned in that chapter. Sometimes this feature involves a hypothetical situation for which the student must apply a psychological principle to find a solution. In other cases, the student can apply psychology to improve some aspect of his or her life.

13. **Glossary:** A standard glossary containing all boldfaced terms is provided at the end of the book.

14. **References:** All footnoted references numbered within the narrative are listed at the back of the textbook, by chapter and number within that chapter.

15. **Index:** Finally, we have included a single index that consists of both names and subjects.

Supplements to This Textbook

1. **Instructor's Guide:** The Instructor's Guide to accompany *Fundamentals of Psychology: Applications for Life and Work* is available to help in lecture preparation and presentation. For each text chapter there is a chapter overview and outline followed by suggestions for discussion and assignment. Ideas for lectures, classroom discussion, and student assignments and activities are provided to stimulate learning. The Instructor's Guide also includes an answer key to the Questions for Review and Discussion found at the end of the each chapter, brief chapter tests with answer keys, and transparency masters for classroom illustration.

2. **Computerized Test Bank:** Chapter tests and answer keys are provided on disk in Macintosh and DOS formats.

3. **Study Guide:** For the student, a softcover study guide is available which focuses on chapter objectives and a chapter outline in which students can fill in pertinent information about each section of the chapter. A key terms worksheet is provided for each chapter wherein important terms are listed and space is provided for students to write in their definitions. Finally, the Student Study Guide contains a pretest for each chapter consisting of 10 True/False, 10 multiple choice, and 5 short-answer questions.

Acknowledgments

The development and production of this text required hard work and a great expenditure of time by many people including the authors. We gratefully acknowledge the efforts and expertise of Delmar senior editor Mary McGarry, who was overseer of the project, and developmental editor, Bob Nirkind, whose knowledge and critical eye helped us to create and fine-tune the manuscript to its final form.

We also thank the following individuals for their review of the manuscript and for their feedback and suggestions.

- Ronald Basil, Pearl River High School; Pearl River, NY
- Steve Childres, Apollo College; Phoenix, AZ
- Sandra Ciccarelli, Gulf Coast Community College; Panama City, FL
- Larry Dohrn, San Antonio College; San Antonio, TX
- Ben Engelberg, PCI Health Training Center; Dallas, TX

- Brenda Martin-Smith, Edgewater High School; Orlando, FL
- Jim Matiya, Carl Sandburg High School; Orland Park, IL
- Christopher Potter, Harrisburg Area Community College; Harrisburg, PA
- Richard Stride, Lamar Community College; Lamar, CO
- Beth Wirick, Davis Junior College of Business; Toledo, OH
- Maria Witkus, Glenbard North High School; Carol Stream, IL

Last but not least, we are grateful to our families whose patience and support was an important ingredient in the preparation of this book.

About the Authors

Joseph Culkin is a professor in the Department of Social Sciences at Queensborough Community College of the City University of New York, where he has taught since 1979. Professor Culkin teaches courses in introductory psychology, abnormal psychology, childhood disorders, adjustment, and personality. After receiving his doctorate in psychology from the Graduate Faculty of the New School for Social Research in 1980, Dr. Culkin pursued postgraduate training in behavioral psychotherapy and marriage and family counseling, and he has accrued extensive clinical experience through his work as a psychotherapist. With Dr. Perrotto he is coauthor of the textbook *Exploring Abnormal Psychology* (Harper Collins, 1993). His research interests include depression, family psychopathology, nonverbal communication, and gender roles. Dr. Culkin is a New York State-licensed psychologist and a member of the American Psychological Association, New York State Psychological Association, and Queens County Psychological Association.

Richard S. Perrotto is a professor in the Department of Social Sciences at Queensborough Community College of the City University of New York, where he has taught since 1978. Professor Perrotto teaches courses in abnormal and physiological psychology and personality as well as introductory psychology. He received his doctorate in psychology from the University of Delaware in 1979. Professor Perrotto is a New York State-licensed psychologist with postdoctoral training in behavioral psychotherapy, and he has extensive experience in the evaluation and treatment of many types of client problems. He has published scientific articles in the areas of abnormal psychology and physiological psychology and is coauthor with Dr. Culkin of the textbook *Exploring Abnormal Psychology* (Harper Collins, 1993). Professor Perrotto is a member of the American Psychological Association and the Queens County Psychological Association.

FUNDAMENTALS *of* PSYCHOLOGY

Applications for Life and Work

Chapter 1

Introduction to Psychology

After completing this chapter, you should be able to:

1. Define psychology and identify its goals.

2. Identify the main specializations and career areas in modern psychology.

3. Summarize the ideas of the major schools of psychology.

4. Distinguish among the research methods of naturalistic observation, case study, survey, and correlation.

5. Explain how a controlled experiment is conducted in psychology.

6. Identify the major ethical principles in psychological research.

▼

psychology—*science of behavior and mental processes*

Imagine an extraterrestrial scientist who has been sent to our planet to study what we call psychology. This scientist seeks out some famous psychologists to ask them about their work and receives some of the following answers:

▶ "I treat people who are mentally ill and cannot cope with everyday life."

▶ "I guide employers in selecting workers who will be productive."

▶ "I examine the brain activity of rats and mice to understand how they learn."

▶ "I test schoolchildren to determine whether they need special help in reading."

▶ "I investigate the biological mechanisms that control our emotions and personality."

▶ "I study why people forget."

Faced with such diverse answers, our visitor might be very puzzled about this field called psychology. As you begin this book, you are in a position similar to that scientist. You will learn in the coming chapters that psychology encompasses all of the preceding interests and many more. To begin your exploration of this curious field, let us first consider the definition and goals of psychology.

The Nature of Psychology

Psychology today is a science with many faces. Like other modern sciences, psychology is very specialized, and the activities of specialists in one part of the field may have little or no connection with those in other parts. Despite its diversity, psychology is a unified field in terms of its basic definition and goals.

Defining Psychology

What is psychology? You might offer many answers to that question. Because psychology is a complex and broad field, several of your definitions would probably fit. Today, most psychologists agree that **psychology** is the science of behavior and mental processes. According to this definition, psychology studies both your observable objective actions, or *behavior*, and your unobservable subjective actions, or *mental processes*.

The scope of modern psychology is enormous: it touches upon virtually all aspects of human and animal activity. Because psychology includes so many topics, it overlaps considerably with other disciplines. As you will learn in the chapters to come, psychology has a close relationship with the fields of biology, medicine, philosophy, and the social sciences.

The goals of psychology are to describe, explain, predict, and control behavior and mental processes. *Description* is the first goal in any science. Achieving this goal requires that psychology answer the questions what, when, and where in regard to its subject matter. If you were to ask questions such as the following, you would be seeking to describe some psychological events:

▶ What was the child's reaction to stress?

▶ When did the student first solve a problem?

▶ Where are the conditions best for learning?

The science of psychology seeks to describe, explain, and predict the complexities of human behavior and mental processes.

Description is important in its own right, but it is also necessary in order to explain behavior and mental processes. Answering what, when, and where questions in a precise manner helps in developing an explanation. The goal of *explanation* in psychology is pursued by attempts to understand the causes and consequences of psychological events. In other words, you try to answer the question why? Such questions may include:

▶ Why are some people addicted to drugs?

▶ Why do certain traits run in families?

▶ Why does your memory fail?

In exploring why questions, psychology seeks to discover the laws that explain general patterns or principles behind events. If you can explain the causes of psychological events, then you can speculate about other events that might occur. The goal of *prediction* leads psychologists to imagine how people might think, act, or feel in some future situations. There are many reasons to want to predict events in psychology:

▶ Will a criminal have a violent outburst?

▶ Will a student succeed in her educational efforts?

▶ Will couples learn to communicate better?

How well you are able to predict events depends on how accurate your explanations are. If behavior and mental processes are predictable, then they may also be controllable. The goal of *control* means that psychology attempts to influence the course of events. Efforts at control in psychology are often directed at solving practical problems:

▶ How can self-defeating thoughts be changed?

▶ How might retarded children be educated?

▶ How could work conditions improve employee health?

Can you think of some practical applications that might be possible if behavior and mental processes could be controlled? Despite its potential value, control is an idea that some people find offensive because it suggests an image of a mad scientist interfering with people's minds and lives. In fact, psychology's goal of control is pursued in the service of human welfare and is guided by a code of ethics that protects human rights and dignity.

Specializations and Careers in Psychology

Modern psychology has grown in the past century from a small academic field to an enterprise that influences your life as well as the lives of many people around you. Today, in the United States, more than 100,000 psychologists work in dozens of specialty areas. At present the American Psychological Association (APA), the main professional organization for psychologists in the United States, has 48 divisions, reflecting the enormous diversity in modern psychology (see Table 1.1). The distribution of APA members in major fields is depicted in Figure 1.1.

Throughout this text many aspects of psychology will be examined, but you will not be reading about all 48 specializations—that would take a dozen books! You will instead learn about the fundamental areas to provide you with a good overview of modern psychology. Table 1.2 summarizes the major areas of specialization that you will be reading about in the chapters to come.

Table 1.1 Divisions of the APA

General Psychology	Military Psychology	Psychology of Women
Teaching of Psychology	Adult Development and Aging	Psychology of Religion
Experimental Psychology	Applied Experimental and Engineering Psychology	Child, Youth, and Family Services
Evaluation, Measurement, and Statistics	Rehabilitation Psychology	Health Psychology
Physiological and Comparative Psychology	Consumer Psychology	Psychoanalysis
Developmental Psychology	Theoretical and Philosophical Psychology	Clinical Neuropsychology
Personality and Social Psychology	Experimental Analysis of Behavior	American Psychological-Law Society
Psychological Study of Social Issues	History of Psychology	Independent Practice
Psychology and the Arts	Community Psychology	Family Psychology
Clinical Psychology	Psychopharmacology and Substance Abuse	Study of Lesbian and Gay Issues
Consulting Psychology	Psychotherapy	Study of Ethnic Minority Issues
Industrial and Organizational Psychology	Psychological Hypnosis	Media Psychology
Educational Psychology	State Psychological Association Affairs	Exercise and Sport Psychology
School Psychology	Humanistic Psychology	Peace Psychology
Counseling Psychology	Mental Retardation and Developmental Disabilities	Group Psychology and Group Psychotherapy
Psychologists in Public Service	Population and Environmental Psychology	Addictive Behaviors

Figure 1.1 Specializations of APA Members

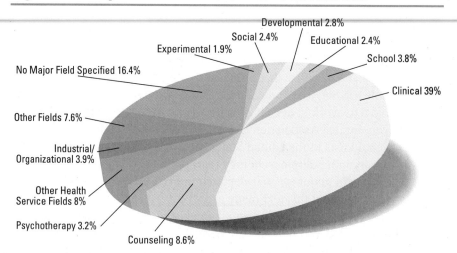

The percentage of members of the American Psychological Assocoation who report a major specialization.

Source: Adapted from American Psychological Association Education Directorate (1991). Current Major Field of APA Members by Membership Status, 1991. Washington, D.C.: Author

Table 1.2 Selected Major Specializations in Psychology

Specialization	Interests
Applied Psychology	Applications of psychological theory and research in everyday life and work
Clinical Psychology	Causes and treatments for abnormal behavior or mental disorders
Cognitive Psychology	Cognition or thinking, including problem solving, language, memory, intelligence, and creativity
Developmental Psychology	Individual development over the lifespan from conception to death
Experimental Psychology	Experimental study of sensation, perception, learning, emotion, and motivation
Health Psychology	Use of psychological principles and practices in understanding and promoting health
Personality Psychology	Personality, individual differences, and personality assessment
Physiological Psychology	Biological basis of behavior and mental processes in nervous system activity and genetic mechanisms
Social Psychology	Social behavior, attitudes, and social influences on individuals and groups

As modern psychology continues to expand, the variety of careers in this exciting field also grows. Today, the largest concentration of psychologists is in mental health careers. Over half of APA members report mental health settings as their primary place of employment. These professionals work in hospitals, health service agencies, clinics, counseling centers, and in independent practice. Psychologists in mental health professions perform a variety of duties. They evaluate adults and children, diagnose mental disorders, and conduct therapy. In addition, they administer tests of personality, aptitudes, and emotional states and perform evaluations for legal matters such as child custody cases.

Clinical psychologists in mental health settings often work with other health professionals such as psychiatrists and social workers as members of mental health care teams. Although their activities sometimes overlap, there are some important educational differences among these mental health professionals, as indicated in Table 1.3.

Table 1.3 Mental Health Professions

Profession	Education
Clinical Psychologist	Master's (M.A., M.S.) or doctorate (Ph.D., Psy.D.) degree with clinical training
Psychiatrist	Medical degree (M.D.) with residency in a psychiatric facility
Social Worker	Bachelor's (B.S.W.) or master's degree (M.S.W.) with a clinical internship

Education and Employment in Psychology

Students often remark that psychology is a fascinating topic, but they wonder, "What can I do with it?" Actually, studying psychology can provide you with a foundation for career options in both psychology and other fields. Certainly most students who take an introductory course in psychology do not become psychologists, and even most psychology majors will work in other fields. The study of psychology can offer you many opportunities for employment, depending on your level of education.

Associate's Degrees (A.A., A.S.) generally require two years of full-time study at a junior or community college. Some possible jobs for an associate's-level individual include:

►health service aide	►mental health aide
►alcoholism counselor	►education paraprofessional
►drug abuse counselor	►laboratory assistant

Bachelor's Degrees (B.A., B.S.) usually take four years of full-time study at a college or university to complete. With a bachelor's degree in psychology the following jobs may be available:

►human service caseworker	►public health assistant
►recreational therapist	►occupational therapist
►high school teacher	►family services worker
►special education teacher	►laboratory technician
►research assistant	►personnel officer

Nearly one-third of all psychologists work primarily in a school or academic setting. Many teach at colleges and universities and conduct research in their specializations. You may have had contact with *school psychologists* in elementary or high school, where these individuals are involved in testing and counseling students. Also in the field of education are *educational psychologists*, who study teaching methods and develop programs to improve classroom instruction.

Careers for psychologists in business and industry have grown rapidly in recent years. Many companies employ *industrial and organizational psychologists* to conduct evaluations of employees and their job requirements and to correct job-related problems, such as accidents and absenteeism. *Consumer psychologists* work with businesses to innovate effective advertising and marketing strategies. For instance, a consumer psychologist

Master's Degrees (M.A., M.S., M.Ed.) typically are conferred after two years of full-time study beyond the bachelor's degree. A master's degree expands the professional opportunities that are open in psychology:

- psychotherapist
- vocational counselor
- school psychologist
- probation officer
- college teacher

- educational counselor
- personnel psychologist
- marriage counselor
- family counselor
- health care administrator

Doctorate Degrees (Ph.D., Psy.D., Ed.D.) are obtained after three to five years of full-time study after a master's degree. Professional work in all specializations is open to those with this level of education:

- private practitioner
- college teacher
- research director

- health care administrator
- academic administrator

Even if you pursue a career in a field that is not directly related to psychology, you will find that the study of psychology can be helpful. No matter what career path you take, you will almost certainly be working with or for other people. The study of psychology will give you a better understanding of yourself and others, and that will be an advantage to you in any line of work.[1,2]

would study your buying habits and attitudes to design an effective advertising campaign for a new product.

New careers regularly arise in psychology as its ideas are extended to emerging areas. For example, in recent years *sports psychologists* have begun to apply psychological principles to help athletes improve their performance. At present, the majority of psychologists work either in mental health or educational settings, as shown in Figure 1.2, but in the future psychologists will certainly find other areas to develop. Anywhere that you find an interest in human behavior and mental life (and that's nearly everywhere), you will also find potential careers for psychologists. In *Issues and Applications: Education and Employment in Psychology*, you will learn about some of the many opportunities for work in this growing field.

Figure 1.2 Primary Work Settings of APA Members

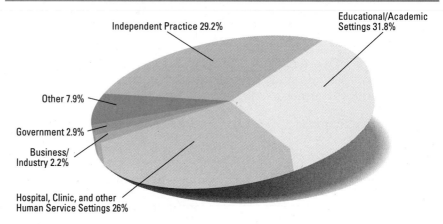

Independent Practice 29.2%

Educational/Academic Settings 31.8%

Other 7.9%

Government 2.9%

Business/Industry 2.2%

Hospital, Clinic, and other Human Service Settings 26%

The percentage of members of the American Psychological Association who report working professionally in a specific setting.

Source: *Adapted from American Psychological Association Office of Demographic, Employment, and Educational Research (1991). Employment Characteristics of Members by Type of APA Membership (1989). Washington, DC: Author.*

Schools of Psychology

Scientific psychology has existed for only slightly more than a century. But the seeds of modern psychology were sewn long before by philosophers whose ideas grew into contemporary science and by natural and social scientists whose work prepared the ground for the emergence of psychology in the nineteenth century. By the late 1800s the new science of psychology emerged through the efforts of several groups of researchers who organized themselves into the early *schools of psychology*. Each school proposed a unique definition of psychology's subject matter and methods.[3] Table 1.4 summarizes the interests of the major schools.

Table 1.4 Major Schools of Psychology

School	Interests
Structuralism	Study of elements of the conscious mind through introspection
Functionalism	Adaptive functions of mind and behavior
Behaviorism	Objective study of observable behavior
Gestalt Psychology	Organized wholes or forms in behavior and mental life
Psychoanalytic School	Study of the unconscious mind by clinical methods
Humanistic Psychology	Individual uniqueness and development

Structuralism

The first school of psychology was **structuralism**, which sought to describe the structure of the conscious mind. In 1879 Wilhelm Wundt, often called the father of psychology, established the first psychological research laboratory in Leipzig, Germany, marking the beginning of modern psychology. Wundt and his colleagues conducted pioneering studies in vision, hearing, touch, and memory. One of Wundt's students, E. B. Titchener (1867-1927), taught for many years at Cornell University in New York State, where he tried to expand structuralism into a general theory of psychology.

structuralism—school that studies the structure of conscious mind through introspection

Biography: Wilhelm Wundt

Wilhelm Wundt (1832–1920) was the youngest of four children of a pastor in a rural German village. Wundt was an isolated child with no friends his own age. He was also a chronic daydreamer who did poorly in school. Failing out of a local high school, he transferred to a school in a larger town and despite mediocre grades won encouragement from his teachers because of his hard work. After high school Wundt began premedical studies, but he did so poorly in his first year that he had to start over the next year at another university. His determination and effort eventually were rewarded when he graduated at the top of his medical class at Heidelberg in 1855. After a year of training in physiology in Berlin, Wundt set out on a professional career that would last 65 years and propel him from an unknown laboratory assistant to international fame.

In the late 1850s Wundt began to teach and conduct research in physiology. His *Principles of Physiological Psychology* (1874) set the stage for experimental psychology by suggesting that consciousness could be scientifically studied through introspection. That book won him an appointment as professor of "scientific philosophy" at the university in Leipzig, where he remained for the next 42 years. The opening of his research laboratory (actually a small room for introspection studies) in 1879 marked the birth of psychology. At the time, university officials worried that Wundt's students might go insane from too much introspection. Their fears were unfounded, and Wundt's reputation grew.

Wundt was a tireless researcher and writer whose lifetime publications total nearly 60,000 pages. You would need almost three years to read it all at a rate of 50 pages a day! Many areas of psychology were advanced by Wundt's studies in sensation, perception, memory, thinking, language, and social psychology. His initiative was carried on by his students, many of whom also became important psychologists.[4]

William James

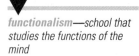

functionalism—school that studies the functions of the mind

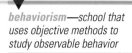

behaviorism—school that uses objective methods to study observable behavior

The structuralists studied the mind through the method of *introspection*. In introspection, you observe and analyze your subjective mental experiences, such as sensations and feelings. The structuralists hoped to discover the elements of consciousness in this manner and thereby to understand the mind. By the 1920s the influence of structuralism had diminished, because its methods and findings were considered too unreliable and subjective. Structuralism, however, had set the foundation for further developments in the study of sensation, perception, memory, and emotion.

Functionalism

In the late 1800s, while Wundt was establishing structuralism in Germany, an American philosopher and psychologist named William James (1842–1910) developed the basis for another school of psychology. James assumed that structuralism missed the truth of mental activity, which is a constantly changing "stream" of consciousness. James's **functionalism** emphasized the study of the functions of the mind, not its structure. The functionalist school considers how your mind works to be more important than what it contains.

This school was also influenced by the writings of biologist Charles Darwin, whose theory of *evolution* proposed that species evolve according to their ability to adapt to the environment. Functionalists such as John Dewey (1859–1952) assumed that psychological processes, as well as biological ones, have adaptive value, enhancing our ability to interact with our environments. In exploring these adaptive abilities, the functionalists studied normal mental processes in everyday life and changed the course of psychology in the fields of education, learning, and social behavior.

Behaviorism

The American psychologist John B. Watson (1878–1958) introduced **behaviorism**, a school that insisted that psychology must employ objective methods to study observable behaviors. Since its introduction in the early 1900s, scientific measurement and experimentation have been hallmarks of the behavioristic approach. Watson was dismayed by the subjectivity of structuralism and functionalism, and he believed that mental processes could never be studied scientifically. For behaviorism, psychology must replace the study of the mind with the study of behavior. In their research, behaviorists rely on objective methods by which they hope to uncover the laws of behavior.

Later behaviorists such as B. F. Skinner (1904–1990) developed this school into a dominant perspective in psychology. Skinner's *radical behaviorism* rejects the idea that mental events influence behavior and seeks instead to explain behavior in terms of objective events in the environment. Behaviorism has explored many issues in human and animal behavior, and its studies have revealed basic principles of learning and motivation that have led to applications in teaching, therapy, business, and everyday life. In later chapters you will learn more about modern behaviorism, particularly in the study of learning in Chapter 5.

Gestalt Psychology

In the early 1900s several German psychologists, including Max Wertheimer (1880–1943) and Wolfgang Köhler (1887–1967), were conducting creative studies of visual perception. Their school, called **Gestalt psychology**, emphasized the study of organized patterns in mental activity. In German, *Gestalt* means an organized whole or form. The Gestalt psychologists' studies of vision showed that a perceived whole (*Gestalt*) is different from the sum of its parts. When you look at a painting, for instance, your impression of it is not simply a combination of its parts, such as colors and objects, but a more general perception of the whole work. You will learn more about the Gestalt principles of perception in Chapter 3.

The Gestalt school employed scientific methods to study mind and behavior as organized activities of the whole person. In the years before World War II, the leading Gestaltists came to the United States, where they and their students expanded the school to include the psychology of personality, motivation, art, and problem solving.

*Gestalt (geh-**shtalt**) psychology*—school that studies organized patterns or wholes in mental activity

Psychoanalytic School

If you recognize only one name from the history of psychology, it is probably Sigmund Freud (1856–1939). You might not have realized, however, that Freud was a psychiatrist, not a psychologist. After being trained as a physician, he practiced psychiatry and developed the ideas that have had a significant impact on the course of modern psychology. Freud's **psychoanalytic school** explained psychological events as the result of unconscious mental forces. Psychoanalysts assume that your conscious mind is just the "tip of the iceberg," and that most of your mental activity is unconscious.

The psychoanalytic school relies on *clinical methods*, or strategies for treating mentally disturbed individuals. For example, a psychoanalyst would use dream interpretation as a method to explore the hidden wishes and needs of your unconscious mind (see Chapter 4). Few individuals have had as much impact on modern psychology as Freud. Since the late 1800s, the psychoanalytic school has grown into one of the dominant views on personality, development, abnormal behavior, and psychotherapy. You will learn more about this school in Chapters 10 and 12.

*psychoanalytic (sye-koh-anna-**li**-tik) school*—school that emphasizes unconscious forces in behavior and mind

Humanistic Psychology

Humanistic psychologists such as Abraham Maslow (1916–1972) and Carl Rogers (1902–1987) developed their school as an alternative to both the psychoanalytic school and behaviorism. **Humanistic psychology** focuses on the individual's uniqueness and capacity for healthy development. This school rejects both the behavioristic idea that you are controlled by your environment and the psychoanalytic concept of unconscious control. By contrast, humanistic psychology proposes that free will is important in your behavior, and thus you have responsibility for your actions.

Like the philosophy of *humanism* on which it is based, humanistic psychology promotes respect for the uniqueness and value of each individual.

humanistic psychology—school that focuses on individual uniqueness and development

In studying human behavior, the humanistic school emphasizes the need to understand the subjective experiences of the individual. This school has had considerable influence on the psychology of motivation (see Chapter 9) and personality (see Chapter 10), as well as on the treatment of abnormal behavior (see Chapter 12).

Modern Trends in Psychology

The early schools of psychology were responsible for establishing many of the basic principles and controversies that are found in psychology today. Some schools continue to influence modern psychology. For example, behaviorism, psychoanalysis, and humanistic psychology are still major perspectives. Although other schools no longer enjoy the status they once had, many of their ideas have been incorporated into the field.

In recent times a few other perspectives have emerged to take important places in the drama of psychology. The *cognitive perspective* stresses the importance of mental activities such as thinking, decision making, and interpretation in shaping your behavior. As you might expect, this view dominates the field of cognitive psychology, but it also affects other areas, such as personality and clinical psychology. In addition, this perspective has produced effective forms of treatment for some mental disorders.

Another modern trend in psychology is found in the *physiological perspective*, which looks to physiological mechanisms for explanations of behavior and mental processes. This view assumes that the primary causes of your thoughts, feelings, and actions lie in bodily activities, especially in your brain. The physiological perspective has produced studies that reveal the biological foundations of your behavior, emotions, motivation, and thought.

Many psychologists today recognize that ideas from both the early schools and modern perspectives have value. A thorough explanation of complex psychological events, however, often requires ideas from many sources. Contemporary psychologists are willing to borrow concepts from several viewpoints in order to understand behavior and mental processes. *Eclecticism* is an approach that combines the ideas of different schools or perspectives, rather than relying on a single point of view. As you will see in the chapters that follow, you often need to consider several points of view in order to understand human behavior.

Research in Psychology

Progress in psychology is governed by the rules of scientific research. Most of the information in this text is derived from research, and as the scope of psychology expands into new areas, more and more of your life and work will be affected by psychological research (see *Issues and Applications: On Being an Educated Consumer of Psychology*). Consequently, you will need to know how research is conducted and how to interpret it. In this section you will learn about the scientific method in psychology, as well as several research strategies, including naturalistic observation, case study, survey research, correlational research, and experimental research.

Scientific Method

While its interests are different from those of other sciences, psychology uses a method of study and discovery common to all sciences. The **scientific method** is a strategy of observation, theory formation, and hypothesis testing.

The fundamental activity of science is *observation*. By observing animals and people, psychologists hope to answer questions about the nature, causes, and consequences of behavior and mental processes. Answers to these questions are the basis of a *theory*, a general and logical explanation that organizes concepts and facts. To evaluate a theory you must test it against the evidence. A *hypothesis* is a testable prediction or assumption that you deduce from a theory. Let us say that you believe that intelligence is inherited. How can you prove or disprove your theory? You must first specify its hypotheses and then test them to see if they are correct. For example, one hypothesis would be that if intelligence is inherited, then your intellectual abilities would be more similar to your parents' abilities than to those of an unrelated person. This hypothesis flows logically from your theory and can be tested by collecting evidence about your intelligence, your parents' intelligences, and the intelligence of people unrelated to you.

Theories rise or fall according to whether they generate good hypotheses. Although theories are not true or false, they are more or less useful, depending on the accuracy of their hypotheses. A hypothesis is tested by accurate measurement of its terms. In psychological research, any measurable characteristic or term is called a *variable*. An **operational definition** is an objective measurement of a variable. For instance, to test your hypothesis about intelligence, you would probably use the standard operational definition of that variable: an IQ test.

To test a hypothesis, you must collect data from a **sample**, a group of research participants or subjects. The accuracy and usefulness of the research are affected by the selection of the sample. If you test your hypothesis about intelligence on only yourself, your parents, and your two best friends, you will not learn much about intelligence in the general population. Ideally, a research sample should be large and varied enough so that it is representative of the population. Most psychological research has relied on samples that do not adequately represent women, African Americans, and other minority groups. Recent guidelines to correct these biases have been recommended, and there appears to be improvement in balancing research for gender, but, the study of African American subjects has actually declined since the early 1970s.[5,6,7]

The science of psychology is an adventure that constantly changes and, in changing, alters our knowledge about ourselves and others. In this way, the scientific method proceeds: Observations lead to theories, hypotheses are tested to evaluate the theories, evidence is collected, theories are refined, and more hypotheses are tested. Scientific research in psychology depends on several methods that are summarized in Table 1.5.

▼
scientific method—strategy of observation, theory formation, and hypothesis testing

▼
operational definition—objective measurement of a variable

▼
sample—a group of research subjects

On Being an Educated Consumer of Psychology

You might not realize it, but you will almost certainly be a consumer of psychology during your life. In fact, you may already be one if you have ever used any services or engaged in activities that psychological research has influenced.

When you shop for groceries, psychology is probably the farthest thing from your mind. Nevertheless, your choice of a new breakfast cereal or soft drink is likely to have been anticipated by researchers who have tested shoppers' reactions to various package designs. Market researchers often use surveys and experiments to develop the best appearance for a product. The next time you buy something, consider how your decision has been shaped by research on consumer decision making and persuasion.[8]

Did you know that nearly 15 percent of the U.S. population receives some mental health services during a typical year? In addition, many others seek counseling for vocational or personal reasons. Perhaps you have sought counseling for some reason, or maybe you have bought a self-help book from your local bookstore. If you have, you

Table 1.5   Research Methods in Psychology

Method	Purpose
Naturalistic Observation	Study behavior in natural, real-life settings
Case Study	Examine in depth the life of one person or group
Survey	Collect information by interview or questionnaire
Correlation	Estimate statistical associations between variables
Experiment	Discover cause-and-effect relationships between variables

have benefited from psychological research on mental health and personal adjustment.

Even in the classroom, you may be influenced by psychological studies. Research helps educators design teaching aids to increase students' mastery of academic subjects. Standardized testing of academic skills and intelligence is also a part of many students' school experience. Such activities reflect the efforts of investigators from many fields, including psychology.

As you can see, psychological research has influence in many areas of everyday life. Not everyone, however, is pleased with the widespread influence of psychology. Some critics argue that the growing intrusion of psychology into modern life can have harmful effects on our education, family life, mental health, and spirituality.[9] Despite such criticism, psychology is here to stay, and it certainly will have some impact on your life. The simple fact that you are reading this book indicates that you are a consumer of psychology. For your part, the best strategy to follow is to know as much as you can about psychology so that you will be able to use that knowledge for your benefit.

Naturalistic Observation

The study of behavior in its natural setting or environment is called **naturalistic observation**. This method provides descriptions of how behavior occurs in everyday life. If you were interested in studying aggression in children, you would witness it firsthand by observing groups of children in their natural settings, such as a schoolyard.

▼
naturalistic observation— study of behavior in natural settings

Although naturalistic observation can yield real-life facts about behavior, there are problems with this method. Suppose that you were being observed by a researcher studying classroom behavior. You might not act as you usually do, because you know that someone is watching. The problem of *reactivity* means that subjects react to the fact of being observed and thus do not behave as they ordinarily would. As a result, the researcher obtains evidence that is invalid. *Observer bias* may further distort the observations because of the observer's prior expectations or attitudes. For example, if you as a researcher assume that boys are more aggressive than girls, you might pay more attention to boys' aggression and reach a conclusion that reflects that bias.

The Case Study

The **case study** is an in-depth investigation of an individual or group. Case studies reveal detailed personal or biographical information about their subjects and provide insights into their behavior. Historically, case studies have been important in research on abnormal behavior and personality. Freud, for example, used case studies of his patients to support his psychoanalytic theories. Today, this method is most often employed in clinical psychology to detail an individual's abnormal development and functioning.

The case study, too, may be influenced by observer bias. Freud, for instance, interpreted the evidence from his case studies in a way that supported his theories. Not only are case studies open to observer bias, but their findings may not necessarily apply to anyone other than the subject of the study. No matter how much you know about one person or group, that knowledge may not tell you much about other people. This lack of *generalizability* limits the usefulness of case studies in discovering general principles of behavior.

case study—in-depth investigation of individual or group

Survey Research

A **survey** is a method of collecting data by conducting interviews with or administering questionnaires to subjects. This method is a relatively direct means of acquiring information about attitudes, behaviors, and perceptions. Marketing researchers and political pollsters, as well as psychologists, rely on surveys to gather information.

A drawback to surveys is the questionable accuracy of the results. The *validity* of the results depends on the subjects' giving complete and honest answers. Suppose you were surveying your peers about whether they practice safe sex; you might find that they are not perfectly frank about such personal matters. A survey's validity also depends on how good a sample is chosen. Small, unusual, or biased samples will distort the results. For instance, if your safe sex survey included only your immediate circle of friends who have similar interests, habits, and backgrounds, its findings would not have much generalizability.

survey—method of data collection by interview or questionnaire

Correlational Research

Are drug abuse and mental illness related? Is there a link between poverty and crime? Do intelligence and creativity go together? If you ever wonder about such things, you are questioning the relationships between psychological variables. Psychologists, too, question the relationships among the many variables of behavior and mental life. **Correlational research** is a method for describing those relationships by analyzing statistical associations, or *correlations*, between variables. Several procedures measure correlation by estimating the strength and type of relationship between variables. A *correlation coefficient* is an estimate with a value between -1 and $+1$. The strength of correlation is shown by the value of the number, with larger numbers showing stronger associations. The type of association is shown by the plus (positive) or minus (negative) sign.

correlational research—method to describe statistical associations between variables

A **positive correlation** means that the variables have values that change in the same direction: They tend to increase or decrease together. If you were in a class where a positive correlation existed between attendance and final grades, your attendance and final grade would rise or fall together. High attendance would correspond to a high grade, and low attendance to a low grade. By contrast, in a **negative correlation** variables tend to change in opposite directions: As one increases, the other decreases. For instance, a negative correlation between test failure and confidence means that students with more test failures would have lower confidence, and those with fewer failures would have higher confidence.

Correlations tell you about associations between variables, but they do not completely explain them. Even a strong correlation informs you only about a *general trend*, not about the exceptions. You may find a positive correlation between class attendance and final grades, but there probably will be exceptions: Students who rarely attend class and get good grades, and those who always attend but fail. In addition, correlations do not give you definite conclusions about cause-and-effect relationships. If you find a negative correlation between test failure and confidence, you do not know why it exists. Do failures cause a lack of confidence? Perhaps, but maybe a lack of confidence causes failure. In addition, the *third-variable problem* may be at work; for example, another variable, such as test-taking anxiety, may affect both failure and confidence. Ultimately, a correlation always leaves you with uncertainty about cause-and-effect relationships between variables.

Experimental Research

Although correlations do not answer the question of *causation*, researchers are often interested in causal relationships between psychological variables. An **experiment** is a method that examines cause-and-effect relationships through controlled manipulations and observations. A typical psychology experiment involves three procedures: *manipulation*, *observation*, and *control*. Figure 1.3 diagrams the major steps in an experiment.

To judge whether a cause-and-effect relationship exists, you must carefully manipulate one variable and observe the effects of your manipulation on another variable. The manipulated variable is called the **independent variable** and is assumed to be the cause in the cause-and-effect relationship. The variable that is observed for changes that follow the manipulation is the **dependent variable**, which is thought to be the effect. In order to judge the influence of the independent variable on the dependent variable, you must first be certain that nothing else is affecting the dependent variable. In addition to the independent variable, many other factors, called **extraneous variables**, may influence the dependent variable; they must be controlled to lessen their impact.

Suppose you are conducting an experiment to test a vitamin that is intended to boost memory. Your independent variable, the vitamin, would be administered to some subjects. The dependent variable, memory, could be tested by having them recall a list of words. In this experiment you would try to control any extraneous variables that might influence memory, such as the subjects' age, intelligence, language ability, and health. Can you imagine any other extraneous variable that you would want to control in this study?

positive correlation—values of associated variables change in same direction

negative correlation— values of associated variables change in opposite directions

experiment—method that examines cause-and-effect relationships between variables

independent variable—the manipulated variable in an experiment, assumed to be a cause

dependent variable—the variable in an experiment observed for changes after a manipulation and assumed to be an effect

*extraneous (ex-**tray**-nee-us) variables—factors besides independent variable that affect dependent variable*

Figure 1.3   Diagram of an Experiment

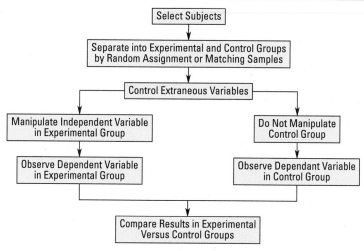

The main steps in conducting a psychology experiment. Subjects are selected; then the experimental and control groups are created through random assignment or matching. Extraneous variables are controlled while the experimental group is manipulated and the control group remains unmanipulated. Finally, the results in the experimental and control groups are compared.

In an experiment, control is a critical element. The difference between a good experiment and a poor one is often the amount of control imposed on the variables. A basic control strategy is the use of at least two subject groups. Subjects who receive the manipulation of the independent variable are the **experimental group**. In the **control group** are subjects who are not manipulated. The control and experimental groups are compared to evaluate the effects of the manipulation. The experimenter tries to ensure that subjects in both groups are equivalent except for the manipulation. These groups may be created by two strategies:

experimental group—
subjects in an experiment who
are manipulated

control group—subjects in
an experiment who are not
manipulated for comparison
purposes

▶ *Random Assignment:*   Subjects are put in the control or experimental group by random selection, such as by picking red or blue marbles from a box.

▶ *Matching Method:*   Subjects in one group are matched with those in the other group by relevant characteristics, such as age, gender, or race.

In some experiments the expectations of the experimenter and the subjects can influence the outcome. For example, a famous study by psychologists Robert Rosenthal and Lenore Jacobson demonstrated that often when teachers are led to expect poor performance from a child, the child's behavior conforms to the low expectations.[10] A control strategy to overcome this problem is the *double-blind design* in which neither the experimenter nor the subjects know who is in the experimental or control group. When the participants are blind to the possible effects of the manipulation they cannot be influenced by expectations about it.

In experimental research, the **placebo effect** is a special problem in which a manipulation works because subjects believe it will work. The word *placebo* is Latin for "I will please," and this effect is most likely in experiments with manipulations that subjects expect will benefit them. For instance, in the earlier study of a vitamin to boost memory the subjects' belief in the vitamin's potential may actually cause improved memory. To control for this effect, the experimenter would give a *placebo group* a false manipulation—one that the subjects believed would affect them. In the vitamin study you could include a placebo group that receives what they think is the memory vitamin but is just a sugar pill. If the results in the placebo and experimental groups are similar, you have evidence that mere belief in the vitamin, not any physical effect, is at work in improving memory.

placebo (plah-***see***-bow) ***effect***—a manipulation works because subjects believe it will work

Experimental research is a powerful tool in scientific psychology, but there are limits to what it reveals. No psychology experiment has perfect control. At best, an experiment minimizes the impact of extraneous variables, but it can not completely eliminate it. Given the complexity of human subjects, it is unlikely that a perfectly controlled experiment will ever be done. Even when they are very well controlled, experiments in psychology often lack *realism*. Control in an experiment requires the use of laboratory conditions and manipulations that are artificial and contrived. Critics of psychology contend that such research has little relevance to everyday life because it gathers evidence in highly unrealistic settings.

Ethics in Research

In a famous experiment on obedience, social psychologist Stanley Milgram found that a majority of ordinary people would obey an order to give dangerously strong electrical shocks to a complete stranger simply because they were told that the study required it (see Chapter 13). Of course, the subjects were not really shocking anyone. Milgram had deceived them, but even when the truth was revealed, many were shaken by what they had done.[11] This study generated a heated controversy over the ethics of psychological research and led to closer scrutiny of many common practices in experiments that used human subjects.

Milgram's obedience experiment provoked concerns over the ethical treatment of subjects in psychology experiments

Today, research in psychology is guided by a set of **ethical principles** that emphasize protecting the subjects' rights and dignity.[12] Manipulations that jeopardize the physical or mental well-being of subjects are not permitted. In Milgram's study, for example, many subjects were emotionally distressed during and after the experiment. A subject's right to privacy must also be protected. Researchers cannot violate the confidentiality of the subject's identity by revealing information about the individual.

Researchers must obtain the subject's *informed consent* to participate in a study. In order to give informed consent, a subject must have a reasonable understanding of the nature of the research, including any potential harmful effects of participation and must voluntarily agree to take part. A subject may withdraw the consent and end participation at any time. Sometimes researchers employ *deception*, as you saw in the Milgram study. Deception contradicts the principle of informed consent, but it may be allowed when it is justified by the potential value of the research and when no alternative exists. If deception is used, subjects must be informed of the truth, or "debriefed," as soon as possible.

Psychology's ethical code also outlines the proper care and use of animals. Because many studies use animal subjects, psychologists are required to provide humane treatment for all research animals. Manipulations that expose animals to pain or distress are allowed only when the potential value of the study justifies such treatment and when no other procedures are available.

Summary

1. Psychology is the science of behavior and mental processes whose goals are description, explanation, prediction, and control. Psychology strives to objectively describe, to explain the causes of, and to predict and control behavior and mental events.

2. Modern specializations in psychology include physiological, experimental, cognitive, developmental, personality, health, clinical, social, applied, industrial and organizational, and environmental psychology. Most careers in psychology are in mental health settings, but many psychologists also work in education, research, business, and industry.

3. The school of structuralism studied the structure of the conscious mind by introspection. Functionalism focused on adaptive functions of mind and behavior. The objective study of behavior defines behaviorism. Gestalt psychology emphasizes organized wholes in behavior and mental life. The psychoanalytic school addresses the unconscious forces of the mind with clinical methods of study. Humanistic psychology attends to the uniqueness and growth of the individual. The physiological perspective assumes a biological basis for behavior and mental processes. In the cognitive perspective, thinking is the focus of theory and research.

4. Naturalistic observation studies behavior in natural, real-life settings. Case studies are in-depth investigations of individuals or groups. Survey research involves questionnaires or interviews to collect information from a sample. Correlational research estimates the statistical association between variables. In a positive correlation, variables tend to change in the same direction, and in a negative correlation, they change in opposite directions.

5. In an experiment, an independent variable is manipulated to determine its effect on a dependent variable. Extraneous variables are controlled by random assignment or matching to reduce their influence on the dependent variable. Experimental groups are manipulated, but control groups are not. Double-blind and placebo designs control for the effects of expectations on the results.

6. The ethical principles in psychology protect subjects' rights and dignity. The ethical principles require informed consent from subjects, the limited use of deception in research, and the proper care and use of research animals.

Questions for Discussion

1. How is psychology defined, and what are its goals?

2. What are the main specializations and career areas in psychology?

3. What are the ideas of the major schools of psychology?

4. How do researchers use the methods of naturalistic observation, case study, survey, and correlation?

5. What are the elements of controlled experimental research in psychology?

6. What are the ethical principles in psychological research?

Applying Psychology

Imagine that you have received a large grant to conduct an experiment on the effect of caffeine consumption on performance in a psychology course. You are the chief experimenter and it is your responsibility to design and carry out this study. Discuss how you would proceed. Remember that you need to consider several key questions:

▶ How would you select the sample of students who will participate in the study?

▶ How would you manipulate your independent variable?

▶ How would you measure your dependent variable?

▶ How would you identify and control all of the potential extraneous variables?

▶ How would you follow the ethical principles of psychological research in your study?

Fundamentals of Psychology

Chapter 2

The Biological Roots of Behavior

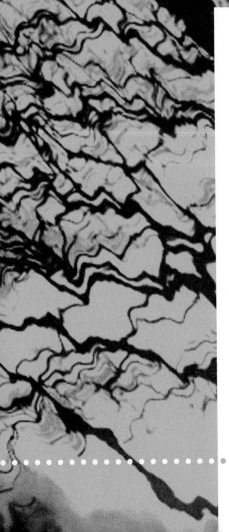

1. Describe the structures and functions of a typical neuron.

2. Summarize the chemical events that occur at the synapse.

3. Identify the major neurotransmitters and describe their functions in behavior.

4. Outline the major divisions of the nervous system.

5. Explain the functions of the medulla, pons, cerebellum, reticular formation, hypothalamus, thalamus, and limbic system within the brain.

6. Identify the activities of the four lobes of the cerebral cortex.

7. Describe "split-brain" studies and the different functions of the left and right cerebral hemispheres.

8. List the major endocrine glands and explain how their hormones influence behavior.

9. Distinguish among family, twin, and adoption studies used in behavior genetics research.

"A young man, known in psychology as H. M., suffered a head injury at the age of seven. The injury resulted in uncontrollable muscle movements, or epilepsy. Eventually disabled from the epileptic seizures, he underwent brain surgery to correct the problem.

Ten months after the surgery his parents moved to a new house only a few blocks from the old one. A year later, he still had not learned his new address nor could he find his way home. He would always go to his old house. Other memory problems were also evident. For example, H. M. would do the same jigsaw puzzles repeatedly without showing any improvement with practice.

One day, the doctors testing H. M. gave him a simple three-digit number to remember. After 15 minutes he was asked to recall the number. He replied, "584." When asked how he was able to remember, he said "It's easy. You just remember 8. You see 5, 8, and 4 and add to 17. You remember 8; subtract it from 17 and that leaves 9. Divide 9 in half and you get 5 and 4, and there you are: 584. Easy." A minute later, H. M. could not remember 584 and did not even remember that he had been given a number to remember!"[1]

When you remember something simple, such as a telephone number, name, or address, you probably take it for granted and never question how you were able to do it. It seems so effortless and automatic. Yet every thought, emotion, and behavior is possible because of events happening within your nervous system and particularly your brain. When the brain is damaged or malfunctions, as it did with H. M., you become aware of the complex relationships between the brain, mind, and behavior.

Physiological psychologists study the nervous system, especially the brain, because it is the basis of all your behavior. Modern brain science has taught us much about the nervous system, but there is certainly much more to be learned. How you move, learn, remember, think, use language, sleep and dream, and express your motivations and emotions are just some of the abilities that psychologists have begun to understand. Studying the brain has also provided new and exciting insights into the biological basis of mental disorders and has led to effective treatments and the hope of more. New technologies have even enabled us to look inside the brain as it functions and promise eventually to expand our knowledge in this area.

The Neuron

The fundamental unit of the nervous system is the **neuron**, a cell that is specialized to receive and transmit information. In this section you will discover what neurons are, how they work, and how their activity is related to mental events and behavior.

▼
neuron (noo-ron)—a cell specialized to receive and transmit information

Though the neurons in your nervous system come in many shapes and sizes, they have certain common features as shown in Figure 2.1a and Color Plate 2.1. The *cell body* is a part of your neuron that contains much of the "machinery" necessary for the cell to perform its activities. A very important component of the cell body is the *nucleus*, in which the genetic material of the cell is found. The nucleus determines how the neuron looks and how it works.

Figure 2.1   A Typical Neuron and the Synapse

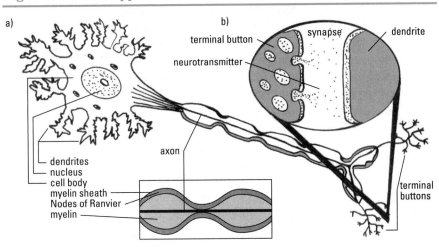

(a) A typical neuron consists of a cell body with a nucleus, branches called dendrites, and an axon that ends in enlargements called terminal buttons. Some axons are covered by a myelin sheath interrupted by nodes of Ranvier. (b) Neurotransmitters send information to other neurons across a tiny space called the synapse.

Extending from the cell body are numerous fine branches called *dendrites*, which receive messages from neighboring neurons. Projecting in the other direction is the *axon*, which carries information away from the cell body. Unlike those of animals such as rats, birds, and fish, nearly 50 percent of your neurons are covered by an insulating material called the *myelin sheath*, which is interrupted by spaces called *nodes of Ranvier*. Finally, the axon branches and ends in little swellings, *terminal buttons*, that contain the chemicals your neurons use to send messages to one another.

How Neurons Work and Communicate

Neurons work by producing small electrical currents. When a neuron is stimulated, the electrical currents change, and these signals are sent to neighboring neurons by way of specific chemicals. Physiological psychologists try to understand your behavior by determining how these signals are generated and transmitted across large numbers of neurons.

In order for your neurons to send messages, they must first be charged up like a battery. The electrical charge is due to a difference in the concentrations of *ions*, electrically charged particles, inside and outside the neuron. There are an abundance of positively charged potassium ions and a low concentration of sodium ions inside the neuron, but the fluid that surrounds the neuron is different. It has a low potassium concentration and a high concentration of sodium. The electrical difference between the interior and exterior of the neuron is called the *resting potential*, which equals −70 millivolts (mV; 1 mV = $\frac{1}{1,000}$ volt). This means that the inside of the neuron is negatively charged like the negative pole of a flashlight battery.

When a neuron is stimulated, the concentrations of potassium and sodium begin to reverse. Sodium ions enter the cell, and potassium ions exit at a slower rate, making the interior more positively charged. If enough sodium enters the neuron for the resting potential to change to approximately −55 mV, the neuron reaches its *threshold*, or firing point. This electrical **neural impulse**, or *action potential*, is conducted down the length of the axon. The entry of sodium ions continues unchecked until the interior reaches 40 mV compared to the outside. At that point, the neuron returns to its resting state. Just as a gun fires with its full force when the trigger is pulled, so does a neuron fire completely when its threshold is reached. The fact that a neuron fires at full strength each time is known as the *all-or-none law*.

How do your neurons send messages to other neurons? Because your neurons do not actually make contact with each other, action potentials cannot jump from one neuron to the next. Instead, each neuron is separated by a microscopic space called the *synapse*. Action potentials force the terminal buttons to release chemicals into the synapse. The chemicals attach to the dendrites of the next neuron like a key fits into a lock (refer to Figure 2.1b). In this way neurons communicate with each other.

Neurotransmitters, Mind, and Behavior

The chemicals released into the synapse are called **neurotransmitters**. How they determine mental events and behavior depends on their effect on other neurons. Some neurotransmitters stimulate other neurons to increase their firing rate and the release of neurotransmitters from their terminal buttons. At many synapses, however, neurotransmitters influence neurons to reduce their firing rate and decrease the amount of neurotransmitter that they release. Thus, your neurotransmitters can have either an excitatory or inhibitory effect at the synapse depending on whether they increase or decrease the activity of other neurons. Just as gas and brake pedals control the speed of a car, this pattern of excitation and inhibition regulates the overall activity of your neurons and ensures that they work normally.

Neurotransmitter activity is associated with many of your mental experiences and behaviors. In addition, brain scientists have learned that many

neural impulse—the electrical activity or firing of a neuron

neurotransmitters— chemicals released at the synapse to communicate between neurons

drugs that influence your thoughts, emotions, and behavior exert their effects by modifying neurotransmitter functions. Thus far, about 50 neurotransmitters have been identified, and it is suspected that there are many more.[2]

There are three classes of neurotransmitters: *amines*, *amino acids*, and *neuropeptides*. Table 2.1 summarizes the types and functions of these neurotransmitters.

Table 2.1 **Neurotransmitters and Their Functions**

Neurotransmitter	Functions
Amines	
Acetylcholine (Ach)	Movement, memory
Dopamine (DA)	Arousal, movement
Norepinephrine (NE)	Arousal, wakefulness, learning and memory, mood
Serotonin (5-HT)	Sensation, sleep, mood
Amino acids	
Gamma-aminobutyric acid (GABA)	Inhibitory: movement, relaxation
Glutamate, aspartate	Excitatory: movement, arousal
Neuropeptides	
Substance-P	Pain sensations
Endorphins	Pain relief, emotional well-being, drug addiction

Acetylcholine, dopamine, norepinephrine, and serotonin are amines. *Acetylcholine* (Ach) is found in the synapses between the neurons and muscles that make you move. Curare, a potent drug used in hunting by native people of South America, blocks Ach at the synapse and kills the victim by paralyzing its respiratory muscles. In your brain, Ach is involved in memory formation, as shown in studies of individuals with Alzheimer's disease. These individuals experience memory impairment due to the destruction of brain neurons that contain Ach.

Dopamine (DA) is responsible for arousing your brain and helping you start and coordinate your movements. If you have an older relative with Parkinson's disease you might be interested to know that the shaking muscles and stiffness come from the destruction of DA-containing neurons in the brain. (See *Issues and Applications: Neural Grafts as a Therapy for Brain Disease*) Abnormalities in the DA system also play a major role in some forms of schizophrenia, a severe mental disorder characterized by abnormalities in thinking, perception, and emotion that you will learn about in Chapter 12.

Norepinephrine (NE) helps you learn and remember, and it is also important in arousing your brain, awakening you, and controlling your mood. Many drugs used to treat depression produce their mood-elevating effects by influencing NE activity. Cocaine, derived from the coca plant of South America, produces its stimulant and mood elevating effects by making more NE and dopamine available at synapses in your brain.

Finally, *serotonin* (5-HT) is involved in your sensory experiences, sleep, and moods. Some of the newer antidepressant drugs, such as Prozac work by making more serotonin available at your brain synapses.

Amino acid neurotransmitters include glutamate, aspartate, and glycine. The best understood is *gamma-aminobutyric acid* (GABA), which controls your movements and helps you relax. The convulsions, or uncontrollable muscle movements, suffered by epileptic patients like H. M. occur when certain GABA neurons work abnormally. GABA's effects are also responsible for your ability to relax. Tranquilizing drugs produce relaxation by increasing the effectiveness of GABA at the synapse.

Issues and Applications

Neural Grafts as a Therapy for Brain Disease

If you know someone who suffers from Parkinson's or Alzheimer's disease, you probably realize how disabling and ultimately fatal these conditions are. In both diseases, many neurons die and cannot be replaced naturally. Drugs offer some relief, but eventually they become ineffective and often produce terrible side effects. On the basis of animal research, scientists have explored the possibility of implanting healthy neurons into the brains of humans as a more effective treatment for such crippling brain diseases.

Now there is hope on the horizon for people with brain diseases, especially Parkinson's. Swedish doctors have been experimenting with the grafting of dopamine neurons from aborted fetuses, and two Americans have received fetal transplants with remarkable success.[3] These individuals had awakened one morning to find themselves totally unable to move, as if they were frozen. They became invalids, unable to feed or dress themselves. It was discovered that their Parkinson's-like symptoms resulted from the destructive effects of tainted homemade heroin they had injected the night before. Standard drug therapy was ineffective, and worse, the drugs made them see things that were not there. Since the surgery, they have been leading relatively normal lives and amazingly, one of the patients was even able to ride a bicycle!

Similar operations are now being performed on a limited basis in the United States, but progress has been slow because of a federal ban on the funding of fetal tissue research. The ban was enacted in 1988 by President Bush in response to abortion critics who argued that such research was immoral and might encourage more women to have abortions to make money. President Clinton, however, lifted the ban shortly after he took office in January 1993. The long-term therapeutic effects of fetal tissue transplants are unknown, and the ethical and moral issues remain unresolved. Nevertheless, neural transplants offer hope for the future of people with brain diseases.

The best known neuropeptides are substance-P and the endorphins. *Substance-P* transmits pain sensations from your body into the nervous system, and the *endorphins* relieve pain and control your emotional well-being. Taking drugs such as cocaine, heroin, and alcohol produces pleasure by influencing parts of the brain that contain endorphins. Because of these findings, it is believed that the endorphins are involved in drug addiction.

The Nervous System

Your nervous system is composed of two major divisions: the *peripheral nervous system* and the *central nervous system* (see Figure 2.2). In this section you will examine these divisions of the nervous system, how they work together, and their relationships to behavior.

The Peripheral Nervous System

The peripheral nervous system (PNS) consists of all the neurons found outside your brain and spinal cord, organized into bundles of axons called *nerves*. The *somatic division* of your PNS contains *sensory nerves*, which carry information from your sense organs into the brain and spinal cord, and *motor nerves* which relay commands from the brain and spinal cord to the muscles of the body that allow you to move.

peripheral nervous system—nerves outside of the brain and spinal cord

The **autonomic nervous system** (ANS), the other division of the PNS, regulates your internal organs such as the heart, lungs, and blood vessels. Psychologists have a special interest in the ANS because of its role in emotions and stress reactions. Suppose you are being stalked by a mugger or some other menacing creature. You would probably experience increased perspiration, pulse, blood pressure, and respiration. Your mouth would

autonomic nervous system—division of the peripheral nervous system that regulates internal organs

Figure 2.2 **The Nervous System**

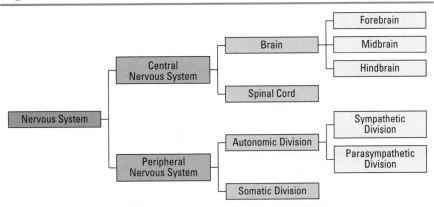

The nervous system is divided into the peripheral nervous system and the central nervous system. The peripheral nervous system consists of the somatic and autonomic divisions. The central nervous system is composed of the spinal cord and the brain.

become dry, your palms would get clammy, and you would feel flushed and frightened. The part of your ANS that is responsible for these "fight or flight" reactions is known as the *sympathetic division*, and the part that allows your body return to its normal level of physiological functioning after the emergency is resolved is known as the *parasympathetic division*. As you can see, the sympathetic and parasympathetic divisions of the ANS work in a complementary fashion.

The Central Nervous System

central nervous system—
the brain and spinal cord

Your **central nervous system** (CNS) consists of the spinal cord and the brain (See Color Plate 2.2). In general, your CNS interprets impressions coming in from your senses and relays commands back to your sense organs, muscles, and internal organs.

Your *spinal cord* relays information from the PNS to the brain and from the brain to the PNS. An understanding of the spinal cord is important to psychologists because it provides a model of a simple behavior, the spinal reflex, which is an automatic movement or response to stimulation. A good example of a *spinal reflex* is the knee-jerk reflex (see Figure 2.3). When the doctor taps your kneecap, sensory neurons in the surrounding tendon excite motor neurons in the spinal cord. The result is a contraction of thigh muscle, which makes your lower leg jerk upward.

Figure 2.3   **The Knee-Jerk Reflex**

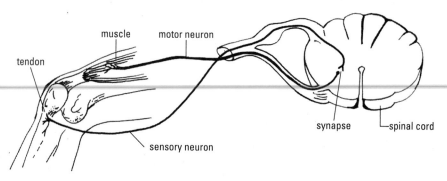

When your knee tendon is tapped, sensory neurons in the surrounding tissue excite motor neurons in the spinal cord. The motor neurons contract the thigh muscles, which, in turn, make your lower leg jerk upward.

brain—*complex structure consisting of 100 billion neurons*

Did you know that there are as many neurons in your **brain** as there are stars in our galaxy? Your brain, composed of approximately 100 billion neurons, is the most complex structure in the known universe (See Color Plate 2.3). Many experimental techniques, summarized in Table 2.2, are used to determine the functions of the different structures in the brain.

medulla—*a hindbrain structure involved in vital and sensory functions*

The brain is divided into the hindbrain, midbrain and forebrain (Figure 2.4). Just above your spinal cord is the *hindbrain*, which consists of the medulla, pons, and cerebellum. The **medulla** controls functions vital for

Table 2.2   Techniques for Studying the Brain

Technique	Description
Electrical recording	Use of electrodes, fine metal probes, to record electrical activity from a single neuron or groups of neurons
Stimulation	Use of small electrical currents or of chemicals to stimulate neurons to fire
Lesion and ablation	Destruction of area or segment of brain tissue
Brain imaging Computed axial tomography (CAT scan) Magnetic Resonance Imaging (MRI) Positron emission tomography (PET scan) (See Color Plate 2.4)	Computer-generated picture of structure (CAT, MRI) or function (PET) of brain region

survival, including your heart rate, respiration, digestion, and salivation. The medulla also interprets information from your senses of taste and hearing as well as touch, pain, and temperature from your head. The **pons**, too, participates in sensory interpretations, vital functions, and allows you to move your jaw. Located behind the medulla and pons is the **cerebellum**, which is involved in motor coordination and memory. If you suffered damage to your cerebellum you would have trouble with balance and might experience tremors (shaking muscles) or a lack of muscle tone.

▼

pons—a hindbrain structure involved in vital and sensory functions and facial movements

▼

cerebellum (se-ruh-bell-um)—a hindbrain structure involved in movement and memory

Figure 2.4   **The Human Brain**

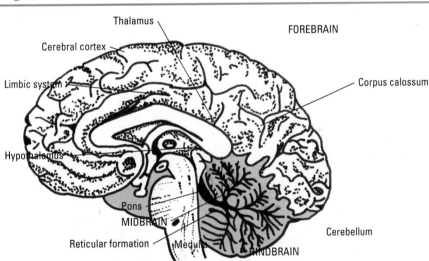

Thalamus

Cerebral cortex

Limbic system

Hypothalamus

FOREBRAIN

Corpus calossum

Pons

MIDBRAIN

Reticular formation

Medulla

HINDBRAIN

Cerebellum

A view of the brain cut in half, lengthwise. Visible from back to front are hindbrain structures including the cerebellum, medulla, and pons. The reticular formation projects into the midbrain and to forebrain structures including the hypothalamus and thalamus. Other forebrain structures that are visible include the limbic system, corpus callosum, and cerebral cortex.

Next is the *midbrain*, which connects the hindbrain with the forebrain. Your **reticular formation**, extending from the hindbrain up through the midbrain into your lower forebrain, is important in arousal, attention, and sleeping and waking. The midbrain also contains neurons that allow you to reflexively turn your head and pay attention to stimuli you see and hear. For example, if you hear a loud noise, neurons in your midbrain make you automatically turn your head in the direction of the sound source. This is called an *orienting reflex*.

The remaining brain structures are part of the *forebrain*, which is large and highly developed in humans. At the base of the forebrain is the **hypothalamus**. Though it is no larger than a kidney bean, your hypothalamus performs many important functions. One of the most important is to control the activity of your *pituitary gland*. As you will see later in this chapter, the pituitary gland is part of your endocrine system responsible for the functioning of your organs and the control many of your emotional reactions. Other critical functions of the hypothalamus include the drives behind feeding, aggression, and sexual behavior.

The hypothalamus is part of the physiological foundation for your experiences of pleasure and reward, too. In a classic series of experiments, psychologists James Olds and Peter Milner surgically implanted fine wires called electrodes into the hypothalamus of rats. Each time a rat pressed a bar, a tiny electrical current was delivered to the hypothalamus through the electrode; a phenomenon called intracranial self-stimulation. Rats would "bar-press" hundreds of times per hour, presumably because of the pleasure

In the Olds and Milner experiment, a rat has an electrode placed in its hypothalamus. Each time the rat presses a bar, a tiny electrical current is delivered. In this experiment, the rats would bar-press hundreds of times per hour, presumably because of the pleasure they experienced.

Source: McGill University

they experienced. In fact, one rat bar-pressed more than 2,000 times per hour for 26 continuous hours, slept for one whole day, then resumed bar-pressing at the same rate when he awakened.[4]

Your **thalamus** sends sensory information to higher forebrain regions. It interprets information from all of your senses except smell, and it assists in the control of your movements, sleeping and waking, and emotions. The *amygdala*, *hippocampus*, and *septal area* are parts of the **limbic system**, a brain region responsible for emotions, learning, and memory. Parts of the hypothalamus and thalamus are also components of the limbic system. In the past, portions of the limbic system were destroyed by brain surgeons for the purpose of changing emotions and behavior in emotionally disturbed patients. This medical practice, known as *psychosurgery*, is rarely used today.[5]

*thalamus (**thal**-uh-muss)—a forebrain structure involved in sensation, movement, emotions, and sleep and waking,*

limbic system—a forebrain region involved in emotions, learning, and memory

The Cerebral Cortex

The cerebrum is the largest part or your brain. It is covered by an outer layer known as the **cerebral cortex** or *neocortex*. The cerebral cortex contains almost three-quarters of your brain's neurons and has numerous convolutions, or folds. The cerebral cortex accounts for your ability to reason, create art, calculate, and express yourself through symbolic language.[6]

cerebral cortex—the outer covering of brain responsible for higher mental functions

The Lobes of the Cerebral Cortex

The cerebrum is divided into left and right *cerebral hemispheres*. Your cerebral hemispheres are connected by the **corpus callosum** and each hemisphere is divided into four lobes: *frontal*, *temporal*, *parietal*, and *occipital* (refer to Figure 2.5 and Table 2.3).

*corpus callosum (**cor**-puss kall-**oh**-summ)—a bundle of axons connecting the cerebral hemispheres*

Figure 2.5 Lobes of the Cerebral Cortex

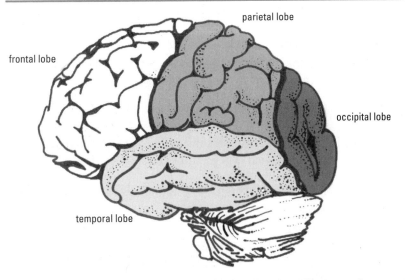

A side view of the four lobes of the cerebral cortex: frontal, temporal, parietal, and occipital.

frontal lobe—brain area
involved in movement and
higher mental functions

Brain-imaging studies show that your **frontal lobe** is responsible for movement and higher mental functions such as intelligence, abstract thinking, language comprehension, and speech (see Table 2.3 and Color Plate 2.5). Movement of the right side of your body is controlled mainly by the left frontal lobe, while left-side body movement is controlled by the right frontal lobe. This arrangement explains, for example, why you would experience muscle weakness on the right side of your body if your left frontal lobe was damaged. Damage to another region of the left frontal lobe could make you speak with difficulty, if at all, and pronounce words poorly though you could comprehend language fairly well.[7]

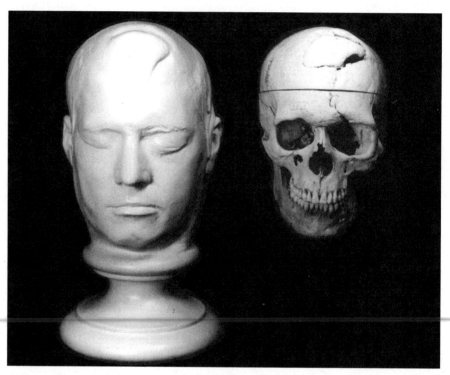

Phineas Gage experienced severe personality and emotional changes after a metal bar was accidentally propelled through his skull, pictured here.

Source: *Warren Anatomical Museum, Harvard Medical School*

Frontal lobe damage often results in dramatic cognitive, emotional, and behavioral changes as well. These problems were evident in the classic case of Phineas Gage, a railroad worker who in 1848 had an iron rod propelled through his skull and frontal lobe by a gunpowder explosion. Although he survived, he became childish, irresponsible, and socially crude. His friends said that he was so changed that he was no longer the old Gage. Some individuals with frontal lobe damage seem uninterested in most things, or they suddenly become happy and excited for no apparent reason. Subtle memory problems and an inability to plan and use foresight are common, too[8,9]. Because of its clear involvement in emotions and personality, cutting of the frontal lobe, called *lobotomy*, was a psychosurgical technique used in the 1940s and 1950s to treat a wide range of psychiatric problems[5].

Your **temporal lobe** allows you to hear and understand spoken and written language. It is also involved in the perception of complex patterns such as faces, and some aspects of emotional expression. People with temporal lobe damage may have difficulties in understanding spoken and written words.

The **parietal lobe** interprets sensory information from your skin, muscles, and joints, allowing you to experience feelings of touch, pressure, temperature, and the contraction of your muscles. If you had parietal lobe damage you might be unable to identify an object by touching it, and you would be clumsy and neglectful of the side of your body opposite the damage. For example, a man with left parietal damage might shave only the left side of his face. Your parietal lobe is also responsible for your association of visual information and spatial information, which helps you to realize that an object is the same even if you look at it with your head tilted.[7]

Your **occipital lobe** is the primary visual area of your brain and is responsible for your ability to perceive and remember colors, shapes, depth, and motion. If an occipital lobe were damaged, you would be permanently blind even though your eyes worked normally.

Your *association areas*, located within the four lobes, put information together from different senses with your motives, emotions, and memories. These activities permit you to carry on complicated tasks such as planning, decision making, and using language. Most of the neurons in each lobe are devoted to association activities.[10]

temporal lobe—brain area involved in hearing, language comprehension, visual perception, and emotions

parietal lobe (puh-**rye**-eh-tull)—brain area involved in skin sensations and visual and spatial associations

occipital lobe (ox-**si**-pi-tull)—the primary visual area of the brain

Table 2.3 **Cortical Lobes and Their Functions**

Lobe	Function
Frontal	Higher cognitive processes, speech, movement
Temporal	Hearing, auditory memory, language comprehension, emotions
Parietal	Body sense interpretation, visual-spatial associations
Occipital	Vision, visual memory and associations

Hemispheric Specialization

Each of your cerebral hemispheres functions differently, a fact known as **hemispheric specialization**. Ordinarily the hemispheres communicate via the corpus callosum (see Figure 2.4), allowing you to experience a unified consciousness. But when the corpus callosum is cut, each hemisphere works independently.

In the early 1960s, neurosurgeons helped some otherwise untreatable epileptic patients by cutting their corpus callosum. Called *commissurotomy*, this surgical procedure permanently separates the left and right hemispheres.

hemispheric specialization—the fact that each cerebral hemisphere has different functions

After the surgery, patients seemed to be quite normal; their personality, emotions, and cognitive abilities seemed unchanged. Later though, the patients were tested under controlled laboratory conditions by scientists Roger Sperry and Michael Gazzaniga, who discovered that these "split-brain" patients responded to stimuli differently than people whose hemispheres were connected.[11,12,13]

In a typical split-brain experiment, the subject is asked to focus on a small spot in the center of a projection screen, and visual images are projected either to the right or to the left (see Figure 2.6). Because of the eye's neural pathways to the brain, images shown to the left of the spot are sent entirely to the right hemisphere. Images projected to the right of the spot are sent to the left hemisphere.

Figure 2.6   Split-Brain Experiment

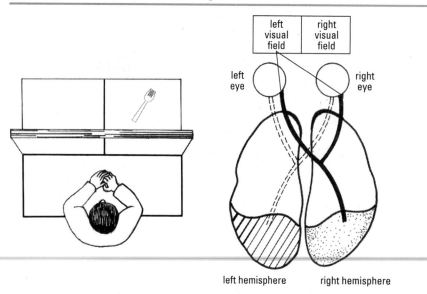

In a split-brain experiment, the subject focuses on a spot while images are projected to either the left or the right of the spot. Images presented to the left are relayed to the right hemisphere, and images flashed to the right are relayed to the left hemisphere.

Ordinarily, your two hemispheres communicate with each other via the corpus callosum, but such communication is impossible in the split-brain patient. As a result, each hemisphere is unaware of what the other is experiencing. For example, if the image of a fork is projected to the right of the spot, the subject can identify the object, say the word *fork*, and then write *fork* with the right hand. The subject is able to do this because the left hemisphere is specialized for language and controls movements on the right side of the body. If the fork is projected to the left visual field, however, the subject cannot find the correct word and cannot write *fork* with the right hand because the right hemisphere does not speak well and cannot move the right hand. You can get some idea of the consciousness of split-brain patients by looking at an actual case of a woman after commissurotomy.

"I decide what I want to wear then I go to the closet to take out a dress. As I reach for the dress with one hand, the other hand takes control and picks an article of clothing I don't want. Then, the original hand grabs the dress from my other hand and throws it on the floor. I become so frustrated I don't even want to get dressed."[14]

Split-brain studies and research with normal subjects have yielded some rough generalizations about the functional differences between the left and right cerebral hemispheres (see Table 2.4). In general, your left hemisphere processes information in sequence and analytically, which means that it handles information by breaking it down into its parts, one piece at a time.

Biography: Roger Sperry

Roger Wolcott Sperry (1913-1994) was born in Hartford, Connecticut. After completing high school in the suburbs of Hartford, Sperry attended Oberlin College in Ohio on a scholarship, where he received a bachelor of arts degree in English in 1935 and a master of arts degree in Psychology in 1937. Pursuing his fascination with zoology, Sperry attended the University of Chicago, where he received his doctorate in 1941.

Roger Sperry's work with the cerebral hemispheres began while he was a research associate of the famous psychologist Karl Lashley at the Yerkes Laboratory of Primate Biology in Florida. At Yerkes, then later when he returned to the University of Chicago to assume a professor's position,

Sperry used animals in split-brain experiments that laid the foundation for his research with humans.

In 1954, Sperry became Hixon Professor of Psychobiology at the California Institute of Technology in Pasadena, California. Later, he collaborated with two

neurosurgeons, Joseph Bogen and Phillip Vogel, to develop the testing procedures used to evaluate mental functioning in split-brain patients. Roger Sperry's research on split-brain patients changed psychology's view of consciousness, mental processes, and hemispheric specialization in particular. For these contributions, Sperry was awarded half the prestigious Nobel Prize in Medicine or Physiology in 1981. He has also received many other awards and honors.

Sperry was married in 1949 and had a son and a daughter. His hobbies included camping, sculpting, ceramics, folk dancing, paleontology, and what he called "human problems." He strongly believed that science can no longer remain in conflict with basic human values.[15]

Is It Possible to Educate Each Hemisphere of the Brain?

The idea that each hemisphere of the brain is specialized to perform different functions is deeply ingrained in popular culture, as reflected in cartoons and advertisements. One magazine cartoon depicted an attractive woman sitting at a bar. A man asks her for a date, and she replies: "My left brain says yes, but I'm waiting to hear from my right brain." Many magazines offer paper-and-pencil tests to help you determine whether you are "left- or right-brained." Knowing your dominant hemisphere is also claimed to be important in determining the type of career you should pursue. Training courses designed to develop the left or right hemisphere abound for would-be executives as a way of landing the desired position.

The idea of hemispheric specialization also has filtered into our educational systems. For example, you may have been told in school that a certain assignment will help you develop your right hemisphere. Many critics bemoan the American educational system's focus on "left-brain" analytic skills to the neglect of "right-brain" creativity. They

For example, your left hemisphere would recognize a face by analyzing individual facial features such as the shape of the eyes, lips, and nose. The left hemisphere is responsible for language and speech, calculation, and other logical skills. By contrast, your right hemisphere processes information simultaneously and holistically, that is, as a whole. It is good at nonverbal tasks such as recognizing shapes and faces, visual-spatial skills such as solving a jigsaw puzzle, generating emotions, and is the source of artistic ability. (See *Issues and Applications: Is It Possible to Educate Each Hemisphere of the Brain?*)

Table 2.4 Functions of the Cerebral Hemispheres

Left Hemisphere	Right Hemisphere
Language comprehension	Visual-spatial skills
Speech	Shape and face recognition
Verbal memory	Emotional expression
Calculation	Artistic ability
Writing	Visual imagery
Right-side movement and touch	Left-side movement and touch

contend that society's problems are far too complex to be solved by training children in reading, writing, and arithmetic alone.

Do the scientific data really support the idea that you can build up one hemisphere of your brain independently of the other? Sally Springer, an award-winning psychologist, thinks not, because the evidence that people are right-or left-brained is weak at best.[16] Although one hemisphere may be better than the other at certain skills, research shows that your two hemispheres complement each other and that their functional differences are not absolute. For example, your left brain excels at constructing and comprehending speech, but your right brain can understand some simple speech and is also involved in determining the emotional content of spoken words.[17,18] Brain-imaging research reveals that the two sides of your brain work together, even at the simplest tasks. There is no solid scientific basis for the claim that creativity is the domain of the right brain, nor are there any real differences between the performances of people such as lawyers and artists on tests that measure hemispheric specialization. For now, we can conclude that it is unlikely that one hemisphere can be trained separately.

There are interesting exceptions to these generalizations. Many left-handers, who make up about 10 percent of the population, have a different brain organization than right-handers. An estimated 30–40 percent of them have language functions in their right (rather than their left) hemisphere, and most of them actually have language abilities in both hemispheres.[19] Thus, unlike that of "righties," language ability in "lefties" could be impaired from damage to either hemisphere.[20]

If you are bilingual, your right hemisphere may be more involved in your second language than is your left hemisphere, especially if you learned the second language informally outside the classroom. If the second language is learned formally—that is in class—the left hemisphere is most responsible.[21]

Men and women differ not only in their physical characteristics, but also in their cognitive and perceptual abilities. Researchers have found that women are more adept at verbal skills and arithmetic calculation. Women also do better than men at perceptual speed tasks such as finding words that begin with a specific letter. Men, by contrast, consistently outperform women in spatial tasks, such as arranging blocks to match a geometric figure, mathematical reasoning, and in finding their way through a route. These differences appear before puberty and are probably due, in part, to hormonal influences on the structure of the developing brain. These observations have led to the suggestion that male and female brains are organized differently, with men showing more specialization than women. That is, men may be more likely than women to have specific functions strictly separated into one hemisphere or the other.[22]

Psychologist Doreen Kimura has offered an alternative interpretation for these findings. Her research indicates that the male brain is not more specialized than the female brain, but that its functions are organized differently within each hemisphere. Language abilities in women, for example, are served by areas closer to the front of the brain, but are farther to the rear in men. Furthermore, the rear part of a female's corpus callosum is larger than that of a man, an anatomical fact that may enhance the transfer of information between hemispheres in women.[22]

The Endocrine System

You have already learned that your behavior is tied to the activity of your nervous system. Despite its great importance, however, your nervous system is not the sole influence on your behavior. Your behavior is also determined by your **endocrine system**—a collection of glands that *secrete* (produce and send) *hormones* directly into your bloodstream.

The Endocrine Glands

The *endocrine glands* control your behavior by the production of **hormones**—chemicals that regulate the activity of specific organs in your body. When your endocrine system is working at peak efficiency you are able to maintain a state of internal equilibrium, or *homeostasis*. Some of the major endocrine glands are the *pituitary*, *adrenal glands*, *thyroid*, *pancreas*, and *gonads*. Their location in the body is illustrated in Figure 2.7, and the hormones they secrete are listed in Table 2.5.

▼

endocrine system—a collection of glands that secrete hormones

▼

hormones—chemicals that regulate body organs

Table 2.5   **The Endocrine Glands and Their Hormones**

Endocrine Gland	Hormone
Pituitary	Adrenocorticotropic hormone (ACTH)
Adrenals	Adrenalin, noradrenalin, corticosteroids
Thyroid	Thyroxin
Pancreas	Insulin

Gonads
  Ovaries
  Testes
	
	Estrogens, progesterone
	Androgens

Figure 2.7 The Endocrine Glands

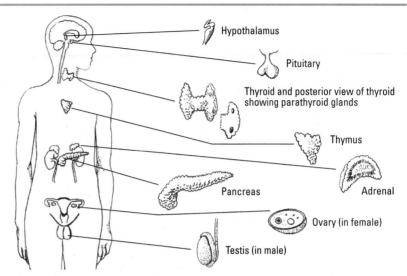

Hypothalamus

Pituitary

Thyroid and posterior view of thyroid showing parathyroid glands

Thymus

Pancreas

Adrenal

Ovary (in female)

Testis (in male)

Endocrine glands secrete hormones that control physiology and behavior. This figure shows the locations of the pituitary, thyroid, and adrenal glands and the pancreas, ovaries, and testes.

Hormones and Behavior

One of the most important pituitary hormones to psychologists is *adrenocorticotropic hormone* (ACTH). Levels of ACTH increase when you face an emergency, thereby stimulating your adrenal glands to release *corticosteroids*, which help you cope with stress. Yet, corticosteroids ultimately make you vulnerable to infections and other physical problems, as you will see in Chapter 11.

Your adrenal glands also produce *adrenalin* (epinephrine) and *noradrenalin* (norepinephrine), whose levels also increase in stressful situations. You do not have to be in grave danger for your stress response to be activated, however. Riding in a commuter train, doing factory work, or taking an exam can increase your levels of epinephrine as well.[23]

Your thyroid gland secretes *thyroxin* which regulates the rate at which your body burns energy. Abnormally low amounts of thyroxin often result in sluggishness and apathy; increased levels can make you irritable and nervous.[9]

Insulin, secreted by your pancreas, lowers the amount of glucose in your blood. Some individuals are unable to produce sufficient insulin and suffer from a disease called diabetes mellitus. Their blood glucose rises to abnormally high levels, harming their eyes, kidneys, and nerves. Too much insulin results in hypoglycemia (low blood sugar), a state sometimes associated with nervousness, fatigue, and depression.

The gonads are the hormone-producing sexual organs in women and men that are responsible for reproductive behaviors as well as the production of eggs and sperm. During prenatal (before birth) development, your gonadal hormones influence the structure and function of the brain, which may affect your sexual identity later in life. As you have already seen, sex hormones may account for some of the hemispheric differences between men and women. The ovaries of women secrete *estrogens* and *progesterone*. Estrogens control aspects of sexual development such as breast development and a widened pelvis as well as the development of the egg, or ovum. Progesterone is responsible for menstruation, and it is believed to play a role in premenstrual syndrome (PMS), a condition marked by depression, irritability, tension, mood changes, sluggishness, and some physical symptoms as well.[24] *Androgens* are male sex hormones produced by the male gonads, or testes. One androgen, *testosterone*, stimulates many of the changes seen in males at puberty, including hair growth, deepening of the voice, genital size, and the rough-and-tumble behavior typical of males.[9]

*H*eredity and Behavior

Psychologists are interested in heredity because all your behaviors are ultimately determined by the interactions of your heredity and environment. In this section you will study basic genetics and learn about the methods psychologists use to determine the hereditary influences on behavior.

Basic Genetics

Genetics is a branch of biology concerned with heredity and the variation of organisms. Genetics explores how certain traits are transmitted from parent to offspring.

Physical traits are passed on to offspring through the transmission of specialized structures called *genes*. Genes contain the code for the manufacture of thousands of proteins that make up your physical characteristics such as eye color, height, and the structure of the brain, to name a few.

Your genes are positioned on *chromosomes*, which are twisted strands of genetic material composed of a complex molecule called *deoxyribonucleic acid* (or DNA). All your genetic information is determined by the precise patterns of these DNA molecules. You have 23 pairs of chromosomes. Twenty-two pairs carry all the genetic information that accounts for your physical traits, and the remaining pair, the *sex chromosomes*, determine whether you are male or female. Females have two X chromosomes, and males have an X and a Y. Each of your parents contributed one chromosome from each pair at the moment you were conceived. The virtually infinite number of genetic possibilities helps explain the variety of individual physical differences that you see in people (see Color Plate 2.6).

Whether a certain trait will be expressed depends on factors other than genetic transmission. For example, a person who has genes for tallness might not grow tall unless he eats the correct foods during childhood and adolescence. Thus, genes may determine your potential, but the environment can determine whether you reach that potential.

▼

genetics—*a branch of biology concerned with heredity*

Behavior Genetics

Behavior genetics is the study of the hereditary basis of behavior. A behavior (or any other trait) is said to exhibit **heritability** if it is influenced by heredity. Behavior geneticists use several methods to determine if a particular behavior has a hereditary basis, including family studies, twin studies, and adoption studies.

In *family studies*, the researcher selects subjects who exhibit a particular behavior or trait, for example shyness. Next, the researcher searches for the presence of the trait among the subjects' family members. If shyness has a hereditary basis, it should be more prevalent (more commonly found) in family members than in the general population. Family studies, however, cannot separate the effects of heredity and environment because the trait similarities observed in family members may not be due to hereditary factors but to the sharing of a similar family environment instead.

Twin studies examine the prevalence of behaviors and traits among twins. Monozygotic (identical) twins are genetically identical because they developed from the same fertilized egg (zygote), which split after conception. Dizygotic (fraternal) twins are no more similar, genetically, than other sibling pairs, because they developed from two fertilized eggs. If shyness is hereditary, then its presence in both twins should be higher among monozygotic than among dizygotic pairs. Twin studies are generally more powerful than family studies in determining hereditary influences, but they still do not rule out environmental influences on behavior.

One way to disentangle the effects of heredity and environment is to conduct an *adoption study*, which studies people who have been raised by adoptive rather than biological parents. If shyness is hereditary, the best predictor of shyness should be the children's biological, rather than adoptive, parents.

Behavior genetics studies have demonstrated a definite link between inheritance and behavior. The most studied trait is general cognitive ability, or intelligence (see Chapter 7). When the results of family, adoption, and twin studies involving more than 10,000 pairs of twins were considered together, roughly 50 percent of intelligence could be attributed to inherited factors. Personality traits such as emotional reactivity (neuroticism) and sociability-shyness (extraversion) also have a substantial hereditary component (see Chapter 10).[25,26]

Behavior genetics studies have also revealed that some abnormal behaviors may be heritable. Apparently, heredity plays a significant role in mental disorders such as schizophrenia, bipolar disorder (manic-depression), some anxiety disorders, and alcoholism.[25,26] You will learn more about the hereditary basis of mental disorders in Chapter 12.

▼

behavior genetics—the study of the hereditary basis of behavior

▼

heritability—the degree to which heredity influences a behavior or trait

Summary

1. A typical neuron consists of a cell body, fine branches called dendrites, and a tubelike extension, the axon. Axons terminate with enlargements called terminal buttons. Neurons function by conducting small electrical currents called action potentials.

2. When action potentials reach the terminal buttons, neurotransmitters are discharged into a tiny space, the synapse. Neurotransmitters attach to postsynaptic dendrites and change the electrical activity of the postsynaptic neuron.

3. Neurotransmitters are categorized into three types: amines, amino acids, and neuropeptides. Amines include acetylcholine, norepinephrine, dopamine, and serotonin. Acetylcholine (ACH) is involved in movement and memory. Norepinephrine (NE) regulates brain arousal and mood. Dopamine (DA) is involved in arousal and movement. Serotonin regulates sensations, sleep, and mood. GABA, an amino acid, is involved in movement and relaxation. Two neuropeptides are substance-P, which transmits pain sensations, and the endorphins, which are involved in pain relief, pleasure, and drug addiction.

4. The nervous system consists of two main divisions, the peripheral and the central nervous systems. The peripheral nervous system is made up of nerves outside the brain and spinal cord. It has a somatic and an autonomic division. The central nervous system consists of the brain and the spinal cord.

5. Within the brain, the medulla and pons regulate vital and sensory functions. The cerebellum controls muscle coordination. The reticular formation is involved in brain arousal. The hypothalamus helps control body physiology through its control of the pituitary gland and it is involved in feeding, aggression, sexual behavior, and pleasure. The thalamus is the main source of sensory input to the cerebral cortex and is also involved in movement, sleeping and waking, and emotions. The limbic system controls aspects of emotional expression, learning, and memory.

6. The four lobes of the cerebral cortex are the frontal lobe, the temporal lobe, the parietal lobe, and the occipital lobe. The frontal lobe controls higher mental functions and movement. The temporal lobe is involved in hearing, language comprehension, emotions, and recognition of visual patterns. The parietal lobe interprets information from our body senses and is involved in visual-spatial associations. The occipital lobe is the primary visual area of the brain.

7. In a "split-brain" study, the subject focuses on a spot while images are presented to either the left or the right visual field. These studies are used to determine hemispheric specializations in the disconnected brain. The left hemisphere is specialized for analytic functions such as language and calculation. The right hemisphere performs holistically and is specialized for visual-spatial and other nonverbal skills.

8. Major endocrine glands include the pituitary, adrenals, thyroid, pancreas, and gonads. Adrenocorticotropic hormone (ACTH), secreted by the pituitary gland, stimulates the adrenal glands to secrete corticosteroids during stress reactions. Epinephrine and norepinephrine are secreted by the adrenal glands during stress. Thyroxin, secreted by the thyroid, regulates metabolism, and insulin from the pancreas lowers blood sugar. The ovaries release estrogens, which control sexual development in women, and progesterone, involved in menstruation. The testes are the male gonads. They secrete androgens, hormones important in male development and behavior.

9. Several methods are used in behavior genetics to determine if a behavior has a hereditary basis. Family studies seek to determine heritability by estimating the prevalence of a behavior or trait in family members. Twin studies attempt to determine heritability by assessing the prevalence of a behavior in both members of a twin pair. Adoption studies separate heredity from environmental influences by studying people who have been raised by adoptive, rather than biological parents.

Questions for Discussion

1. What are the structures and functions of a typical neuron?

2. What are the chemical events that occur at the synapse?

3. What are the major neurotransmitters and their roles in behavior?

4. What are the divisions of the nervous system?

5. What are the functions of the medulla, pons, cerebellum, reticular formation, hypothalamus, thalamus, and limbic system?

6. What are the functions of the four lobes of the cerebral cortex?

7. How are "split-brain" studies conducted, and what do they reveal about the functional differences between the left and right cerebral hemispheres?

8. What are the major endocrine glands, and how do their hormones influence behavior?

9. How do the behavior genetics methods of family, twin, and adoption studies inform us about heritable traits and behavior?

Applying Psychology

Kelly is a 30-year-old left-handed woman who had a split-brain operation six months ago. Since her operation she has been trying to get her life back together. Ken asked her to dinner, and afterward they went back to her place. While watching television, Ken got fresh with Kelly. She reached under the couch with her left hand, pulled out a gun, and shot him dead. When the police arrived she admitted shooting Ken.

Pretend that you are on the jury during Kelly's trial and therefore are responsible for making a decision about her fate. Your job, as ordered by the judge, is to determine whether Kelly is guilty of murder, which requires that she understood the seriousness of her actions, or of manslaughter, meaning that the shooting was an impulsive act. On the basis of your knowledge of split-brain research and hemispheric specialization, how would you decide? What additional information would you ask for to help you make a decision?

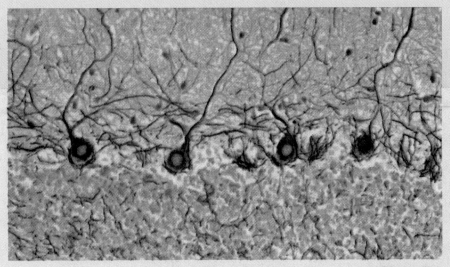

Plate 2.1
Neurons

Behavior is determined by the neural impulses carried by neurons. The brain neurons shown here were treated with a special stain to make them stand out from the surrounding tissue.

Source: © Biophoto Associates/Photo Researchers, Inc.

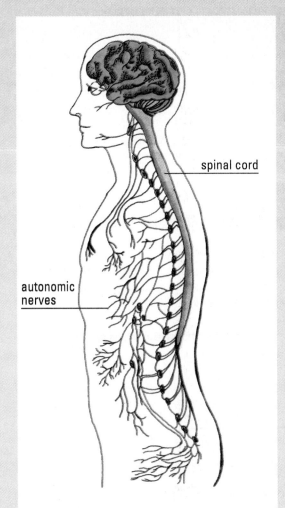

spinal cord

autonomic nerves

Plate 2.2
Central Nervous System

Nerves from the autonomic nervous system, depicted here, project from the central nervous system to involuntary muscles and organs such as the heart, liver, stomach, and the adrenal glands.

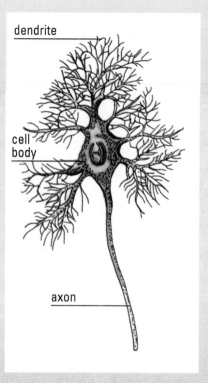

Plate 2.3
Neurons in the Brain

Neurons come in all shapes and sizes. The neuron illustrated here is a typical neuron found in the cerebral cortex.

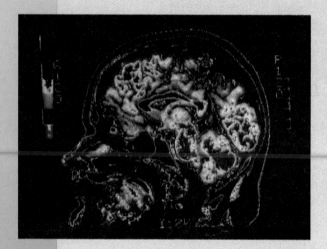

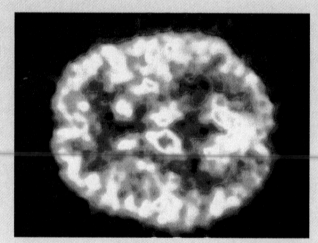

Plate 2.4

MRI

Magnetic Resonance Imaging (MRI), shown here, allows scientists to visualize the activity of brain cells by detecting the small magnetic fields that they generate.

Source: © 1994 John Meyer/Custom Medical Stock Photo

PET Scan

Positron Emission Tomography (PET scan) uses radioactive chemicals to measure the amount of neural activity in the brain.

Source: © 1994 Michael Fisher/Custom Medical Stock Photo

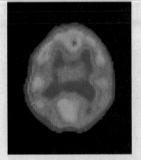
A. Resting State

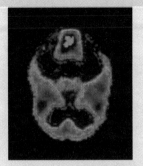
B. Visual

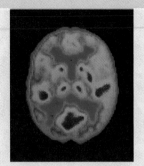
C. Music

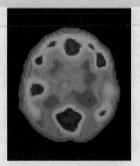
D. Language

Plate 2.5

PET Scans of Normal People, Showing Differences During Various Tasks

Red areas show the greatest amounts of brain activity and blue indicates the least. The PET scans pictured here show brain activity: (a) during rest; (b) while viewing an object; (c) while listening to music; and (d) during speech.

Source: Plate 2.5A, 2.5C, and 2.5D • Mazziotta et al/SPL/Photo Researchers, Inc.
        Plate 2.5B • NIH/Science Source/Photo Researchers, Inc.

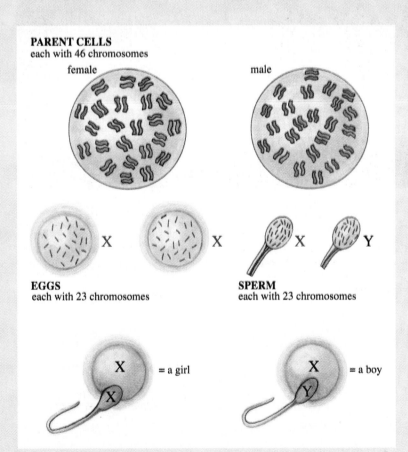

PARENT CELLS
each with 46 chromosomes
female   male

EGGS
each with 23 chromosomes

SPERM
each with 23 chromosomes

X = a girl

X
Y = a boy

Plate 2.6

Hereditary Mechanisms Determine an Individual's Sex

Females have two X chromosomes and males have an X and a Y chromosome. One chromosome was contributed by each parent, the mother contributing an X chromosome and the father contributing an X or a Y.

Plate 3.1
Retina

In this photo of a retina, a short wide cone receptor is surrounded by more numerous long thin rod receptors. The rods and cones absorb and respond to light stimuli.

Source: © Omikron/Photo Researchers, Inc.

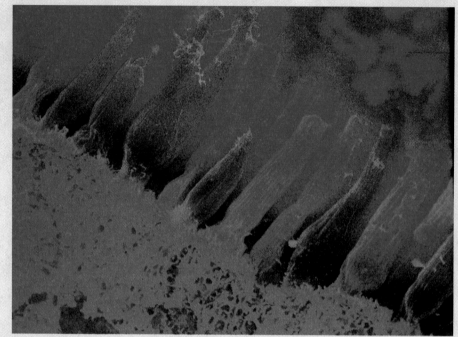

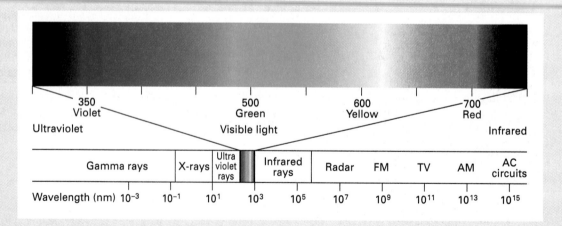

350 Violet	500 Green	600 Yellow	700 Red
Ultraviolet	Visible light		Infrared

Gamma rays	X-rays	Ultra violet rays	Infrared rays	Radar	FM	TV	AM	AC circuits

Wavelength (nm) 10^{-3} 10^{-1} 10^1 10^3 10^5 10^7 10^9 10^{11} 10^{13} 10^{15}

Plate 3.2
The Visible Spectrum

The visible spectrum of light makes up only a small portion of the entire electromagnetic spectrum. The wavelength of a light stimulus determines its perceived color.

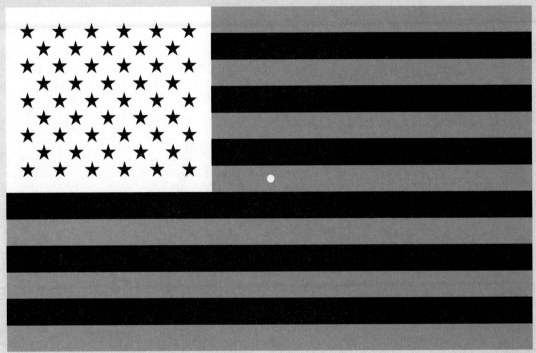

Plate 3.3

A Negative Afterimage

After staring at the dot in the center of this flag for a minute look at a blank white page. You will perceive an image made up of the flag's complementary colors. This phenomenon is known as a negative afterimage.

Plate 3.4

Auditory Hair Cell Receptors

These auditory hair cells are the sensory receptors for hearing and are sensitive to soundwave stimulation.

Source: Professor P. Motta/Department of Anatomy, University "La Spienza" Rome/ SPL/Photo Researchers, Inc.

Plate 3.5

Cross Section of Skin

Many structures are found in the human skin, including several kinds of sensory receptors to detect touch signals.

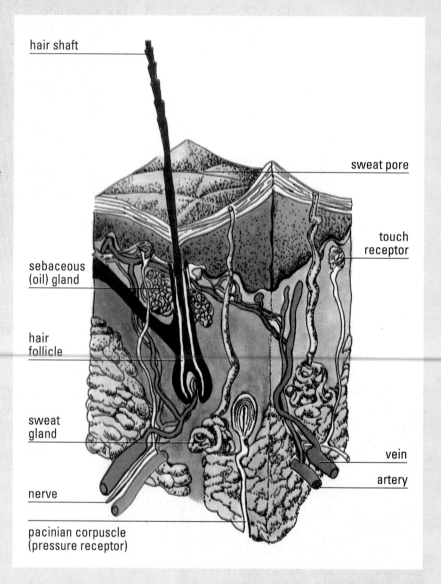

hair shaft

sweat pore

touch receptor

sebaceous (oil) gland

hair follicle

sweat gland

vein

artery

nerve

pacinian corpuscle (pressure receptor)

Plate 8.1
Sperm Penetrating Egg

At conception, a sperm cell penetrates the egg and the genetic material of sperm and egg combine in the fertalized cell, called a zygote.

Source: © d. w. Fawcett/Photo Researchers, Inc.

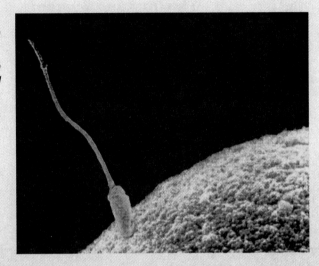

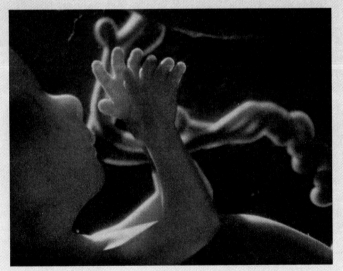

Plate 8.2
Fetal Stage of Development

This 22 week old female fetus is about 10 inches long and has clearly developed bodily features, but she will need 16–18 weeks more before she is ready to be born.

Source: © Petit Format/Nestle/Science Source

Plate 11.1
The Immune System

The immune system eliminates foreign substances, like viruses and bacteria, from the body by the actions of antibodies. This photo shows an antibody destroying a bacterial cell in the throat.

Source: © David M. Phillips/Photo Researchers, Inc.

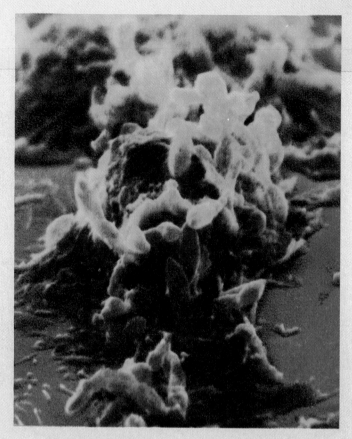

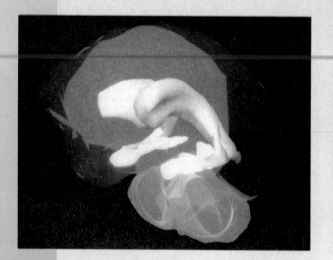

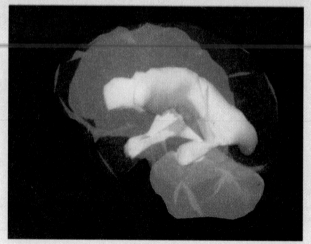

Plate 12.1
MRIs of Normal and Schizophrenic Brains

Many schizophrenic individuals have brain damage involving the frontal lobe and limbic system. The left figure shows normal brain structure. The right figure shows a three-dimensional MRI reconstruction of a shrunken limbic system structure, the hippocampus (yellow), and enlarged ventricles (white), which are fluid-filled chambers in the brain.

Source: Nancy C. Andreasen/University of Iowa

Chapter 3

Sensation and Perception

After completing this chapter, you should be able to:

1. Define sensation and perception and describe their relationship.

2. Outline the visual system and discuss its functions.

3. Identify the mechanisms of color vision.

4. Discuss the perception of forms.

5. Explain perceptual constancy.

6. Identify the cues for distance and depth perception.

7. Describe the auditory system and its functions.

8. Discuss the perception of pitch, loudness, and sound location.

9. Identify the functions of the skin and body senses.

10. Describe the mechanisms of taste and smell.

sensation—process by which senses detect and respond to stimuli

sensory receptors—neurons specialized to detect physical stimuli

Deprived of sight and hearing by an illness during infancy, Helen Keller nevertheless became a celebrated author, educator, and activist. Despite her sensory limitations, she developed a remarkable awareness of the world around her, as she described in her autobiography:

"It seems to me that there is in each of us a capacity to comprehend the impressions and emotions which have been experienced by mankind from the beginning...and blindness and deafness cannot rob him of this gift from past generations."[1]

Most people certainly never experience sensory problems like Helen Keller, and ironically, the average person rarely thinks about his or her senses although they are such obvious and natural elements of daily life. As you will learn in this chapter, your senses and the perceptions to which they give rise involve a complex interplay of biological and psychological factors that provide you with the rich world of sight, sound, touch, smell, and taste.

The Nature of Sensation and Perception

You are constantly exposed to stimulation from your environment and your own body. Sensation and perception detect and interpret these external and internal events, or *stimuli*, enabling you to understand and adapt to your world. Because they lay the foundation of your knowledge of the world, your sensory and perceptual abilities are also essential to your thinking, emotions, and behavior.

Sensation

While you read this sentence, you are receiving thousands of stimuli from your environment. Light stimuli are reflected by the page to your eyes. In addition, you are probably also receiving signals about sounds, smells, and other stimuli. **Sensation**, the processes by which your senses detect and respond to stimuli, is the initial step in understanding those signals. Your senses detect and analyze stimuli through the action of **sensory receptors**, highly specialized neurons in your sensory organs that provide your nervous system with its first information about the world (see Table 3.1).

Table 3.1 **The Senses**

Sense	Sensory Organs	Sensory Receptors
Vision	Eyes	Rods and cones
Hearing	Ears	Hair cells
Touch	Skin	Cold, warmth, pain, and pressure receptors
Movement	Muscles	Proprioceptors
Balance	Semicircular canals	Vestibular hair cells
Smell	Nasal passages	Olfactory receptors
Taste	Taste buds	Sweet, sour, salty, and bitter receptors

Your sensory receptors transform stimuli into neural responses by a process called *transduction*. In each sense, transduction involves unique mechanisms, and it is just the first of many steps in your nervous system's translation of stimuli. From your sensory organs *sensory pathways* carry information about the stimuli through higher levels of your nervous system, eventually arriving at the sensory areas of your cerebral cortex (see Chapter 2).

Your sensory receptors are most efficient in responding to a new stimulus or a change in stimuli. You have probably noticed that after a period of exposure to a stimulus it seems less intense than at first. For example, when you first enter an air conditioned room it feels very cool, but soon you do not even notice the temperature. This reduced responding of your sensory receptors to a prolonged stimulus is called *sensory adaptation*. These experiences of sensory adaptation indicate that the senses have evolved to take most notice of the novel and changing events in the stimulus world.

Stimulation from your environment and your own body is constantly affecting your senses and providing you with a basis for your perceptions.

Even before the beginning of modern psychology, researchers had established the basic principles of **psychophysics**, a field that studies the relationships between physical stimuli and sensations. Psychophysics examines how experiences in vision, touch, and other senses correspond to features of the stimuli that the senses detect. For example, how does the brightness of an object depend on the intensity of the light reflected by the object? To answer such questions, psychophysics uses several methods for measuring sensations.

What is the least light that you can see? The slightest sound that you can hear? The lightest touch that you can feel? Questions about the limits of the senses have long been of interest to psychophysics. Many studies have sought the absolute threshold of sensation, the minimum stimulus energy required to produce a sensation. The *absolute threshold* is measured as the smallest stimulus value that you can detect 50 percent of the time. Table 3.2 shows the estimated absolute thresholds for several senses.

Table 3.2 Estimated Absolute Thresholds

Vision	A candle flame from 50 kilometers away on a dark night
Hearing	A tick of a watch from 6 meters away in a quiet room
Touch	A bee's wing falling on your cheek from a height of 1 centimeter
Smell	A drop of perfume diffused through a three room apartment
Taste	A gram of table salt in 500 liters of water

Source: *Adapted from McBurney, D. H., and Collings, V. B. (1977). Introduction to Sensation and Perception (p. 19). Englewood Cliffs, NJ: Prentice Hall.*

Psychophysics also looks at the ability of the senses to detect a change in or a difference between stimuli. The smallest detectable difference between stimuli is the *difference threshold*, also called a "just noticeable difference." This threshold is measured as the smallest value of stimulus difference that you notice 50 percent of the time. Difference thresholds, however, depend on the relative values of the stimuli. For example, imagine that you are holding a brick in one hand and a dime in the other. Which hand would require more added weight for you to notice the change? The hand with the brick, of course, because its weight was so much greater to begin with. This principle was first described in 1834 by physiologist Ernst Weber. According to *Weber's law*, the difference thresholds for stimuli are relative to their original values. The more intense a stimulus is, the more change is needed for you to notice the change.[2]

Modern psychophysics has been challenged by studies that question the mechanisms responsible for sensation. According to **signal detection theory**, your sensory thresholds result from both your sensory activities and your decisions about stimulus events. In this view, sensation involves a decision about whether you detect a stimulus (*signal*) in a setting with other background stimulation (*noise*). Both the stimulus and the noise influence your decision. For example, if you tried to judge whether your friend had whispered your name in the middle of class, your decision would depend on the loudness of her voice (the signal) and the loudness of other sounds in the room (noise).

Although signal detection theory is most relevant to studies of sensation, it can be applied to other areas as well. When you judge the presence or absence of something—a stimulus, an event, or a behavior—your decision usually involves some uncertainty because of background factors or noise. Signal detection theory is useful in analyzing the decisions that people make in a variety of settings, such as in scanning a radar screen, diagnosing a disease, or testing for defects in an airplane's structure.[3,4]

Issues and Applications

Subliminal Persuasion

How would you like to lose weight, stop smoking, or overcome your inhibitions? Wouldn't it be wonderful if you could accomplish these goals by just listening to a message hidden in a musical recording or video? You may have heard such claims and even seen the products that promise those changes at your local bookstore. Many people believe that behavior is influenced by *subliminal messages*, which are not detected consciously, but are registered in your unconscious mind. Despite popular belief in the power of subliminal persuasion products, research does not usually support their claims.

In the 1950s, moviegoers in a New Jersey theater were exposed to subliminal advertising messages spliced into a film. The messages passed too rapidly to be noticed, but the theater owner claimed that refreshment sales increased. During the 1970s, a popular book, *Subliminal Seduction*, argued that sexual and emotional messages are subtly woven into many ads to stir consumer interest. But controlled studies of subliminal messages question their value in advertising.[5,6,7,8]

More recently, interest in subliminal persuasion has been renewed by the marketing of self-help tapes with subliminal messages embedded in music or video presentations. These tapes are intended to promote weight loss, self-esteem, smoking control, and other types of behavior change. Despite their profitability, those subliminal tapes do not live up to their promises. Studies show that subliminal messages have no significant impact beyond that due to the placebo effect. In other words, the tapes work only because the people using them believe they will help.[9]

These findings do not mean that subliminal messages have no influence. Many studies find that subliminal messages can subtly affect your emotional responses, perceptions, and memory. Whether subliminal messages can significantly affect everyday behavior is another matter. For now, the evidence does not support the conclusion that subliminal persuasion can change your actions in a lasting way.[10,11,12]

Like that of the radar operator, your ability to detect stimuli is based on your decisions about the presence of sensory signals in settings with background noise.

Perception

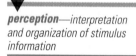

Sensation is only the start of a remarkable process by which you come to understand your world. **Perception** is your interpretation and organization of stimulus information. Your perceptions depend on sensations, but they are also influenced by other psychological activities. A perception is constructed when your brain integrates sensations, memories, and expectations into an organized, meaningful experience. When you think about your perceptions, you probably consider only your conscious awareness of events. Many of your perceptual activities, however, occur in an automatic and unconscious manner, which may affect you without your realizing it (see *Issues and Applications: Subliminal Persuasion*).

Your perceptions are strongly influenced by factors other than sensations, such as memory, expectations, emotions, and culture. It is easier to perceive familiar objects than to perceive unfamiliar ones because you have information about them stored in memory. In addition, you can more readily perceive a stimulus that you expect to perceive because your anticipation prepares you mentally to recognize its features. Emotional states, too, shape perceptions. For example, your perception of pain is shaped not only by pain sensations from an injury but also by your emotional arousal. In a state of emotional distress you will experience greater pain than if you are relaxed because anxiety or fear tends to magnify your feelings of pain.[13] Culture plays a role in perception, as well as in so many other areas of your life. Your perceptions of other people are especially prone to cultural influences. For instance, your attitudes about body weight, height, and skin color are molded by your culture and affect how you perceive the attractiveness of other people.

Perception generally provides you with reasonably accurate and useful information about the stimulus world. But your perceptions are sometimes deceptive and invalid. In an **illusion** you experience a false or distorted perception that does not correspond to the stimulus reality (see Figure 3.1). Oddly enough, illusions can help to explain the normal perceptual activities of the brain. When nearly everyone makes the same false perceptual interpretation of a stimulus, the underlying brain processes behind that perception may be revealed. By examining illusions you can learn about some important mechanisms of perception.

illusion—a false or distorted perception

Figure 3.1 Two Illusions of Size

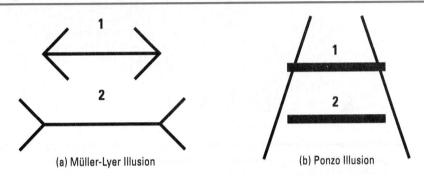

(a) Müller-Lyer Illusion   (b) Ponzo Illusion

Two common illusions of size. (a) In the Müller-Lyer illusion, line 2 appears to be longer than line 1, although the two are actually the same length. The direction of the angles at the ends of the lines is responsible for the illusion. (b) In the Ponzo illusion, bar 1 seems longer than bar 2 despite their actual equality because of the angled lines on their sides.

Researchers generally distinguish sensation and perception according to where in the nervous system their mechanisms are located. Sensation typically refers to mechanisms in the peripheral nervous system at the level of sensory organs. By contrast, perception usually involves the central nervous system, especially the brain. Although this distinction is sometimes useful, it is also somewhat artificial. In everyday life your experiences of the world result from integrated *sensory-perceptual systems* that combine sensory and perceptual mechanisms for detecting, organizing, and interpreting stimulus events. In this chapter you will study the fundamental principles of your major sensory-perceptual systems: vision, hearing, skin and body senses, and the chemical senses.

Vision

In many respects, vision is your dominant sense. The average person tends to depend more on vision than on any other sensory-perceptual system. The dominance of vision in your experience is a consequence of the unique evolution of the human species, in which visual abilities played a critical role. Modern psychology has devoted much more research to vision than to the other senses, and consequently, you will find in this chapter more extensive treatment of this sense.

The Visual System

Your visual system has three major parts: the eyes, the visual pathways, and the visual cortex (see Figure 3.2).

Figure 3.2 The Major Structures of the Eye

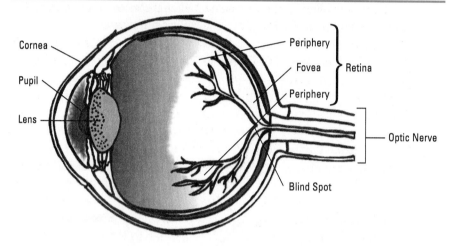

Light enters through the cornea and pupil and is focused by the lens onto the retina, which is composed of the fovea and periphery. The optic nerve emerges from the eye at the blind spot, where no rod or cone receptors are found.

Light enters your *eye* through a transparent membrane called the *cornea* and then passes through your *pupil*, an opening that controls the amount of light that enters your eye. Incoming light is focused onto the inner surface of your eye by the *lens*, which acts similar to a camera lens. Like a camera lens, your eye's lens sends an image into your eye that is both upside-down and reversed with respect to left and right, such as when you look into a mirror. The inner surface of your eye is called the **retina**, which is composed of several layers of neurons including the sensory receptor cells for vision, the rods and cones.

Your rods and cones both contain light-sensitive chemicals, called *visual pigments*, that enable you to detect light stimuli. Because their pigments are different, rods and cones react differently to light stimuli. **Rods** are visual receptor cells that respond to the overall brightness of stimuli and are most sensitive to lower intensities of light. Consequently, rods are good at detecting light in dark or dim settings, allowing you to see at night or in a dark room. By contrast, your **cones** are visual receptors that detect and analyze color information and are most sensitive to higher intensities of light. You may have noticed how at dusk colors seem to fade. That happens because your cones are less responsive to the lower light intensity, (See Color Plate 3.1).

Open your eyes and look around. The light images that form on your retina define your *visual field*, the portion of the visual world that you can see at any given moment. Your retina is divided into two portions, the fovea

retina—*the inner surface of the eye containing the rod and cone receptors*

rods—*visual receptor cells that respond to brightness and low light intensity*

cones—*visual receptor cells that respond to color and high light intensity*

and the periphery. The **fovea** is a small region in the back of your retina where thousands of cones are packed tightly together, but no rods are found. Your *foveal vision* is the center of your visual field, in which objects are the clearest and most detailed. Your fovea analyzes the features of visual stimuli very effectively because the cones lie so close together. While you read this sentence the light is focused on your fovea, allowing you to perceive the small details of these letters and words.

The *periphery* is the largest part of your retina, containing all 120 million rods and most of the 6 million cones in each eye. *Peripheral vision* is not as precise as foveal vision because the receptor cells in the periphery are farther apart than are those of the fovea. If you look straight ahead, holding an object in the center of your visual field gradually moving it to the side, its image will become fuzzier as it enters the periphery. Despite lacking detail, the periphery does provide information about the sides of your visual field and is effective in dim light because of the rods' sensitivity.

Just beneath the fovea is the *blind spot*, a region with no rods or cones. This is the exit point of the *optic nerve*, the visual pathway that carries signals from the eye to higher regions of the brain. Since there are no receptor cells at the blind spot, any light focused there will not be detected. You can use Figure 3.3 to locate your blind spot.

Figure 3.3 **Blind Spot Demonstration**

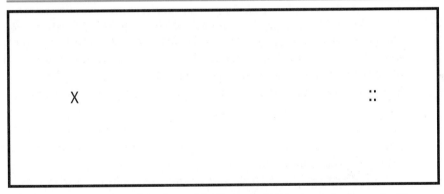

To demonstrate the location of your blind spot, hold this page about one foot from your face. Close your left eye, and slowly move the page closer to you while staring at the X with your right eye. The pattern of dots will disappear when it projects onto your blind spot.

Your optic nerves proceed from each eye to the *optic chiasm*, where nearly half the nerve fibers from each eye cross over to the opposite side of the brain. The visual pathways continues to the *thalamus*, from which signals are transferred to their last stop in the cortex. Disruption of these pathways can cause serious problems of perception. For example, people with *dyslexia* have trouble perceiving the form and order of letters. If you had this reading disability, you might misperceive a *b* as a *p* or see the word *dot* reversed as *tod*. Dyslexia is sometimes due to timing problems in signals arriving at the cortex from a visual pathway.[14,15]

Chapter 3 • Sensation and Perception

As you learned in Chapter 2, the visual areas of the cortex are in your occipital lobes; they perform the final analysis, organization, and perception of visual information. The visual area of the cortex contains specialized neurons called **feature detectors**, which respond to very specific features of stimuli, such as their shape, color, and movement. For instance, shape detectors in the cortex respond selectively to lines, angles, and other elements of a stimulus. Feature detectors receive signals from small regions of the retina known as *receptive fields*. Some researchers believe that feature detectors control the brain's analysis of all visual stimuli. Different aspects of visual stimuli are interpreted by specific regions of the cortex. Specialized regions have been found for interpreting information about movement, color, and forms.[16,17]

▼

feature detectors—cortical neurons that respond to specific features of visual stimuli

Color Vision

Imagine a world without color, where everything looked like an old black-and-white TV show. Your appreciation of art, fashions, and the beauty of the natural world depends strongly on your ability to see color. Color vision involves mechanisms at several levels of your visual system that enable you to distinguish the many thousands of types and shades of color.

To understand color vision, one must first understand light. Light is a stimulus composed of wave patterns that the eye can detect. The range of light wavelengths that your eyes respond to is known as the *visible spectrum*. The major color types along this spectrum are called *hues*, which are based on the wavelength of light reflected by objects (see Color Plate 3.2). The longest wavelengths are at the red end of the spectrum, and the shortest at the violet end. To remember the hues think of the fictional *ROY G. BIV*, whose name abbreviates the colors of the spectrum: *R*ed, *O*range, *Y*ellow, *G*reen, *B*lue, *I*ndigo, *V*iolet. In addition to hue, color also has two other features. Color *brightness* depends on the intensity of light that an object reflects: More intense stimuli yield brighter colors. The mixture of light wavelengths reflected by an object determines its color *purity*. Few objects have pure colors, consisting of a single wavelength. Rather, most objects reflect combinations of many wavelengths. White light, for example, has the least purity, being composed of equal amounts of all wavelengths.

How your visual system interprets these features of light is the basis of color vision. In fact, color vision involves mechanisms throughout your visual system. The **trichromatic theory** explains color vision according to the responses of three kinds of cones in the retina. These cones contain different visual pigments that affect their reactions to different wavelengths of light. The *S-cone* responds best to short wavelengths, the *M-cone* to medium wavelengths, and the *L-cone* to long wavelengths. The combined responses of these three cones are the first translation of color by your visual system.[18]

Mechanisms beyond the retina also shape color perception. In your thalamus, groups of neurons called *opponent-pairs* process color information in terms of mutually opposing reactions to color pairs: *red-green, blue-*

▼

trichromatic (try-crow-mat-ik) theory—explanation of color vision in terms of actions of three cone types

David Hubel, born in 1926, is a respected neurobiologist who has made major contributions to our understanding of the brain mechanisms for vision. He is best known for discovering the feature detectors in the visual cortex.

Born in the Canadian province of Ontario, his family moved to Montreal when he was three years old. He developed his love of science from his father, a chemical engineer, and from a young age he exhibited a talent for chemistry and music. Although he never took a biology course in college, Hubel began medical training at McGill University in Montreal, graduating in 1951.

In 1953, Hubel became an American citizen. While

conducting research at Walter Reed Army Institute in Washington, D.C., he devised a method for measuring the electrical responses from neurons in the brain. During the 1950s Dr. Hubel and his col-

league Torsten Wiesel studied the visual cortex of cats. They discovered that groups of specialized neurons, the feature detectors, analyze and respond to many specific characteristics of visual stimuli.

Since 1959 Dr. Hubel has been at Harvard University, where he has continued his investigation of visual mechanisms. In 1981 he and Dr. Wiesel shared half of the Nobel Prize for Medicine or Physiology for their discoveries in the area of visual information processing. Dr. Hubel's work has been very influential in expanding our understanding of how the visual cortex analyzes stimuli and constructs perceptions of form and movement.[19]

yellow, and *black-white*. For example, in the red-green opponent-pair one member of the pair is excited by red and inhibited by green, while the other member is excited by green and inhibited by red. You see the result of these opponent mechanisms in a *negative afterimage*, as illustrated in Color Plate 3.3. For instance, after viewing a red stimulus, the cells excited by red become fatigued, and when you turn your gaze away the opponent green-responding cells become excited, producing an illusion of that color.[20]

Color is finally analyzed by the cerebral cortex, which integrates signals from lower mechanisms and performs a comparative analysis of light wavelengths. For example, if you wear green-tinted sunglasses, you see all the hues of the spectrum even though your retina is awash with green light. Your cortex filters out the green tint by comparing ratios of wavelengths from different objects.[21]

Like most people, you are probably a *trichromat*, that is, you have all three types of cones and normal color vision. However, about 8 percent of males and less than 1 percent of females have visual defects that cause *color blindness*, a deficiency in color perception. Color blindness is usually due to hereditary factors that prevent formation of some cone pigments. The most common color blindness, the *red-green type*, is due to a lack of the L-cone pigment. A person with red-green blindness cannot discriminate hues from the upper end of the spectrum corresponding to red, orange, yellow, and sometimes green. The *blue-yellow type* of blindness results from a

Figure 3.4 **The Gestalt Laws of Perception**

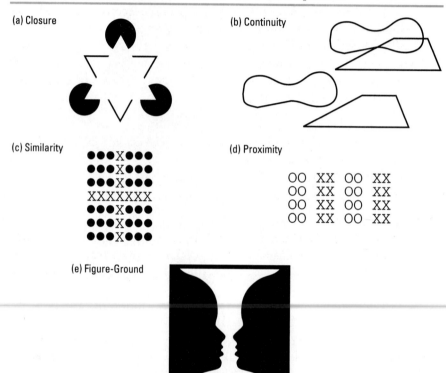

(a) The subjective figure of a white triangle in this display is an example of the law of closure. Your visual system fills in the missing parts of the black "circles" and "triangle," by constructing an illusory image of the triangle. (b) The law of continuity is illustrated when you perceive the parts of this figure as the two forms shown on the bottom. These forms are defined by their continuous, smoothly flowing outlines. (c) In this figure you see a central cross pattern made up of Xs. According to the law of similarity, the similarity of the Xs leads you to perceive them as belonging together. (d) The law of proximity indicates that stimuli that are close together, such as the groups of Os and Xs in this figure, will be seen as belonging together. (e) This vase-faces figure demonstrates the law of figure-ground organization. In a reversible figure like this, there are two possible perceptions. When you see the vase, the faces recede into the background, and when you see the faces, the vase becomes the background.

deficiency of S-cone pigment. Total color blindness is a very rare condition found in people called *monochromats* who have none of the usual cone pigments. A monochromat perceives the world in neutral colors, or shades of black, white, and gray.

Visual Organization

A quick look around your immediate environment will show you one of the most obvious facts of visual perception: The world is organized into distinct objects and groups of objects. This *visual organization* is the result of mechanisms that determine your perception of the forms of objects by interpreting sensations from your eyes. As you learned in Chapter 1, the Gestalt school began by studying how people perceive organized wholes. Those early studies revealed the **Gestalt laws** of visual organization, principles describing how perceptions of objects and groups of objects are formed (see Figure 3.4). The Gestalt laws describe some basic facts about the visual field, but they do not explain exactly how visual organization occurs. Today, there is still no complete physical explanation of how these principles work.[22,23] The Gestalt laws are:

▶ *Closure*: You tend to see objects as complete or fully formed, even when visual information is incomplete. Your visual system "fills in" gaps in stimuli, as in the case of your blind spot.

▶ *Continuity*: You see objects as having continuous, unbroken outlines or boundaries.

▶ *Similarity*: You perceive objects as belonging together in a group when they are similar in shape, color, motion, or other features.

▶ *Proximity*: You see objects that are close together as belonging to a group.

▶ *Figure-Ground*: Your visual field is organized into *figures*, objects that stand out in the front of the field, and *ground*, background objects.

In addition to the Gestalt laws, your perception of forms is influenced by several other factors, such as the retinal image of the object and the context in which you see the object. An object projects an image onto your retina, providing the basic information about its form. The retinal image is essential to form perception, but it does not always match the perceived form. For example, in a *subjective figure* you see a form illusion that does not exactly correspond to the image on your retina, (see Figure 3.4a).[24] In the subjective figure, the *context* of visual stimuli gives you misleading cues that support the illusion. Context also influences the perception of real, as well as illusory, forms. As you see in Figure 3.5a, the squares look very different depending on the surrounding frame. Your perception of *ambiguous stimuli* is especially affected by the context in which they appear, (see Figures 3.5b and c).[25,26]

▼
Gestalt laws—principles that describe the visual organization of objects and groups

Figure 3.5 **The Perception of Form**

(a) The small squares on the left and right actually have the same shape, but you perceive them as being different because of the different contexts in which you look at them. (b) How you perceive the form of the stimulus in the center of this display depends on the setting. Reading from left to right, you will perceive it as the letter **B**, but reading from top to bottom you perceive it as the number **13**. (c) In this ambiguous figure you can see either an old woman or a young woman. The form that you perceive will be influenced by your expectations. If you looked at several drawings of old women before viewing this figure, you would likely see the old woman more easily.

Sources: (a) Kaufman, L. (1979) Perception: The World Transformed (p.159). New York: Oxford University Press. (c) Kaufman, L. (1974) Sight and Sound: An Introduction to Visual Perception (p.496). New York: Oxford University Press.

Perceptual Constancy

Much of the time your visual experiences occur as you move around in your environment. When you are in motion your perceptions are constantly adjusted to account for the ever-changing stimuli streaming into your eyes. Although retinal images change from moment to moment, your perceptions usually do not reflect those changes. This tendency to perceive constant features of objects despite changes in their retinal images is called **perceptual constancy**.

perceptual constancy
tendency to perceive constant features despite retinal image changes

An important example of perceptual constancy is *size constancy*. You see objects as having constant size even though their retinal images have different sizes depending on their distance. The closer an object is to you, the larger its retinal image will be. Yet, you do not typically see a change in an object's size as it moves closer because your brain adjusts the perception of size by accounting for the object's distance. Size constancy does not apply in all conditions. If you are in an airplane at 20,000 feet, objects on the ground seem very tiny—much smaller than you know is correct. At such great distance, size constancy fails because the brain is a poor judge of distance. At that distance, your size perception is based mainly on the retinal image, which is very tiny.

Perceptual constancy is also found in shape, color, and movement perception. Those features of retinal images also change without your perceiving corresponding changes in the object. For instance, if you stand in front of a door and move slowly to the right, the shape of the door's image on your retina changes, but you will still see it as a rectangle. Considered from the point of view of evolution, perceptual constancy is very adaptive. If you saw objects exactly as they are on your retina, your perceptions would be in turmoil: Every move you make would cause a change in how objects appear.

Distance and Depth Perception

Your ability to judge spatial relations between objects in the visual world depends on your distance and depth perception. Distance and depth perception is based on your brain's interpretation of two types of information called monocular and binocular cues. Either your left or right eye can provide significant information about distance and depth through the **monocular cues** that are available from just one eye or the other. The major monocular cues are:

▼
monocular cues—distance and depth cues that are available from one eye

- ▶ *Interposition*: Closer objects block out portions of the images of farther objects.

- ▶ *Detail*: You perceive closer objects in greater detail than farther objects.

- ▶ *Shadowing*: Shadows cast by objects provide depth information.

- ▶ *Linear Perspective*: The image of parallel lines receding into the distance appears to you as lines coming closer together.

- ▶ *Familiar Size*: Your memory of the familiar size of an object influences your judgments about how distant it is.

- ▶ *Motion Parallax*: As you and objects move with respect to each other, the images of closer objects move faster than images of farther ones.

Numerous distance and depth cues are available in these photographs. Refer to the cues described in the text and see how many of them you can pick out of these pictures.

binocular cues—distance
and depth cues that are
available when both eyes work
together

Distance and depth information available only when your two eyes work together are the **binocular cues**. *Retinal disparity* is a powerful binocular cue based on the fact that your left and right retinas have slightly different images of the world. Your brain notes their differences and unifies them into a single image with three-dimensional properties. If you have ever seen a "3-D" movie, you have observed an illusion due to retinal disparity. The glasses you wear to watch the movie deliver different images to your left and right eyes in a way that mimics how the images might actually appear if you were to really look at the scene. Another binocular cue called *convergence* results from the movement of eye muscles that focus your eyes on objects. In order to focus on an object, your eyes must be turned at just the precise angle, but that angle depends on the object's distance. Extend your arm and focus on a finger as you move your hand closer to your face. The muscles that turn your eyes to keep your focus on the finger signal your brain about its distance.

Hearing

Every moment of the day your sense of hearing, or *auditory sense*, is showered with sound. Even if you block your ears, sound vibrations carry through your head and are heard. Sound from the environment can invade your sleep and become part of your dreams. Your auditory sense gives you experience of the great variety of music, voices, noises, and all other features of the world of sound.

The Auditory System

The main components of your auditory system are your ears, auditory pathways, and auditory cortex. The ear is divided into three parts: outer, middle, and inner ear (see Figure 3.6). Your *outer ear* channels sound

Figure 3.6   The Auditory System

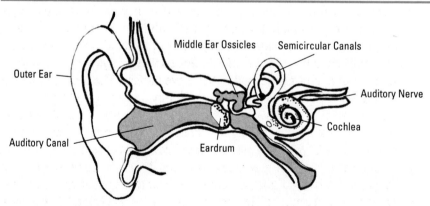

The auditory system includes structures of the outer ear, middle ear, and inner ear. Sound waves travel from the outer ear through the auditory canal to the eardrum, from which they are sent through the middle ear ossicles to the interior of the cochlea.

waves from the environment through the *auditory canal* to your *eardrum*, a sensitive membrane that vibrates in response to sound stimuli. Your eardrum's movement causes vibrations of three tiny bones, or *ossicles*, of your *middle ear*. The motion of the ossicles transfers sound vibrations to your *inner ear*. In some people, particularly the elderly, the middle ear bones fail to conduct sound properly, resulting in a hearing impairment called *conduction deafness*. With conduction deafness, there is a loss of sensitivity to sound.

Vibrations in the ossicles are sent to the inner ear and received by the **cochlea**, an organ shaped like a snail shell. Your cochlea contains fluid surrounding the *basilar membrane*, a sensitive membrane that vibrates in response to incoming sound signals. Along the basilar membrane is the *organ of Corti*, a structure that contains the sensory receptors for hearing, the **hair cells**. Tiny fibers on the hair cells move in response to basilar membrane vibrations and trigger neural impulses that translate the sound waves, (see Color Plate 3.4). From the inner ear those impulses are passed to your *auditory nerve* and carried to the brain. *Nerve deafness* is a hearing impairment due to auditory nerve damage from diseases or genetic factors. The degree of hearing impairment can vary from total deafness to partial hearing loss. Overexposure to very loud noise can also damage your hair cells and cause a loss of sensitivity to sound. People who work around intense noise, such as airport employees and rock musicians, risk some loss of hearing sensitivity.

After leaving your ear, some auditory nerve fibers cross over to the other side of your brain, so signals from each ear are represented on both hemispheres. Before reaching your cortex, sound signals are processed by structures in your midbrain and thalamus, which are important for attending to and analyzing the stimuli. Your temporal lobes contain the *auditory cortex* that performs sophisticated interpretations of sound, as in your perception of music and speech.

cochlea—*inner ear organ containing basilar membrane and hair cell receptors*

hair cells—*sensory receptors for hearing*

Perceiving Sound

Your perception of sound depends on the detection, analysis, and interpretation of sound wave stimuli. A sound wave stimulus has two properties, known as amplitude and frequency. The *amplitude* of a sound wave is its intensity, as measured by units called *decibels*. Sound wave *frequency* is defined by the number of cycles per second in the wave pattern. The measurement unit for frequency is *hertz*: 1 hertz (Hz) equals 1 cycle per second (cps).

Perceived sounds vary in their *pitch*, the quality of sharpness or dullness in the sound. For example, a siren has a high pitch, whereas a bass drum's pitch is very low. Pitch is based mainly on the frequency of the sound wave, with a higher pitch corresponding to a higher frequency. Played from left to right on a piano keyboard, the notes you hear will extend from about 27.5 Hz (low A) up to 4,186 Hz (high C). The average person can hear a range of frequencies from a low of 20 Hz to a high of 20,000 Hz. How your auditory system translates sound wave frequency is described by frequency theory and place theory.[26,27]

According to **frequency theory,** your hair cells respond to a sound wave at a pace that matches its frequency. For instance, a 50-Hz sound wave will trigger 50 impulses per second from your hair cells. This frequency mechanism is very efficient, but it is limited by the inability of your hair cells to respond at a fast pace for a prolonged time. For frequencies of 100 Hz or more, no single group of hair cells can respond fast enough to translate the stimulus. Two or more groups of receptors, however, can coordinate their responses to different parts of the sound wave. This variation of frequency theory is the *volley mechanism*. Fibers of the auditory nerve add up the volleys of hair cell responses and send this information to the brain.

Place theory explains hearing in terms of the sensitivity of parts of the basilar membrane to different sound wave frequencies. One end of your basilar membrane responds most to very high frequencies, and the opposite end responds best to very low frequencies. Pitch is determined by the hair cells on the region of the basilar membrane that is most affected by the stimulus. Place theory is the most general explanation of how you perceive pitch, especially for sound wave frequencies over 5,000 Hz.

Consider the difference between a scream and a whisper. What you hear is a difference in *loudness*, the perceived intensity of sound. Loudness is due mostly to the sound wave's amplitude, with a higher amplitude causing a louder sound (see Table 3.3). High-amplitude stimuli cause more vibration of the basilar membrane, resulting in responses by many auditory receptors. If someone screams in your ear, thousands of hair cells are set into action; whereas relatively few hair cells react to a whisper. The distance of the sound's source also affects its loudness. A sound wave's amplitude lessens as it travels, so it will seem loudest when you are very close. Sensory adaptation also affects your perception of loudness. Remember the last party you attended? When you first arrived the noise probably seemed very loud, but a few minutes later it seemed less intense. Prolonged exposure to sound leads to adaptation by the hair cell receptors and a perception of reduced loudness.

Table 3.3 **Sound Wave Amplitudes**

Amplitude (dB)	Example
180	Rocket launch from 150 feet away
140	Loud rock group
100	Shouting at close range
80	Busy street
70	Normal conversation
50	Quiet conversation
30	Soft whisper
20	Country area at night

Source: *Adapted from Moore, B. C. J. (1977). Introduction to the psychology of hearing. Baltimore: University Park Press.*

If you were blindfolded in a room full of talking people, how would you know where your friend's voice came from? *Sound localization*, your ability to locate a sound in space, depends on the fact that you have one ear on each side of your head. Because your ears are separated, sound waves do not usually arrive at both ears simultaneously. Unless the sound comes from directly in front or in back of you, it will be picked up first by either your left or right ear, depending on which ear is closer to the source of the sound. If your friend is standing to your left side, her voice will arrive at your left ear just before it reaches your right ear, and the different time of detection will be interpreted by your brain as a sign of her location. Besides different arrival times, there are also loudness differences in the sounds detected by your ears. The ear closer to the source receives a slightly louder sound than the farther ear, providing your brain with information about where the sound originated.[28]

Skin and Body Senses

Like those of most people, your sensory experiences of the external world are dominated by vision and hearing. But, your awareness of the world is also shaped by your *skin senses*, or touch, which yield information about external stimuli, and your *body senses* which detect signals about your body's motion and position. The skin and body senses often work together, allowing you to better coordinate interaction with the environment.

Skin Senses

Your **skin senses** detect information about temperature, pressure, and pain. Touch depends on several kinds of receptors contained in your skin, (see Color Plate 3.5). You detect temperature sensations with receptors called *free nerve endings*, which respond to warmth and cold. When you perceive a hot stimulus, your perception is based not on a single receptor's action, but on the combination of signals from your warmth and pain receptors. Different receptors control your sensations of pressure and skin movement and those receptors typically work together. If an ant crawled on your hand, *Meissner* and *Pacinian corpuscles* in your skin would detect the pressure and vibrations caused by the ant's movement. Touch receptors are not distributed equally, but are concentrated more on your palms, fingers, lips, and the soles of your feet.

Your experience of *pain* is a complex perception that depends on skin sensations and on higher-level activities, such as attention and emotion. Free nerve endings in your skin are the receptors for pain caused by skin damage, such as from a cut or burn. According to the **gate-control theory**, pain sensations from the skin are channeled to the brain by "gate" mechanisms in the spinal cord. When excited ("opened"), the gates allow pain signals to pass upward to the brain, but when inhibited ("closed"), the gates block those signals and they are not perceived.[29] *Acupuncture*, a method for pain control by turning needles inserted into the skin, may work by closing

skin senses—senses that detect temperature, pain, and pressure through touch

gate-control theory—theory of pain sensation in terms of spinal cord "gate" mechanisms

Chapter 3 • Sensation and Perception

the spinal pain gates. Pain involves many levels of your nervous system. What happens when you step on a tack in your bare feet? Pain sensations from your skin are sent to your spinal cord by nerves with substance-P, a neurotransmitter that conducts pain signals. Passing through your spinal gates, signals enter your brain, causing the release of *endorphin* neurotransmitters, the brain's natural pain killers.[30]

This individual is obviously experiencing pain, which is influenced by a physical injury and probably also by emotional distress.

More than other sensory-perceptual systems, the pain system is closely associated with your emotions. The experience of pain typically includes a negative emotional state, as well as the pain sensations. Studies of people with serious pain problems—for example, chronic back pain—show that their level of suffering is a matter of emotional responses as well as sensory processes. In a person in a state of emotional distress, such as anxiety, the feeling of pain is magnified.[13] In addition, cognitive factors, such as attention and memory, also affect your pain perception. If you ever had a painful injury, you probably know that the pain increases when you think about or pay attention to it. The role of memory in pain is shown by an illusion, *phantom limb pain*, which is sometimes felt by amputees in their missing arms or legs. Phantom pain and other touch illusions such as itches, felt by amputees result in part from the false recognition of signals as sensations from the missing limb.[31]

Body Senses

body senses—*senses of body movement, position, and balance*

Walking, bending, reaching, and all bodily actions generate signals that are detected by your **body senses**, which interpret your muscle movements and body position as well as your body equilibrium, or balance. Close your eyes and touch your index finger to your nose. In order to do this you rely on

Fundamentals of Psychology

your sense of muscle movement, or **proprioception**. In your muscle tissues thousands of sensory receptors, called *proprioceptors*, respond to the stretching and tensing of muscle fibers, informing you of the whereabouts and actions of your body parts. You need to have constant proprioceptive feedback from your muscles about their movements in order to carry out any coordinated behavior.

Another body sense, the **vestibular sense**, controls your bodily equilibrium, or balance, by detecting how your head moves. If you tilt your head left or right, forward or back, you cause reactions in the *vestibular organs* in your inner ear. The vestibular organs each contain three *semicircular canals* (see Figure 3.6) and two *otolith organs*. These structures are fluid-filled chambers lined with *vestibular receptors*, which are hair cells similar to those used in hearing. When your head moves, the fluid in those structures is disturbed, causing responses by your vestibular receptors, whose signals communicate to your brain the direction and speed of your head's movement. Fast spinning or body rotation, as on an amusement park ride, disturbs your vestibular receptors and can lead to dizziness and loss of balance.

proprioception (proh-pree-oh-sep-shun)—sense of muscle movement

vestibular (ves-tib-you-ler) sense—sense that controls balance

Chemical Senses

Smell and taste are known as the **chemical senses** because they detect chemical stimuli. The chemical senses were the earliest to evolve in ancient organisms, but despite their primitive origins, the taste and smell senses in people are quite sophisticated. How many different kinds of foods and odors are you able to distinguish with your chemical senses?

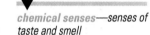

chemical senses—senses of taste and smell

Smell

Take a whiff of air through your nose, and you will flood your nasal passages with millions of aromatic stimuli. Your sense of smell, or *olfaction*, detects those chemical stimuli in the air through receptors lining your upper nasal passages (see Color Plate 3.7). An estimated 12 million odor receptors enable you to detect approximately 10,000 different smells. Although you can distinguish thousands of smells, like most people you probably have a limited vocabulary for naming them. How many different "smell labels" can you think of? Unlike other senses, smell does not channel signals directly to your cortex. Their link with the brain is powerful, however, because smell signals are sent to the *olfactory bulbs*, small strips of tissue under your frontal lobes.[30]

Who has never been moved emotionally by the beautiful scent of a flower or the stink of rotting garbage? Your sense of smell is strongly associated with your emotions and memory because of connections with the limbic system (see *Issues and Applications: Being Led by Your Nose*). In some species, drives and behavior are regulated by smell. For example, many animals give off chemical signals, called *pheromones*, whose smell triggers sexual responses in others of their species. Whether humans also

Being Led by Your Nose

You have probably heard someone exclaim, "This job stinks!" Modern sensory researchers are giving new meaning to that old lament. Although unhappy workers usually do not mean to comment on workplace odor, studies are finding that there may be a link between how the environment smells and your mood and behavior on the job.

For many years, traditional healers and aroma therapists have claimed that certain smells can influence emotional states. Peppermint and lemon scents, for example, have a stimulating effect on people, while a whiff of lavender or sandalwood is soothing. The impact of scent on mood and perception has long been recognized by the fragrance and perfume industries. More recently, smell researchers have begun to explore these links by controlled studies. Although most claims of aroma therapy's effectiveness have not been proved, the evidence of a smell-emotion connection is mounting steadily from studies of natural and synthetic odors. For example, researchers have found in human sweat a chemical with calming effects on those who smell it. Other evidence suggests that compounds in mothers' body odors act as natural sedatives for their infants.[32]

have pheromones is uncertain, but we definitely have body odors that can provoke emotional reactions in one another. Although modern American culture generally frowns on body odors, they may represent an ancient signal system that your remote ancestors depended on for survival.[32]

In his famous work *Remembrance of Things Past*, the French author Marcel Proust detailed extensive childhood memories that were triggered by smelling a tea biscuit. Like Proust, you have probably experienced the power of smells over your memory. Odor memory is exceptionally good and durable in most people. Even after a prolonged absence, many people can identify by smell an article of clothing worn by a close relative. From an evolutionary view, odor memory is a terrific advantage. Animals that remember smells of food that made them ill might just avoid them later and live longer.[35,36,37]

Taste

The sense of taste, or *gustation*, is based on responses of receptors located in the 3,000 or more *taste buds* on your tongue and in the roof of your mouth. Each taste bud contains as many as 100 *taste receptors* that are sensitive to specific properties of chemical stimuli. The responses of your taste receptors give you the experience of four basic *taste qualities*: sweet, sour, salty, and bitter. Different regions of your tongue are most sensitive to the four qualities of taste. The front of your tongue is most sensitive to sweet and salty stimuli, the sides to sour stimuli, and the back to bitter tastes (see Figure 3.7).[38]

You probably assume that your sense of taste controls how you perceive the flavor of food. If so, you are partly correct. Actually, taste and smell interact

How might odors affect your work performance? Studies at the University of Cincinnati tested subjects' concentration on a computer task and found that both a stimulating peppermint scent and a relaxing lily-of-the-valley odor improved their performance. Other studies have shown that certain fragrances can increase brain arousal and induce pleasurable feelings. Conceivably, if odors enhance your attention and arousal and put you in a better mood, they may help you do your job better.[33]

Although there is no clear proof of a direct effect of odor on work behavior, some companies are already implementing fragrance manipulations in the workplace. In Japan, for example, one corporation varies the scent from a stimulating lemon smell in the morning to a more relaxing odor in the afternoon.[34]

The next time you are at work, notice the smell and consider how the odor affects your mood and thinking. Keep in mind, though, that odors are often too subtle to perceive consciously. Some researchers think that those subliminal odors are even more effective. With that in mind, you might want to bring your own air freshener.

to produce the experience of *flavor*. To demonstrate the importance of a food's odor for its flavor, try the Jelly Bean Test. Take four different-colored jelly beans, close your eyes, and eat one while holding your nose. Guess which jelly bean you ate. Your perception of flavor will be very limited when you cannot smell the jelly bean. Food contains more than 5,000 *flavor compounds*, chemicals that influence food's smell and taste. Chocolate alone has about 500 compounds that affect its flavor. In creating new products, chemists in the food industry pay as much attention to the odor of a substance as to its taste, knowing that if a food does not smell right its flavor will not be good.[39,40]

Figure 3.7 **Taste Areas on the Tongue**

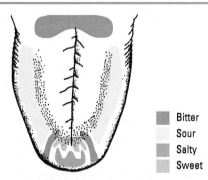

■	Bitter
■	Sour
■	Salty
■	Sweet

The areas for tasting sweet and salty lie near the front of the tongue, the sour areas are on the sides, and the bitter tastes are detected on the back of the tongue.

Source: *Adapted from Sekuler, R. & Blake, R. (1990) Perception, (2nd ed.) New York: McGraw Hill*

Summary

1. Sensation involves sensory receptors that detect stimuli and transduce them into neural responses. Perception is the interpretation of sensations that involve higher-order activity such as attention and memory. Sensory-perceptual systems integrate sensation and perception in vision, hearing, skin and body senses, and chemical senses.

2. The visual system includes the eyes, visual pathways, and visual cortex. Light stimulates rods and cones in the retina. Foveal vision controls detailed analysis of light, and peripheral vision detects changes in levels of light. Visual pathways bring signals from the eye through the thalamus to the brain. Feature detectors in the visual cortex analyze characteristics of images, including color, form, and movement.

3. The trichromatic theory explains color in terms of responses in three types of cones in the retina. Opponent neural mechanisms in the thalamus analyze color in terms of opposing responses of black-white, blue-yellow, and red-green neural pairs. The cortex interprets color in terms of color detector responses and the relative wavelengths of light.

4. Visual organization is described in the Gestalt laws of closure, continuity, similarity, proximity, and figure-ground. In the perception of forms, the shape of the retinal image as well as the context and familiarity of the stimulus are taken into account.

5. Perceptual constancy is a tendency to see an object's features as constant despite changes in the features of the retinal image. In vision, perceptual constancies are found for size, shape, and several other features of visual events.

6. Distance and depth perception informs us of spatial relationships among objects. Monocular cues are interposition, shadowing, linear perspective, detail, familiar size, and motion parallax. Binocular cues are retinal disparity and convergence.

7. The auditory system includes the ears, auditory pathways, and auditory cortex. The ear is divided into outer, middle, and inner ear sections. The cochlea holds the hair cell receptors along the basilar membrane. Hair cells detect sound waves and send them to the brain along the auditory nerve. The auditory cortex in the temporal lobes interprets the qualities of sounds.

8. Pitch perception is due to sound wave frequency. Frequency theory describes how hair cell response rates match sound wave frequency. The volley mechanism combines groups of hair cell responses to different parts of a sound wave. Parts of the basilar membrane respond to different frequencies according to place theory. Perceived loudness is a function of sound amplitude. The time of arrival and loudness of sounds at each ear affect sound localization.

9. Skin senses include touch and pain. Touch receptors detect warmth, cold, and pressure. Pain is registered by free nerve endings and conducted through spinal gates to the brain. Pain perception is influenced by emotional states, memory, and brain endorphins. The body senses are proprioception and the vestibular sense. Proprioception informs us of muscle movement through receptors in muscle tissue. The vestibular sense controls balance by detecting head movement.

10. Smell and taste are the chemical senses. Olfactory receptors in the nasal passages detect smells, which are interpreted by olfactory bulbs. Smell is linked with memory and emotion by mechanisms in the limbic system. Taste receptors in the tongue and mouth produce sweet, sour, salty, and bitter taste qualities. Taste and smell interact to produce the perception of flavor.

Questions for Discussion

1. What are sensation and perception? Explain their relationship.

2. What are the main parts of the visual system and how do they function in vision?

3. What are the features of color vision and the mechanisms behind it?

4. How does visual organization take place?

5. What is perceptual constancy?

6. What are the major distance and depth cues?

7. How do the main parts of the auditory system work?

8. How does the perception of pitch, loudness, and sound location occur?

9. What mechanisms control the skin and body senses?

10. What are the mechanisms of smell and taste?

Applying Psychology

Suppose you were given an experimental drug that changed your perceptions of the visual world so that you saw objects in a way that matches exactly their images on your retina. Discuss how the world might look to you and how you could use your other senses to test your visual perceptions.

▶ Be sure to mention your perception of forms, size, distance and depth and your visual organization.

▶ Discuss how your hearing, touch, vestibular sense, and proprioception might help you determine whether your visual perceptions were accurate or illusory.

Chapter 4

States of Consciousness

Learning Objectives

After completing this chapter, you should be able to:

1. Outline the stages and functions of sleep.

2. Discuss the major theories of dreaming and findings of dream research.

3. Distinguish among the disorders of sleep and dreaming.

4. Summarize the characteristics of the hypnotic state.

5. Discuss the uses of hypnosis.

6. Identify the major depressant drugs and summarize their effects.

7. Describe how stimulants influence behavior and consciousness.

8. Discuss the opiates and their effects.

9. Name the major hallucinogens and describe how they alter consciousness.

10. Summarize the mental and behavioral changes caused by marijuana.

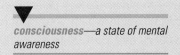

consciousness—a state of mental awareness

In 1959, Peter Tripp, a New York disk jockey, stayed awake for 200 consecutive hours (over eight days) in order to raise money for a charity. By the 100-hour mark he was experiencing serious mental difficulty, including memory, attention, and perceptual problems. Near the end of his sleepless marathon, his mental state deteriorated to the point where he was disoriented, hallucinating, and quite irrational. He actually believed that the doctor who tried to examine him was an undertaker coming to bury him alive. Upon reaching his goal of 200 hours without sleep, he slept for 13 hours and awoke recovered except for a depression that lasted three months.[1]

Although an extreme case, Tripp's experience illustrates how fragile and changeable states of consciousness can be. You are unlikely ever to do what Tripp did, but you are certain to exhibit changes of consciousness every day as you shift between waking, sleeping, alertness, daydreaming, and other states.

What is consciousness? A century ago, the famous psychologist William James described consciousness as an everchanging stream of thought, and psychology has since struggled to define this concept. **Consciousness** refers to a state of mental awareness. Your awareness may be of external events, such as other people and objects, or of your own internal processes, daydreams and memories, for instance. Experience shows that your consciousness occurs on different levels. Sometimes a state of consciousness occurs without your realizing it at the time. Remember your last dream? When you were having it, you probably did not realize that you were dreaming, yet later you could recall the experience.

Your states of consciousness have many variations. They include waking states in which you are fully aware of your surroundings and yourself, as when you are speaking to a friend or reading a book. Consciousness also includes *altered states*, or changes from your ordinary waking frame of mind, such as sleep, trance, and drug-related states. As you will learn in this chapter, the many variations of consciousness illustrate the richness and flexibility of the mind.

Sleep and Dreams

If you live to age 75, you will spend about 25 years sleeping! In fact, you probably spend more time sleeping than socializing, studying, or even working. Most of us sleep about one-third of our lives, but we know surprisingly little about what goes on during that time. In the past few decades, however, researchers have found that sleep is a remarkably complex state defined by the rhythms of activity in both mind and body.

The Stages of Sleep

On waking from a night's sleep, you may have only a vague sense of what you experienced. Although it is not apparent, you have progressed through a sequence of mental and physiological changes known as the **sleep cycle**. Your sleep cycles usually last about 100 minutes, and on an average night you move through four to six cycles.

While you sleep, your brain undergoes regular changes in its electrical activity. Researchers use the *electroencephalograph* (EEG) to measure brain wave patterns that mark the stages of sleep as well as other states of consciousness. *Slow waves*, known as theta and delta, have low frequency and occur mostly in sleep. Beta and alpha patterns are known as *fast waves* because of their higher frequency, and they typically accompany waking states. Your sleep cycle is divided into two main stages, NREM and REM sleep, which are distinguished by their unique brain activity. (See Table 4.1 for a summary of brain wave patterns.)

Table 4.1 **Brain Waves and Mental States**

Wave	Frequency (cps)	State of Consciousness
Beta	13-30	Awake, alert
Alpha	8-12	Awake, relaxed
Theta	4-7	NREM sleep; deep meditation
Delta	1-3	NREM sleep

In the 1950s, researchers discovered a link between brain wave patterns in sleep and erratic, involuntary, *rapid eye movement* (REM). The state of fast, irregular brain activity accompanied by rapid eye movements was dubbed **REM sleep**. Slower brain waves unaccompanied by rapid eye movement was called **NREM sleep**, or *non-rapid-eye-movement sleep*. When you fall asleep, the sleep cycle begins with NREM sleep, in which your muscles relax, your heart and breathing rates decrease, and your body's metabolism slows to a pace that is well below normal. NREM sleep is divided into four distinct stages, each with unique brain wave patterns. Because low-frequency theta and delta waves are most prominent in NREM sleep, it is sometimes called *slow wave sleep*.[2]

As shown in Figure 4.1, the EEG records from the stages of sleep vary dramatically. As you enter NREM sleep, your brain waves change from a relaxed alpha state to *Stage 1* in which slower theta waves begin to dominate. In *Stage 2*, theta waves are accompanied by occasional bursts of high-frequency waves and wave fluctuations. Delta waves appear in *Stage 3*, and some high-frequency bursts continue. In *Stage 4*, delta waves dominate

sleep cycle—*a sequence of mental and physiological changes involving NREM and REM sleep stages*

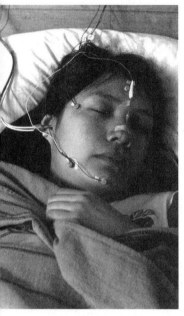

Sleep researchers use the EEG to obtain data about brain activity during the sleep cycle.

REM sleep—*sleep stage with rapid eye movement, fast, irregular brain waves, and dreaming*

NREM sleep—*four stages of non-rapid-eye-movement sleep with slow brain waves*

your brain's activity, and you are in the deepest stage of sleep, meaning that it is most difficult for you to awaken. You move through these stages in about an hour, and then your brain's activity level increases and you repeat the stages, moving from Stage 4 to Stage 1. When you return to Stage 1, your brain shifts suddenly from slow wave activity to the fast waves of REM sleep.

Figure 4.1 EEG Records of Sleep

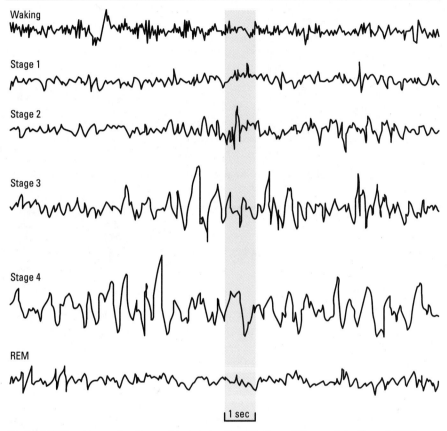

Typical EEG patterns for the waking state, NREM sleep (Stages 1 to 4), and REM sleep. The change from Stage 1 to Stage 4 is marked by a transition from theta to delta wave patterns, indicating a lowering of brain arousal. The fast irregular waves in the REM pattern show an increase of brain activity to a level similar to that in the waking state.

Source: *Bridgeman, B.,(1988). The Biology of Behavior and Mind. New York: Wiley*

After briefly returning to Stage 1, your brain jumps into "high gear," with irregular fast waves that mark the start of REM sleep (see Table 4.2). You also show the rapid eye movement from which REM sleep gets its name. If you can imagine what your eyes do while you watch a table tennis match, you have an idea of how they move in REM sleep. Your heart and breathing rates also increase, and there is a loss of muscle tone and arousal of your sexual organs. A curious feature of REM sleep is that the brain's activity in this stage somewhat resembles its activity when you are awake. In fact, your brain's electrical pattern in REM sleep is more like that found in waking states than in the other stages of sleep.

An important psychological event in REM sleep is dreaming. If you are awakened during REM sleep, you will report dreaming 80–90 percent of the time. Your most vivid and memorable dreams occur during REM sleep. You also dream in NREM Stages 1 and 2, but those dreams are not as clear, organized, and memorable as the dreaming of REM sleep.

Table 4.2 **The Stages of Sleep**

Stage	EEG Pattern	Characteristics
1	Theta waves	Reduced heart and breathing rates; bodily relaxation; dreamlike imagery
2	Theta waves; high frequency bursts	Lowered metabolic rate; unorganized dreamlike thoughts
3	Delta waves; high frequency bursts	Sleepwalking; sleep talking; sleep terrors
4	Delta waves	Deep sleep; hard to awaken; sleep-walking; sleep talking; sleep terrors
REM	Irregular fast waves	Dreaming; rapid eye movements; loss of muscle tone; sexual responses

Your sleep cycles change as the night progresses, and you spend varying amounts of time in each stage (see Figure 4.2). On an average night, you spend 20–25 percent of sleep time in REM sleep, 40–50 percent in Stage 2, and the rest in other NREM stages. As you proceed from early to later sleep cycles, your REM sleep time expands and NREM sleep shrinks. By your second cycle, REM sleep replaces Stage 1 and is then called *Stage 1/REM*. Your later sleep cycles are dominated by REM sleep and Stage 2. You are most likely to recall the dreams you had just before waking because you just ended your longest REM period in your last sleep cycle.

When was the last time you slept as long as you wanted in a completely soundproof room with constant temperature and no distractions? You probably have never done that, but subjects in sleep studies do. The highly controlled conditions in a sleep laboratory are quite different from conditions in real life. In your usual sleep conditions, many factors influence the sleep cycle. Environmental noise, physical discomfort, emotional distress, and illness can all inhibit the natural flow of your sleep stages. Individual sleep habits, such as "catnapping," also shape the course of sleep. If you take brief catnaps during the day, you will generally need less sleep at night. Individual differences in sleep needs are shown by studies of *long-sleepers*, who need nine or more hours of sleep, and *short-sleepers*, who need six hours or less. If you are a short-sleeper, you spend more time in REM sleep

Fundamentals of Psychology

Figure 4.2   Changes in the Course of Sleep

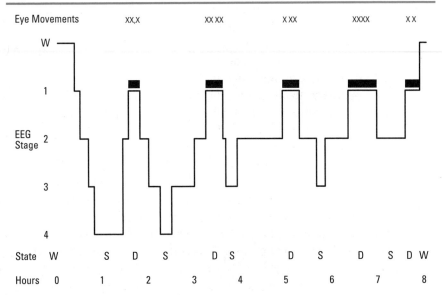

REM sleep is shown by thick horizontal bars, and NREM sleep is shown by thin lines. With each subsequent cycle, the amount of time spent in NREM sleep decreases and REM sleep time increases. NREM Stages 1, 3, and 4 gradually diminish, but Stage 2 and REM sleep continue. W, waking; S, NREM (slow wave); D, REM (dream sleep)

Source: *Thompson, R.F., (1975). Introduction to Physiological Psychology. New York: Harper and Row.*

and Stage 4 than do long-sleepers, and your sleep cycles are more efficient, giving you the same benefits in less time.

Sleep patterns also change over your life span. As you age, you spend less time asleep, and the relative amount of REM sleep time declines. When you were a newborn, you slept about 16 hours a day, nearly half of which was REM sleep. By age 20, your total sleep time and REM sleep are half of what they were in infancy. After age 60, overall sleep and REM sleep time are further reduced.[3]

The Functions of Sleep

Many animals sleep and rest, but the pattern of alternating NREM and REM sleep is distinctive in mammals. Sleep, like hunger and sex, is a basic biological need in mammals, but its exact purpose remains a mystery. Have you ever stayed up all night and felt awful the next day? Although the effects of sleep loss show the need for sleep, there is still no specific answer to the question: Why do we need sleep?

Since the 1950s, researchers have tried to understand the functions of sleep by preventing subjects from sleeping and observing the effects of *sleep deprivation*. Remember Peter Tripp, the disk jockey who experienced extreme effects of sleep deprivation? Early studies suggested that sleep loss can cause mental disruption like Tripp experienced, but later research has disputed those findings. For example, in 1964 17-year-old Randy Gardner stayed awake for 264 hours to get his name in the *Guinness Book of World Records*. Although he had some memory, concentration, and irritability problems, Gardner did not show bizarre extremes as Peter Tripp had, and later Gardner had no lingering ill effects.[4]

Researchers today assume that moderate sleep deprivation produces temporary impairments of attention, perception, and memory, but rarely results in extreme, damaging effects. The negative consequences of sleep deprivation are mainly due to a loss of REM sleep and Stage 4. After a period without sleep, subjects spend an above-average portion of their sleep in REM sleep and Stage 4. These changes are known as *rebound effects*, and they occur first for Stage 4, then for REM sleep. Rebound effects hint that critical functions are served by those sleep stages.[5,6] What do sleep deprivation studies tell us about those functions? They confirm commonsense beliefs that sleep is essential, but they do not tell us why. Attempts to explain why sleep is important are found in sleep theories that are based mainly on animal studies and emphasize the biology of sleep.

According to the **restoration theory**, sleep allows your body to recover from the effects of waking life by renewing its physical resources. Restoration theory claims that while you sleep your body conserves energy and restores a balance in brain activity. Sleep may allow your brain to replenish its supply of key neurotransmitters, such as serotonin and norepinephrine, which are depleted through the stress of everyday life. In addition, sleep appears to refresh your immune system and improve its functioning. Animal studies show that prolonged sleep deprivation can cause death from either general metabolic collapse or failure of the immune system, which opens the door to serious infections.[3,7]

Two theories emphasize a possible role of REM sleep in your brain's memory systems. One characterizes REM sleep as a "housekeeping" operation in which unnecessary information is cleaned out of your memory. Imagine how crammed with useless memories your mind would be if you never forgot anything! In this view, you sleep to forget unimportant daily experiences, such as the lunch menu at the cafeteria. A second theory proposes that sleep strengthens crucial memories from your waking life. Animal studies show that activity in the brain's limbic system during REM sleep involves memory structures that are essential in forming new memories. Although these two theories emphasize different aspects of sleep's role in memory, they both suggest that sleep makes your memory more efficient and adaptive.[8,9]

Dreaming

For thousands of years poets, philosophers, and ordinary people have wondered where dreams come from and what they mean. In modern times, two perspectives on dreams have emerged, one emphasizing their psychological functions and another their biological basis.

In his classic work *The Interpretation of Dreams*, Sigmund Freud opened the modern era of dream theory. His **wish fulfillment hypothesis** argued that dreams express your unconscious wishes, needs, and drives. Freud believed that feelings and ideas that you block from awareness while awake are released in your dream fantasies. Your dreams disguise unconscious wishes by presenting them as symbols. Freud suggested that the remembered portion or *manifest content*, of a dream is a symbolic expression of its unconscious, hidden meaning, or *latent content*. The latent content is discovered by associating dream emotions and images with your life experiences and personality (see Table 4.3).[10]

wish fulfillment hypothesis—Freud's theory that dreams express unconscious wishes, needs, and drives

In a famous case study, Freud analyzed the dream of a young woman, Dora, who was troubled by the sexual advances of Mr. K, a friend of her father. In her dream, their house was on fire and Dora's mother wanted her father to save her jewelry case. Freud interpreted the jewelry case as a symbol for Dora's genitals, concluding that Dora wanted her father to rescue her from the sexual threat of Mr. K.[11]

Table 4.3 Freudian Dream Symbols

Manifest Dream Symbol	Latent Dream Meaning
Gun, knife, snake	Male sexual organ
Container, box, tunnel	Female sexual organ
Injection, stabbing	Sexual intercourse

Freud's psychoanalytic theory emphasized the sexual drive and often interpreted dreams as having hidden sexual meaning. Since Freud, psychological theories have considered several different purposes of dreaming. The psychiatrist Carl Jung (1875–1961), an early colleague of Freud, proposed that dreams help to establish a healthy balance between the conscious and unconscious parts of your mind. Jung saw dreams as messages from the unconscious, informing the conscious mind of personality and behavioral imbalances which it could then correct.[12]

Psychologist Rosalind Cartwright offers a **network model**, which contends that your dreams are a type of unconscious mental activity used to solve problems from everyday life.[13] Cartwright finds that dreams often contain ideas about your most pressing emotional concerns. For example, women experiencing the stress of divorce are likely to express those concerns in dreams, as in the dream of a 35-year-old mother of four whose husband had recently left her:

network model—theory that unconscious problem solving activity occurs in dreaming

"Jim picked up a gold sock and hurled it into a corner of the room. I was shocked and said, "Why did you do that?" He said, "It has a hole in it. I don't want it anymore!"[14]

The imagery in this dream reflects the dreamer's experience of being rudely discarded by her husband like an old unwanted sock. The network model suggests that dreams may also offer you advice about how to cope with life's problems. If you are caught up in a troubling situation in your personal life, relationships, or school, your dreams may reflect your unconscious efforts to come up with a solution.

A biological view of dreams is found in the work of J. Allan Hobson and Robert McCarley, whose **activation-synthesis theory** describes dreams as the result of the enormous brain arousal during REM sleep. When you enter REM sleep, your brain's fast wave patterns indicate a high level of cortical *activation*, which stimulates your memories, feelings, and perceptual images. Upon waking, you recall an organized dream that is the product of your brain's *synthesis*, or combining, of the experiences stimulated during REM sleep. The activation-synthesis theory assumes that dreams do not necessarily have any psychological purpose, although they may reflect personal issues relevant to the dreamer.[15]

Despite theoretical disagreements about why we dream, the fact remains that most of us dream every night. Although some people claim never to dream, they probably just do not remember dreaming. Sleep research shows that the average person has up to two hours of REM sleep each night, and much of that time is spent dreaming. However, what you dream about depends on your unique psychological makeup. As Rosalind Cartwright's studies show, dreams reflect the current emotional concerns of the dreamer. When you are happy, frustrated, or depressed, your dreams convey those emotional themes. The next time you remember a dream, try to understand how it reveals the important issues in your life.

Dreams are also related to your age and gender. Children's dreams mirror their immaturity in the lack of complex plots and imagery. By midadolescence your dreams are more mature and better organized. At any age, your dreams will reflect themes that pertain to your developmental stage. For instance, teens are more likely to dream about dating problems, whereas kindergartners dream about scary monsters in the closet. Gender differences in dream contents are also consistent with general male-female differences in interests and personality. Females tend to dream more about other people and relationships with friends and family. By contrast, males are more likely to dream of work, achievement, and aggression.[13,16,17]

What if you could actually control your dreams? Studies of lucid dreaming suggest that for some people dream control is possible. In a **lucid dream**, you are aware of being in a dream and are able to influence the course of events in your dream. Some lucid dreamers can change their dreams and can even signal observers that they are in the middle of a lucid dream. Studies of lucid dreams hold out promise for their use in improving problem solving and creativity.[18] (The "Applying Psychology" section at the end of this chapter provides an exercise in learning lucid dreaming.)

activation-synthesis theory—biological view of dreaming as a result of brain arousal in REM sleep

lucid dream—dream in which the dreamer is aware of and influences the course of dreaming

Fundamentals of Psychology

Biography: Rosalind Cartwright

Born in 1922 in New York City, Rosalind Cartwright grew up in Toronto, Canada, as the third of four children. Her father was a lawyer, actor, and builder, and her mother was a poet. She attributes her understanding of dreams in part to her mother's poetic images, which were often drawn from her dreams. She became interested in psychology because it was a topic of dinner conversation in her family, and, as a child she read works by Freud, Jung, and Adler from her family's bookshelves. After receiving her bachelor's and master's degrees at the University of Toronto, she took her doctorate in social psychology from Cornell University in 1949.

Cartwright's interest in sleep and dreams began in the 1950s while she was doing psychotherapy research with the famous humanistic psychologist Carl Rogers at the University of Chicago. But, she became a serious dream researcher in response to her own mid-life crisis following a divorce that left her depressed and gave her anxiety-filled dreams. Examining her own dreams and those of many others going through crises led her to conclude that dreams often display our mental troubles and help to test ways of coping with them.

Currently, Dr. Cartwright is the chairman of the Department of Psychology and Social Sciences at Rush University and director of the Sleep Disorder Service and Research Center at Rush-Presbyterian-St. Luke's Medical Center in Chicago. The author of more than 100 professional articles and chapters, as well as five books, Dr. Cartwright has explored several areas, including psychotherapy, social psychology, and most particularly sleep and dreaming. Her work on dreams combines both scientific rigor and useful clinical insights. She has served on the editorial boards of several major professional publications and on many committees of the National Institute for Mental Health. In addition, she has received many awards, including the research prize of the American Personnel and Guidance Association (1955 and 1958), Eminent Woman in Psychology (1988), and the Award for Distinguished Contributions to Basic Research in Psychology (1993).

Disorders of Sleep and Dreaming

On most nights, you flow naturally through your NREM and REM stages because of the innate coordination of psychological and biological processes. When that coordination is disrupted, you may experience one or more disorders of sleep and dreaming.

Remember the last time you had trouble falling asleep or found yourself tossing and turning and waking up repeatedly during the night? You were experiencing a bout of **insomnia**, a sleep disorder involving a delay in the start of sleep or a problem in staying asleep. Insomnias are the most common sleep disorders, and they usually result from stress or emotional arousal. If you are worried about an important exam tomorrow, you might have trouble falling asleep tonight because you cannot stop thinking about the material and the test questions.

Although insomnia is typically caused by emotional distress, it may also result from other factors. Drugs such as caffeine and other stimulants increase brain arousal and prevent the sleep cycle from beginning. Persistent insomnia is sometimes a sign of serious mental disturbance. Chronic sleep difficulties are often associated with severe psychological problems such as depression and schizophrenia (see Chapter 12).

Some people suffer from insomnia caused by **sleep apnea**, a condition in which the sleeper's breathing rhythm is disrupted or temporarily stopped. The respiration centers of the brain malfunction, causing the sleeper to awaken, gasping for air. Sleep apnea is most common in middle-aged men, but it can occur at other ages. It is suspected that apnea may be the cause of some cases of *sudden infant death syndrome*, or "crib death."[19,20]

An unusual sleep disorder is **narcolepsy**, a type of *hypersomnia* (excessive sleep) with sudden, irresistible attacks of sleep that may cause a loss of consciousness. In narcoleptics, the mechanisms that ordinarily suppress REM sleep during waking states fail, and they begin dreaming as in a normal REM state. Narcolepsy is more common in males than in females and may have a hereditary basis.[3]

The last time you woke in a cold sweat from a terrifying dream you were responding to a *nightmare*, a REM sleep event marked by extreme anxiety and frightening imagery. Nightmares are most likely to occur during stressful periods in your life, and they usually do not indicate serious mental discord. From his studies of chronic nightmare sufferers, however, psychiatrist Ernest Hartmann concluded that people with frequent nightmares are inclined toward severe psychological disturbances, as well as greater creativity.[21]

Unlike nightmares, which occur in REM sleep, sleep terrors and sleepwalking are disorders of NREM sleep. In a *sleep terror* the person remains asleep but shows excessive movement and may even cry out as if in pain. Sleep terrors usually appear in NREM Stage 4 and thus are not associated with dreams. *Sleepwalking* is an NREM disorder in which the person performs complex behaviors without awakening. Sleepwalkers may

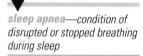

insomnia—sleep disorder involving delay in the start of sleep or problems staying asleep

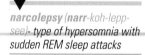

sleep apnea—condition of disrupted or stopped breathing during sleep

narcolepsy (narr-koh-lepp-see)- type of hypersomnia with sudden REM sleep attacks

wander around, talk to you, watch television, and even prepare a snack while asleep, but later if you remind them of the episode, they will usually have no recollection of it. Sleepwalking and sleep terrors are both most common in pre-adolescent children, most of whom grow out of these disorders by their teenage years[22].

Hypnosis

You have probably seen movies depicting characters who appear to be in a zombielike state after they have been hypnotized by staring at a swinging watch or crystal. Such fictional presentations do more to foster misconceptions about hypnosis than to illustrate how it works. In fact, **hypnosis** is a procedure that alters your consciousness and makes you more open to new ideas and suggestions. As you will learn, hypnosis is a flexible, useful tool that has many applications in psychology.

The peculiar history of hypnosis is responsible for many misconceptions about it. The modern era of hypnosis began in the 1700s with Franz Anton Mesmer (1734–1815), an Austrian physician who used *"mesmerism"* to treat his patients. Mesmer thought that their ailments were cured by magnetic forces that he channeled into their bodies. In 1784, a scientific panel debunked his claims, and the popularity of mesmerism declined. The term *hypnotism* was introduced by James Braid (1785–1860), a Scottish physician who believed his patients were put into a sleeplike state. Braid named this state after *Hypnos*, a god of sleep, and caused a lasting confusion between hypnosis and sleep. In the late 1800s, the French psychiatrist Jean Martin Charcot (1825–1893) used hypnosis to treat mental illness, and his student Sigmund Freud adopted it as a therapy method. Freud soon abandoned hypnosis in favor of his own psychoanalytic methods. Interest in hypnosis was renewed in the 1960s when researchers began to explore its effects on memory, perception, and emotional states. Therapeutic uses of hypnosis also revived, and today it is a popular method in psychology and psychiatry.

hypnosis—a procedure that alters consciousness and increases openness to suggestions

Although later discredited, Anton Mesmer's use of "mesmerism" paved the way for the modern therapeutic applications of hypnosis

The Hypnotic State

Some experts contend that hypnosis produces a *trance state* distinct from normal consciousness. According to **neodissociation theory**, the hypnotic trance state is defined by a divided consciousness in which your perceptions, thoughts, and behaviors are dissociated, or split apart, from one another. In trance, dissociated mental abilities can operate independently. If you were in a trance, you could put your hand in a bucket of ice water and notice the sensation of cold, but feel no pain and later have no memory of the experience.[23] If you have ever been caught up in a daydream in class, you have firsthand experience of some features of trance. While daydreaming, you lose yourself in fantasy and may even lose track of time altogether until you "return to earth." Studies of the hypnotic state indicate several important characteristics:

neodissociation (nee-oh-diss-so-see-ay-shun) theory—view that hypnosis causes a trance state of divided consciousness

- ▶ Increased openness to suggestions
- ▶ Highly focused attention or concentration
- ▶ Distorted sense of time and self
- ▶ Diminished self-consciousness
- ▶ Nonrational, metaphoric thinking[24,25]

Critics of neodissociation theory argue that hypnosis does not produce a distinctive state of consciousness with clear psychological or physiological features. In addition, some researchers argue that the effects of hypnosis can be explained by factors other than a special trance state. They maintain that the behavior of hypnotized subjects can result from other factors in the hypnosis situation. For example, if you were a hypnosis subject, your response to the hypnotist's suggestions might reflect your beliefs about how you are supposed to act or your motivation to comply with the suggestions. Your beliefs and motives, not a trance state, would explain your behavior.[26,27]

Whether due to a trance state or to the subject's beliefs and motives, a central element in hypnosis is **suggestibility**, the openness and responsiveness to suggestions. When you are hypnotized, you are unusually receptive and responsive to suggested ideas. In order to identify good hypnosis subjects researchers have devised several methods for measuring suggestibility. For example, the *Stanford Hypnotic Susceptibility Scales* assess a subject's behavioral responses to different suggestions, such as being unable to move your arm and imagining a fly buzzing around you.[28] Although not everyone can be hypnotized, most people can to some degree. Your hypnotizability is unrelated to specific personality traits, but it is linked with some cognitive abilities, including imagination, attention, and creativity. Consider the following questions. If you answer yes to all of them, you are probably a good candidate for hypnosis.

suggestibility—openness and responsiveness to hypnotic suggestions

- ▶ Do you have a vivid imagination? For example, can you close your eyes and "see" a colored object?
- ▶ Are you are able to focus your attention clearly? For example, can you totally concentrate on an object for 5 minutes?
- ▶ Do you have a holistic, or synthetic, type of thinking? For example, can you perceive the patterns in music and visual stimuli?

The Uses of Hypnosis

Since its revival in the 1960s, hypnosis has been extended to many practical applications, including pain control, memory improvement, and therapy.

Laboratory and clinical studies indicate that hypnosis can help relieve pain. Imagine having a cavity filled or getting stitches without pain medication. Hypnosis can produce a reduced sensitivity to pain, called *analgesia*, and it has sometimes proved better than acupuncture and medications for short-term pain relief. Exactly how hypnosis reduces pain is not well understood, but the shifting of attention away from pain signals plays a central role.[24,29]

Law enforcement agencies have used hypnosis to aid eyewitness memory. In a famous 1976 case, a hypnotized school bus driver remembered several license plate numbers of kidnappers who had taken his busload of children. His recollection helped solve the case and stimulated interest in the use of hypnosis to enhance memory. A later study by the Los Angeles Police Department found that in most of 400 cases, hypnotized witnesses recalled some helpful information.[30]

But, the validity of memories obtained by hypnosis has been disputed because of cases in which distorted and false memories have been recalled. If you tried to recall an event while hypnotized, you might recall a mixture of fact and fantasy, and not be able to distinguish between them. In addition, memories obtained with hypnosis might be influenced by hypnotic suggestions, and thus their accuracy is questionable.[31,32]

Numerous applications of hypnosis are found in the treatment of emotional and behavioral problems. Hypnotic suggestions aid people in overcoming undesirable habits such as overeating and smoking. If you were trying to lose weight, you would be given suggestions about changing your eating habits and visualizing yourself as a slimmer person. Successful *hypnotherapy* has been reported for many psychological disorders, including phobias, depression, sexual problems, and multiple personality. Hypnosis can also improve coping with stress and, like meditation (see *Issues and Applications: Meditation*), it helps control mental and physical tension.[4,33]

Drugs and Consciousness

How many people do you know who have used drugs to alter their state of consciousness? Considering that most adolescents and adults in the United States have used consciousness-altering drugs at least once, you probably know quite a few (see Table 4.4). Although you may think of drug use as a

Table 4.4 **Drug Use in the United States**

Drug	Estimated Lifetime Use*	
	Number of people (millions)	**Percent of population**
Alcohol	171.8	84.7
Cigarettes	147.5	72.7
Any illegal drug	75.3	37.1
Marijuana	67.6	33.4
Cocaine	23.7	11.7
Hallucinogens	16.6	8.2
Heroin	2.8	1.4

Based on responses from a nationwide sample of subjects 12 years of age and older

Source: *Adapted from National Institute of Drug Abuse. (1991) National household survey on drug abuse: Population estimates 1991. Rockville, MD: Author.*

very modern behavior, it is nothing new. The use of drugs for medicinal, spiritual, and recreational purposes goes back to ancient times in many cultures throughout the world.

Whether in a mild form like the caffeine in your cola and coffee or in more potent forms like cocaine and heroin, drugs that alter consciousness are commonplace in modern life. A **psychoactive drug** changes your feelings, thoughts, perceptions, and behavior mainly because of its effects on the nervous system. Many psychoactive drugs work by interrupting the way your brain's neurotransmitters work; others have more general effects on several physiological systems.

The impact of psychoactive drugs on consciousness is also influenced by psychological factors. Your beliefs and expectations about a drug's effects influence your response to it. Marijuana smokers, for instance, typically report experiences that they think "pot" is supposed to create, and other drugs, too, are subject to such *expectancy effects*. Furthermore, emotions also modify the drug's influence on your state of mind. For example, depressed people who get drunk often get even more depressed. In addition, the situations in which drugs are used set the stage for different experiences. "Getting high" is usually more enjoyable in a safe, friendly atmosphere with friends than in unfamiliar or threatening settings.[34,35]

Today, millions of people use psychoactive drugs as part of their social and recreational activity. But, excessive use may cause harmful changes in your mind and body. In some cases, drug abuse results in a state of psychological and physical dependence. **Addiction** is drug dependence in which the person has a physical need for the drug, as indicated by tolerance and withdrawal. *Tolerance* means that your body adapts to the drug and requires it to function, and, when drug use stops, unpleasant physical symptoms of *withdrawal* appear.[22] The disorders of psychoactive drug use will be examined further in Chapter 12.

Psychoactive drugs are typically grouped according to their psychological and physical effects. In this section you will learn about five major types of drugs: *depressants*, *stimulants*, *opiates*, *hallucinogens*, and *marijuana* (see Table 4.5).

▼

psychoactive drug—a drug that changes feelings, thoughts, perceptions, and behavior

▼

addiction—drug dependence with physical need, tolerance, and withdrawal

Table 4.5   **Major Psychoactive Drugs and Their Effects**

Types	Psychoactive Effects
Depressants: alcohol, sedatives	Slow neural activity; disrupt higher mental processes; have a calming effect
Stimulants: cocaine, amphetamines	Increase neural activity; induce excitement, elation and pleasure
Opiates: opium, morphine, heroin	Induce a narcotic euphoria and drowsiness; relieve pain
Hallucinogens: LSD, mescaline, PCP	Induce hallucinations and sensory distortions; have psychedelic mind-alteration effects
Marijuana	Induces relaxation, euphoria, and sensory alterations

Meditation

For thousands of years, Hindus and Buddhists have practiced *meditation*, a method of altering consciousness for spiritual enlightenment. Today, many psychologists and psychiatrists are interested in the benefits of meditation for mental health, and researchers are exploring its physical and psychological dimensions. Studies of meditation show it to have these beneficial effects, especially when used regularly:

Increased	Decreased
►relaxation	►stress and anxiety
►self-esteem	►blood pressure
►subjective well-being	►need for sleep
►alpha wave activity	►drug use

Several strategies of meditation developed from different traditions. The most common types—for example, *zen*, *yoga*, and *transcendental meditation* (TM)—require that you sit in a quiet place and concentrate on one specific stimulus, for example, a word or sound (called a *mantra*) that you repeat over and over. Another form, *tai chi*, involves repetitions of slow methodical body motions. By focusing on the mantra or body motion, your mind is freed from distracting thoughts and feelings and you experience a peaceful state of consciousness.

Suppose you are ready to try meditation. A few simple instructions are enough to get started:

►Find a quiet room and sit in a comfortable position. Loosen tight clothes or shoes.

►Allow yourself to breathe in a gentle rhythm. Do not force your breathing.

►Repeat your mantra silently to yourself. The mantra can be any word or sound, for example, "one," "calm," "shh."

►When your mind drifts, return to your mantra. Expect to have distracting thoughts and do not let yourself be bothered by them.

With some practice, you will find that regular meditation for 15 minutes a day can lead to a healthier and calmer state of mind.[4,36,37]

Depressants

A drug that slows down or suppresses the activity of the nervous system is a **depressant**. Depressants include the most widely used drug, alcohol, as well as sedatives such as barbiturates and tranquilizers.

Produced by the fermentation of sugar, **alcohol** is the most popular psychoactive drug in history. Since ancient times, people have drunk alcoholic beverages made from fruits, honey, grains, and vegetables.[38] In the United States, over 80 percent of the population uses some alcohol during their lifetime. The effects of alcohol depend largely on your *blood alcohol level* (BAL), the percent of your blood that is alcohol. Your BAL is affected by several factors: the amount and potency of alcohol consumed, body weight, and the rate of alcohol breakdown in the body.[39] To examine the effect of BAL on behavior, consider a hypothetical case of an average 150 pound, 18-year-old named Tom who goes to a party and drinks 12-ounce cans of beer:

▶ 1 drink (BAL 0.01): Tom begins to feel in a better mood after one drink. He starts to relax and loosen up, and he experiences a mild decrease in his eye-hand coordination.

▶ 3 drinks (BAL 0.10): Tom's reaction time is slowed, and his coordination obviously is impaired. He begins to lose control of his emotions and becomes too loud and boisterous. He can be considered legally drunk in many states.

▶ 6 drinks (BAL 0.20): Tom's loss of coordination is extreme. He stumbles and cannot see clearly. His speech is slurred and makes little sense. He is rambling, confused, irrational, and probably nauseous.

▶ 9 drinks (BAL 0.30): Severely intoxicated, Tom is feeling sleepy and struggling to keep awake. His attention, perceptions, and judgment are very poor. He finds even simple actions, such as walking, difficult.

▶ 14 drinks (BAL 0.50): Tom is either in or near an unconscious state. He may lapse into a coma.

Alcohol can significantly impair behavior and mental functioning.

Because it suppresses brain arousal, alcohol disrupts most behavior and mental activity, including reasoning, judgment, self-control, learning, and memory. At first, alcohol relaxes you and relieves emotional tension. After drinking a moderate amount, you may feel carefree and less inhibited and self-conscious. But, alcohol sometimes releases negative emotions, too, such as anger and hostility. Alcohol alone probably does not cause aggression, but it is associated with many instances of violent antisocial behavior, such as sexual assaults and child abuse. In high doses, alcohol may cause you to lose consciousness and have a *blackout*, or memory loss, for the period of intoxication. Because alcohol is an addictive drug, long-term use can lead to a state of physical dependence, or *alcoholism*. Alcoholics have above-average rates of serious mental and medical problems, such as depression and liver disease. For a severe alcoholic, alcohol withdrawal includes *delirium tremens* (the DTs), shown by irrationality, confusion, and bodily tremors ("the shakes").[40]

Drugs with a calming or relaxing effect are called **sedatives**. *Barbiturates* are strong, addictive sedatives that generate feelings of well-being and relaxation. Their general psychoactive effects are similar to those of alcohol. When barbiturates and alcohol are combined, the depressant effects are magnified and may cause loss of consciousness, coma, and death by breathing failure.

Tranquilizers are sedatives that are prescribed mainly for relieving anxiety and stress. Common tranquilizers such as diazepam (Valium) have limited use as recreational drugs because they do not create a significant "high." They are, however, quite addictive, and when taken with other drugs, such as alcohol, they can produce a state of severe intoxication.[41]

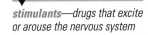

sedatives—depressants with a calming or tranquilizing effect

Stimulants

Caffeine, nicotine, cocaine, amphetamines, and other drugs that excite or arouse the nervous system are known as **stimulants**. The most apparent result of stimulant use is an increased feeling of energy (see *Issues and Applications: Drugs in the Workplace*). For example, the lift you get from your morning coffee is from *caffeine*, the stimulant in coffee, tea, colas, and chocolate. Causing increased alertness in modest doses, caffeine can also lead to anxiety and agitation in higher dosages. An ingredient of tobacco, *nicotine* is a psychoactive drug with mild stimulant effects. Although it does not cause any obvious intoxication, nicotine is very addictive, as shown by the millions of cigarette addicts worldwide.

stimulants—drugs that excite or arouse the nervous system

Cocaine and *amphetamines* are much more powerful stimulants, with prominent physical and psychological consequences. They raise your heart and breathing rates, increase your blood pressure, and boost your energy level. In addition, they produce a state of emotional elation, exhilaration, and alertness, as well as heightened activity, restlessness, and talkativeness. In high doses, they generate intense anxiety and sometimes a state of extreme suspiciousness, or paranoia.

Cocaine has become an especially prominent drug since the 1970s. Found in the South American coca plant, it was once used in health "tonics," including the original Coca Cola. Cocaine increases your feelings of pleasure, sex drive, and self-confidence and produces a state of excessive alertness or vigilance. Cocaine is exceptionally addictive, particularly in the form of *freebase* or *crack*, both of which are associated with violent behavior.[42]

Opiates

The poppy plant is the source of the narcotic drugs called **opiates**, which include *opium, morphine, codeine, and heroin*. Used medically for pain control, opiates also have pronounced psychological effects. A drowsy state of euphoria, or extreme pleasure, is the most distinctive emotional feature of opiate intoxication. These drugs influence the brain areas that regulate pain and pleasure by stimulating neurons that use endorphin and dopamine neurotransmitters.

Heroin, the most abused opiate, was introduced in 1874 as a substitute for the painkiller morphine, but it soon proved to be a bigger problem. Heroin gives an intense "rush" of pleasure followed by several hours of dreamy contentment and sedation. For heroin addicts, painful withdrawal symptoms may begin within a few hours and thus prompt further use to relieve the discomfort. Since the early 1990s the availability of high grade, inexpensive heroin has increased its use, especially among adolescents and young adults.[43]

opiates—narcotic drugs such as opium, morphine, codeine, and heroin

Hallucinogens

As their name indicates, **hallucinogens** are drugs that cause hallucinations, or false perceptions. They also have other prominent effects, however, including psychedelic mind alterations and unpredictable emotional changes. Hallucinogens distort your perceptions and produce shifting images of color, form, and movement in ordinary objects and scenes.

hallucinogens—drugs that cause hallucinations and psychedelic mind-alterations

Issues and Applications

Drugs in the Workplace

In the 1600s, Spanish conquistadors in South America supplied their slaves with coca leaves to energize them, enabling them to work harder and longer with less food. Long before the conquistadors arrived, however, native people chewed coca leaves to increase their energy and endurance. Historically, drugs and work have a long relationship in many cultures where people have used drugs to enhance their work performance.[38]

Every day millions of people take a coffee or cola break at work and school to "recharge their batteries." During your next caffeine break, stop and consider what bearing the stimulant has on your state of mind and behavior. Mild stimulants such as caffeine increase your attention and energy and can improve your performance on some work tasks. Most psychoactive drugs, however, disturb your mental abilities and interfere with job skills, especially those involving complex behavior. You have certainly heard about accidents in which workers have been injured or caused injury to others because of drug intoxication. Such incidents are only the most visible signs of the dam-

Natural hallucinogens such as *mescaline* have long been taken by some Native Americans in their religious rituals. Many hallucinogen users report having spiritual insights and mystical experiences under their influence.[44]

Phencyclidine (PCP) is a synthetic hallucinogen, first used as an animal tranquilizer, that creates profound sensory and cognitive disruptions as well as emotional agitation and a loss of coordination. Often called "angel dust," PCP has been responsible for numerous cases of irrational behavior and violence.

Another synthetic hallucinogen, *lysergic acid diethylamide* (LSD), became popular in the 1960s because of its supposed "mind-expanding" effects. Feelings of insight and creativity, distortions of sensory images and time, and euphoric moods are commonly reported by LSD users. Albert Hoffman, the chemist who invented LSD in 1938, described its effects in the following passage:

"On arriving home, I lay down and sank into a kind of drunkenness which was not unpleasant and which was characterized by extreme activity of imagination. As I lay in a dazed condition with my eyes closed…there surged upon me an uninterrupted stream of fantastic images of extraordinary plasticity and vividness and accompanied by an intense kaleidoscope-like play of colors."[45]**

Although Hoffman described several typical LSD experiences, not everyone has a "good trip." Many cases of serious emotional and behavioral disturbances have also resulted. Like other hallucinogens, LSD is not addictive, but with prolonged use can lead to psychological dependence.

aging effects of drugs in the workplace. Much more of the damage is subtle, as in drug-related absenteeism and health problems.

Experts estimate that 15 percent of adult Americans have a drug or alcohol problem, and millions more use drugs occasionally. Most drug users are also members of the workforce, and the cost of their drug use to society is staggering. The economic cost of alcohol use alone is over $100 billion per year, much of that due to lost productivity. Drug use not only reduces productivity, but also increases the worker's chance of injury, illness, and psychological disturbances, all of which impair job performance.[44]

In an effort to deal with this problem, more employers are developing drug education programs for their workers and providing drug treatment for the more severely impaired. If you are now a member of the workforce or plan to be someday, in all likelihood your job performance and perhaps your personal safety will be affected by someone's drug use. You and other members of society will also be responsible for addressing this widespread dilemma.

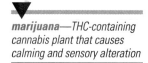

marijuana—THC-containing cannabis plant that causes calming and sensory alteration

Marijuana

The most common illegal drug in the United States is **marijuana**, which is obtained from the leaves and flowering tops of the *Cannabis* plant. Long used as a medicine for its calming effects, marijuana is mentioned in Chinese documents nearly 5,000 years old. The chemical in marijuana that causes its psychoactive effects is *tetrahydrocannabinol* (THC). Marijuana produces feelings of emotional well-being and sensory alterations, such as enhanced music perception. Marijuana also disrupts your attention and memory temporarily until the THC is passed from your body.

Although uncommon, some marijuana users experience dramatic fear and panic reactions. While there is no evidence that marijuana is addictive, chronic abusers develop psychological dependence. Prolonged abuse of marijuana can cause apathy, reduced sex drive, and respiratory problems.[46]

Summary

1. The sleep cycle consists of REM sleep and four stages of NREM sleep. As sleep progresses from NREM Stage 1 to Stage 4, brain arousal decreases, and then an increase in brain arousal accompanies progress back from NREM Stage 4 to Stage 1. REM sleep has irregular fast waves, rapid eye movement, muscle inhibition, and dreaming. Sleep deprivation studies indicate that sleep is essential. Restoration theory states that sleep replenishes the brain's resources for waking activity. Other theories claim that sleep aids memory by removing unneeded memories and storing useful memories.

2. Freud's wish fulfillment hypothesis explains dreams as wish fulfillment fantasies that serve unconscious needs. Jung thought that dreams help set a balance between the conscious and unconscious mind. The network model views dreaming as unconscious emotional problem solving. In activation-synthesis theory cortical arousal during REM sleep is considered the basis for dreams. Research finds that dreams reflect dreamers' current emotional concerns, developmental levels, and gender-related issues. In lucid dreams dreamers control the events in their dreams.

3. Insomnias are disorders of sleep due to stress, sleep apnea, and emotional disorders. Hypersomnia is excessive sleep. A sudden attack of REM sleep defines narcolepsy. Nightmares are frightening REM sleep dreams, and sleep terrors and sleepwalking are abnormalities of NREM sleep.

4. According to neodissociation theory, hypnosis produces a trance state in which mental activities are dissociated from one another. The hypnotic state includes suggestibility, nonrational thinking, focused attention, and distortions of self-awareness and time. Hypnosis is influenced by the subject's beliefs and motivation to comply with suggestions.

5. Hypnosis is used in controlling pain by helping subjects distract themselves from pain signals. The use of hypnosis for memory improvement has had some success, but the validity of the memories is often questionable. Hypnosis is helpful in therapy for emotional and behavioral problems, such as habit control, anxiety, and depression.

6. Psychoactive drugs alter your thinking, emotions, and behavior. Depressants are psychoactive drugs that suppress or slow neural activity, especially in the brain. Alcohol is a depressant that relieves tension, releases positive and negative emotions, impairs judgment and perception, and disrupts coordination. Depressants such as barbiturates and tranquilizers are called sedatives because they cause relaxation and anxiety reduction.

7. Stimulants are psychoactive drugs, such as amphetamines, cocaine, caffeine, and nicotine, that increase neural arousal and feelings of energy. The most powerful stimulants, amphetamines and cocaine, produce emotional excitement, heightened alertness, and excessive activity, and they are addictive.

8. The opiates are drugs derived from opium, including morphine, codeine, heroin, and methadone. Opiates are highly addictive drugs that create narcotic euphoria and drowsiness as well as a reduced sensitivity to pain.

9. Hallucinogens are drugs that cause hallucinations, psychedelic mind alterations, and emotional disruptions. The hallucinogenic class includes naturally occurring drugs, such as mescaline, as well as synthetic drugs such as PCP and LSD.

10. Marijuana is obtained from the *Cannabis* plant and contains a drug called tetrahydrocannabinol (THC). The psychoactive effects of marijuana include a relaxed and pleasurable mood state as well as mild alterations of sensory experiences.

Questions for Discussion

1. What are the stages and functions of sleep?

2. What are the major theories and research findings about sleep?

3. What are the main disorders of sleep and dreaming?

4. What are the characteristics of the hypnotic state?

5. In what ways is hypnosis used today?

6. How do the depressants alter consciousness?

7. What psychoactive effects result from use of stimulants?

8. In what way do the opiates affect mental activity and behavior?

9. How do hallucinogenic drugs influence consciousness?

10. What are the effects of marijuana on mind and behavior?

Applying Psychology

You have probably had the experience of realizing that you are dreaming while your dream is taking place. When this happens most people find it curious, funny, or sometimes scary. What if you could influence the dream and put it to some good use? In lucid dreaming that is exactly what happens. Strange as it sounds, you can learn to develop this ability with a few simple activities.

▶ *Step 1: Practice recalling your dreams.* On waking in the morning, spend a few minutes remembering any dream or part of a dream. Keep a dream journal and record your dream recollections. Be patient and practice faithfully every day.

▶ *Step 2: Use self-suggestions for dreaming.* Before going to sleep, remind yourself how very much you want to remember your dreams. Tell yourself to remember to realize that you are dreaming when the dream unfolds.

▶ *Step 3: Rehearse lucid dreaming.* When you recall a dream in the morning, review it several times and visualize yourself in the dream being aware that you are dreaming. Suggest to yourself that you intend to be aware in your dreams the next time you sleep.

▶ *Step 4: Direct your dreaming to solve a problem.* After practicing steps 1–3, you will be ready to apply lucid dreaming to a problem. Pick a simple, concrete, real problem—for instance, overcoming procrastination. Use self-suggestions (step 2) and dream rehearsal (Step 3) focused on the problem to prepare yourself to direct your lucid dreaming and create a solution.

After completing this chapter, you should be able to:

1. Outline and describe the elements of classical conditioning.

2. Explain the principles of extinction, spontaneous recovery, generalization, discrimination, and higher-order conditioning in classical conditioning.

3. Provide two applications of classical conditioning to human behavior.

4. Define the roles of positive and negative reinforcers and punishment in operant conditioning.

5. Describe the different schedules of partial reinforcement.

6. Discuss the application of operant conditioning principles to human behavior.

7. Define cognitive learning and explain how it differs from classical and operant conditioning.

8. Discuss how Köhler's work on insight learning and Tolman's latent learning experiments provide evidence of cognitive learning.

9. Discuss Bandura's observational learning experiments and identify the principles of observational learning.

10. Describe applications of observational learning in life and work.

▼

learning—*a change in behavior as a result of experience*

► You see an advertisement in a magazine showing one of your favorite dishes prepared just the way you like it, and your stomach begins to growl.

► Your experience tells you that if you improve your study techniques you will receive higher grades on your exams.

► You are watching a movie or television program, and later you behave just like one of the actors or actresses you observed.

The situations above illustrate **learning**, a change in behavior as a result of experience. You are capable of performing many behaviors that allow you to adapt to changes in the environment. Some are unlearned and reflexive, such as jerking your knee when it is tapped or blinking your eyelid when dust touches your eye. Feelings such as hunger, anger, or sexual desire are also unlearned in the sense that the ability to experience those feelings is built into your nervous system. Unlike that of many animals, however, whose behavior is controlled largely by unlearned patterns of behavior called *instincts*, your behavior is influenced more by your experiences.

In defining learning as a change in behavior due to experience many psychologists, called behaviorists, define behavior as observable actions. Others, known as cognitive psychologists, consider mental events, such as thoughts and attitudes, too. Psychologists distinguish learning from the effects of maturity. Consider riding a bicycle. If you placed a six-month-old infant on a bike for 16 hours a day, he still could not ride it. Why? Because he does not possess the physical maturity to coordinate his muscles. Later, when he matures a little more, he will be able to ride the bike. You can see in this example that some behavioral changes depend not only on learning, but on maturity as well.

Psychologists also distinguish between learning and performance. Learning is a hypothetical process that is measured by performance, but performance is not necessarily an accurate measure of learning. Say you learn most of the material in this chapter, but when you take the exam you have other, more pressing things on your mind that make you perform poorly. In this case, as in many others, you may have learned more than you are able to show by your performance.

In this chapter you will study three major types of learning: classical conditioning, operant conditioning, and cognitive learning. You will also learn how these types of learning are applied to everyday life and work situations.

Classical Conditioning

You are watching a horror movie, and your heart begins to pound and your body tenses up. You have probably noticed that such reflexive responses occur automatically and involuntarily. The fact that you can be frightened by a horror movie shows that your reflexes are linked to stimuli in the environment. **Classical conditioning** is a kind of learning in which a new stimulus comes to produce a reflexive response by its association with another stimulus that naturally triggers the reflex. In this section we will trace the early development of classical conditioning, explain its principles, and show how it applies to human behavior.

Pavlov's Experiments

The roots of classical conditioning lie in the work of the Russian physiologist Ivan Pavlov (1849–1936). While studying digestion in dogs, Pavlov noticed that the dogs' salivation reflex became conditioned to Pavlov's own behavior. Spurred on by these observations, Pavlov began a series of experiments that formed the basis of *classical*, or *Pavlovian, conditioning*.

In order to study digestion, Pavlov put tubes in a dog's mouth. When the dog was given some meat, its saliva passed through the tubes and into containers, where it was collected and measured. After presented with meat many times, the dog began to salivate when Pavlov walked into the room, even before the meat was presented. Originally, Pavlov considered these "psychic secretions" to be an annoyance, but later he decided to study them systematically because they looked similar to the physiological reflexes he was interested in.[1,2]

In Pavlov's classical conditioning experiment, the dog was placed in a harness with tubes leading from its mouth. A tuning fork was struck, and then meat was given to the dog. At first, the dog only salivated at the food, but after repeated pairings of the tone and the meat, the dog salivated at the tone, even before the meat was presented.

In a typical experiment, Pavlov placed the dog in a harness with tubes leading from its mouth. Then he struck a tuning fork and gave the dog some meat about a half second later. At first, the dog salivated only at the meat, but after repeated pairings of the tone and the food the dog began to salivate at the tone, even before the meat was given. Eventually, Pavlov found that many different stimuli could be paired with the food and elicit, or produce, the salivation reflex.

Principles of Classical Conditioning

Pavlov's pioneering experiments with the salivation reflex led to the basic principles of classical conditioning. Over the years, psychologists have employed these principles to help us understand the learning of many animal and human behaviors.

In Pavlov's experiments, the dogs learned to associate the tone with the food (see Figure 5.1). In this situation, food is the **unconditioned stimulus** (US), defined as any stimulus that naturally elicits a reflexive response. The reflexive response to the US, in this case salivation, is known as the **unconditioned response** (UR). Remember that no learning occurs here because a dog does not have to learn to salivate when food is given. Learning occurs when a neutral stimulus, one that ordinarily cannot produce the reflex such as the tone, is paired with the food. The neutral stimulus, in this case the tone, is known as the **conditioned stimulus** (CS). It is defined as a stimulus that comes to elicit a reflex after repeated pairings with the US. The reflexive response produced by the CS is the **conditioned response** (CR). The elements of classical conditioning are summarized in Table 5.1.

unconditioned stimulus—a stimulus that naturally elicits a reflexive response

unconditioned response—a reflexive response to an unconditioned stimulus

conditioned stimulus—a neutral stimulus that eventually elicits a reflexive response by repeated pairings with an unconditioned stimulus

conditioned response—the reflexive response to the conditioned stimulus

Figure 5.1   **The Classical Conditioning Model**

Procedure:

Neutral Stimulus (Tone)
+
Unconditioned Stimulus (Food)   ➡   Unconditioned Response (Salivation)

Result:

Conditioned Stimulus (Tone)   ➡   Conditioned Response (Salivation)

In classical conditioning, a neutral stimulus (tone) is repeatedly paired with an unconditioned stimulus (food), and an unconditioned response (salivation) is produced. Eventually, the tone becomes a conditioned stimulus, capable of producing a conditioned response (salivation) by itself.

The process whereby the CR becomes stronger through repeated pairings of the CS and US is known as **acquisition**. The time interval between the CS and US is an important factor in acquisition. Pavlov observed the strongest CR if the tone preceded the food by $\frac{1}{2}$ second. Researchers have found that time intervals of 2–4 seconds or more work well, too.[1]

acquisition (ack-kwi-zi-shun)—the strengthening of a conditioned response by repeated pairings of the conditioned and unconditioned stimuli

Table 5.1 Elements of Classical Conditioning

Unconditioned stimulus (US)	Stimulus that naturally elicits a reflexive response
Unconditioned response (UR)	Response produced by the US
Conditioned stimulus (CS)	Previously neutral stimulus that elicits a reflexive response by association with US
Conditioned response (CR)	Reflexive response produced by CS

What do you think would have happened if Pavlov had repeatedly sounded the tone without offering the food after it? One of the most important observations made by psychologists is that learned behaviors can be inhibited, or weakened. The process whereby a response weakens and is eliminated is called **extinction** (see Table 5.2). When the CS no longer elicits the CR, we say that the CR has been extinguished because the association between the CS and US has been disrupted.

extinction—the weakening and elimination of a conditioned response

Another important discovery is that although extinguished behaviors may be inhibited, the associations are not always lost. One week after Pavlov extinguished the conditioned salivation response he went back into the laboratory, struck the tuning fork, and the dog salivated, though at a weaker intensity. These observations illustrate the principle of **spontaneous recovery**, which is the reappearance of an extinguished response without retraining. These recovered responses extinguish rapidly, however.

spontaneous recovery—the reappearance of an extinguished response without retraining

Do you think Pavlov's dog would have salivated if other tones had been presented? Pavlov presented other tones to the dog and found that it would salivate to them. These findings led Pavlov to propose the principle of **stimulus generalization**, in which a conditioned response follows a stimulus that is similar to the original stimulus used in training. The strength of the CR depends on how similar the new stimuli are to the original such that the greater the similarity, the stronger is the response. **Stimulus discrimination** occurs when the subject perceives a difference between two or more stimuli and responds only to one. For example, if Pavlov had substituted an arm movement for the tone, the dog would have noticed the difference between the two and would have responded only to the tone.

stimulus generalization—a response to a stimulus that is similar to the conditioned stimulus

stimulus discrimination—the selective response to a specific stimulus

Suppose that you go to the dentist to have a cavity filled without an anesthetic. As the drill burr digs into your tooth, you experience intense pain and are afraid to continue. In this case, you learn to associate the sound of the drill with pain and fear so that the sound of the drill becomes a conditioned stimulus. The next time you visit the dentist to have a cavity filled, you hear music that you did not hear the first time. The music becomes associated with (conditioned to) the sound of the drill and acts as a conditioned stimulus itself, so that both the sound of the drill and the music can elicit the same fear response. Your experience is explained by **higher-order conditioning**, which is the pairing of a neutral stimulus with a conditioned stimulus so that they evoke the same conditioned response. Higher-order conditioning shows that new learning can be built upon prior experience.

Table 5.2 **Principles of Classical Conditioning**

Acquisition	Creation of CS-US association by pairing CS with US
Extinction	Weakening of CR by presenting CS alone (no US)
Spontaneous recovery	Reappearance of extinguished CR without retraining
Stimulus generalization	Carryover of CR to stimuli similar to CS
Stimulus discrimination	Responding selectively to specific CS
Higher-order conditioning	Use of prior conditioning to create new CS-CR association

Applications of Classical Conditioning

By now you must be wondering how the study of salivation in dogs has any relevance to human behavior other than bad experiences in the dentist's office. Psychologists have applied classical conditioning principles to explain many human behaviors and to modify a variety of behavioral problems. In this section you will learn about the application of classical conditioning principles to explain phobias, taste aversions, and drug abuse.

In 1920, the psychologist John B. Watson and his research assistant Rosalie Rayner showed that humans could learn emotional responses. They explained these findings using principles of classical conditioning. The subject of Watson's experiment was an 11-month-old boy, "Little Albert." Watson gave Albert a white rat (CS) to play with. At first Albert seemed to enjoy the rat, then Watson evoked fear (UR) in him by repeatedly striking two metal bars (US) behind his head. Soon thereafter, Albert showed fear in the presence of the rat, indicating a *conditioned emotional response* (CER). Worse, Albert's fear generalized to other white furry objects such as rabbits, a woman's coat, and a Santa Claus mask. Whether Albert ever unlearned his fear of rats is unknown, but it is likely that extinction eventually occurred. Though Watson's methods were unethical by today's standards, he showed that humans could learn to fear stimuli that they previously had not.

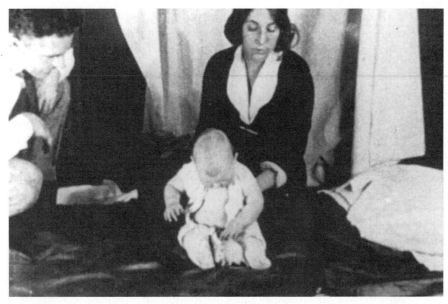

"Little Albert" was given a rat to play with. Watson made a loud noise that frightened Albert, and as a result Albert learned to fear the rat, which previously he had seemed to enjoy. This experiment demonstrated that humans could learn fear through classical conditioning.

Since Little Albert, psychologists have shown that many other emotional responses could be learned through classical conditioning. If you have ever developed a dislike for a food you previously enjoyed, you have firsthand knowledge of CERs in humans. Imagine that you become nauseous (UR) and vomit shortly after eating an "everything" pizza (CS). Even though you realize that your nausea is not caused by the pizza but by an intestinal virus (US), you nevertheless associate your nausea with the last food you ate, the pizza. Thereafter, the mere thought, sight, or smell of pizza can act as a conditioned stimulus and make you nauseous (CER), and you may never be able to eat pizza again! This conditioned nausea is known as a *conditioned taste aversion* (CTA). Researchers have found that CTAs may play a role in *anorexia nervosa*, an eating disorder in which the person refuses to eat enough food to maintain a normal body weight.[3]

Drug use and relapse have been explained by classical conditioning, too. Consider a person who abuses heroin or cocaine. You might know that taking these drugs requires the use of "equipment" such as a syringe, a needle, "cooking" apparatus, or perhaps a pipe for smoking. Many drug abusers say that these stimuli, the sight of certain people, or hearing a song may be conditioned to the drug and stimulate cravings and relapse after an extended period of not using the drug.[4] See if you can identify the CS, US, UR, and CR in the above example.

Classical conditioning is the basis for therapies designed to eliminate undesirable behaviors, especially irrational, disabling fears called *phobias*. For example, if you were treated for a phobia you would probably be taught to relax while exposed to the feared stimulus, until the stimulus no longer made you afraid. You will study this type of therapy, called *exposure therapy*, in more detail in Chapter 12.

Current Views of Classical Conditioning

Thus far, you have examined classical conditioning as a simple mechanical process in which the CS and US are associated because they are presented together. According to this model, any neutral stimulus could act as a CS as long as it was paired with the US. Modern experiments have revealed, however, that it is not quite that simple and that some stimuli may be more capable of eliciting a CR than others. These observations have led psychologists to propose an explanation of classical conditioning based on mental processes.

The current view is that the important element in classical conditioning is the information that the CS provides to the subject. This idea, called *contingency theory*, states that conditioning involves the learning of relations among events. In other words, a CS will be associated with a US only when the CS predicts the presence of a meaningful unconditioned stimulus.[5,6]

Support for this idea came from a study by psychologist Leonard Kamin in which two groups of animals received two conditioned stimuli—a tone and a light—before they received the US. One group was conditioned so that the light signaled the US; for the second group, there was no prior conditioning. The tone became well conditioned for the second group but apparently provided no additional information for the first group. Although both the light and tone were paired with the US for each group, only the light was consistently capable of producing the CR in the group that was pretrained with the light. This observation is known as a *blocking effect*. Traditional classical conditioning theory would predict that both stimuli would be equally effective in eliciting the CR since both were presented just before the presentation of the US. The blocking effect shows, however, that a stimulus does not automatically become a CS just because it is paired with the US. Instead, the meaning of the stimulus is most important in conditioning.[7]

Operant Conditioning

The study of classical conditioning is important in the history of psychology, but it represents only one type of learning. In classical conditioning you learn how stimuli are related to produce a reflexive response. Many of your important behaviors are not reflexive, however. Instead, they are *emitted*, meaning that they are produced by you rather than being automatically elicited by a stimulus. Emitted behaviors are acquired by **operant conditioning**, a type of learning in which *operants*, responses that operate on the environment, are strengthened or weakened by their consequences.

▼

operant conditioning—a type of learning in which responses called operants are strengthened or weakened by their consequences

Thorndike's Instrumental Conditioning

In 1898, the American psychologist Edward L. Thorndike (1874–1949) proposed a theory of learning called **instrumental conditioning**, in which behavior is directed toward a goal. His theory was based on research in which a hungry cat was placed in a "puzzle box." If the cat was able to unlatch the door of the box, it could escape and receive a food reward. Thorndike's measure of learning was *response latency*, or how long it took the cat to escape. Initially, the cat's behavior was totally ineffective; it would run through many irrelevant behaviors until, by trial and error, it unlatched the door. Each time the cat was placed in the box it escaped more quickly, until eventually, it unlatched the door almost immediately. Thus, unlatching the door was instrumental in reaching a goal (refer to Figure 5.2).

▼

instrumental conditioning—a type of learning in which behavior is directed toward a goal

Figure 5.2   **A Hungry Cat in Thorndike's Puzzle Box**

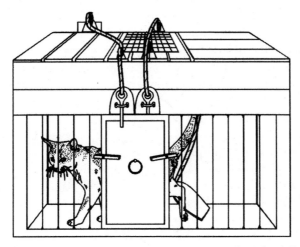

If the cat was able to unlatch the door, it could escape and get food. Demonstrations like this one led Thorndike to propose that learning was goal-directed.

Thorndike's puzzle box experiments led him to formulate the **law of effect**, which stated that responses followed by satisfying effects are strengthened, or "stamped in," and those that produce unsatisfying effects are weakened, or "stamped out." Thus, if you like the consequences of your behavior, you will probably show the same behavior when you are in the same situation again. If the consequences are unpleasant, however, you will be less likely to perform that behavior again. You may recognize that the law of effect describes the consequences of what are more commonly known as reward and punishment.[1]

▼

law of effect—rule that behaviors followed by satisfying consequences are strenghtened and responses followed by unsatisfying consequences are weakened

Skinner's Operant Theory

B. F. Skinner is one of the most prominent figures in the history of psychology. Influenced by giants like Pavlov, Watson, Thorndike, and others before him, Skinner analyzed a few conditioning events and used this knowledge to study more complex forms of behavior. On the basis of his research with animals, Skinner proposed a version of instrumental conditioning that he called **operant theory**. Like other theories that emphasize learning principles to explain behavior, operant theory is a type of *behaviorism* based on several assumptions:

▶ The main goals of psychology are the prediction and control of behavior.

▶ Behavior is lawful and determined, meaning that it is controlled or caused by factors in the environment and can be scientifically understood.

▶ Psychology should be confined to observable behavior. "Mentalism," or looking into the mind to explain behavior, has no place in scientific psychology. [8,9,10,11]

Skinner studied learning by using an apparatus he called the *repeating problem box*, better known as the Skinner box. The *Skinner box* is a simple soundproof box with a small lever, or bar, extending from one wall. The bar is connected to a recording system that tallies response rate, measured as the number of bar-presses per time period. A hungry rat is placed in the box and presses the bar, automatically releasing a food pellet into a food cup. Skinner found that if bar-pressing was followed by food, the probability that the rat would press it again would increase, thereby strengthening the relationship between the response and its consequence. Skinner labeled this process of strengthening a response *reinforcement* and defined a **reinforcer** as any stimulus that increases the probability of a response.[1]

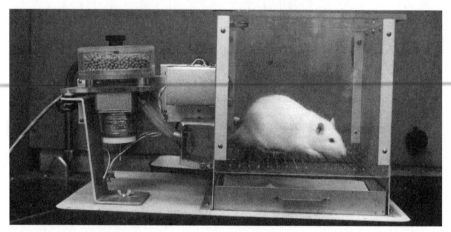

A hungy rat is placed in a Skinner box, a device which Skinner used to measure learning. If it presses a bar, food reinforcement is delivered.

There are two types of reinforcers: positive and negative. A **positive reinforcer** is a stimulus that, when applied after a response, increases the probability that the response will be repeated. Say that you can receive extra credit in your psychology course by completing a short paper. Extra credit would be a positive reinforcer if it increased the chances of your completing a paper each time you were given the opportunity. A **negative reinforcer** is a stimulus that, when removed after a response, increases the probability that the response will be repeated. A headache would be a negative reinforcer because if it disappeared after you took an aspirin, the probability that you would take an aspirin to relieve the headache pain would be increased. Notice that both positive and negative reinforcers increase the likelihood that a behavior will occur. The difference is that a positive reinforcer is added after a behavior occurs and a negative reinforcer is removed.

Positive reinforcers are classified as primary or secondary. A *primary reinforcer* is one that satisfies a biological need. Food would act as a primary reinforcer for you if you were hungry by increasing the chances of your eating. A stimulus that is rewarding because of its association with a primary reinforcer is known as a *secondary reinforcer*. Because the rewarding qualities of secondary reinforcers are learned, they are often called *acquired reinforcers*. Money is a good example of a secondary reinforcer; it cannot satisfy any biological need, but you can "cash it in" for a primary reinforcer such as food. You can readily see from this example that secondary reinforcers are important in controlling your behavior.

The chances that you produce a behavior also depend on how soon afterward it is reinforced. In general, reinforcement is most effective when it is delivered immediately after the response. Delayed reinforcement, by contrast, allows other stimuli to come between the response and its consequence, making it difficult for you to figure which stimulus is the consequence of behavior. For example, suppose you are training your dog to shake hands. Each time he gives you his paw, you wait 10 minutes before you give him a biscuit. Do you think your dog will associate shaking hands with receiving the biscuit? Probably not. Delayed reinforcement may help explain why some behaviors weaken. For example, you may find it difficult to study because the positive consequences of studying, such as getting good grades or landing a better job, are not provided very quickly.

Another way to change behavior is by *punishment*. A **punisher** is a stimulus that decreases the probability that a response will occur. Unlike positive and negative reinforcers, which are used to strengthen behaviors, punishers are designed to eliminate behaviors. Though it may seem to you that punishment is an effective way to eliminate undesirable behavior, its use is controversial. Some early studies by Skinner showed that punishment worked as long as it was in effect, but the punished behavior often recovered fully when punishment was removed. You probably know someone who was regularly punished but resumed punished behavior, in defiance, when the punishment was lifted. Imagine a teenager who is punished for staying out late by having to come home two hours earlier than usual. That teenager is likely to stay out later than ever when punishment is no longer in effect.

punisher—*a stimulus that decreases the probability of a response*

Many studies show that punishment can work to suppress behavior, but it must be used correctly. Despite the unpleasantness of punishment, it has a role in controlling behavior, especially dangerous behavior—for instance putting your finger in an electrical outlet—and other behaviors that must be stopped quickly.

Biography: B.F. Skinner

Burrhus Frederic Skinner (1904–1990), was born in Susquehanna, Pennsylvania. His father was a self-taught lawyer, and his mother was a housewife. His mother's sense of right and wrong had a strong effect on Skinner, who once said, "I was taught to fear God, the police, and what people think. As a result, I usually do what I have to do with no great struggle." As a youngster, Skinner played the piano and saxophone and earned pocket money playing in a dance ensemble. He was also mechanically inclined, building scooters, see-saws, blow guns, and a steam cannon. Skinner tried in vain for years to build a glider that he could fly.

Skinner received his bachelor's degree in English from Hamilton College in New York in 1926. He took a variety of college courses, including a philosophy course taught by one of Wilhelm Wundt's students, yet, ironically, he never took psychology. A brief literary career followed, but he realized that he had nothing to say. He was so disenchanted that he almost consulted a psychiatrist.

Skinner entered Harvard University's graduate psychology program and received his Ph.D. degree in 1931. He went on to the University of Minnesota and then became chairman of the psychology department at Indiana University in 1945, before moving back to Harvard where he finished his career. During these years he developed his operant theory and established himself as a prominent experimental psychologist.

While in Minnesota, he designed a "baby tender" for his daughter Deborah. Though it was nothing more than a climate-controlled playpen, he was accused of raising Deborah in a cage like an animal.

B. F. Skinner stands alone in psychology. His contributions in operant theory, research methodology, and the breadth of applications of his work have left a lasting impression on modern psychology and culture. He received more than 30 honorary degrees from universities around the world and was the recipient of many professional awards. He authored numerous journal articles and wrote several famous books, including *The Behavior of Organisms* (1938), *Walden Two* (1948), and *Beyond Freedom and Dignity* (1971). Perhaps Skinner's greatest distinction came in 1989, when a bust of him was unveiled at Harvard. Shortly before, he found out that his name had been cited more often than Freud's in the psychological literature.[12,13,14,15]

Some general rules apply to the appropriate application of punishment:

▶ The behavior that is to be punished should be defined as specifically as possible. For example, punishing a child for being a "bad girl" may not teach her which of several possible behaviors is the inappropriate one.

▶ Punishment must be delivered immediately after the behavior occurs, and it should be consistent; that is, the punishment should be delivered each time the behavior is present.

▶ The punishment should fit the behavior. Parents who punish a child while they are angry might give a punishment that is too severe or unreasonably long.

▶ The use of punishment should not be the principal means of modifying behavior. Punishing a child for doing the wrong thing and rarely rewarding the child for good behavior may cause resentment. Besides, punishment tells a child what not to do, but it does not tell him what he should do. Only reinforcement can strengthen the appropriate behavior.

Principles of Operant Conditioning

Many learning principles discovered in classical conditioning, such as extinction, generalization, and discrimination, also apply to operant conditioning. In this section, you will learn about these principles and how behavior is modified through shaping and the scheduling of reinforcement.

Behaviors usually are not performed correctly at first. If you ever tried to play a musical instrument, you know that many skills must be mastered before you can play well. A process fundamental to learning in operant theory is called **shaping**, the reinforcement of successive approximations to the correct response. Reinforcing successive approximations means reinforcing a behavior that is not yet precise but is getting closer and closer to the desired response. When your music teacher praises you for a good attempt at playing the correct notes, she is shaping your behavior.

shaping—the reinforcement of successive approximations to the correct response

Like conditioned responses, operants can also be eliminated. The gradual disappearance of a response caused by the removal of reinforcement is called *operant extinction*. If a child has a temper tantrum to get his way, a parent might try ignoring the behavior rather than reinforce the behavior by paying attention to it. Consistently ignoring temper tantrums may gradually extinguish them.

Operants can generalize to other stimuli besides the stimulus used in training. Imagine that a pigeon is trained in a Skinner box to peck at a green disc in order to obtain food. As the experimenter gradually varies the shade of green, the pigeon will continue to peck at the disc. The fact that the pigeon pecks at a colored disc that is similar to the original disc demonstrates *stimulus generalization* in operant conditioning. The pigeon would exhibit *stimulus discrimination* if it perceived a difference between green and red discs and pecked only at the green. A stimulus indicating that a response is likely to be reinforced is a *discriminative stimulus*, and we say that the response is under stimulus control. Many daily situations require you to make decisions on the basis of the presence or absence of certain stimuli. For example, suppose that you are planning to ask your boss for a raise. You might be more likely to ask for the raise if she is smiling than if she is scowling, because you have learned that you are more likely to get a raise if she is in a good mood. Table 5.3 summarizes the features of operant conditioning.

Table 5.3 Features of Operant Conditioning

Positive reinforcer	Stimulus added after a response that increases the chances that the response will be repeated
Negative reinforcer	Stimulus removed after a response that increases the chances that a response will be repeated
Punisher	Stimulus that decreases the probability that a response will occur
Shaping	Reinforcement of successive approximations to a correct response
Operant extinction	Disappearance of a response due to removal of reinforcement
Stimulus generalization	Response to stimulus that is similar to original stimulus
Stimulus discrimination	Selective responding to a specific stimulus

Everyday life and work are not like a Skinner box; reinforcers are not delivered regularly and consistently. Certainly you do not receive praise each time you perform a good deed, and paychecks rarely come every day. Yet behaviors persist despite the uncertainty of reinforcement. In one of his experiments, Skinner ran low on food pellets and could reinforce the rats only once per minute, no matter how many times they pressed the bar. Under these conditions, he observed that the rats pressed even more frequently than when they were reinforced for every response. These observations led Skinner to speculate that changing how reinforcement was scheduled could be a potent way to control behavior.[2]

There are two types of *reinforcement schedules*. A **continuous reinforcement schedule** is one in which every correct response is reinforced. If you got a pat on the back every time you helped a friend, you would be reinforced on a continuous reinforcement schedule. By contrast, behavior is reinforced occasionally on a **partial reinforcement schedule** (also called *intermittent reinforcement schedule*). Skinner experimented with many types of intermittent schedules and found that behaviors reinforced on these schedules do not undergo extinction as easily as responses reinforced continuously (refer to Figure 5.3).

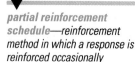

continuous reinforcement schedule—reinforcement method in which each correct response is reinforced

partial reinforcement schedule—reinforcement method in which a response is reinforced occasionally

Figure 5.3 Schedules of Reinforcement

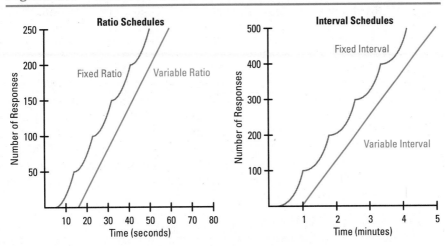

Response rates on ratio and interval schedules of reinforcement. Ratio schedules deliver reinforcement after a specified number of responses; interval schedules deliver reinforcement for the first response after a specified time period. Fixed-ratio and fixed-interval schedules, as shown, produce high rates of responding as the moment of reinforcement approaches, then reduced rates of responding just after reinforcement is delivered. Variable-ratio and variable-interval schedules produce more even rates of responding.

Source: Adapted from Rachlin, H., (1992). Introduction to Modern Behaviorism (3rd ed.). New York: W.H. Freeman

Ratio schedules give reinforcement after a specified number of responses. With a *fixed-ratio schedule*, the number of responses that the subject must give before being reinforced does not change. For example, if you were given a bonus for every 100 items you sold at work, you would be on a fixed-ratio schedule. If the number of items you had to sell to get a bonus changed from 100 to 125 to 75, you would be reinforced on a *variable-ratio schedule*. If you still doubt that responses reinforced on ratio schedules resist extinction, consider playing a casino slot machine. Even though slot machines pay on the basis of a variable-ratio schedule, the profits made by casinos provide ample evidence that pulling the lever is a behavior that is not weakened too readily.

Interval schedules are designed to reinforce the first correct response after a specified amount of time has elapsed. With a *fixed-interval schedule*, the amount of time that must elapse remains constant. Fixed-interval schedules usually produce high rates of responding near the end of the interval and low rates of responding just after the interval period is over. Many students study more just before an exam and very little after the exam is over. How do you think your study habits might change if instructor gave exams without notice? Not knowing when you would be tested, you would probably study some every day. A schedule in which the amount of time that must elapse before reinforcement changes is called a *variable-interval schedule*.

Operant Conditioning in the Workplace

If you have ever been disturbed by a boss who criticizes and humiliates you at work, you must have said that there has to be a better way. Perhaps there is. The success of businesses and organizations depends on the people who make up their workforce. When employees and management personnel are properly trained and motivated to perform, businesses and organizations operate at peak efficiency. Because of the recognition of the human element, psychologists have a long-standing involvement in studying how behavior affects business and organizational performance.[16]

Poor worker motivation, turnover, and absenteeism can have negative effects on productivity, and these effects are strengthened by destructive criticism. Fortunately, however, they can be modified through reinforcement.[17] In general, research shows that worker motivation and satisfaction can be improved if jobs are attractive and interesting. One study of 1,500 American workers, for example, found that they considered interesting work, good pay, availability of needed resources, hav-

Applications of Operant Conditioning

The principles of operant conditioning have been used to explain numerous aspects of learning, including infant memory, language and perceptual development, personality, and abnormal behavior.[20] The principles of operant conditioning have also been applied to raising children, the treatment of abnormal behavior, and performance in the workplace (see *Issues and Applications: Operant Conditioning in the Workplace*). Operant conditioning has even found a place in outer space. Before sending astronauts into space, the Air Force sent chimpanzees into orbit in 1961 to see if space travel would have a harmful effect on behavior. The chimps performed an assortment of operant tasks without any performance problems. The results of those experiments were influential in making the decision to send humans into space.[21]

Principles of operant conditioning are used to modify students' behavior in the classroom and as a teaching tool. In *behavior modification*, points or stars used as tokens are awarded for desired behavior such as completed homework, staying in the seat, or finishing class work on time. At the end of each week, tokens are traded for certain classroom privileges. In such behavior modification systems, inappropriate behavior is eliminated because it is ignored and cannot earn tokens. With *computer-assisted instruction*, students are instructed to respond to computer-generated questions about a particular topic or lesson. Correct answers are immediately reinforced, and the student is allowed to move on to the next question. Thereby students are

ing some authority, and friendly and cooperative co-workers to be important rewards to increase motivation.[18]

In order to improve job satisfaction, psychologists have recommended making jobs more challenging, as well. A study of 90 clerical workers showed that job enrichment improved workers' attitudes and decreased absenteeism and turnover.[18] Traditional rewards such as promotions and pay raises were found to be less effective in motivating professionals and high-tech employees than were wealth-building and wealth-sharing plans such as stock options and profit sharing.[19]

It is clear that reinforcement in the workplace should be delivered immediately, if possible, and it should depend on your performance rather than on merely showing up for work and doing just enough. For example, tying incentive pay to your performance, such as sales or parts completed, is an effective way to boost productivity.[18] When you are looking for your next job, it might be a good idea to consider features of the job besides pay and schedule. Otherwise, you might get stuck with a job you cannot tolerate.

informed about their performance. Punishment takes the form of not being permitted to move on.[22]

In 1948, Skinner published a utopian novel, *Walden Two*, in which he talked of a fictional community based on his social values. In this community, there were no class distinctions, men and women were equal and could pursue the same tasks, and there was a strong emphasis on education. In contrast to a free market economy in which goods are produced for profit, in *Walden Two* people conserved and shared their resources. Skinner viewed *Walden Two* as a psychological laboratory in which his behaviorist ideas could be tested.

Many critics reacted strongly and negatively to Skinner's philosophy. Nevertheless, in the early 1970s, a Mexican psychology student read *Walden Two* and founded a Walden-like community in the Mexican desert 175 miles south of the U. S. border. In *Comunidad Los Horcones*, 26 adults and children live the principles of operant theory. There is a written code of behavior detailing community lifestyle. Goals are planned, and each member shares in the responsibility of helping the community reach its goals. All adults are parents to all children, and all the clothes are stored in one building because possessiveness is discouraged. Since its founding, more than 60 people have come and gone from Los Horcones. People who leave usually mention jealousy and their individualistic natures for leaving.[23,24]

A more ambitious application of Skinner's ideas is the ongoing *Juniper Gardens Children's Project*. The project began in the mid-1960s as an effort to improve the development of disadvantaged children living in a housing project in Kansas City, Kansas. On the basis of Skinner's notion that behavior is determined by factors in the environment, the project effectively uses operant techniques to improve language, social and academic skills, as well as parenting skills. Stimulus control procedures are aimed at reducing dangerous behaviors and increasing patient compliance with medical treatments. The Juniper Gardens Children's Project is just one more example of Skinner's contributions to psychology and society.[25]

Cognitive Learning

Classical and operant conditioning emphasize learned associations between observable stimuli, responses, and consequences while failing to explain the underlying mental processes such as attention and thinking. These behavioristic approaches assume that mental events either are unimportant or cannot be understood scientifically. By contrast, **cognitive learning** is concerned with unobservable mental activities such as paying attention, perceiving, thinking, and remembering.

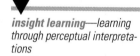

cognitive learning—theory of learning concerned with unobservable mental activity

Insight Learning

In 1913, the Gestalt psychologist Wolfgang Köhler studied the problem-solving abilities of chimpanzees. In a typical study, a banana was fixed to the ceiling of a cage. The chimp could reach the banana by standing on a box and jumping up to knock down the fruit. Most chimps found this task difficult, and only Sultan, the most intelligent, could solve the problem without help.

In the most difficult case, Sultan could reach the fruit only by stacking two boxes, climbing the boxes with two sticks joined together, and knocking the fruit down. After many unsuccessful attempts, Sultan eventually obtained the fruit accidentally. Once he "got the idea," he was able to insert one stick into the other and repeatedly get the fruit.[1]

Köhler's interpretation of these findings was that the chimpanzees solved the problems through perceptual interpretations, or insight, and labeled this activity **insight learning**. Insight allowed the animals to suddenly realize that the boxes and sticks could be used as tools needed to reach the goal.

insight learning—learning through perceptual interpretations

Latent Learning

Additional evidence for cognitive processes in learning came from Edward Tolman's maze-learning experiments with rats in 1930. In a typical experiment, hungry rats were divided into three groups, and for 10 days they explored the maze. The rats in group 1 received a food reward each time they reached the goal box, but the rats in groups 2 and 3 were not rewarded for reaching the goal. By the end of the tenth day it was apparent that the rewarded rats made many fewer errors than the nonrewarded rats, suggesting that they had learned more than the nonrewarded rats (refer to Figure 5.4). On the eleventh day the rats in group 2 received a food reward for finding the goal box and quickly performed as well as the rats who had been rewarded all along.

Figure 5.4　**Latent Learning**

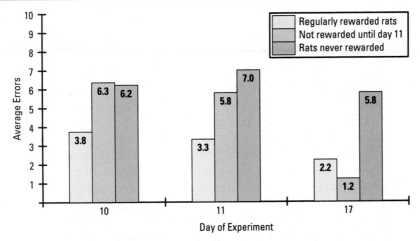

Maze-running performance in Tolman's latent learning experiment. Rats in group 1 were rewarded for successfully running a maze; rats in groups 2 and 3 were not rewarded. After 10 days, the rats in group 1 performed better than rats in groups 2 and 3. On the eleventh day, the rats in group 2 received a food reward and promptly improved their performance so that they made fewer errors than the rats who had been rewarded all along.

Source: Adapted from Hilgard, E.R. & Bower, G.H., (1975). Theories of Learning (4th ed.). Engelwood Cliffs, NJ: Prentice Hall

Tolman interpreted these findings to mean that the nonrewarded rats must have learned just as much as the rewarded rats, but did not show what they had learned until they were given an incentive to perform. Tolman called this **latent learning** because the amount of learning was hidden, or latent, and was revealed only when an incentive was provided. Tolman's findings highlight the distinction between learning and performance discussed at the beginning of this chapter.

Tolman's latent learning experiments were important to cognitive psychology for several reasons. First, they indicated that, contrary to the principles of operant conditioning, learning was possible in the absence of reward. Second, demonstrating later what was learned earlier showed that the rats must have developed and maintained mental images or memories of the maze. Tolman called these images *cognitive maps*. More recent studies of animal learning also support the notion that animals use varied cognitive processes to solve problems.[6]

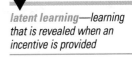

latent learning—learning that is revealed when an incentive is provided

Social Learning Theory

In the 1960s, cognitive psychologists began to shift their focus away from animal research and toward human learning in social situations. This approach, known as **social learning theory**, emphasizes the interaction of cognitive and environmental factors in learning. Unlike traditional learning theories, social learning theory proposes that direct experience is important but not sufficient to explain the richness of human learning. Social learning theorists purport that much of what you learn comes vicariously, that is, by observing the behavior of

social learning theory— theory of learning based on the interaction of cognitive and environmental factors

other people called *models*. Also, social learning theory strives to carefully analyze the cognitive activities that are part of the learning process.

The most prominent social learning theorist is the psychologist Albert Bandura. He proposed a theory of **observational learning**, which requires the observation and imitation of models. There are four steps in observational learning. First, you must pay attention to particular behavioral characteristics of the model. Second, you must mentally organize and remember the observed behavior. Third, you must perform the behavior. Fourth, on the basis of feedback you receive, you must decide whether to repeat the behavior.

In Bandura's classic study, kindergarten children watched a film in which an adult model beat an inflatable "Bobo" doll. Later, the children were placed in a similar situation and were observed by researchers through a one-way window. The results showed that children who had observed the aggressive model were likely to imitate the model's behavior, whereas children who had not observed the aggressive model were less likely to beat the Bobo doll. Apparently, the children learned how to be aggressive through observation.[26] (See *Issues and Applications: The Effects of the Media on Children's Behavior*.)

Bandura's research showed that the relationship between observation and performance was influenced by several variables. Children who had observed the aggressive models being punished were not likely to perform aggression themselves, even though they had learned aggression. But,

Issues and Applications

The Effects of The Media on Children's Behavior

Have you ever wondered if watching television or movies can affect your behavior? In 1993 a five-year-old boy set his home on fire, killing his baby sister, after watching the MTV cartoon characters Beavis and Butt-Head talk about setting fires. Shortly thereafter, one teenage boy was killed and another paralyzed after imitating scenes from a movie—*The Program*—in which college football players showed their mental toughness by lying in a busy highway. Since Bandura's observational learning experiments in the 1960s, the effects of media on behavior, especially aggressiveness in children, has been a hotly debated topic in society and psychology.

Many studies conducted in real-life settings have shown that media violence leads to aggression in children and adolescents and that the effects may accumulate with repeated exposures. One study, for example, showed that the more television children viewed at age 8, the more likely they were to be convicted of serious crimes by age 30.

What do you make of these studies? Do you believe that viewing media violence necessarily and automatically leads to aggression? If you

children who had observed the aggressive models being rewarded not only learned to act aggressively, but they also performed what they had learned. As you saw previously in Tolman's latent learning experiments, whatever is learned may not be performed unless an incentive is provided.

Other factors that can affect the performance of observed behavior include the age, sex, and status of the model. In general, you are most likely to imitate the behavior of a model who is of the same sex and age as you or whom you perceive to be someone of high status. You may not realize it, but your behavior has been influenced by your exposure to many models since childhood. At any rate, Bandura's research tells us that behavior is learned even if it is not performed. This is an important point to consider in child development. Parents may drink, smoke, overeat, or act aggressively; and when the child imitates them they may say; "Do as I say, not as I do." If Bandura's research is any indication, then it informs us that children may very well do both!

Social learning has been used to explain many behaviors (such as sex-role behaviors and family violence), attitudes (such as prejudice), abnormalities (such as drug abuse, depression, and phobias) and their treatment. For example, if you have a phobia, your therapist might use *modeling* techniques to help you overcome your problem by having you observe a model demonstrate appropriate behavior. Modeling is also an important part of training in business and industry to help build feelings of competence and expectations of success in trainees and managers alike. For example, one study showed that behavior-modeling training increased sales performance by 7 percent, while sales decreased by 3 percent during the same period for individuals who had not been trained.[27]

think it does, then how could you explain the fact that many children who view aggression on television do not act aggressively? Many other children must have watched Beavis and Butt-Head talk about fire without setting a fire themselves. It should be clear to you that the relationship between media violence and behavior is not a simple one, because aggression is determined by many interacting factors such as age, gender, and other social factors as well as the observation of violence. Do you think you would imitate television violence if you were not attracted to violence already? One hypothesis suggests that media violence has its greatest impact on people who are already most prone to aggression. In this view, aggressive individuals may be drawn to depictions of aggression in the media, and continued viewing of media violence may act as a rehearsal for aggression.[28]

The relationship between viewing media violence and aggressive behavior is difficult to determine. One thing is certain, however. Though you may not actually behave aggressively after watching violence on television or in the movies, it is clear that you nevertheless learn to act aggressively by viewing it.

Chapter 5 • Learning

Summary

1. In classical conditioning, the unconditioned stimulus elicits a reflex called the unconditioned response. The conditioned stimulus, a previously neutral stimulus, is repeatedly paired with the unconditioned stimulus until it eventually elicits the conditioned response.

2. Extinction is the gradual weakening of the conditioned response when the conditioned stimulus is no longer followed by the unconditioned stimulus. Spontaneous recovery is the reappearance of the conditioned response without retraining after it has been extinguished. In generalization, the conditioned response is evoked by stimuli that are similar to the conditioned stimulus. In discrimination, the new stimulus is perceived as different from the original conditioned stimulus, so the conditioned response is not evoked. Higher-order conditioning involves pairing new stimuli with the conditioned stimulus to elicit the conditioned response.

3. Classical conditioning has been applied in the explanation of phobias. A person learns to associate a previously neutral stimulus with one that naturally elicits fear. In drug relapse, previously neutral stimuli are associated with taking the drug, thereby evoking drug craving and relapse.

4. In operant theory, a reinforcer is any stimulus that increases the probability of a response. Reinforcers are used to strengthen behaviors. A positive reinforcer is a stimulus applied after a response that increases the probability that the response will be repeated. A negative reinforcer is a stimulus that, when removed after a response, increases the probability that the response will be repeated. A punisher is any stimulus that decreases the probability of a response. Punishers are used to suppress behavior.

5. Schedules of partial reinforcement are classified into two types. With fixed- and variable-ratio schedules, reinforcement is delivered after a specified number of responses occur. Fixed- and variable-interval schedules deliver reinforcement for the first response after a certain time period has elapsed.

6. Operant conditioning has been applied to many aspects of human behavior. It is used in education for classroom management and in computer-assisted instruction. Its principles have been applied to social programs such as the Juniper Gardens Children's Project, in which it is used to improve the behavior and academic performance of disadvantaged children.

7. Cognitive learning focuses on the mental processes, such as thinking, perceiving, and planning, that underlie learning. By contrast, classical and operant conditioning are more mechanical views of learning that minimize or ignore mental processes in learning.

Fundamentals of Psychology

8. In Köhler's experiments, chimpanzees realized how to obtain fruit. Köhler interpreted these findings as evidence that the chimpanzees solved the problems through perceptual interpretations, or insight. In Tolman's latent learning experiments, rats showed what they had previously learned when they were given an incentive to perform. Tolman concluded that they must have kept a cognitive map of the maze.

9. Bandura conducted experiments in which children observed aggressive models on film. Later, Bandura found that observing the aggressive model led to aggressive behavior when children were placed in a similar situation. From these studies Bandura concluded that much of what we learn is learned vicariously, through the observation and imitation of behaviors performed by models.

10. Observational learning principles have been applied to help people with phobias cope with their problems. In business, modeling helps managers and trainees build expectations of success that lead to improved performance.

Questions for Discussion

1. What are the elements of classical conditioning?

2. What are extinction, spontaneous recovery, generalization, discrimination, and higher-order conditioning?

3. What are two applications of classical conditioning?

4. What are the roles of reinforcement and punishment in operant conditioning?

5. What are the different schedules of partial reinforcement?

6. How is operant conditioning applied to human behavior?

7. What is cognitive learning, and how does it differ from classical and operant conditioning?

8. How did Köhler's insight learning experiments and Tolman's latent learning studies provide evidence for cognitive learning?

9. How did Bandura study observational learning, and what are the principles he developed?

10. How are the principles of observational learning applied to life and work?

Applying Psychology

Imagine that you are working in an after-school child-care center in which you are responsible for 15 children ages 6 to 10. Because they sometimes become unruly, your supervisor asks you to help her with a behavior management program. How would you set up this program in order to strengthen positive behaviors and eliminate negative behaviors? In designing the program, be sure to consider the principles of operant conditioning including reinforcement, punishment, shaping, extinction, generalization, and discrimination. Also, discuss how observational learning might be used as part of the program.

Chapter 6

Memory

After completing this chapter, you should be able to:

1. Describe the memory processes of encoding, storage, and retrieval.

2. Summarize recall, recognition, and relearning tests of memory.

3. Describe the information-processing model of memory.

4. Discuss the characteristics of sensory memory.

5. Explain the features and processes of short-term memory.

6. Outline the organization of long-term memory.

7. Explain the processes of long-term memory.

8. Distinguish among decay, interference, retrieval errors, and motivated forgetting.

9. Discuss the biological bases of memory.

▼

memory—mental abilities for acquiring, retaining, and accessing information

In August 1982, Lenell Geter, a 25-year-old engineer, was arrested for the robbery of a Kentucky Fried Chicken restaurant in Texas. Although he was at work when the robbery occurred and his boss and co-workers supported his alibi, five eyewitnesses identified him as the culprit. On the basis of their testimony, he was convicted and sentenced to life in prison. After serving 16 months, Geter was released when another man was arrested for the crime. Four of the eyewitnesses changed their minds and identified the other man as the robber. In an interview on the *60 Minutes* television program Geter wondered, "How could five people be so wrong?"[1]

That is a tough question. Like Geter, you might also wonder how so many eyewitnesses could fail so badly in such a serious matter. Psychologists, too, are puzzled about such problems and have devoted considerable effort to unraveling the mysteries of memory. In this chapter you will learn about how memory works and how it fails.

An Overview of Memory

As was true of the eyewitnesses who misidentified Lenell Geter, memory may yield remarkably unreliable results. Sometimes, however, memory is amazingly accurate. Psychologists use the term **memory** to mean the mental abilities that you use to acquire, retain, and access information about your experiences. Whether your memory works well or not, its activity is characterized by three basic processes:

▶ acquiring information, or *encoding*

▶ retaining information over time, or *storage*

▶ accessing information, or *retrieval*

Encoding processes put information into your memory through *memory codes*, ways of representing information. For instance, as you read this sentence, it enters your memory in a code based on the meaning of the words. Other memory codes represent perceptual and emotional experiences. Information in memory is retained over time by storage processes. Have you ever tried to remember a definition by repeating it several times? When you do that, you are using a common storage process. Like other aspects of memory, storage is imperfect, and many memories are retained only temporarily.

By the way, do you remember the name of the unfortunate man mentioned at the start of this chapter? The state where he was arrested? The number of eyewitnesses? To gain access to stored memories you use your retrieval processes. If you recalled that Lenell Geter was arrested in Texas and misidentified by five people, your retrieval processes are in good working order. Like storage, retrieval, is often less than perfect. You may have remembered his last name only or thought that his first name was Lenny or Lionel. As you will learn later in this chapter, retrieval is likely to malfunction for a variety of reasons.

How Memory Is Measured

In the late 1800s, the German psychologist Hermann Ebbinghaus (1850–1909) began the scientific study of memory, with himself as a subject, using *nonsense syllables*, or meaningless letter combinations, such as *QOP* and *XAH*. Since Ebbinghaus, memory researchers have employed many methods to measure memory, but most studies have relied on three kinds of tests: recall, recognition, and relearning.

A test of *recall* requires you to search for some information in your memory and judge how accurate the possibilities are. For instance, a recall test in your psychology class might ask, Who is called the father of psychology? To answer this question you must gain access to the part of your memory that contains facts about the early history of psychology and search for names of possible figures. When you retrieve some names—Freud?, Wundt?, James?—you must judge how likely they are to be correct.

By contrast, a *recognition* test asks you to identify the familiarity or correctness of some information. Multiple-choice exams are recognition tests. You must pick the right answer from several options by comparing each with your stored memories. Your psychology exam is a recognition test if it asks, Which of the following people was the founder of behaviorism: a) Wertheimer, b) Titchener, or c) Watson? Recognition tests are usually easier than recall tests because you do not have to search your memory for the answer, and you can always guess.

Relearning tests measure the time you saved in learning some information for a second time. Ebbinghaus called relearning the *savings method*. If you memorize the names of the founders of the early schools of psychology today, you may forget a few of their names in two weeks. If you memorize them again at that time, you will notice that the process takes less time. The time savings in relearning is an indication of how strong your initial memory was.

Hermann Ebbinghaus

The Information-Processing Model of Memory

Today, the most widely accepted view of memory is called the **information-processing model**, which describes three stages of memory in which information is encoded, stored, and retrieved in distinctive ways. Figure 6.1 shows the features of this model.

▼
information-processing model—view of memory as having sensory, short-term, and long-term stages

Figure 6.1 The Information-Processing Model of Memory

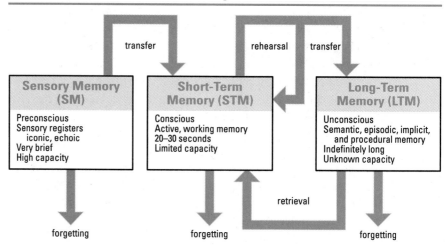

The three stages of memory—sensory, short-term, and long-term—and their relationships. Information first enters SM and is transferred to STM, from which it is transferred to LTM. Retrieval transfers information from LTM to STM. At each stage, information is lost by forgetting.

First, information enters your *sensory memory* (SM), then it is processed further in your *short-term memory* (STM), and finally it is deposited into your *long-term memory* (LTM). But, memory is not a simple, automatic passing of facts from stage to stage. At each stage, information is altered by your memory processes and some of it is forgotten. Although the stages are separate, they interact and influence each other. For example, when you learn a new phone number and retrieve it a minute later, you are transferring information from STM to LTM when learning and back again from LTM to STM when retrieving.[2,3,4]

Sensory Memory

Imagine how good your grades would be if you had a perfect memory for everything you saw or heard. Believe it or not, you do have a near-perfect memory, but it lasts only briefly and is not consciously known. **Sensory memory** (SM) is your brief, but nearly complete memory for data received by the senses. Unfortunately, your SM is *preconscious*, meaning that the sensory data have not yet been consciously processed, and much of your sensory input is lost even before you become aware of it.

Iconic Memory

Your sensory memory for visual stimuli is known as **iconic memory**. Psychologist George Sperling discovered iconic memory by studying how subjects recall stimulus displays like the one in Figure 6.2.[5] To test the

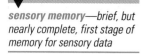

sensory memory—brief, but nearly complete, first stage of memory for sensory data

iconic (eye-konn-ik) memory—sensory memory for visual stimuli

number of letters available in memory immediately after the presentation of the display, Sperling used a *partial report method* that involved three steps:

1. The subject observed a display of letters that was presented very quickly.
2. The subject was given a cue or signal to recall only a part of the display of stimuli.
3. The subject reported the letters only from the cued part of the display.

If you were a subject in this study, different tones would cue you to recall different rows of letters: high-pitch tone top row; medium-pitch tone middle row; and low-pitch tone bottom row. If the tone cues were given within a quarter of a second after the display was removed, you would show nearly perfect recall for all the letters. This remarkable memory disappears rapidly, however, and unless it is transferred to STM the information is lost.

Figure 6.2 Partial Report Method of Studying Sensory Memory

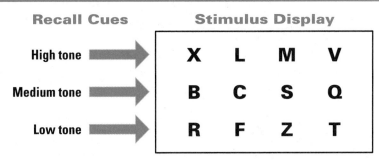

In Sperling's partial report method of studying sensory memory, subjects were given a display similar to this and their recall was tested at different intervals by giving recall cues (tones) to indicate which part of the display they were to remember.

The Sensory Registers

Following Sperling's lead, researchers looked for sensory memory in the other senses. In addition to iconic memory, they found several sense-specific mechanisms, or *sensory registers*, that are separate and independent. There is no apparent interaction between the sensory registers of different senses. In addition, the features of your sensory registers vary from sense to sense. In contrast to iconic memory, which retains visual information for a split second, your *echoic memory*, the sensory register for hearing, can last as long as a few seconds.

Many unanswered questions about sensory memory remain. Except in vision and hearing, the features of the sensory registers are not well defined. Some researchers even argue that sensory memory is really an aspect of sensation, not a separate stage of memory. Others believe that sensory memory has two phases, one very brief, like iconic memory, and another more durable and linked with short-term memory.[4,6,7,8]

Short-Term Memory

How often have you done any of the following:

- ▶ Sung along with a song on the radio?
- ▶ Repeated a phone number while waiting to dial it?
- ▶ Tried to memorize the definition of a new term?

When you engaged in those activities, you were using your **short-term memory** (STM), the stage in which you actively and consciously perform memory tasks. Also known as *working memory*, STM enables you to obtain information from sensory memory (singing along with a song), hold it in your awareness (repeating a phone number), and transfer it to long-term memory (memorizing a definition).[9,10]

Attention

Many times each day you pay attention to events in your environment. While conversing with your friends, reading a magazine, listening to music, doing your homework, or engaging in other common activity, you rely on your ability to attend to certain stimuli and ignore others. Everyday experience shows that your memory depends on **selective attention**, the ability to selectively focus on specific stimuli. You might be surprised to learn that such an important and obvious ability as attention has long been a puzzle to psychologists.

Imagine that you are at a noisy party, where the loud music and voices make it hard to hear what your friend is saying to you. How do you pay attention to her voice and understand her without being distracted by the

In a stimulus-rich environment, selective attention abilities enable you to filter out irrelevant information and process stimuli that are meaningful.

surrounding noise? According to the *filter model*, your selective attention acts as a filter to block some stimuli and allow others to pass through to awareness. Exactly how attention mechanisms select the stimuli that pass through to your awareness is unknown, but their selection is affected by the meaning they have to you. The effect of meaning on attention is shown by the *cocktail party phenomenon*: While you are talking at that noisy party, you suddenly hear your name spoken by someone several feet away. Although you were not really listening to the speaker and did not mean to eavesdrop, your selective attention keyed into the voice because of the personal significance of what it said.[11,12,13,14]

In contrast to the filter model, the *capacity model* explains attention as a general information-processing resource controlled by your higher cognitive abilities. Complex mental tasks use more of your attention capacity than do simpler tasks. You can test this difference easily by comparing the effort required to keep in mind four license plate numbers (complex) and a friend's name (simple). Support for this model comes from studies of *divided attention*, in which subjects must pay attention to two or more sources of information at the same time. If you have tried to listen to two friends talking to you at the same time while trying to catch the traffic report on your car radio, you have experienced how difficult it is to divide your limited attention capacity.[8,15,16]

The Features of Short-Term Memory

Because you perform many of its activities consciously, STM has several features that can be readily examined. Researchers have clearly defined the characteristic duration and capacity of STM, as well as the processes that make this memory "workbench" so important.

As its name suggests, short-term memory holds information for only a short time, typically about 20–30 seconds. But, the duration of STM is qualified, because you can keep items in STM as long as you pay attention to or rehearse them. A classic example of STM research is a 1959 study by psychologists Lloyd and Margaret Peterson, who estimated STM duration by employing a *distractor task* to stop their subjects from rehearsing. Subjects tried to remember three consonants (for example, *MBN*) while counting backward by 3 from a designated number (for example, "811, 808, 805…"). While they were counting, the subjects could not rehearse the consonants. Try this task with a friend and see how hard it is to rehearse even three letters. By testing recall at different time intervals, the Petersons found that their subjects usually forgot the letters in about 20 seconds.[17]

Like its duration, STM capacity is also limited, because your memory workbench has only so much space for work to be done. On the average, STM holds between five and nine items, and thus, the capacity of STM is often called the "magic number 7±2." You can confirm this estimate by rehearsing sets of randomly chosen words. When you attempt to rehearse more than seven words at a time, the task becomes very difficult. Your STM is nearly filled, and a new word can be fit in only by displacing one already there.[18]

Estimates of STM capacity are also qualified because organization affects the number of items that can be held. Consider these letters: *CIAHBOFBIMTV*. If you see them as 12 separate items, you will have trouble keeping them all in STM. Now, try thinking of them in the following way: *CIA-HBO-FBI-MTV*. The task is easier when you treat the letters as four sets of information, called *chunks*, and even easier when each is a familiar abbreviation. This is an example of **chunking**, or organizing information into larger, more meaningful items. As you can see, STM capacity depends on the type of chunks that you use.

▼
chunking—STM process that organizes information into larger, meaningful items

Short-Term Memory Processes

As you have learned, STM allows you to pay attention to, consciously retain, and organize information. In addition, STM processes also promote more permanent, long-term memories.

How do you memorize names, phone numbers, addresses, or new facts? You probably repeat them several times until they are firmly set in your mind. This type of rehearsal through repetition is known as **maintenance rehearsal**, and it is an effective STM process for learning and establishing durable long-term memories. Too much maintenance rehearsal however, can cause information to lose its meaning and thus be easily forgotten. Try taking an unfamiliar definition—that of maintenance rehearsal, for example and repeating it 100 times; long before you get to the hundredth repetition, the definition will have lost any meaning and will be just senseless noise.[19]

▼
maintenance rehearsal—rehearsal by repetition of information

Issues and Applications

Improving Your Study Skills

What better way could there be to appreciate memory research than by using its findings to improve your grades? By applying three basic strategies in your studying, you will be able to learn, retain, and recall information much more effectively.

1. The *SQ3R Method* of textbook study involves these five steps: survey, question, read, recite, review.
   ▶ *Survey*: Get a general idea about the material by scanning the outline and organization of chapters and the sections of chapters.
   ▶ *Question*: Ask questions about the material and keep them in mind when you start to read.
   ▶ *Read*: Carefully read the material and try to find the answers to your questions. Taking notes and underlining text are helpful practices.
   ▶ *Recite*: After reading the material, recite what you recall of the main ideas and facts.
   ▶ *Review*: Go over your notes and questions and re-read whatever material is unclear.

A more effective STM strategy is **elaborative rehearsal**, in which you associate new information with familiar facts or with knowledge already in your memory. For example, if you learned about positive reinforcement (see Chapter 5) by relating it to an experience of training your dog or cat you would be using elaborative rehearsal and your memory would last longer. Although it requires more effort than maintenance rehearsal, in the long run elaborative rehearsal produces more meaningful and durable memories.[20]

From time to time, we rely on little gimmicks to remember names, facts, lists, and other information. When you do this, you are employing a **mnemonic**, or strategy to reorganize information to improve recall. Perhaps you already know these common mnemonics:

▶ ROY G. BIV: A nonsense name to remember the colors of the spectrum—**R**ed, **O**range, **Y**ellow, **G**reen, **B**lue, **I**ndigo, **V**iolet

▶ **E**very **G**ood **B**oy **D**oes **F**ine: A mnemonic sentence to order notes on a musical staff—E, G, B, D, F

The key to mnemonics is changing the material to be remembered into a new and more memorable pattern. The above mnemonics reorganize the information with new verbal patterns: an abbreviation (ROY G. BIV) and a sentence (Every Good Boy Does Fine). Another powerful mnemonic is to represent the information by *imagery* based on perceptual experiences. Creative images can help you remember simple information, such as someone's name. Suppose you meet someone named Robert for the first

elaborative rehearsal—strategy of associating new information with familiar facts

▼
*mnemonic (nee-**mon**-ik)—strategy to reorganize information to improve recall*

2. The strategy of *distributed practice* means that you break up study time into small, efficient periods. If you read an entire chapter in one sitting, you will probably soon forget most of it. Spend a brief period, about 20 minutes, studying one section and then do something else for a while. Later do another 20 minutes, and so on, until you complete the chapter. Cramming too much material at once is a waste of your time and energy.

3. *Overlearning* is a method of strengthening your memory by continuing to perform maintenance rehearsal (repetition) of the material even after you have first learned it. For example, after you master a new definition, *read it*, *repeat it*, and *write it* several more times. If you use this multiple rehearsal strategy of reading, speaking, and writing, your memory will be much more durable.

Although these methods do not guarantee that you will get better grades, if you use them regularly they will help you to retain more of what you study.

time. Find an image to link with his name, for example, visualize him with a mask like a "robber," and associate that image with your memory of him.

A striking example of imagery mnemonics is found in the case of S., a Russian *mnemonist*, or memory expert, who memorized long lists of words, names, and numbers by visualizing associations between them and familiar places. When he wanted to recall them, he would mentally "walk down the street" and "see" the information right where he had put it. This mnemonic is called the *method of loci* (places), and it has been a trick of memory experts since ancient times. Perhaps you can test this method next time you have to memorize a list of names or objects.[21] (See *Issues and Applications: Improving Your Study Skills*.)

Long-Term Memory

Everything you know—every word, name, fact, date, experience, definition, and skill—is contained in your **long-term memory** (LTM), where information is stored unconsciously for an extended period of time. How long do your memories last in LTM? No precise answer can be given. LTM duration can be as brief as a few minutes and as long as a lifetime. Many people believe that LTM is permanent, but the evidence is not conclusive. The duration of LTM depends on several factors, including the strength of the memory, its meaning, and how much it is used.[22]

How much do you know? If you started to remember everything in your LTM right now, you would probably spend the rest of your life and not finish. If STM is a memory workbench with limited space, your LTM is a vast warehouse of information with no apparent limit. Surely there are millions of items stored in your LTM, but researchers have no way of estimating the maximum capacity of LTM. Although its upper limit is unknown, your everyday experience tells you that LTM holds an astounding amount of information.

The Organization of Long-Term Memory

The enormous LTM warehouse contains many types of knowledge, and its contents are highly organized in terms of several qualities of those memories. Four aspects of LTM have been identified and named: *semantic*, *episodic*, *procedural*, and *implicit* memory. These aspects of LTM organization are summarized in Table 6.1.

Table 6.1 Organization of Long-Term Memory

Semantic memory	Impersonal facts based on semantic, or verbal, codes
Episodic memory	Personal, autobiographical facts; flashbulb memories
Procedural memory	Skills, habits, stimulus-response associations
Implicit memory	Memories learned and retrieved without conscious effort

Language is an essential part of your memory. Factual knowledge based on words, phrases, sentences, and other verbal information is contained in your **semantic memory**. Like a dictionary, your semantic memory is based on *semantic codes*, representations of information in terms of the meaning of words. To appreciate the scope of semantic memory, just consider the many definitions, names, formulas, and other facts that you have learned since elementary school. Your semantic memory does not exist as thousands of independent bits of knowledge, but is organized by complex *association networks*, or groups of memories linked together on the basis of meaning.

As a demonstration, start with a familiar word, *dog* and call to mind every word association you can, for example, *pet, companion, mammal*, and so on. Then, do the same for each of those associations, and for all the associations linked to them, and so on. Before long, you will realize that the web of your word associations is almost endless. These complex semantic associations control your ability to understand and remember language-based facts. Remember elaborative rehearsal from the section on STM? Elaborative rehearsal works so well as a learning strategy because it creates meaningful association networks.[23,24]

Your semantic memory is impersonal, lacking any obvious connection with specific life experiences. For instance, when you remember $2 + 2 = 4$ you probably do not connect it with the situation in which you first learned it. By contrast, your **episodic memory** contains very personal, autobiographical facts—facts that are tied to episodes in your life and often ones that contain significant emotional meaning. Think of the birth of your younger siblings, a great party you attended, a family tragedy, and other events from your personal past—these recollections reveal your episodic memory.[25]

A special type of episodic memory is a *flashbulb memory*, a vivid recollection of an emotionally powerful event.[26] Your flashbulb memories seem like moments frozen in time, and their emotional associations are thought to be responsible for their vividness. For example, some people report flashbulb memories for January 28, 1986, the day the space shuttle *Challenger* exploded, killing the crew, while broadcast nationwide on television. Many flashbulb memories are more personal, such as the death of a close friend or the day you won the lottery. Although they seem very clear, flashbulb memories are not necessarily accurate, and people often recall with confidence false details of those events.[27,28,29]

Your memory for learned responses and action patterns is **procedural memory**. Learned skills and behaviors, as well as stimulus-response associations, are contained in your procedural memory. Countless everyday activities depend on procedural memory, as when you drive a car, play the piano, use a tool, or carry on a conversation. As you read in Chapter 5, such behavior may be acquired through conditioning and cognitive learning. In addition, procedural memory controls your automatic conditioned responses to stimuli. The next time you experience fear upon entering your dentist's office, you can thank your procedural memory for the reminder.[25]

Semantic and episodic memories are sometimes called *declarative memory*, which requires conscious effort to learn and retrieve. For example,

semantic memory—memory for *factual knowledge* based on *verbal information*

episodic (epp-ee-sod-ik) memory—memory for *personal, autobiographical facts*

procedural memory—memory for *learned responses* and *action patterns*

People often develop vivid flashbulb memories for emotionally intense events, such as the tragic explosion if the space shuttle Challenger.

you must exert conscious effort to memorize a new formula in math (semantic memory). Many memories however, are acquired and remembered automatically with little or no conscious involvement. These make up your **implicit memory**. In fact, a lot of procedural memory is implicit, such as conditioned fears and other emotional responses. You do not consciously control their acquisition or activation by stimuli.[30,31,32]

Research on the *priming effect* illustrates that implicit memory controls your unconscious retrieval of stored information. In a typical study, subjects are "primed" by exposure to some stimuli, and later their memory is tested without asking them to consciously remember the stimuli. Priming improves their memory despite the subjects' lack of awareness of learning or remembering the stimuli. Imagine that you are in such a study: You are shown some words (the priming list), which you must identify as nouns or verbs (see Table 6.2). Later, another series of words (the test list) is presented very rapidly, and you are asked simply to indicate which words you perceive. You are most likely to perceive the test list words that were on the priming list even though you did not try to memorize or retrieve them.[31,32,33,34]

Table 6.2 **Priming Effect Study of Implicit Memory**

Priming List	Test List	Primed Implicit Memory
rabbit	bird	rabbit
swim	rabbit	write
car	write	
write	house	

Although implicit and declarative (semantic and episodic) memory have distinctive features, they are not completely independent. Rather, these aspects of LTM interact to provide you with richly integrated memories. Do you remember how to ride a bicycle? If you can describe this skill in words (semantic memory), recall yourself doing it in a specific situation (episodic memory), and show it in action (procedural memory), you are illustrating the integrated facets of your LTM. Recent studies suggest that declarative and implicit memory work together to create complex abilities and knowledge, such as learning the rules of language usage and classifying your experiences into organized concepts.[32,35] (See Chapter 7.)

Long-Term Memory Processes

As you have learned, LTM contains many types of stored information. The complex organization of knowledge in LTM depends on a number of factors. The **depth-of-processing** model explains the strength and durability of LTM as the result of encoding processes. In this view, a "deep" memory is acquired by semantic codes that represent facts through language. Without semantic codes, memory is "shallow" and quite easily forgotten. A deep memory is more lasting and meaningful than a shallow one, and it is easier to recollect. This model suggests that memories based on several codes are deeper than those based on a single code.[20,36]

▼
depth-of-processing model—view that memory strength depends on encoding processes

Research on combined semantic codes and imagery supports this notion. This effect may be illustrated by a *paired-associates recall task*, in which you are given word pairs to remember (for example, *house-pencil, fish-tree*), and later you must recall one of the words when the other is presented. For instance, when shown *tree* you must say *fish*. If you use visual images along with the words to encode the paired associates, your recall is improved, especially for concrete words like those in Figure 6.3.[37,38]

In 1932, British psychologist Frederick Bartlett proposed that memories are reconstructions of events based partly on fact and partly on *schemas*, or personal beliefs about reality. In his classic study, he read a Native American folktale to his English subjects and later asked them to remember it. Their memories of the story showed changes that reflected their culture-based schemas. For instance, instead of recalling that the Indians hunted for seals in canoes, some subjects remembered that they were fishing in boats.[39]

In the tradition of Bartlett, many psychologists today consider **reconstructive memory** to be an act of remembering in which facts, personal beliefs, guesses, and inferences are all woven together. In reconstructing a past event, you often fill in the gaps with "facts" that you believe, on the basis of your personal schemas, might have occurred. In addition, you rely on familiar patterns of events stored as *memory scripts* that give you a framework for remembering. Try to remember what you did at 4:00 P.M. exactly six months ago. If it was a Wednesday during the school year, you might find yourself using your "typical-Wednesday-afternoon-at-school" script to reconstruct what you probably did.[21,40]

▼
reconstructive memory—remembering affected by schemas, personal beliefs, and inferences

Eyewitness Memory

Regardless of the work you do, from simple manual tasks to complex mental activity, you rely on your memory to perform your job properly. In law enforcement and other legal professions the role of memory is especially critical. Earlier, you read about Lenell Geter who was misidentified by five eyewitnesses. Unfortunately, what happened to him is not a rare, isolated case, but just one example of many failures of eyewitness memory. Sometime in your life you may be required to judge an eyewitness memory, if you work in law enforcement or mental health, serve as an officer of the court, or sit on a jury. Keep in mind that eyewitness memories are just as prone to error and distortion as other memories are, and perhaps even more so.

Eyewitnesses often give accurate reports, but they can also provide dangerously false recollections. Their accuracy depends on several factors, especially the circumstances at the time of the event and at the time they remember it. Their memories are easily influenced by emotional states, such as fear and surprise, that impair their accuracy. How well would you recall details of an incident in which an armed robber

Figure 6.3 **Imagery in a Paired-Associates Recall Task**

House • Pencil   **Fish • Tree**

The depth-of-processing model suggests that a combination of semantic and image codes will produce a deeper memory than will a single code. When subjects use visual images and word pairs to encode the information, their memory for the word association improves.

held up a store while you were working there? Fear can disrupt encoding and storage processes, resulting in inadequate memory. Surprise also plays a role; few eyewitnesses expect to see what they see, and thus they are not attending clearly to what happens. The personal schemas of the eyewitnesses can further distort their memories. Geter, an African American, was misidentified by five white eyewitnesses. As in the Geter case, when the people involved are of different races misidentifications increase. After-the-fact suggestions, too, influence recollections. What eyewitnesses remember is affected by later information, such as that contained in leading or suggestive questions. As shown by the Loftus and Palmer car accident study (see below), the wording of questions can suggest different facts.[41,42,43]

Controlled research and real life provide reasons to question the validity of eyewitness memory. If your work ever requires you to judge an eyewitness account, remember to be cautious, consider all the facts, and bear in mind the many variables that might have influenced the recollection.

Have you ever noticed that each time you tell a story it is a little different than the last time because you add new elements or drop old details with each telling? Facts learned after a memory is formed can change it, and even the act of remembering sometimes alters the memory being recalled. Reconstructive memory is also open to the power of suggestion, as shown in a study by psychologists Elizabeth Loftus and John Palmer in which subjects saw a filmed car accident and were later asked how fast the cars were going. The questions were phrased either in terms of when the cars "hit" or when they "crashed." Subjects who were asked the "crashed" version recalled much higher speeds because the wording suggests that the cars were moving faster.[44,45,46] (See *Issues and Applications: Eyewitness Memory*.)

Your ability to retrieve a memory often depends on having the proper cues at the time you try to remember. When your retrieval is influenced by stimulus cues, you show evidence of **cue-dependent memory**. Two forms of cue-dependent memory are context-dependent memory and state-dependent memory.

If you try to recall some information in a situation that is similar to the one in which you learned that information, you tend to perform better than when you try in a situation that differs from the learning one. This phenomenon, called *context-dependent memory*, is the result of associations formed between situational cues and the information at the time it is learned. An example of context-dependent memory is a study of scuba divers who learned some words under water and later recalled them better when under water than on land. You can examine context-dependent memory in yourself by studying some material while listening to music and later testing yourself on half of the material with the same music playing and on the other half without any music. You should find that your memory is better when the music is playing.[47,48]

cue-dependent memory—memory influenced by cues in the situation or emotional state

The power of situational cues may explain a curious phenomenon called déjà vu (French for "already seen") in which you feel that you recognize someone or some place with no basis for the memory in your experience. For example, on entering a house for the first time, it may seem familiar, as if you had been there before. Deja vu is a false recognition due to subtle cues in the situation. Perhaps something about the house, such as an odor or room design, triggers partial memory of another place in which similar cues were present, thus giving you the feeling of familiarity.

Have you ever noticed that when you are happy you remember many experiences with a similar happy feeling, or that when depressed you recall other depressing events? Such observations point to *state-dependent memory*; your state of mind influences you to retrieve memories that were formed in a similar state. Studies of state-dependent memory show that emotional states prime your retrieval of experiences with similar emotional features.[49,50]

Forgetting

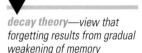

forgetting—failure to remember because of problems in one or more memory processes

How many times have you forgotten something? Obviously, no one can answer this question, but forgetting is an ever-present part of your experience. Psychologists use the term **forgetting** to indicate failures to remember due to problems in your encoding, storage, or retrieval processes or some combination of them. In this section, you will learn about several types of forgetting, summarized in Table 6.3.

Table 6.3 **Explanations of Forgetting**

Decay theory	Gradual weakening of memory due to passage of time and disuse
Interference theory	Memories interfere with one another, proactively and retroactively
Retrieval failure	Processes that retrieve memories fail because of emotions or physical factors
Motivated forgetting	Disturbing memories are blocked from consciousness

Decay Theory

decay theory—view that forgetting results from gradual weakening of memory

Common sense tells you that your memories simply grow weaker over time. According to **decay theory**, forgetting results from the gradual weakening, or decay, of information in memory. Decay occurs mainly from the passage of time and disuse of a memory. Do you recall the names of all the children in your first grade class? Probably not—too much time has passed. In addition, you probably have not thought much about all those names in a long time. Unused memories decay more rapidly than those you use regularly.

Decay occurs rapidly in SM, as Sperling's partial report studies showed. The Petersons' distractor study suggests that STM decay happens within 20 to 30 seconds. Whether decay has a significant role in LTM is still uncertain. Over time, decay may promote a gradual loss of LTM strength, but some research shows that information in LTM remains remarkably intact over very long periods. Although decay theory is applied to many instances of forgetting, the exact mechanisms behind it are still unknown.[8,51,52]

An unusual memory ability called *eidetic imagery*, or photographic memory, calls into question the mechanisms of decay. A person with eidetic imagery can look briefly at a complex stimulus such as a drawing or a dictionary page and later remember it in precise detail. Long after SM and STM have decayed in most people, eidetic imagery persists. The basis of eidetic imagery is uncertain, but it is more common in children than adults and usually disappears in adolescence.[53]

Interference Theory

Did you ever try to remember someone's name, only to think of the wrong name, or to recall a term's meaning and come up with another definition? These common mistakes indicate a type of forgetting due to confusion among different memories. **Interference theory** purports that forgetting is caused by the interference of memories with one another. When older, more established memories interfere with newer, more recent memories you are experiencing *proactive interference*, which increases forgetting of the more recent information. For instance, if you learn a second language, you will probably experience some difficulty because of proactive interference from your native language. By contrast, *retroactive interference* is present when newer memories inhibit your older memories, causing forgetting of the older information. For example, what you have learned in this chapter might cause you to forget material from earlier chapters because of retroactive interference.

▼
interference theory—view that forgetting is caused by interference of memories with each other

Interference causes forgetting in both STM and LTM, and it is greatly affected by the similarity and timing of older and recent memories. The more similar and closer in time they are, the greater is the interference. If you memorized two similar lists (for example, names of U.S. cities) within a few minutes of each other, you would experience a great deal of interference when you tried to recall each list separately. See Figure 6.4 for a test of proactive and retroactive interference.[54,55,56]

Figure 6.4 **Testing for Interference**

List 1	List 2
Chicago	Miami
Albany	Houston
Sacramento	Denver
Baltimore	Atlanta
St. Louis	New Orleans
Pittsburgh	Milwaukee
Portland	Boston
Phoenix	Oakland

(a) To test for proactive interference:
Learn List 1 ⟶ Learn List 2 ⟶ Recall List 2

(b) To test for retroactive interference:
Learn List 1 ⟶ Learn List 2 ⟶ Recall List 1

In the test for proactive interference, two lists are learned and the second list is recalled. If items on the second list are forgotten, then proactive interference from the first list is blamed. In the test for retroactive interference, two lists are learned and the first list is recalled. If the items on the first list are forgotten, then retroactive interference from the second list is blamed.

Interference research suggests a few useful study hints. Do not cram too much studying into a short time; cramming increases interference, especially if you are studying similar subjects. Instead, study one topic and take a break before starting another. Studying just before going to sleep also improves your memory for the studied material by reducing retroactive interference on those new memories.[57]

Retrieval Failure

How many times have you forgotten an answer on a test, a phone number, or an appointment only to remember it afterward when it is too late? These kinds of *retrieval failure* are annoyingly common instances of forgetting. At times, retrieval failure is partial and only some of the memory is forgotten. The *tip-of-the-tongue (TOT) phenomenon* provides an example of partial retrieval failure in which some elements of a memory are recalled while others are missing despite their being "on the tip of your tongue." What was the name of the falsely accused man in the opening story of this chapter? If you can remember that his first name began with L and had two syllables, then you are showing a TOT phenomenon (by the way, he was Lenell Geter).[58]

Poorly organized, meaningless, and uncued memories are the most difficult to retrieve. In addition, retrieval failures may be due to emotional states, such as stress or anxiety. Students with test-taking fears often temporarily forget what they know because they are distracted by their emotional distress. Problems in retrieval also result from physical factors, such as illness, fatigue, and drug intoxication.

Motivated Forgetting

One day in 1989, 28-year-old Eileen Franklin-Lipsker suddenly remembered the look on her childhood friend's face before Eileen's father murdered her. With her therapist's help, she gradually recalled more about the murder. Could a memory hidden for so long really be true? A California jury thought so and convicted her father of a homicide he had committed more than 20 years earlier. Although a dramatic example, Eileen's case shows that **motivated forgetting** can cause the loss of emotionally disturbing memories. Freud's psychoanalytic theory explains motivated forgetting by *repression*, a defense mechanism that keeps memories out of conscious awareness to protect you against emotional pain.[59] You will learn more about defense mechanisms in Chapter 10.

motivated forgetting—forgetting of memories that are emotionally disturbing

Many mental health professionals assume that repressed memories are authentic. In recent years considerable attention has been devoted to cases in which repressed memories of sexual abuse in early childhood are recovered in therapy. All recovered memories do not prove accurate, but enough do to support the idea of motivated forgetting. In more ordinary instances, you may block out an unpleasant memory because unconsciously you do not want to think of it. Perhaps when you forgot to attend class for your last exam, it was because you really did not want to take the test anyway.[60,61]

Elizabeth Loftus, professor of psychology at the University of Washington, is a leading expert in the field of memory research and eyewitness testimony. Best known for her work on reconstructive memory and the accuracy of eyewitness recall, Dr. Loftus has helped to popularize the study of memory through her accessible and interesting books, including *Eyewitness Testimony* (1979),*Witness for the Defense* (1991) and *The Myth of Repressed Memory* (1994).

Born in 1944, she was raised in Los Angeles. She attended the University of California–Los Angeles and graduated in 1966 with a dual major in psychology and mathematics. While a graduate student at Stanford University, she became intrigued with memory research, and since receiving her doctorate. in 1970 she has investigated numerous aspects of human memory. As one of the foremost experts on eyewitness memory, Dr. Loftus has provided testi-mony or was a consultant in some of the most controversial legal cases of recent years, including the Hillside Strangler and Ted Bundy serial killer cases and the McMartin Preschool child abuse case. Her eyewitness research has emphasized the role of memory and its limits in real-life circumstances. Recently, she has turned her attention to the problem of repressed memories, particularly of early abuse.

A prolific writer, Dr. Loftus has authored 19 books and more than 200 professional articles. In addition, she has served on editorial boards for several important journals in psychology and law and has been a consultant to both government agencies and private industry.

The Biological Basis of Memory

Do you remember the case of H. M. who was described at the beginning of Chapter 2? After brain surgery to correct his seizures, H. M. was unable to transfer new information from STM to LTM. Consequently, he forgot simple facts very shortly after learning them.[62] In H. M. you see evidence of *biogenic amnesia*, a memory loss due to biological factors. Several types of biogenic amnesia result from brain damage due to injury or disease.

Brain-damaged subjects provide many clues about the biology of memory and bring into focus two fundamental questions: Where are memories located in the brain? What neural mechanisms control memory?

How Memory Is Stored in the Brain

▼

engram—physical form or trace of memory in the brain

Since the 1920s, researchers have searched for the location of memory in the brain on the assumption that memory is grounded in a physical form called an **engram** or memory trace. Karl Lashley (1890–1958), a pioneer in animal memory studies, concluded that engrams are spread throughout the brain rather than being located in one particular area.[63] Today, researchers recognize that, as Lashley suspected, memory is not stored in one place but is regulated by many brain structures. However, the structures that control memory differ for various types of memory (see Table 6.4).

Table 6.4 **Memory and the Brain**

Brain Structures	Memory Functions
Hippocampus	STM → LTM transfer; semantic memory
Cerebellum	Implicit memory; procedural memory
Frontal lobes	STM; episodic memory
Temporal lobes	STM; semantic memory

Your hippocampus, temporal lobes, and frontal lobes influence STM. Damage to the hippocampus or temporal lobe, as in H. M., prevents the transfer of new learning from STM to LTM. STM activity requires a high degree of arousal in your frontal lobes, and different regions of those lobes process different stimulus features, such as their color and location.[64] Because LTM is a more complex stage of memory, more brain structures are involved. Semantic and episodic memories rely on your hippocampus, cortical lobes, and thalamus. New memories are held by the hippocampus for up to two weeks while they are being stored in the cortex as more permanent long-term memories. Because they regulate language, the temporal lobes are essential for your semantic memory. Episodic memories, however, are more affected by the frontal lobes, which control your personal self-awareness. The cerebellum, a hindbrain structure involved in movement regulation, governs much of procedural memory. Implicit memory also relies on your cortex, but does not seem to involve the hippocampus.[32,65,66,67]

Neural Mechanisms in Memory

▼

consolidation hypothesis— view that memory is based on the formation of reverberating neural circuits

Since Lashley, many researchers have tried to define the engram by examining the neural mechanisms in memory. In 1949, psychologist Donald Hebb (1904–1985) proposed a **consolidation hypothesis**, which explains memory in terms of *reverberating neural circuits* established by learning and strengthened by repetition. These circuits are sets of neurons and their connections that are activated by stimuli. When you learn something, a neural circuit forms in your brain, and when you use the memory the circuit is reinforced. Consolidation theory does not clearly define the nature of these memory circuits, but it has prompted numerous investigations on that issue.[68,69]

One line of research identifies structural changes in the brain from learning experiences. Studies of rats raised in enriched learning environments show that the formation of memories depends on the growth of new connections (synapses) between neurons.[70] In addition, biochemical changes in memory formation have also been found in classical conditioning research on sea snails. The conditioning of simple movements in these creatures causes the sensitivity of neurons to signals from neighboring neurons to increase, creating a physical basis for the new stimulus-response association.[71,72,73]

The biology of memory strongly involves your brain's neurotransmitters. Learning and memory are regulated by several neurotransmitters including *acetylcholine* (Ach), *dopamine* (DA), *norepinephrine* (NE), and *glutamate*. Diseases, such as Alzheimer's disease, and drugs, such as stimulants, that disrupt these neurotransmitter systems can have profound effects on memory. Because they interact with neurotransmitters and influence brain activity, hormones also influence memory. Epinephrine (adrenaline) and vasopressin are hormones that enhance performance on some memory tasks. The vividness of your flashbulb memories may be due to the impact of hormones, such as epinephrine, that are released in a state of emotional arousal.[27,74]

Summary

1. There are three memory processes: encoding, storage, and retrieval. Encoding enters information into memory through memory codes. Storage processes retain memories over time. Retrieval processes bring information out of memory as in recall and recognition.

2. Memory is measured by tests of recall, recognition, and relearning. A recall test requires a memory search with few cues. A recognition test asks for judgments of familiarity or correctness. Relearning measures the savings in learning information again.

3. The information-processing model of memory has three stages: sensory memory (SM), short-term memory (STM), and long-term memory (LTM). SM is a very brief first stage that transfers information to STM for active processing and transfer to LTM, the final stage. The stages interact in transfer and retrieval, and forgetting occurs at each stage.

4. Sensory memory is a very brief, but complete, preconscious memory for raw sensory data. The sensory registers in each sense are independent and have unique features. Visual SM is called iconic memory, and SM in hearing is echoic memory. The mechanisms of SM are not well understood.

5. Short-term, or working, memory is an active, conscious stage. Attention is an STM activity that is viewed as either a stimulus filter or cognitive capacity. STM has a capacity of 5–9 chunks and a duration of 20–30 seconds without rehearsal. Maintenance rehearsal is the repetition of information to keep memories in STM and transfer them to LTM. Elaborative rehearsal associates new memories with old familiar ones. Mnemonics are strategies to improve memory by reorganizing information.

6. Long-term memory is a relatively permanent stage with unknown capacity. Consciously acquired and retrieved facts make up declarative memory. Semantic memory is factual knowledge based on semantic (verbal) codes. Personal, autobiographical facts are in episodic memory. Procedural memory is memory for behaviors and conditioned associations. Implicit memory is acquired and retrieved with little or no conscious effort, as shown by the priming effect.

7. The strength of LTM depends on encoding, according to the depth-of-processing model. Semantic codes and multiple codes produce deep memories. Remembering is a reconstruction of events, based on facts and personal schemas. LTM may be distorted by biases, inferences, scripts, and suggestions. Retrieval from LTM is affected by the cues available in the context of remembering and the subject's state of mind.

8. Decay theory explains forgetting as a weakening of memory over time. Interference is found when memories interfere with one another proactively or retroactively. Forgetting results from retrieval failures due to inadequate cues, emotional distress, or physical factors. Motivated forgetting blocks painful memories from awareness by repression.

9. Many brain structures influence memory. STM is controlled by the hippocampus and temporal and frontal lobes. Semantic and episodic memory depend on the cortex and hippocampus. Procedural memory and implicit memory involve the cerebellum. In consolidation hypothesis, the biological basis of memory is a neural circuit in the brain. Structural changes in neural connections, neurotransmitters, and hormones also play a role in memory.

Questions for Discussion

1. What are the memory processes and what does each do?

2. What are recall, recognition, and relearning tests of memory?

3. How does the information-processing model describe memory?

4. What are the characteristics of SM?

5. What are the features and processes of STM?

6. How is LTM organized?

7. What processes influence LTM?

8. How do decay, interference, retrieval failure, and motivated forgetting differ?

9. What are the biological bases of memory?

Applying Psychology

Your autobiography is defined by your episodic memories. As an exercise in episodic memory, take a few minutes to recollect the very first memory of your entire life. Try to find your earliest actual memory, not something that others have told you about. Jot down what you recall, and consider how this recollection might have been influenced by these forces:

▶ *Emotional Factors*: You will probably notice that the memory is charged with either positive or negative feelings. Why does that matter?

▶ *Personal Schemas*: Your recollection is probably shaped by your current beliefs or attitudes about yourself. How do they influence this memory?

▶ *After-the-Fact Suggestions*: Your memory probably reflects things that you have been told throughout your life. Can you tell what is true and what is due to suggestions?

Learning Objectives

After completing this chapter, you should be able to:

1. Define thinking and show how it is related to images and concepts.

2. Identify the four steps in problem solving.

3. Describe the structure of language.

4. Discuss the relationship between language and thought.

5. Define intelligence.

6. Explain the intelligence theories of Spearman, Thurstone, Guilford, Gardner, and Sternberg.

7. Describe the mental abilities tested in the Stanford-Binet Intelligence Scale and the Wechsler Adult Intelligence Scale.

8. Identify the characteristics of giftedness and mental retardation and their relationship to intelligence.

9. Discuss the role of heredity and environment in determining intelligence.

▼

thinking—the act of mentally representing information

"**T**hree missionaries and three cannibals are on a riverbank waiting to cross the river. They have at their disposal a boat that can fit only two people. There is one major problem. If there are more cannibals than missionaries on either side of the river, the cannibals will eat the missionaries. How can all six people get to the other side of the river without endangering the missionaries?"[1] (Solution on page 167.)

In order to solve this problem you must understand it and think it through to completion. Your ability to comprehend language and use your thinking skills to solve problems is part of your overall intelligence. In this chapter you will learn about the nature of thinking, language, and intelligence and how they allow you to adapt to problems in everyday life and work.

Thinking

As you learned in earlier chapters, you are capable of acquiring a wealth of information through your senses and organizing and storing that information in your memory. This information forms the basis of your *thoughts*, or mental models of the world you experience. **Thinking** is the act of mentally representing information in images, words, symbols, or ideas. As such, thinking is at the heart of cognitive psychology because it involves many high-level mental abilities such as memory retrieval, language comprehension, reasoning, problem solving, and decision making. Thinking is also an important ingredient of your intelligence.[2,3]

Thinking and Images

What comes to mind when you think of yourself swimming in an ocean or lake? No doubt you have a "mental picture" in which you are having fun, stroking and kicking through the water. You also might "feel" the water surrounding your body, "hear" the water moving around you, and "taste" it. You can see from this example that your thoughts are composed of *images*, or sensory impressions.[4,5] The Greek philosopher Aristotle stated that thought is impossible without an image. In psychology, one of the hottest debates has been whether images are fundamental components of thinking or simply a product of our verbal descriptions of things and events.

Get a stopwatch, or any watch with a second hand, and ask a friend to look at a geometric shape like those shown on the left of A, B, C in Figure 7.1. See how long it takes for your friend to determine whether the figures on the right are the same as those on the left. In a famous experiment, psychologist Roger Shepard did just that and found that the amount of time subjects needed to respond depended on how much the geometric shape was rotated. When it was rotated slightly, subjects responded immediately, but when the object was turned upside-down, the subjects needed much more time to judge if the two objects were the same. Shepard interpreted these results as evidence that images were fundamental components of thinking and that the subjects made decisions by mentally rotating the objects much as they would if they actually had the objects in their hands.[6]

Figure 7.1 Shepard's Mental Rotation Experiment

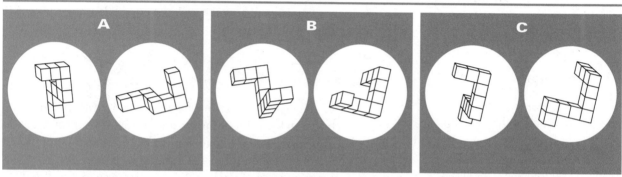

Subjects were asked to look at the geometric shapes similar to those on the left in a, b, and c and then to judge whether the shapes on the right were the same. The time it took to judge depended on the degree to which the second object was rotated, indicating that subjects were mentally rotating the objects.

Source: Adapted from Shepard, R.N., & Meltzer, J. (1971). Mental rotation of three-dimensional objects. Science, 171, 701–703.

Thinking and Concepts

What do a Chevy, a Toyota, and a Porsche have in common? If you like one or another, at first you might say that they have little in common, but, of course, they all are automobiles. One of the most obvious features of your thinking is that you organize information into categories. A category is the basis of a **concept**, an idea that represents a group of things, or events that have features in common. The use of concepts allows you to organize and lend meaning to your experiences. Even though Chevys, Toyotas, and Porsches are different automobiles, they are automobiles nonetheless. Because they are automobiles you have expectations about how they work and what they can and cannot do.

Concepts are often formed around a *prototype*, a representative example of that category that shares most of the features, or attributes, with other members of that category. You easily recognize a trout as a fish (and maybe a tasty meal) because it shares most of the attributes of a prototypical fish.

concept—an idea that represents a group of things or events that have features in common

By contrast, you might less easily recognize an eel as a fish because it does not clearly fit the prototype of a fish. It may seem more like a snake to you and not as appetizing as the trout. You can see from this example that categories have "fuzzy" rather than clear boundaries.

Concepts are arranged from the specific to the more general. You know that trout (specific) are fish (less specific) along with eels and bass. They are also aquatic creatures (general) categorized with other animals such as whales, crabs, and snails. The concept animals (more general), groups trout along with land-dwelling animals such as lions, birds, and people. As you can see, forming and using concepts is a way of making sense of your experiences.

Problem Solving

You face many problems in your everyday life; some are easy to solve, others are more difficult. In this section you will learn about the steps in problem solving, potential barriers to problem solving, and creative problem solving.

Steps in Problem Solving.   Imagine that you are a doctor treating a patient with a malignant stomach tumor. Operating on the tumor is impossible, but you know that a certain type of high-intensity X-ray can destroy it. The problem is that the X-rays will also destroy the surrounding healthy tissue. If the tumor is not destroyed, the patient will certainly die. What a predicament! How can you destroy the tumor and save the patient's life?[7]

Research shows that if you want to solve this or any other problem, you must follow a sequence of four steps: preparation, production, incubation, and evaluation. (See Table 7.1, and *Issues and Applications: Thinking and Problem Solving by Business Executives*.) The first step in solving a problem is *preparation*, during which you identify and define the problem on the basis of available facts. With the X-ray problem, at first you might conclude that the problem is impossible to solve and the patient will die. Preparing to solve a problem often requires that you reformulate, or refigure, it. You might be better able to solve the X-ray problem by reformulating the goal; to destroy the tumor, while avoiding high-intensity X-ray contact with the surrounding healthy tissue. By restating the problem in this way, you might discover the solution: Pass low-intensity X-rays from different directions and have them add together as they meet on the tumor.

Table 7.1   **Steps in Problem Solving**

Preparation	Gather information needed to solve the problem.
Production	Try possible solutions to the problem using trial and error or hypotheses
Incubation	Take a rest from the problem if it hasn't been solved after many attempts.
Evaluation	Look at the outcome to determine whether the problem has been solved.

During the second step, *production*, you try to solve the problem by taking action. With complex problems you might try many tactics by trial and error until something works. In the X-ray problem, you might think that the tumor could be destroyed by passing X-rays through the throat or by first moving the tumor closer to the outside of the body. Although such solutions will not work, they show that you are formulating tentative hypotheses about a remedy. In general, the more hypotheses you propose, the better your chances of finding a solution.

Two ways of forming hypotheses and solving problems are by using algorithms and heuristics. An **algorithm** is a formula for solving a problem. When you use a simple formula to solve a math problem you are employing an algorithm. But you would probably find it impossible to use algorithms to solve more complex, ill-defined problems such as world hunger or finding a cure for AIDS.

An alternative to using algorithms is to limit the number of possible solutions. A **heuristic** is a procedure used to simplify problem solving. Unlike an algorithm, a heuristic does not guarantee a solution to a problem but offers a solution or "rule of thumb" that is good enough most of the time. For example, in playing chess or checkers you can try out several

▼

algorithm—a formula for solving a problem

▼

heuristic (you-riss-tick)—a rule of thumb

Issues and Applications

Thinking and Problem Solving by Business Executives

One of the most telling applications of your ability to think and solve problems is in your performance at work. Business executives are often confronted with difficult tasks and problems, and their careers can depend on finding successful solutions. If you hope to have a career in the business world, you may be interested in how business executives solve problems.

Researchers who study thinking and problem-solving techniques of successful executives have identified several cognitive characteristics. One of the most important is *opportunistic thinking*. Opportunistic thinkers respond to opportunities, develop ideas before a situation has been defined clearly and a strong judgment has been formed, and draw conclusions based on the available information. A good example of an opportunistic thinker is Bill Gates, who developed his Microsoft computer software company into one of the most successful corporations anywhere.[8]

Successful corporate general managers emphasize five activities in their work.[9] They:

moves in your head before you actually move the piece, then use the strategy in playing other chess or checkers games.

Whether you use algorithms or heuristics, once you have tried all the possible solutions in vain, it is time to take a rest from the problem. This step of problem-solving is *incubation*. Here you step back from your efforts so that you can take a fresh look at the problem later.

The final step in problem solving is called *evaluation*, during which you look to see whether the problem has really been solved. If it has not, you must return to step one, preparation.

Barriers to Problem Solving.

Solving a problem is not quite as easy as applying the four steps described earlier. Aside from not having sufficient information to solve a problem, other factors can interfere with your problem solving abilities. Two barriers are *mental set* and *functional fixedness*.

To see how problem solving can be impaired, try to solve the nine-dot problem illustrated in Figure 7.2. Your job is to connect all nine dots. Sounds easy, right? You must connect the dots using only four line segments and without lifting your pencil off the page. Do you think it's impossible? Well,

1. Set goals and policies in the face of uncertainty
2. Balance their time and energy among different business functions
3. Control different activities so that they can identify and solve a variety of problems rapidly
4. Develop an agenda for completing tasks
5. Develop and maintain a network of interpersonal relationships that they use to collect information and accomplish the agenda

Studies of good managers show that they are able to break down a problem into its component parts and then put the pieces back together in a unique and useful way. Finally, successful business executives follow certain "rules of thumb." For example, "recognize problems before they become serious," and "take a second look at first impressions."

Developing these problem-solving strategies may enhance your ability to be a successful business executive, and it can also help you in school and in your relationships.[10]

it would be if you used old problem-solving techniques to figure it out. The tendency to approach new problems in old and rigid ways is called **mental set**. To solve the nine-dot problem you must "break set," or change your assumptions about what is specified in the instructions. If you cannot figure out how to connect the dots, look at the solution on page 167.

Figure 7.2 **The Nine-Dot Problem**

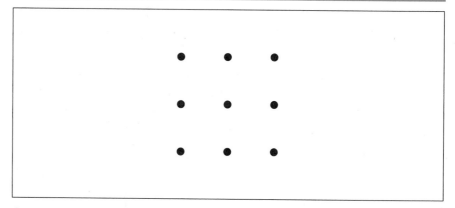

Connect all nine dots without lifting your pencil off the page. Use only four line segments.

Another barrier to problem solving is **functional fixedness**, the tendency to look at an object according to its typical use or function. You usually use coins to buy things, and your fingernails are things, that you polish or bite. If you have ever used a dime or a fingernail as a screwdriver, you have overcome functional fixedness.

Creative Problem Solving. The solution to some problems requires that you approach the problem in a unique way. Do you:

- ▶ Make up rules as you go along?
- ▶ Have a free spirit?
- ▶ Have the ability to put old information together in a new way?
- ▶ Appreciate the arts?
- ▶ Follow your feelings in making decisions after weighing the pros and cons?
- ▶ Question the rules of society?
- ▶ Find yourself motivated by goals?

If you answered yes to most of these questions, you exhibit **creativity**, the ability to solve problems in unique ways.[1] You can solve many problems by using *convergent thinking*, in which the facts are narrowed to find a solution using logic. However, researchers have discovered that creative problem-solving is more often associated with *divergent thinking*, or thinking of many possible solutions to a problem. One example of divergent thinking used in advertising is *brainstorming*, in which a group of individuals contributes many different ideas toward the solution of a problem. Brainstorming encourages wild, unrestrained ideas that group members are urged to build upon until an advertising concept is ready to be presented to a client.[11,12]

*L*anguage

Language is an organized system of using symbols such as sounds, images, and gestures to communicate thoughts and feelings. As an expression of thinking, language is one of our most important cognitive abilities. In this section you will learn about the structure of language and its relationship to thought.

The Structure of Language

Every spoken language has a unique set of basic speech sounds called *phonemes*. There are more than 40 phonemes in the English language, and some languages have more than 80. A *morpheme* is a combination of phonemes that makes up a unit of meaning. Some morphemes are individual words such as *bird*, *ask*, or *charm*, and others are prefixes, suffixes, or word roots, such as *cran* in *cranberry*.

Syntax refers to the relations among words in a sentence. In English, the usual order of words in a sentence is subject-verb-object. For example, "Marty plays the guitar" is a syntactically correct sentence, whereas "Plays Marty the guitar" is incorrect. *Semantics* is the study of the meaning of words and sentences and reflects the social aspects of language. For example, the question "Is that my coat?" might be interpreted as a request for information or, in other situations, as an implied accusation that the coat was stolen.[13]

The rules by which the elements of language are organized into meaningful expressions of thought is called *grammar*. One popular model proposed by linguist Noam Chomsky is **transformational grammar**, in which each language has a set of rules that determines how a sentence can be transformed into another and how sentences are related to each other. For example, "The mouse was chased by the cat" can be understood as a

People are using language, an organized system of using symbols, to communicate their thoughts and feelings.

transformation of the sentence "The cat chased the mouse." In transformational grammar, the *deep structure* is the real meaning of a sentence. Once you understand the deep structure, you can transform the sentence into its *surface structure*, or actual wording. Chomsky believes that the rules of transformational grammar are an inborn kind of universal grammar that allows us to understand sentences that we have never heard before.[14,15,16]

Language and Thought

Is language a reflection of your thoughts, or is the way you think determined by language? The Dani, Stone Age people of New Guinea, have only two color terms, *mola* for bright, warm colors and *mili* for dark, cold hues. In contrast, the English language has names for 11 major color categories and words for hundreds of intermediate hues. Could it be that the Dani think about colors in a different way than English-speaking people?

The **linguistic-relativity hypothesis**, proposed by linguist Benjamin Whorf, states that language shapes our perception of reality. In other words, the language you use determines how you think about yourself and the world. According to this hypothesis, the fact that the Dani have only two color terms indicates that they must perceive only two colors.

Psychologist Eleanor Rosch challenged the linguistic-relativity hypothesis by showing that the Dani could recognize colors in much the same way as English-speaking people even though their language for color was limited. Now psychologists generally agree that language is a reflection of the way we think rather than its cause.[17]

Intelligence

Intelligence is one of our most treasured attributes. It has been the focus of many controversies for more than a century. This section presents three major issues confronting psychologists today: the nature of intelligence, its measurement, and its determining factors.

What Is Intelligence?

Intelligence is a term we use in our everyday lives to describe certain aspects of our behavior and the behavior of others. Certainly, intelligence is one way of distinguishing among your friends, relatives, classmates, and co-workers as they go about their daily lives, but what is it? In one study, train commuters, university students, and supermarket shoppers were asked to provide their conception of the term. Most of them agreed that intelligence is composed of three main characteristics:

1. Practical problem-solving ability, as observed in logical reasoning
2. Verbal ability, such as good reading skills and speaking well in conversation
3. Social intelligence, which includes being sensitive to social cues and showing interest in the world[18]

A survey of more than 1,000 psychologists and education specialists with expertise in intelligence testing indicated that a majority of experts agreed on some of the important elements of intelligence such as abstract thinking, problem-solving ability, and the capacity to acquire knowledge.[19] These elements are presented in Table 7.2.

Table 7.2 **Important Elements of Intelligence**

Element	Percentage of Experts Who Consider It Important
Abstract thinking or reasoning	99.3
Problem-solving ability	97.7
Capacity to acquire knowledge	96.0
Memory	80.5
Adaptation to one's environment	77.2
Mental speed	71.7
Linguistic competence	71.0
Mathematical competence	67.9
General knowledge	62.4
Creativity	59.6
Sensory acuity	24.4
Goal-directedness	24.0
Achievement motivation	18.9

Source: *Snyderman, M. & Rothman, S. (1987), Survey of expert opinion on intelligence and aptitude testing. American Psychologist, 42, 137–144.*

In psychology, most definitions of intelligence are similar to the definitions used by nonprofessionals. They emphasize your capacity to learn, solve problems, adapt to changing environments, and act purposefully. The definition we will use in this chapter is that of psychologist Robert Sternberg, who defines **intelligence** as the mental management of one's life in a constructive, purposeful way by adapting to, selecting, and shaping the environment. Whether it involves adjusting to a new role at work, resolving disputes with a friend, or getting good grades in school, intelligent behavior allows you to function well in your environment.

In many cases, however, it might be unwise to adapt to an environment that does not promote your well-being. In such cases, the intelligent thing to do might be to select a new environment. For example, if your boss asked you to do something illegal in order to boost sales, you would be better off getting another job.

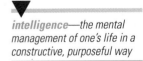

intelligence—the mental management of one's life in a constructive, purposeful way

Realistically, there are times when you cannot adapt to or change environments. In those circumstances, your intelligence would help you shape your environment. For example, of you were dissatisfied with your government, rather than yield to it, or leave the country, you might take a more active role in changing that government by getting involved in politics.[1]

Theories of Intelligence

Early theories of intelligence assumed that intelligence was "something in the head." These theories focused on discovering the factors or components that make up intelligence. Later, psychologists influenced by computer models began to view intelligence in terms of how we process information, think, and behave.

Spearman's Factor Theory.
Charles Spearman (1863–1945) was the first psychologist to study intelligence using the statistical methods of *factor analysis*. These methods allow a researcher to reduce, or "break down," intelligence into its major factors or components by analyzing correlations (see Chapter 1). Although Spearman recognized that specific traits, or *s-factors*, were part of intellectual ability, he concluded that intelligence was composed primarily of one main factor called general intelligence, or the **g-factor**. The *g-factor* is a type of intellectual ability you would use to perform many mental tasks such as solving a math problem, reading and understanding a book, or completing a jigsaw puzzle.

Thurstone's Theory of Primary Mental Abilities.
Psychologist Louis Thurstone (1887–1955) proposed a theory of intelligence based on seven **primary mental abilities** rather than a single g-factor. According to Thurstone, the primary mental abilities are:

▶ Verbal comprehension, or understanding vocabulary words
▶ Verbal fluency, or speech production
▶ Reasoning
▶ Spatial visualization, or the ability to recognize shapes and perceive distances
▶ Numerical ability, or arithmetic
▶ Memory
▶ Perceptual speed

Many of the components of intelligence in Thurstone's theory are often measured in intelligence tests today.

Guilford's Structure-of-Intellect Model.
From his factor-analytic studies of mental ability, psychologist J. P. Guilford (1897–1987) proposed the **structure-of-intellect model**, which identifies 150 intelligence factors organized by the general categories of operations, contents, and products. *Operations* are mental processes; *contents* refers to whether a problem involves words, numbers, or pictures; and *products* are the types of responses required to correctly solve a problem. Guilford represented the interactions of operations, contents, and products in a cube, shown in Figure 7.3.[20]

g-factor—the main component, general intelligence, in Spearman's factor theory

primary mental abilities—Thurstone's seven intelligence factors

structure of intellect model—Guilford's theory of intelligence based on 150 factors

Figure 7.3 Guilford's Structure-of-Intellect Model

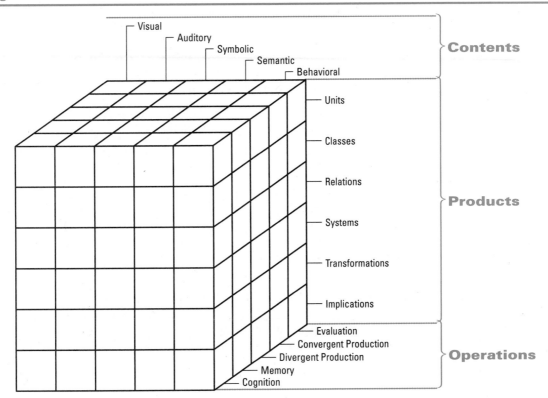

This cube depicts the 150 interacting factors of intelligence. Operations are mental processes. Contents refers to whether a problem involves words, numbers, or pictures. Products are the kinds of responses required to solve a problem.

Source: *Guilford, J.P. (1967). The nature of human intelligence. New York: McGraw-Hill.*

Gardner's Theory of Multiple Intelligences.

Factor theories claim that intelligence is a single "thing" composed of underlying factors. Psychologist Howard Gardner's **theory of multiple intelligences** proposes that there are seven distinct types of intelligence, each with its own forms of perception, learning, and memory. Because each intelligence is distinct, it is possible for you to be intelligent in one area, but not in another. Gardner also believes that intelligence cannot be determined from traditional intelligence tests, but only from studying how you function in your everyday life.[21]

The seven types of intelligences and the kinds of individuals who exhibit them are:

1. *Linguistic*: The ability to understand the meaning and order of words (poets and other writers)

2. *Logical-Mathematical*: The ability to reason and recognize patterns (mathematicians and scientists)

theory of multiple intelligences—Gardner's theory based on seven distinct types of intelligence

3. *Musical*: Sensitivity to musical characteristics such as pitch, melody, rhythm, and tone (musicians and composers)

4. *Bodily-Kinesthetic*: The ability to use your body in a coordinated manner (athletes, dancers, and surgeons)

5. *Spatial*: The ability to perceive things accurately and recreate aspects of the world (sculptors and architects)

6. *Interpersonal*: The ability to understand people and relationships (salespeople and religious leaders)

7. *Intrapersonal*: Having insight into yourself and others (social workers or therapists)

Sternberg's Triarchic Theory.

Convinced that most theories of intelligence were incomplete and irrelevant to everyday life, psychologist Robert Sternberg developed a **triarchic theory** based on three types of intelligence: *componential*, *experiential*, and *contextual*. Triarchic theory strives to understand the relationship of intelligence to your mental world (componential), your experience in coping with tasks (experiential), and your external world or environment (contextual).[1]

Componential intelligence consists of the mental processes, or components, you use in planning and evaluating your behavior; your specific problem-solving skills, such as reasoning; and your learning abilities. When you have insightful solutions to new or unfamiliar problems and when you use automatic cognitive processes such as implicit memory (see Chapter 6), your experiential intelligence is at work. In adapting to and changing your environment, you use your contextual intelligence.

As an example, consider what you do when you begin a new job. Componential intelligence enables you to learn the skills required to perform the work; your experiential intelligence adds your own creative touch and helps make job performance more automatic. Contextual intelligence allows you to adjust to the habits and style of your boss and co-workers. As you can see, the three types of intelligence constantly interact to help you solve problems.[1]

How Intelligence Is Measured

The modern approach to the measurement of intelligence began in 1905 when French psychologists Alfred Binet (1857–1911) and Theodore Simon (1873–1961) devised the *Binet-Simon intelligence tests* to identify retarded children and place them in appropriate educational programs. Several years later, the Binet-Simon tests incorporated the idea of expressing intelligence as an IQ, or **intelligence quotient**, or the ratio of mental age to chronological age multiplied by 100.

$$IQ = \frac{mental\ age}{chronological\ age} \times 100$$

Fundamentals of Psychology

Biography: Robert J. Sternberg

Psychologist Robert Sternberg is one of the most important figures in contemporary psychology because of his contributions to our understanding of intelligence. His triarchic theory of intelligence focuses on how individuals use thinking skills to cope with novel, real-world situations.

Born in 1949, Sternberg grew up in Maplewood, New Jersey. His interest in intelligence was stimulated when he had to take an IQ test with his sixth-grade classmates. His test anxiety was so great that he scored miserably low on the test and had to retake it with fifth-graders. Sternberg later remarked, "If I hadn't known before what it meant to be embarrassed, I did then. I was being told to take a test with a bunch of babies."

Sternberg's seventh-grade science project was to develop a mental test, so he constructed an intelligence test he called the Sternberg Test of Mental Abilities (which nobody took). For practice he got a copy of the Stanford-Binet Intelligence Scale and gave it to his classmates. The mother of one of his subjects reported Sternberg to the principal, and the school psychologist threatened that if Sternberg ever brought the test into school again, he would personally burn it. In high school, Sternberg continued to study intelligence and even devised a physics aptitude test to bolster his low physics grades. The test actually had good predictive validity and was used by his high school for several years.

Sternberg entered Yale University on a National Merit Scholarship, and, when he received a grade of C in his introductory psychology course, he seriously considered switching to mathematics or philosophy.

He remained in psychology, however, and graduated with highest honors in 1972. He went on to receive his doctorate from Stanford University in 1975, then took a professorship at Yale, where he has remained.

Robert Sternberg has written many professional articles and books, including *The Triarchic Mind* (1988), and has served on the editorial board of several professional journals. He has received many professional awards including the American Psychological Association's Distinguished Scientific Award for an Early Career Contribution to Psychology in 1981.[1,22]

For example if a nine-year-old performed like a typical nine-year-old, she would have a mental age of 9 and a chronological age of 9. According to the formula, her IQ would be 100, which is considered average at any age.[23,24]

All major intelligence tests used today are based on several assumptions. First, intelligence is a single entity largely made up of a general intelligence similar to Spearman's g-factor. Second, intelligence is a stable characteristic, meaning that your score should not change much from one time to another. Third, intelligence follows the normal (or bell-shaped) distribution. (See Figure 7.4.)

Figure 7.4 The Normal Distribution of Intelligence

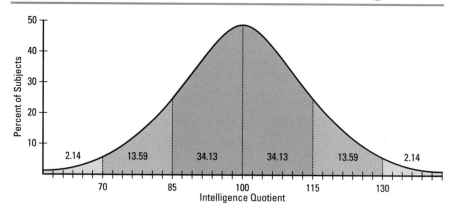

IQ tests assume that intelligence follows the normal distribution, or bell-shaped, curve. This figure shows the percentage of individuals who achieve IQ scores in each range on the Wechsler Adult Intelligence Scale–Revised.

The Elements of Intelligence
Tests.

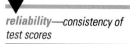
standardization—the specification of the conditions under which a test is taken

Psychological tests provide useful information only if they are standardized. **Standardization** means that the conditions under which the test is given and scored are clearly specified and are always the same. For example, if you take an IQ test, you will be given specific instructions on how to take the test, and time limits and scoring rules will be strictly enforced. Also, standardization means that test norms have been established. Your score on an IQ test can be interpreted only by comparing your score with the scores of others who are similar to you in age, sex, and other important characteristics. The group of subjects used for comparisons is known as the *normative group.*[25,26]

Test reliability and validity are also important elements of intelligence tests. **Reliability** is the consistency of test scores obtained. For example, *test-retest reliability* refers to consistency of scores with repeated administrations of the IQ test. If a test has good test-retest reliability then your score should not vary much each time you take it.

Validity refers to a test's accuracy. A valid IQ test is one that actually measures intelligence. Two important types of validity are *construct* and *predictive validity.* Construct validity is concerned with how well a test measures intelligence. An IQ test would have good construct validity if it

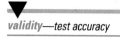
reliability—consistency of test scores

validity—test accuracy

accurately measured the concept intelligence. If your IQ score turned out to be a good predictor of how well you performed in school or at work, the test would have good predictive validity.

Types of Intelligence Tests. In 1916 at Stanford University, psychologist Lewis Terman (1877–1956) revised the Binet-Simon intelligence scales into what remains one of the most widely used IQ tests. The **Stanford-Binet Intelligence Scale** is an individually administered test for ages 2 to adult.[27] Table 7.3 lists the subtests of the Stanford-Binet.

▼

Stanford-Binet Intelligence Scale—IQ test for people ages 2-adult

Table 7.3 **Stanford-Binet Intelligence Scale Subtests**

Name of Subtest	Mental Ability Tested
Vocabulary	Verbal reasoning
Comprehension	
Absurdities	
Verbal Relations	
Quantitative	Quantitative reasoning
Number Series	
Equation Building	
Pattern Analysis	Abstract/visual reasoning
Copying	
Matrices	
Paper Folding and Cutting	
Bead Memory	Short-term memory
Memory for Sentences	
Memory for Digits	
Memory for Objects	

The most widely used individually administered IQ tests are the *Wechsler Scales*, devised by psychologist David Wechsler (1896–1981). The **Wechsler Adult Intelligence Scale–Revised** (WAIS-R), used for people 16 years of age and older, consists of six verbal and five performance (nonverbal) subtests described in Table 7.4.[28]

If you take the WAIS-R you will receive scores for each subtest, a verbal IQ, a performance IQ, and a full scale, or total, IQ. Intelligence classifications for the WAIS-R are presented in Table 7.5. If you have ever taken an IQ test in school, it was probably one of the Wechsler tests or the Stanford-Binet. Wechsler Scales are available for children as well. The *Wechsler Intelligence Scale for Children* (WISC-III) is designed for children ages 6–16 and the *Wechsler Preschool and Primary Scale of Intelligence* is suitable for children from age 4 to $6\frac{1}{2}$.

▼

Wechsler Adult Intelligence Scale-Revised—IQ test for people 16 and older

Chapter 7 • Thinking Language and Intelligence

Table 7.4 Wechsler Adult Intelligence Scale-Revised (WAIS-R) Subtests

Name of Subtest	Mental Ability Tested
Verbal Subtests	
Information	General knowledge of facts
Digit Span	Short-term memory for numbers
Vocabulary	Meanings of words
Arithmetic	Mental calculation
Comprehension	Understanding of situations and sayings
Similarities	Understanding of concepts
Performance Subtests	
Picture Completion	Perception of missing things
Picture Arrangement	Nonverbal reasoning
Block Design	Visual analysis and synthesis
Object Assembly	Ability to assemble a puzzle
Digit Symbol	Memory for symbols

Table 7.5 IQ Classifications for the WAIS-R

Full Scale IQ	Classification	Percent Included
130 and above	Very Superior	2.6
120–129	Superior	6.9
110–119	High Average	16.6
90–109	Average	49.1
80–89	Low Average	16.1
70–79	Borderline	6.4
69 and below	Mentally Retarded	2.3

Source: Wechsler, D. (1981), Wechsler Adult Intelligence Scale (rev.) (p. 28). The Psychological Corporation

The Evaluation of Intelligence Tests.

Psychologists and others who favor IQ tests claim that they are reliable and valid ways of measuring intellectual ability. They are useful in predicting academic performance and in measuring cognitive disability caused by brain damage. They also believe that IQ tests play an important role in job placement, selecting candidates for management training, and placing military personnel. Criticisms come from many fronts, however.

One of the major criticisms of IQ testing is that IQ tests do not fairly measure the entire range of intelligent behavior, especially in everyday situations. Instead, they focus on the verbal and arithmetic skills you need to do well in school. How many people with a high IQ do you know who are struggling in their careers or relationships? These criticisms are not merely of academic interest, because your IQ score can determine whether you are placed in, or excluded from, special school programs or a job.[1,18,29]

Critics complain that IQ test scores are strongly influenced by factors other than your intelligence. Your motivation, moods, values, and personality can all affect your IQ score. For example, if the test result is not important to you, you may not work hard enough to do as well as you could. In addition, the skills of the examiner and the test-taking situation can also influence the test outcome.[1,18,29]

Consistently lower IQ scores for racial minorities in the United States has fueled one of the most fiery complaints about IQ tests—that they are biased in favor of upper- and middle-class whites and against minority groups. Critics claim that many minorities are unfairly placed in special education programs and denied the enriching experiences of programs designed for those with higher IQ. In response, some states have attempted to pass laws that ban the use of IQ test scores as the main basis for placement in special education programs.

One response to cries of bias has been the development of tests in which familiarity with particular aspects of mainstream culture are minimized. An example is psychologist Raymond Cattell's *Culture-Free Intelligence Tests* (CFIT), which downplay verbal skills, cultural background, and educational experience. Having no verbal content, these tests ask subjects to perceive relationships in shapes and figures.[30]

Culture-free tests adequately reduce the effects of cultural bias, but they are used infrequently. The main reason is that even though minorities score higher on these tests than they do on the traditional IQ tests, scores on culture-free tests do not predict academic achievement very well—the very purpose for which IQ tests were developed in the first place.[26]

What conclusions can be drawn from the criticisms of IQ testing? Most psychologists believe that IQ tests do measure certain aspects of your intelligence, especially those that predict academic performance. They also believe, however, that they are somewhat biased and misused. Many psychologists argue that the use of IQ tests as the primary means of making decisions about people in education and work should be discouraged. There is an old saying: "Don't throw out the baby with the bath water." Rather than eliminate IQ testing, psychologists should consider many sources of information in addition to IQ scores and should strive to make IQ tests more valid measures of real life.[18,19]

The Extremes of Intelligence

It is estimated that 3-5 percent of the American population are gifted whereas nearly 3 percent are considered mentally retarded.[31] In this section you will learn about intelligence as it applies to giftedness and mental retardation.

You probably know or have heard of someone who possesses exceptional talents and skills and who solves problems beyond the abilities of ordinary human beings. We often talk of "gifted" athletes like Michael Jordan and Monica Seles, artists like Leonardo DaVinci, or scientific geniuses like Marie Curie. Historically, giftedness was thought to result from supernatural powers, the devil, or mental illness. Beginning with Terman's studies of genius in the 1920s, giftedness was viewed in terms of the upper extremes of intelligence as measured by IQ tests.

Improving Your Intelligence

Since the early 1900s, psychologists such as Spearman, Terman, and more recently Arthur Jensen have assumed that intelligence is largely hereditary in origin and therefore unchangeable. You may have wondered whether it is possible to increase your intelligence. Many studies suggest that you can by learning how to improve thinking skills.[31]

Programs designed to improve intelligence teach strategies used in concept development, understanding cause and effect, drawing inferences, dealing with contradictions, distinguishing facts from opinion, and applying thinking skills in school and real-life situations. One such program, sponsored by the Venezuelan government, was designed to teach seventh-graders the cognitive skills that apply to learning and intelligence independent of the subject matter. The emphasis was on the teaching of observation, classification, reasoning, the critical use of language, problem solving, inventiveness, and decision making. In general, students who participated in the experimental program showed sizable improvements in their intellectual performance.[32]

▼

giftedness—an IQ score of 130 or higher

Despite our common sense and historical conceptions of giftedness, psychologists have been hard-pressed to come up with a definition that satisfies everyone. The definition of **giftedness** most often used for the placement of children in special programs is a score of 130 or higher on a standardized IQ test.[34] An alternative way to look at giftedness is in terms of exceptional abilities. The gifted have high levels of general intelligence and specific abilities in their fields of expertise and make the most of their abilities. They are better at shaping their environments than others, have exceptional problem-solving abilities, and have a talent for being able to develop a "master plan," which they systematically follow throughout their lives.[34]

Table 7.6 Characteristics of Mental Retardation

Level of MR: IQ and Mental Age	Percent of MR Cases	Features
Mild: IQ 50–55 to 70; mental age 11–12	85	Educable up to sixth-grade level; have skills necessary for minimal self-support
Moderate: IQ 35–40 to 50-55; mental age 8–9	10	Educable up to second-grade level; have semi-independent living skills
Severe: IQ 20–25 to 35–40; mental age 5–6	3–4	Educable up to kindergarten level; need supervision; can learn simple hygiene
Profound: IQ below 20–25; mental age 3-4	1–2	Educable up to preschool level; can perform simple tasks under close supervision

Other programs are designed around research that shows that intelligence can be improved if individuals are taught how to learn and access new information. Such programs stress the learning of general skills and strategies used to solve problems rather than techniques that can be used only in limited situations.

Anything you do to improve your thinking skills and problem-solving strategies will probably make you more intelligent. One way would be to use the IDEAL approach to problem solving, in which there are five components: *Identify, Define, Explore, Act,* and *Look.* According to this approach, you must first identify then define the problem precisely. Those steps will lead you to the exploration of solutions and action. Finally, you must look at the results and evaluate whether the problem has been solved.[33]

Although heredity sets limits on your intelligence, your ultimate ability is influenced by how well you use and expand your intellectual potential.

Mental retardation (MR) is a condition characterized by below-average intellectual functioning and deficits in adaptive behavior such as a lack of age-appropriate skills in learning and self-care. When test scores are used, mental retardation is defined as an IQ score of below 70. Table 7.6 describes the characteristics of MR. Many forces, both genetic and environmental are responsible for MR, as you will learn in the following section.

▼
mental retardation—below average IQ and deficits in adaptive functioning

What Determines Intelligence?

What do you think determines your IQ: your genes or your upbringing? Research shows that they both play a role. One of the most enduring controversies in psychology is whether behavior is determined by heredity (nature) or environment (nurture). At the heart of the nature-nurture controversy is the subject of intelligence. In this section you will learn about hereditary and environmental influences on intelligence and the implications for programs designed to improve it.

Early IQ studies assumed that individual differences in intelligence were largely inborn, determined by the genes you inherited from your parents. Such innate intelligence was believed to be fixed, or unchangeable. Indeed, adoption studies conducted in Texas and Colorado show that the IQs of adopted children are generally more similar to those of their biological parents than to these of their adoptive parents.[35]

Behavior genetics studies involving more than 10,000 pairs of twins tell us that about 50 percent of the differences in IQ test scores are due to heredity (Refer to Chapter 2).[36,37] One ongoing study of more than 100 sets of monozygotic (genetically identical) twins reared apart reveals that heredity accounts for 70 percent of the differences in IQ. Genetics also plays a role in some forms of mental retardation. In *Down syndrome*, retardation is due to the presence of an extra chromosome on the twenty-first pair.[38]

Family studies also support the notion that there is a hereditary component to intelligence. In general, the more similar two people are genetically, the more similar are their IQ scores. Your IQ is probably more similar to that of your parents, brothers, and sisters than it is to the IQs of your distant cousins.[39]

Behavior genetics studies of intelligence, must be weighed carefully. Genes do not permanently fix behavior. Their expression depends on the experiences that your environment provides. For example, you may be genetically inclined toward average IQ, but you can improve your cognitive ability through study, practice, and specialized training as discussed in *Issues and Applications: Improving Your Intelligence.*

Today, most psychologists agree that intelligence is determined by the interaction of heredity and environment. If heredity accounts for at least 50 percent of the variation in IQ scores, the environment must account for the other 50 percent. This means that your environment can make a difference of 20–25 IQ points one way or the other.[18]

Intelligence can be negatively affected by environmental factors such as problems during pregnancy, childhood illnesses, and malnutrition. The low intellectual levels observed in the mentally retarded can be caused by rubella (German measles), malnutrition, and the effects of maternal alcohol consumption on the developing fetus. Moreover, inadequate intellectual stimulation during critical learning periods early in life can also lead to retardation in disadvantaged children. The family environment can also have a positive effect on intelligence. Generally, higher IQ is associated with higher social class and higher parental income and education.[40]

The impact of environment on intelligence has been noted in studies in France and the United States in which children from lower-class families were raised in middle-class households. In one study, African American children adopted at birth and raised in white upper-middle-class families scored well above average on IQ tests and clearly better than their counterparts with similar genetic backgrounds who were not raised in middle-class homes.[41]

Special education improves intelligence in the mentally retarded and shows an environmental basis for intelligence. Two special education strategies for the MR are commonly employed. *Mainstreaming* places MR children in classes with nonretarded children and works best with mildly retarded children who can benefit from their exposure to normal children. Children who are at least moderately retarded are usually *segregated* from the mainstream by placing them in classes with other retarded children.

In conclusion, the important question about intelligence is not whether it is determined by heredity or environment, but how much they each contribute and how intelligence can be changed.

Summary

1. Thinking is the act of mentally representing information in images, words, symbols, or ideas. Thinking involves the organization of information into categories, or concepts. Concepts are formed around a prototype, a representative example of a category that shares most of the features of that category. Categories are arranged into hierarchies, from the more specific to the more general.

2. The four steps in problem solving are preparation, production, incubation, and evaluation. Preparation involves using available facts to define the problem. Production involves trying possible solutions. During incubation, you take a rest from the problem so that you can step back and get a fresh view of it. After you have produced a possible solution, you evaluate it to determine whether the problem is actually solved.

3. Language consists of phonemes, morphemes, syntax, and semantics. Phonemes are sounds and morphemes are combinations of phonemes that make up a unit of meaning. Syntax refers to the relations of words in a sentence, and semantics is the study of word meaning. The elements of language are organized by rules called grammar.

4. The linguistic-relativity hypothesis holds that language influences thought and determines one's conception of reality. Today, psychologists generally agree that language is a reflection not a cause of the way we think.

5. Intelligence is defined as the mental management of one's life in a constructive, purposeful way, by being able to adapt to, select, and shape the environment.

6. Spearman claimed that intelligence is composed largely of one factor called general intelligence. Thurstone viewed intelligence in terms of seven primary mental abilities. Guilford offered a structure-of-intellect model based on 150 factors. Gardner formulated a theory of multiple intelligences in which there are seven distinct types of intelligence. Sternberg proposed the triarchic theory, based on three interacting types of intelligence: componential, experiential, and contextual.

7. The Stanford-Binet Intelligence Scale measures four main abilities: verbal reasoning, short-term memory, quantitative reasoning, and abstract/visual reasoning. The Wechsler Adult Intelligence Scale–Revised measures verbal abilities including general knowledge, short-term memory, vocabulary, mental calculation, understand-

ing of sayings and situations, and concepts. Performance abilities tested are perception of missing things, nonverbal reasoning, visual analysis and synthesis, ability to assemble a puzzle, and visual memory.

8. Giftedness is characterized by an IQ above 130 and high levels of specific abilities. The gifted are superior at shaping their environments, problem solving, and following a master plan. Mental retardation is marked by below-average intellectual functioning (an IQ below 70) and deficits in adaptive behavior.

9. Intelligence is determined by the interaction of hereditary and environmental factors. Many studies show that at least 50 percent of the individual differences in intelligence is genetically determined. Environments that are not intellectually stimulating and diseases can interfere with intellectual development, whereas environments that encourage intellectual pursuits may improve it.

Questions for Discussion

1. How are concepts and images involved in thinking?

2. What are the four steps of problem solving?

3. What is the structure of language?

4. What is the relationship between language and thought?

5. What is the definition of intelligence?

6. What are the intelligence theories proposed by Spearman, Thurstone, Guilford, Gardner, and Sternberg?

7. Which mental abilities are tested in the Stanford-Binet Intelligence Scale and the Wechsler Adult Intelligence Scale–Revised?

8. What are the characteristics of giftedness and mental retardation?

9. How do heredity and the environment influence intelligence?

In this chapter you learned about the nature of intelligence and how it is measured in standardized IQ tests. You also learned that definitions of intelligence and the measurement of intelligence have been criticized on many grounds, especially that intelligence is infrequently viewed in terms of how it is expressed in everyday situations.

Your task is to organize into small groups and discuss your conceptions of intelligence by providing definitions, examples of how it is expressed in everyday situations, and how it might be measured other than by using standardized IQ tests.

Answers to Chapter Problems

Solution to the Cannibal/Missionary Problem. The missionaries and cannibals' can cross the river without the cannibals eating the missionaries by following the plan depicted below.

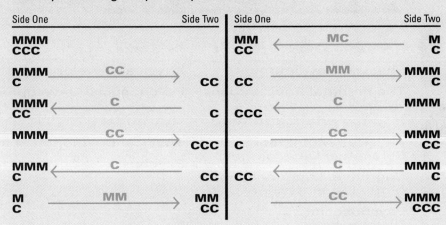

Solution to the Nine-Dot Problem. The nine-dot problem requires breaking set. The instructions do not require, as most people think, that the lines be drawn within the interior boundaries of the nine dots.

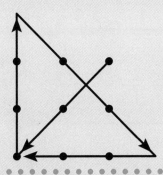

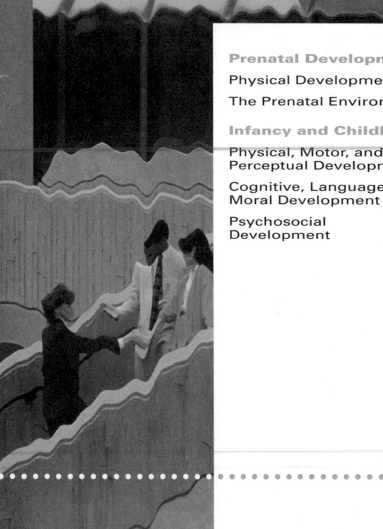

Chapter 8

Human Growth and Development

After completing this chapter, you should be able to:

1. Outline the stages of prenatal development and discuss the effects of the prenatal environment on the developing individual.

2. Describe the features of physical maturation and perceptual and motor development during infancy and childhood.

3. Discuss cognitive, language, and moral development in infancy and childhood.

4. Outline the major psychosocial changes during infancy and childhood.

5. Identify the main physical changes of adolescence.

6. Summarize psychosocial development in adolescence.

7. Discuss the physical changes that occur during adulthood.

8. Describe the major areas of psychosocial development in adulthood.

▼
prenatal stage— the period of development from conception to birth

In his award-winning book *The Broken Cord*, Michael Dorris describes his struggle to raise his mentally retarded adopted son, Adam. Because Adam's mother drank excessively when pregnant, his brain was severely damaged. Dorris's account paints a detailed picture of how alcohol can devastate the brain of the unborn child and cause lasting psychological harm. Adam's story reveals how biological factors set the stage for problems in intellectual, behavioral, and social development. It also reveals how human development is influenced by the constant love and support of a committed family and by the proper educational environment.[1]

Although Adam's story is an unusual one, the lessons it teaches about development, in particular the give-and-take between physical and psychosocial factors, are relevant to everyone. As you will learn in this chapter, the process of human growth and development is influenced by many forces whose interactions mold you into a unique individual.

Prenatal Development

The nine months from the moment you are conceived to your birth is the **prenatal stage** of development during which a single cell develops into a viable human infant. Prenatal development is controlled by your genes as well as by your prenatal environment. Although it is a brief part of your life span, the events that occur during the prenatal period have considerable impact on your later physical and mental capabilities.

Physical Development

Conception, the fertilization of the mother's ovum (egg) by the father's sperm, begins the *germinal stage* of prenatal development, which lasts for about two weeks. The fertilized ovum, called a *zygote*, divides rapidly from a single cell to several hundred cells. About 10 days after conception, the cluster of rapidly dividing cells attaches to the wall of the mother's uterus. At that point in life, you were about the size of the period at the end of this sentence. (See Color Plate 8.1)

The *embryonic stage* extends from two to eight weeks after conception. Rapid cell division continues in the *embryo*, and bodily organs begin to appear. The umbilical cord attaches the embryo to the mother's *placenta*, which exchanges nutrients and waste between the mother and embryo. This stage is called a **critical period** because the embryo is most ready for developmental changes to occur and is very sensitive to its environment. For example, at seven weeks *sexual differentiation* occurs; male and female embryos begin to take their unique shapes as a result of hormonal changes.

From the second month after conception until birth is the *fetal stage*, during which the *fetus* grows rapidly and the bodily organs become more distinct and functional. Reflexive arm and leg responses are noticeable in the fourth month, by which time the fetus has working sensory abilities, as shown by responses to sounds, including human voices, and to touch and pain. (See Color Plate 8.2)

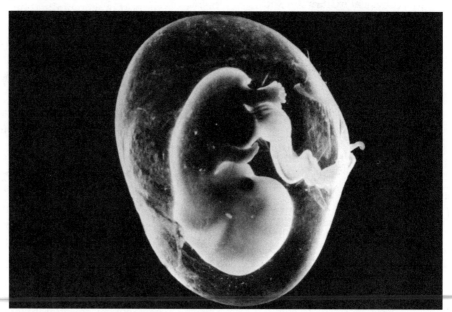

Even before birth, the developing child is highly sensitive to changes in the environment.

Infants born after the normal 38–42 weeks of prenatal development are *full-term infants*. Those born before 38 weeks are *premature infants*, and they are at higher risk for many health problems. A significant factor in the premature infant's condition is body weight. *Low-birthweight* infants, those who weigh under 5 pounds, are more prone to medical complications, such as respiratory failure. With proper medical care, however, most low-birthweight infants can develop normally.[2]

The Prenatal Environment

Even before birth, your environment had an enormous impact on your development. The prenatal environment can exert both beneficial and harmful effects on the unborn child. An important aspect of your prenatal environment was the quality of nutrition that you received. Before your birth you were totally dependent on your mother for nutrients, and her diet was critical to your development. Although the majority of pregnant women in this country have adequate diets, many impoverished women here and in other countries suffer from malnutrition. Approximately one-third of pregnant mothers, and their unborn offspring, have inadequate nutrition. Malnutrition can harm many bodily organs, including your brain, and is a leading cause of learning disabilities and mental retardation, especially in underdeveloped nations.[3,4]

The mother's physical health also determines the health of her child. Some maternal illnesses infect the unborn child and cause damage to developing organs. Diseases that harm the nervous system, such as rubella (German measles), have especially destructive effects on sensory and cognitive abilities. Later problems in development have also been associated with other prenatal illnesses, such as influenza, herpes, and HIV (the AIDS virus).

Because many drugs pass from mother to child through the placenta, the mother's drug use can also affect her child. For example, pregnant women who drink alcohol excessively are at risk for bearing children with **fetal alcohol syndrome**, a condition characterized by brain damage, mental retardation, and other birth defects, such as in the case of Adam mentioned earlier. Experts believe that many learning disabilities and behavior problems in children are due to prenatal drug exposure. Children whose mothers used cocaine while pregnant have high rates of learning and attention problems. Many other drugs including nicotine, marijuana, and heroin also have harmful effects on unborn children. Today, physicians caution pregnant women against drug use because of the potential hazards to their children.[5,6]

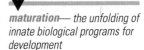

fetal alcohol syndrome— a condition of brain damage and mental retardation due to prenatal alcohol exposure

Children with fetal alcohol syndrome have distinctive birth defects and mental retardation due to the damaging influence of alcohol on their nervous systems before birth.

*I*nfancy and Childhood

The most rapid developmental changes occur during infancy and childhood. *Infancy*, the first two years of your life, was a period of remarkable transition from a helpless newborn to a mobile, self-aware toddler. The period of your *childhood*, between two years of age and puberty, was marked by rapid physical and mental growth as you became a more independent and socialized individual.

Physical, Motor, and Perceptual Development

The emergence of physical changes, motor (movement) skills, and perceptual abilities is guided by innate factors that shape the course of development. The unfolding of these innate biological programs is called **maturation**, which is influenced by both genetic and environmental events.

maturation— the unfolding of innate biological programs for development

Physical Development.   During your first year of life, your physical growth was one of the most obvious areas of development. The average infant grows very rapidly, but growth rates slow in the preschool years. Between ages 6 and 12, children show a steady gain of height and weight, with a growth spurt around age 10. A noticeable sex difference appears in late childhood as girls grow taller faster than boys. This sex difference can cause some embarrassing moments at sixth grade parties and dances when boys and girls do not see "eye to eye."[7]

Although your physical size and rate of growth in infancy and child-hood are affected by genes, diet also has a powerful influence. An under-nourished child grows at a slower rate than a child with the benefit of good nutrition. Children from impoverished families often have delayed physical growth due to their poor diet. Emotional factors, too, may influence the child's growth. Severely abused and neglected children sometimes exhibit a delayed physical maturation, called **failure-to-thrive**, in which there is a severe inhibition of weight and height gain. Failure-to-thrive can be re-versed if the child is placed in a more nurturing environment.[8]

Brain maturation is a critical aspect of physical development in infancy and childhood. At birth, the brain is only one-quarter of its adult size, but by age 2 it is about 75 percent of its full size. Throughout childhood the brain grows steadily until reaching its adult size in adolescence. As the nervous system matures, neural connections in the brain increase, setting the stage for psychological changes.[9]

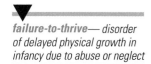

failure-to-thrive— *disorder of delayed physical growth in infancy due to abuse or neglect*

Motor Development. At birth your movements were dominated by simple reflexes such as sucking and grasping objects. Many of those reflexes disappeared in the first few months of your life and were replaced by more complex voluntary movements. Coordinated head, arm, and leg movements are very limited in the newborn, but within the first year of life the infant's motor skills improve dramatically. The major milestones of early motor development are shown in Table 8.1.[10]

Table 8.1 **Motor Milestones in Infancy**

Age	Motor Milestone
1 month	Holding chin up
2 months	Pushing up head and chest
3 months	Reaching for an object
6 months	Sitting up unaided
7 months	Crawling
8 months	Standing or pulling self up with support
10 months	Cruising or walking with support
12 months	Walking unaided for a short distance

Source: *Adapted from Gormly, A. V., & Brodzinsky, D. M. (1993). Lifespan human development (5th ed.). New York: Harcourt Brace Jovanovich.*

Throughout childhood, increased bodily coordination results from the combined effect of brain maturation and muscle growth. *Gross motor skills*—such as walking, running, and climbing—improve steadily, and by age 5 clumsiness gives way to controlled, even graceful action. Boys generally outperform girls in gross motor skills that involve strength and large muscle action, but girls usually do better than boys on tasks involving *fine motor skills* such as printing letters or tying shoelaces, which require finger coordination.

Motor skills depend on the amount and quality of the child's physical activity. Playing, running, and other activities are essential for the fine-tuning of movement abilities. Although most children need no push to become active, many children today seem more passive and sedentary than in the past. Fitness surveys find that today many school children are more overweight, less fit, and exercise less than they should. Pediatricians and child psychologists fear that a generation of "couch potatoes" is in training for a life of poor health.[11]

Perceptual Development.
Not long ago, an infant's perceptions were thought to be a "blooming buzzing confusion." Modern research, however, shows that infants have well-developed perceptual abilities. Although newborns are quite nearsighted, the accuracy of their vision improves quickly in the first year of life. At just a few weeks of age, some infants even demonstrate imitation abilities and will stick out their tongues in response to that behavior in an adult.[12]

Within their first six months, infants show rapid progress in their perception of the world around them. Psychologist Robert Fantz demonstrated that infants see complex forms, colors, and motion in the visual world.[13] In fact, infants prefer complicated designs to simple ones and also show a preference for human forms such as faces. Depth perception appears early in life, as illustrated in the *visual cliff* studies of psychologists Eleanor Gibson and Richard Walk. When infants were placed near the "deep" side of an artificial cliff (actually a box with a clear top), they became upset because they saw that they could fall over the "cliff".[14]

Infants in the visual cliff experiment show fear responses when they are able to perceive depth cues indicating that they are over the deep drop.

The ability to discriminate sounds and voices also emerges in the early months. Infants are particularly good at recognizing the sound of their mother's voice. Touch and pain senses are also ready at birth, but it is not easy to test newborns' experiences of such sensations.[2]

Cognitive, Language, and Moral Development

How children understand their world and themselves is the domain of cognitive development. Cognitive changes are reflected in the child's thinking, problem solving, language, and moral reasoning.

Piaget's Theory of Cognitive Development.

How do children think? That deceptively simple question was the concern of Jean Piaget (1896–1980), a Swiss psychologist whose theory of cognitive development is one of the best known in psychology. According to Piaget, a child's thinking progresses through four stages, with each stage characterized by a unique blend of concepts, called *schemas*, as indicated in Table 8.2.[15,16]

Table 8.2 **Piaget's Theory of Cognitive Development**

Age (years)	Stage	Schemas
0–2	Sensory-motor	Perception and movement, Object permanence
2–6	Preoperational	Symbolic thought, Egocentrism, Animism
6–11	Concrete operations	Conservation, Concrete logic, Concrete concepts
11	Formal operations	Abstract reasoning, Formal logic

▼
sensory-motor stage— stage of cognitive development in which thinking is dominated by immediate sensory impressions and bodily movements

From birth to age 2, the infant is in the **sensory-motor stage**, in which thinking is dominated by the child's immediate sensory impressions and bodily movements. During this period, mental life is tied closely to the child's "hands-on" experiences with people and objects. An important schema that begins to appear by the ninth month of life is *object permanence*, the realization that objects continue to exist even when the infant cannot see or hear them. Before they acquire object permanence, infants act according to the "out of sight, out of mind" rule. You can test object permanence in an infant by hiding a toy in view of the infant; if she searches for the hidden toy, she shows object permanence. At this time infants will also show signs of *separation anxiety* when they are away from their mothers for even a short time. Object performance is fully developed by about 18 months of age.

▼
preoperational stage— stage of cognitive development marked by symbolic thinking, egocentrism, and animism

The **preoperational stage** lasts from about 2 to 6 years of age and is marked by the child's advance to symbolic thinking, especially through language. By age 2 most children acquire language skills quickly, and their ability to think in words blossoms. The preoperational child is not bound to immediate sensory impressions, but can manipulate symbolic thoughts about the world. Preoperational thinking is limited by the child's *egocentrism*. In playing a game, for instance, the child may assume that his way of playing is the only right way. The preoperational child cannot understand the perspectives of other people and cannot take different points of view. A charming quality of preoperational children is their *animism*, a kind of magical thinking in which everything seems to be alive. Remember when you believed in ghosts, had imaginary playmates, or talked to your toys and puppets? Those behaviors show that the preoperational child's view of reality is still very illogical and fantastic.

From age 6 to 11 the child is in the **concrete operations stage**, when logical thinking first appears and the child's concepts become more realistic. The child has entered this stage when he or she solves the problem of *conservation*. Suppose that you fill a short wide glass with water and pour the contents into a tall narrow glass while the child observes. Preoperational children will tell you that there is more water in the taller glass because they confuse the height of the container with the amount it holds. By contrast, the concrete operational child knows that the amount of water does not depend on the shape of the glass and will correctly judge the amount to be the same. The child knows that physical properties such as amount and number are conserved, or constant despite changing appearances. During this stage, children develop more realistic concepts about the world and begin to reason logically. But, the child's thinking remains "concrete," or bound to reality. For example, the child can classify ideas about concrete objects such as animals but does not grasp more abstract notions such as algebra.

Abstract thinking appears in the **formal operations stage**, starting at around 11 years of age. In this last stage of cognitive development, children acquire an understanding of hypothetical concepts and principles, such as those in mathematics and science. The formal operational child reasons according to general logical principles, regardless of how unrealistic the problem seems. Consider this statement: All dogs have wings; trees are dogs; therefore, trees have wings. In this stage, children understand that the conclusion is logical, although ridiculous and untrue because only the form, not the content of the statement matters.

Piaget's theory has been supported by studies on children throughout the world, but it has also been criticized on several grounds. Piaget's critics argue that cognitive development is more gradual and subtle than his model suggests. Transitions between stages are slow, not abrupt, his critics claim, and schemas appear gradually, not suddenly. Some researchers question whether the formal operations stage is universal or a product of classroom education. Adults from many cultures do not show formal operations, perhaps because of limited education. Although the first three stages appear in all cultures, formal operations may be a culturally determined stage due to the type of academic training of Western school children.[17,18]

▼
concrete operations stage— stage of cognitive development marked by conservation and concrete reality-based logic

▼
formal operations stage— stage of cognitive development characterized by abstract thinking and reasoning

Chapter 8 • Human Growth and Development

Jean Piaget, (1896–1980), is best known for his theory of cognitive development, one of the most widely tested and supported theories in the history of psychology. Credited with inventing the field of cognitive development, through his long career he became the most influential figure in developmental psychology.

Piaget was born in Switzerland to an academic family, and his genius was apparent early in life. When he was 10 years old he published an article about sparrows in a respected biological journal and was offered a job at the Geneva Museum of Natural History. Of course, when the directors realized that Piaget was a child the offer was withdrawn. After receiving a degree in zoology from the University of Neuchatel (Switzerland), Piaget began to explore the field of psychology.

For a time he studied child intelligence with the French psychologist Theodore Simon, who with Alfred Binet had developed the first intelligence test, the Binet-Simon Scale. Curious about how children think and the kinds of mistakes they make in trying to solve problems, Piaget conducted his early observations on his own three children. From this modest beginning, he expanded his studies and formulated his famous theory of cognitive development.

During a period when psychology was dominated by the behavioristic emphasis on environmental forces, Piaget maintained that human action was due to interactions between innate factors and the environment. Over time his interactional view became the dominant perspective in the field. An energetic and highly productive individual, Piaget authored dozens of books and many research publications on development, including *The Child's Conception of the World* (1929) and *The Origins of Intelligence in Children* (1952). In addition, he was an influential teacher for an entire generation of developmental psychologists, whose works have extended his ideas into many new areas.[17]

Language Development.   Language is essential for a child's cognitive and social development (See Chapter 7). Language not only permits the child to think symbolically, it also allows communication and the formation of relationships. Between ages 2 and 6 the child's language skills develop faster than at any other period in life. All children learn language at different rates, but there is a general sequence of development in most children. No matter what your native tongue is, your first language was much the same as every other infant: spontaneous babbling and cooing. Through exposure to speech the child shapes vocal expressions to match adult language. Within a few months of your first birthday, you probably uttered your first true word. Months before speaking, However, you could understand some words and instructions spoken to you. A general rule of language development is that comprehension precedes expression: Children understand speech before using it.

Like most children, your first words were probably short one-syllable expressions, such as "No," "Ma," or "Da." These early words, called *holophrases*, convey complex thoughts. For example, an infant's "No" may mean "I don't want it," "Go away from me," or "Don't do it." By age 2, simple two-word *telegraphic speech* conveys the child's thoughts. The telegraphic phrase "Doggie go" may mean "Go get the dog," "The dog went away," or "Where did the dog go?" In early childhood, the length and organization of speech increase quickly. Can you learn 20 new words each day? The average six-year-old acquires language at that amazing pace.

When children first learn the rules of grammar, they often apply them excessively. A four-year-old child is sure that she has two "foots," and yesterday she "goed" to McDonalds for lunch. Such mistakes reflect the child's understanding of general English language rules for forming plural nouns (add *s*) and the past tense of a verb (add *ed*). Improvements in the understanding and use of grammar continue throughout childhood and are affected by exposure to adult speech, as well as by classroom instruction. When children are read to by adults, their language development benefits greatly.[18,19]

Moral Development.

Consider the following situation: You need a large sum of money for medicine to save the life of a close family member. The inventor of the medicine is charging excessively for it and refuses to reduce the price although you offer him much more than his cost to produce it. In desperation you steal the medicine. Did you do the right thing or the wrong thing?

By studying children's ideas about similar dilemmas, psychologist Lawrence Kohlberg constructed a theory of **moral reasoning**, the ways in which people think about right and wrong. In Kohlberg's theory, moral reasoning proceeds through three levels. The *preconventional level* dominates moral reasoning up to age 9. At this level children judge right and wrong by their own personal experiences of reward and punishment from parents and other authorities. For example, a preconventional child might reply that you should not steal the drug because you will probably get put in jail. From about age 10 into adolescence, the *conventional level* of reasoning is most apparent. At this level, the child reasons about morality in terms of the rules or laws of society. A conventional child may justify your stealing the medicine on the grounds that it is your duty to take care of your family. The most mature moral reasoning is found at the *postconventional level*, where decisions about right and wrong are based on your personal principles or values. Postconventional judgments recognize that individuals have different values and people should follow their own conscience.[20]

Kohlberg's theory has been criticized because few people actually exhibit postconventional moral reasoning, even in adulthood. Furthermore,

moral reasoning— thinking or judgments about right and wrong

some researchers question the relevance of Kohlberg's theory to female moral development. Kohlberg's postconventional level focuses on individual rights and conscience, reflecting a male-oriented notion of morality. By contrast, psychologist Carol Gilligan argues that female moral reasoning places more emphasis on relationships and concern for other people. Kohlberg's critics also question the connection between moral reasoning and moral behavior. You may show advanced thinking about moral principles, but still act immorally in your everyday life. Moral action depends on more than just your moral reasoning, such as the forces in the situation in which your behavior occurs.[21,22]

Psychosocial Development

The growth of your personality, gender identity, and interpersonal relationships defines your psychosocial development. The foundations of psychosocial development are set early in life through your interactions with people in your family, neighborhood, and school.

Personality Development.   Psychoanalyst Erik Erikson (1902–1994) offered a popular theory about personality development, emphasizing the formation of **identity**, your sense of self, or self-concept. According to Erikson, you move through eight stages during your life, and at each one you face a developmental challenge to be mastered (see Table 8.3). Success in meeting these challenges helps you to achieve a healthy identity, but failure can cause lasting deficits in your personality and social adjustment. In Erikson's view, your social relationships strongly affect your personality development.[23]

▼

identity— *a stable sense of self or self-concept*

Table 8.3 **Erikson's Theory of Personality Development**

Age	Stage	Developmental Challenge
0–1	Trust vs. mistrust	Learn to trust in people and the world
1–3	Autonomy vs. shame and doubt	Acquire independent will and action
3–6	Initiative vs. guilt	Develop personal responsibility
6–12	Industry vs. inferiority	Master skills and knowledge
12–18	Identity vs. identity confusion	Explore self, values, and roles
Young adult	Intimacy vs. isolation	Form intimate relationships
Middle adult	Generativity vs. stagnation	Care for the next generation
Older adult	Integrity vs. despair	Evaluate life accomplishments

Erikson's theory emphasizes the developmental similarities among people at each stage. Although these similarities exist, many differences do as well. What makes your personality unique? How do your life experiences shape your character? Seeking answers to these questions about personality, psychologists study individual differences among children and find that personality unfolds as a result of forces within the child and from the child's social environment.

Ask your mother what you were like as an infant and she will probably tell you about your **temperament**, your inborn style of emotional and behavioral responding. Within the first months of life, infants show clear temperament patterns. Some are passive and quiet, adapting easily to changes in their environment. Others are decidedly more difficult, irritable, and moody. If there are infants in your family, you can probably characterize their temperaments after a brief period of observation. Your overall activity level and emotionality are basic aspects of your temperament that establish a foundation for your later personality and social traits.[24] Psychologist Jerome Kagan has studied children with an *inhibited temperament*, characterized by anxiety over change and unfamiliar situations. He concludes that early inhibition has a genetic basis and is related to later social behavior and traits, such as shyness.[25,26]

Childhood personality is also affected by early social relationships. The emotional bond between an infant and mother (or primary caretaker) is called *attachment*. This bond is critical to the child's emotional and social adjustment. Children with secure attachments are more self-assured in new situations and with unfamiliar people. By contrast, insecurely attached children are fearful of the unknown and have more difficulty relating to others. Extreme disruptions of attachment, for instance in abused children, have destructive effects. Abused children have higher than average risks for developing serious personality disorders and emotional disturbances.[27,28]

According to developmental psychologist Michael Lewis, a child's identity is governed by *self-schemas*, or beliefs about oneself. By the end of their first year, children show signs of self-awareness and over time develop more elaborate ideas about their abilities and limitations.[29] These self-schemas influence both identity and **self-esteem**, your self-evaluations and feelings about yourself. Children with positive self-esteem have good feelings about themselves and see themselves as valuable and worthwhile. Negative self-esteem, by contrast, is reflected in harsh and critical self-evaluations. Self-esteem influences not only a child's emotional state, but also his social interactions. Children with positive self-esteem are more active socially and more popular with peers.[30] (See *Issues and Applications: Building Your Self-Esteem*)

Parents are especially important in promoting the growth of a child's self-esteem. Harsh treatment from parents is reflected in a child's negative self-evaluations. On the other hand, supportive and approving parental attitudes foster positive self-esteem in their children. Psychologist Stanley Coopersmith found that children with positive self-esteem tended to have parents who were accepting and affectionate, but also set clear limits for the child's behavior.[31]

How did your parents discipline you when you were a child? Children are exposed to many kinds of discipline that affect their personality and social behavior. Researcher Diana Baumrind distinguishes three *parenting styles*, having different developmental outcomes. The *permissive parent* sets few limits and is uninvolved with the child. Consequently, the child has problems in self-control and cooperating with others. At the other extreme, the

temperament— inborn style of emotional and behavioral responding

self-esteem— evaluations and feelings about oneself that influence the sense of personal worth

Building Your Self-Esteem

Take a minute to answer the following questions:

▶ Are you overall a worthwhile person?

▶ Do you like yourself the way you are?

▶ Are you as good as most people?

If you said yes to these questions, you have positive self-esteem, but if you answered no, your self-esteem needs help. A nationwide study of tenth-graders found that only 46 percent of boys and 29 percent of girls report positive self-esteem.[32] Apparently, problems in self-esteem are widespread in American adolescents, particularly girls. These findings are quite alarming considering that self-esteem influences your emotional and social adjustment. Although it may have childhood roots that cannot be altered, your self-esteem can improve if you change your attitudes and behaviors.

Self-esteem reflects your perceptions and evaluations of yourself. Unfortunately, low self-esteem is a trap for many people who set low standards because they expect to do poorly and, consequently, reinforce their low opinion of themselves by achieving little. To break free of this self-esteem trap, follow these principles:

▶ Set goals and standards that are challenging, but reasonable.

▶ Reward yourself for progress, remind yourself when you are doing well, and encourage yourself for trying your best.

▶ Judge yourself rationally and do not always blame yourself when things go wrong.

▶ Identify your strengths and assert them in your social interactions.

▶ Pick friends carefully and develop relationships with supportive and positive people.

▶ Evaluate yourself according to your own principles not by ideas imposed on you by others.

Positive self-esteem tends to feed on itself, and as you see yourself progressing, you will find it easier to further your psychological well-being.

---

authoritarian parent places excessively strict rules and discipline on the child, often using punishment to enforce the rules. As a result, the child is anxious and socially incompetent. *Authoritative parents* set clear standards and values. They discipline with instruction and encouragement, rather than with punishment, and their children are self-confident and responsible as a result.[33]

Gender Identity. Like most people, you have probably had a definite sense of being male or female since you were about three years old. Your **gender identity** is one of the most stable aspects of your personality and social behavior. Once established it rarely changes, although its characteristics are refined during your life. Biological factors are clearly relevant to gender identity. For most people, biological sex, as defined by sex chromosomes and genitals, corresponds to their psychological sense of being male or female. Genetically programmed hormonal influences set the foundation for gender even before birth.[34]

Besides biology, social forces also shape your gender identity. Early in life, *identification* is essential to gender identity. Girls typically identify with their mothers and other female figures, taking into their personalities the attitudes, values, and actions of female role models. Similarly, boys usually identify with their fathers and other male figures, imitating those role models. Identification is not altogether controlled by the child, however. Parents, family, and society encourage imitation of same-sex role models. According to psychologist Sandra Bem, socialization provides children with a set of beliefs about gender, called a *gender schema*, that motivates their sex-role behavior.[35,36]

Although American sex roles have changed dramatically in recent years, children continue to be channeled into different activities according to their gender. Boys receive encouragement to be aggressive and independent, and girls are expected to be nurturing and cooperative. Changing social attitudes have reduced some sex typing by parents, but many "traditional" patterns remain especially with fathers, who are more likely to respond differently to sons and daughters regarding gender-relevant behavior. For example, fathers encourage rough play in their sons but tend to discourage it in daughters.[37]

Social institutions provide powerful messages about gender that shape children's attitudes. Depictions of men and women on television and in films have great impact on the child's view of gender behavior. The occupations of men and women on television are often stereotypes of traditional sex roles. Schools, too, may reinforce stereotypical gender behavior if teachers encourage assertiveness and class involvement more in boys than in girls and if boys receive more support than girls for interest in math and science.

gender identity— the sense of being male or female

Children learn many attitudes and habits by identifying with their parental role models.

Adolescence

Your teenage years are usually considered the boundaries of *adolescence*, a transitional period in which the change from childhood to adulthood occurs. Although this transition is an important part of your development, adolescence is significant in its own right because of its distinctive physical and psychosocial changes.

Physical Development

In adolescence, physical development takes on a dramatic form with the onset of **puberty**, when height and weight increase and *secondary sexual characteristics* emerge. In both sexes, more body hair appears, particularly

puberty— the period of rapid physical and sexual maturation during early adolescence

in the pubic and armpit regions, and, in boys, facial hair grows. Girls' breasts and hips develop, and boys' penises and testes enlarge. These pubertal changes are prompted by increases in two hormones, *testosterone* in boys and *estradiol* in girls. Puberty is usually drawn out over a few years in early adolescence. Both sexes show a growth spurt, but girls usually grow sooner. Girls may begin puberty one to two years earlier than boys. The first menstruation, or **menarche**, marks a clear start a girl's sexual maturation.[38]

A quick look at a sixth-grade class will confirm that the timing of puberty varies quite a bit from child to child. In that class you will probably find a wide range of development in terms of height and sexual characteristics. Early-maturing boys have an advantage over late-maturing peers in physical size, athletic skills, and social activity, especially dating. Although some of those advantages apply to early-maturing girls, they often have some disadvantages as well. A girl whose puberty arrives early often feels self-conscious about her physical appearance, especially if her body is much more developed than her peers.[39,40]

Many adults attribute the occasionally extreme behavior and emotional states of teenagers to their "raging hormones." Despite the popularity of this idea, research does not consistently support the belief that the excesses of adolescents are due directly to hormonal changes. Testosterone is associated with aggressiveness and anxiety, and estradiol appears to be linked with moodiness and depression, but the exact relationship between hormones and behavior is not clear. Adolescent emotions and social behaviors cannot be explained simply in terms of hormones.[41]

Psychosocial Development

With physical maturation in adolescence come changes in personality and social functioning. The transition from childhood to adulthood is psychological and social as well as physical. Three areas of adolescent psychosocial development are particularly important: identity, social relationships, and sexuality.

Identity. Who am I? What do I want to be? These questions touch on issues of personality that are strongly felt in adolescence. Erikson's theory views adolescence as a period in which the main challenge is to establish a stable identity. The teenage years provide opportunities to explore different values, relationships, and roles in the interest of identity formation. The occasional sudden and extreme changes of opinion or style that you see in adolescents can be a healthy and even necessary part of this exploration. Adolescents who have trouble "finding themselves" and who struggle to form a consistent self-concept experience an **identity crisis**.[42] Psychologist James Marcia points out that teens may undergo several changes from *identity crisis* to *identity commitment* before the end of adolescence.[43]

In identity development, the adolescent's family and friends are extremely powerful influences. Parents can foster a healthy identity by providing supportive and open relationships with their teenage child. Although conflicts between parents and teens are inescapable, most teenagers retain basically positive relationships with their parents. In fact, adoles-

▼
menarche (**men**-ark)— a girl's first menstruation

▼
identity crisis— the struggle to establish a stable identity in adolescence

cents usually report general agreement with their parents' fundamental values and moral sentiments. Parent-teen conflict usually springs from the teen's efforts to deal with "normal" developmental problems. For example, adolescents need to seek greater autonomy for themselves in terms of personal independence and emotional separation from their parents. When parents are reluctant to yield their control and permit this growth, conflicts will arise.[44] One area in which independence and also conflict may appear is that of work, as discussed in *Issues and Applications: Teens at Work*.

Issues and Applications

Teens at Work

Rush from school and grab a sandwich or a slice of pizza on the way to work; work several hours and try to find a few minutes for homework; come home and catch some sleep; get up, go to school, and do it all over again. Sound familiar? For many teenagers today this scenario is a way of life. Of American adolescents ages 12 to 17 about 5 million, or 75 percent, work part-time after school. What effect does working have on the adolescent? Research offers no simple answer, but suggests a "good news, bad news" situation for teens at work.[46]

The good news is that work has some clear benefits. Obviously, there are economic advantages for teens and their families. From 1986 to 1991 the annual earning power of American teenagers increased from $65 to $95 billion. Parents of working teens gain some financial relief when their children start to buy things for themselves, and the teens become more independent as a result of their income. Their personal responsibility, dependability, and money management skills also benefit, and for some working teens academic performance and family relationships improve as well.[47,48]

The news is not all good, however. With increasing time spent at work, teens have less time for athletics, socializing, hobbies, family, and school work. A steady decline in grades with increased work time is noted in high school students who work for 10 or more hours a week. Those who work 20 or more hours a week show the most serious effects. They are most likely to have poor grades and high absenteeism from school, as well as greater alcohol use. Many teens get "burned out" trying to meet the demands of their jobs and school. In the pursuit of short-term material advantages, working teens may jeopardize their long-term occupational success by neglecting their academic growth.[46]

Perhaps you know someone who has been able to successfully maintain his or her school work, job, and social life. Many working teens do juggle their obligations masterfully. The key to their success is that they set clear priorities and balance all the elements of their lives.

An important aspect of self-concept is **ethnic identity**, the awareness of and attitudes about your cultural or racial group. Identification with and appreciation of your ethnic heritage can be a source of pride and self-esteem and can provide important social supports. During the teenage years, an increase in ethnic awareness is apparent in most adolescents, particularly among minority group members. Studies of African American, Asian American, and Mexican American teens show that a clear ethnic identity is positively related to overall psychological adjustment.[45]

Ethnic identity provides teens with an important framework for personal growth and group activities.

Social Development.

During adolescence the social life of the average teen takes a more central role. As the teen becomes more independent of family members, relationships with friends and peers assume greater importance for recreation and psychological support.

Social adjustment and competence in adolescence are signs of how well the teen is likely to function in adulthood. In early adolescence, strong same-sex friendships are significant features of social development. In mid to late adolescence mixed sex groups become common, and dating relationships become prominent. Inasmuch as identity formation requires an exploration of personal values and attitudes, social development relies on exploring different relationships. Peer relationships allow a teen to acquire essential social skills that can make the transition to adulthood easier. Communication, cooperation, conflict resolution, and role-playing skills evolve in peer interactions. With your own peers, you surely have seen several roles being enacted: Who is the leader? The decision maker? The eager follower?[49,50]

A common assumption about teenagers is that they are strongly influenced by **peer pressure**, the pressure to comply or conform with members of one's peer group. You surely can find evidence for this belief in your own experiences of going along with your friends in some activity in which you were not too interested. Certainly peer pressure exists, but it is worth remembering that peer groups usually form on the basis of individual choice. You tend to select peers because their traits or interests are similar to your own. Although teens do often conform to their peers' behavior and attitudes, peer pressure is likely to be only part of the reason. Conformity also results from the adolescent's own motives. For instance, teens with low self-esteem are more apt to conform with peers in order to seek acceptance from them, while teens with high self-esteem tend more to act as individuals.[51]

Social development in the teenage years is affected by many forces, including two distinctive attitudes of adolescents: idealism and egocentrism. Teenage *idealism* reflects the adolescent's increased cognitive and moral maturity that is shown in strong beliefs about how the world should be or how people should treat one another, as well as in criticisms of hypocrisy and error in others. The values of the adolescent idealist may lead to productive ends, such as participation in efforts to clean up the environment or political activity. The attractiveness of cults to some adolescents may also be due to idealism because of promises the cults make about a purer or better way of life.[49]

Earlier in this chapter you learned about egocentrism in preoperational children according to Piaget's theory. In adolescents, *egocentrism* refers to their self-absorption and self-consciousness. Adolescents often assume that other people are as keenly interested in them and their ideas as they are themselves. Conflicts in relationships with peers and adults often arise because teens feel that they are not adequately appreciated or understood.[52]

Sexual relationships also develop in adolescence. These relationships are influential in setting a foundation for adult sexuality. In recent decades, American adolescents have shown more sexual behavior at earlier ages. By age 15 most teens have begun to date, and by age 18 most have had sexual intercourse. Greater sexual freedom has not been an unqualified benefit, however, as the sharp rise in rates of AIDS and other sexually transmitted diseases in the teenage population shows. Despite their apparent sexual sophistication, most sexually active American teens do not regularly use birth control. One in 10 American teenage girls becomes pregnant, usually without intending to, and nearly half of those pregnancies end in abortion. The majority of teenage girls who have their babies will raise them as unwed mothers, placing themselves at greater risk of academic failure, underemployment, and poverty.[53]

Adulthood

When does the adolescent become an adult? Legally, adulthood is most often reached at age 18, but psychologically *adulthood* is not so clearly defined. Becoming an adult implies that you are responsible for yourself, are self-sufficient, and accept the roles and obligations of the "grown-up" world.

Psychologist Daniel Levinson offers a model of adult development based on the concept of **life structures**— the underlying patterns or designs of a person's life based mainly on relationships. In adulthood, marriage, family, and work relationships are the focal points of life structures. Levinson's model divides adulthood into three periods: *early*, *middle*, and *late adulthood*. Each of these periods has three life-structure phases, as shown in Figure 8.1. Development in these phases is shaped by the individual's personality, social environment, and physical condition.[54]

Figure 8.1   Levinson's Model of Adult Development

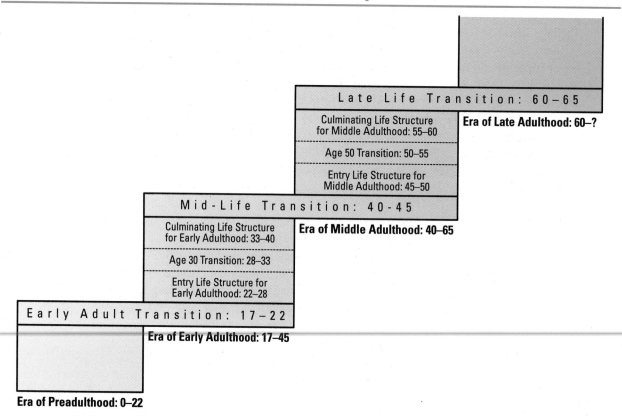

The three main phases ("eras") of adult development: early adulthood, middle adulthood, and late adulthood. Periods of transition between eras are also shown.

Source: Levinson, D.J. (1986). A conception of adult development. *American Psychologist, 41, 8.*

Physical Development

In their twenties and early thirties, young adults reach their physical peak in terms of strength, stamina, and overall physical health. In young adulthood, sensory abilities and bodily coordination are at their best, as illustrated by the performance of athletes who tend to reach their potential at this time. Women in their twenties are at their reproductive peak, and their pregnancies tend to have fewer complications than those of younger or older women.

By middle adulthood, physical capacities begin to diminish. Reaction times slow, visual accuracy declines, and metabolism decreases, often producing a weight gain called the "middle-age spread." Physical appearance changes, too, with graying and thinning hair and wrinkling of the skin. Throughout middle adulthood, there is gradual loss of efficiency in bodily functions, including respiration and heart, and muscle activity. For women, middle age is punctuated by the end of their menstrual cycle, or **menopause**, often called the "change of life."

▼

menopause (men-oh-paws)— stage marked by the end of menstruation in the middle-aged woman

After age 60, when late adulthood begins, there is usually a more rapid decline in physical abilities. With movement into late adulthood, senior citizens experience numerous age-related disabilities. Eyesight, hearing, and coordination problems are normal conditions in this stage. The aging brain produces diminished mental abilities, such as memory difficulty. Age-related diseases are also prominent aspects of late adulthood, when people become more prone to heart disease, arthritis, cancer, and Alzheimer's disease.[55,56]

Psychosocial Development

Adulthood is generally marked by a stabilization of personality, occupation, and social relationships. However, many changes in psychosocial functioning take place as you progress through the phases of adult life.

Personality. After the identity formation of adolescence personality becomes stabilized during early adulthood. In their research, psychologists Paul Costa and Robert McCrae found considerable continuity of basic personality traits and self-concept through adulthood.[57] Although adult personality is stable, it is not set in concrete and some development occurs. Changes in adult personality are most apparent in attitudes and behaviors related to interpersonal relations. For example, increased dependability and responsibility tend to emerge during the adult years.[58,59]

Keep in mind that personality stability does not necessarily mean stagnation. In adulthood, as in other periods of life, personality change can be prompted by changing life circumstances, especially relationships. After divorce, for example, many women become more assertive and independent than they were when married. Daniel Levinson, whose model of adult development was mentioned earlier, considers middle adulthood a time of potential crisis. The **mid-life crisis** of the "fortysomething" adult may appear as strangely uncharacteristic behaviors and attitudes, as well as emotional distress. For instance, a man may abruptly quit his job and separate from his wife and children. This extreme type of mid-life crisis is most likely in someone who is displeased with his current lifestyle and feels that his life goals have been disappointed.

▼

mid-life crisis— a period of uncharacteristic behaviors and attitudes, indicating the distress of middle adulthood

Relationships. As Erikson's psychosocial theory indicates, the major developmental challenge of young adulthood is to form *intimacy* in relationships. Some of Erikson's critics argue that while intimacy follows identity formation for males, just the reverse happens for females. Young women tend to develop intimacy first, and from their relationships develop a sense of adult identity.[60]

Both male and female Americans usually develop intimate romantic relationships in their twenties, and marriage is most prevalent for this age group. For both sexes, young adulthood is usually a time of "settling down" in terms of relationships, family, and work. Developmental psychologist Robert Havighurst outlines several tasks that confront the young adult:[61]

▶ Mate selection

▶ Starting a family

▶ Rearing children

▶ Managing a home

▶ Getting started on a career or occupation

▶ Establishing a network of social relationships

▶ Developing a sense of civic responsibility

Approximately 95 percent of adult Americans will get married, and for many of them marriage will prove to be the most significant relationship of their adult lives. Their marital satisfaction influences their general psychological well-being and personal growth, as well as that of their children. Children raised by parents who have a disturbed marriage are likely to develop emotional and interpersonal problems. Nearly half of all marriages in the United States end in divorce. For most people, divorce is an event with mixed consequences. Stress is almost inevitable during and after divorce for both spouses, but eventually most divorced people perceive their splitting up in positive terms. Most divorced women however, experience significant financial loss due to divorce. In addition to the loss of income from the husband's earnings, divorced women are also likely to be economically burdened by having custody of the children.[55,62,63]

Work.   Freud once remarked that an adult's mental health is based on the ability to "love and work." Along with marital and family relationships, work is an important component of adult life. The work you do helps to define your self-concept, interpersonal relationships, and emotional well-being. Studies show that job satisfaction in adulthood tends to increase gradually over time. How satisfied you are with your career is affected by many factors, including income, personal goals, and relationships with co-workers. In turn, job satisfaction can affect other aspects of your life. For example, people who are extremely unhappy in their work often develop problems both in the workplace and at home.[64]

Since the 1960s, women have entered the American workforce in great numbers. Today, a majority of married women with children work outside the home. Working women typically report greater life satisfaction than nonworking women, but this finding is qualified by other variables. As a group, women earn less than their male counterparts and are more likely to encounter discrimination on the job. In addition, working mothers are usually faced with "double duty" in that they are also more responsible for child care and household chores than their husbands are. For unmarried working mothers the combined stress of work and home obligations is even greater.[65,66]

Aging and Dying.   If you lived during the time of the ancient Roman empire, you would have been middle-aged at puberty because the average life span then was only about 22 years. Today, however, the life expectancy for Americans is around 75 years. Advances in technology and modern health care have made possible not only a longer life, but also a better life for most people. Nevertheless, late adulthood is a time for confronting the approaching end of life and coping with the inevitable effects of aging. During this period of **senescence**, or old age, the body weakens and mental abilities begin to diminish as a result of aging.

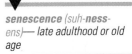

senescence (suh-**ness**-ens)— late adulthood or old age

Erik Erikson proposed that the main task of late adulthood is developing a sense of *integrity*. The elderly person reviews his or her life and evaluates the achievements and failures of a lifetime. The sense of integrity comes from concluding that it was a life well lived and meaningful. To the extent that they remain healthy and active, most elderly adults continue to enjoy life despite the closeness of death. In fact, older adults generally report having less anxiety about death than do younger people.[55]

Old age can also be a stressful time. After age 60, a multitude of illnesses and infirmities begin to appear. In addition, many elderly are economically disadvantaged and struggle to live on meager incomes. Even for financially secure senior citizens, the adjustment to retirement may be quite difficult and promote emotional disturbances. Retirees whose careers were their most important source of self-esteem and social support may find retirement a prison of boredom and emptiness. Many elderly also suffer emotionally from the deaths of their friends and spouses. One indication of the stressfulness of aging is the sharp increase in suicide rates, especially for white males over 65.

Psychiatrist Elizabeth Kübler-Ross has outlined a model of how people cope with the prospect of death.[67] Her theory proposes five stages in the confrontation with this ultimate dilemma:

▶ *Denial*: Initial disbelief that death is near

▶ *Anger*: Resentment against the fact of dying

▶ *Bargaining*: Efforts to bargain for more time

▶ *Depression*: Emotional letdown and despair

▶ *Acceptance*: Resignation to the fact of death

Elisabeth Kübler-Ross

Critics of Kübler-Ross maintain that her theory overlooks the many individual differences in how people face death, and thus, oversimplifies the process. Despite criticisms, Kübler-Ross's model has been widely adopted and has served as the basis for counseling the elderly and terminally ill people and their families.[68]

Summary

1. Prenatal development lasts from conception to birth. The germinal stage lasts from conception to two weeks, the embryonic stage from two to eight weeks, and the fetal stage from 8 weeks to birth. During critical periods in development, the developing individual is particularly sensitive to environmental influences, such as nutrition, diseases, and drugs.

2. Maturation is the unfolding of inborn programs for development. In infancy and childhood, growth is determined by diet and emotional factors. Brain maturation sets the stage for motor and perceptual development, which respond also to environmental influences. In their first year, infants rapidly acquire coordination, locomotion, and sensory abilities, such as shape and depth perception.

3. Piaget's theory of cognitive development has four stages. Sensory-motor thinking is dominated by sensory and movement schemas and object permanence. The preoperational stage is defined by symbolic thinking, egocentrism, and animism. The concrete operations stage is marked by conservation and concrete logic. Abstract reasoning appears in the formal operations stage. Language develops through regular changes in the use and understanding of speech elements and meaning. The preconventional, conventional, and postconventional levels of moral reasoning describe age-related changes in thinking about right and wrong.

4. Erikson's psychosocial development theory describes the growth of identity in an eight-stage model. Inborn temperament patterns of behavior and emotions set a basis for personality. Early attachment is critical for the development of later interpersonal relations. Self-esteem develops in accordance with the treatment received from parents. Parenting styles promote varied developmental outcomes in children. Gender identity results from biology and socialization forces such as identification and sex typing.

5. The changes in puberty promote physical growth and maturation of secondary sexual characteristics. Although puberty is triggered by hormonal changes, the connection between hormones and adolescent behavior is uncertain.

6. Identity development in adolescence is affected by family, peers, and ethnicity. Peer relationships assume significance as teens explore relationships and roles. Social behavior in teens is shaped by peer pressure, idealism, egocentrism, and sexual relationships.

7. Physical ability peaks in young adulthood and then gradually declines during middle and late adulthood. Metabolism slows, and physical strength and sensory capabilities diminish. Over time, age-related health problems, such as Alzheimer's disease, accumulate.

8. Personality is relatively stable in adulthood. Marital and family relationships and work dominate the adult's life structures. Marital and job satisfaction are associated with general well-being and social adjustment. Kübler-Ross's stages of coping with death are denial, anger, bargaining, depression, and acceptance.

Questions for Discussion

1. What are the stages of prenatal development and the main influences on them?

2. How do physical maturation and perceptual and motor development proceed in infancy and childhood?

3. What are the main features in cognitive, language, and moral development during infancy and childhood?

4. What important psychosocial changes take place in infancy and childhood?

5. What are the physical changes of puberty?

6. What are the features of psychosocial development during adolescence?

7. What physical changes take place in adulthood?

8. How does psychosocial development proceed in adulthood?

Applying Psychology

Erikson's theory of personality development states that your identity is shaped by the social relationships that you have at each stage of life. Consider your present stage according to Erikson's model (see page 178) and analyze how your current relationships with family, peers, and others influence your sense of identity. Evaluate the positive and negative effects of those relationships. Form a small group with your classmates and discuss the similarities and differences in your experiences.

Chapter 9

Motivation and Emotion

After completing this chapter, you should be able to:

1. Distinguish among physiological, stimulus, and social motives and give examples of each.

2. Describe the determinants of hunger and sexual motivation.

3. Define achievement motivation and identify the characteristics of individuals with a high need for achievement.

4. Explain instinct theory, sociobiology, and the drive theory of motivation.

5. Identify incentive, arousal, the expectancy-value, and need hierarchy theories of motivation.

6. Describe the nature and range of emotion.

7. Identify three ways in which emotion is expressed and measured.

8. Summarize the James-Lange and Cannon-Bard theories of emotion.

9. Explain cognitive theories of emotion.

▼

motivation—*process that activates and directs behavior toward a goal*

"I pulled up near a gas station. I told the service station guy to give me all of his money. I then took him to the bathroom and told him to kneel down and then I shot him in the head twice. The guy didn't give me any trouble but I just felt like I had to do it."[1]

These horrible words were spoken by Gary Gilmore, who was executed for murder in Utah in 1977. When you hear of such terrible crimes, you must ask yourself "Why would somebody do such a thing"? In asking this question you are asking about *motivation*: What makes people do what they do and think what they think? You might believe that murderers like Gary Gilmore and serial killers like Jeffrey Dahmer, Ted Bundy, David Berkowitz, and Joel Rifkin kill because of hatred. Actually, some are motivated by the thrill of killing or by painful emotions from being abused as a child. Though the behaviors of serial killers are extreme, we are as curious about their motives and emotional makeup as we are about why we act and feel the way we do. In this chapter you will learn about the nature of motivation and emotion and their roles in your behavior.[2, 3]

*M*otivation

When you work hard to make money it may be said that you are motivated by money. Studying all night for an exam might indicate that you are motivated by the desire to succeed in school. These examples show that **motivation** is a process that activates and directs behavior toward a goal.[4] Psychologists distinguish between two types of motivation: extrinsic and intrinsic. When they talk about *extrinsic motivation*, psychologists mean that your behavior is motivated to gain a reward found in the external environment, for example money. In contrast, behavior controlled by *intrinsic motivation* is performed in the absence of an external goal: it is governed instead by factors inside you such as the need to excel. With intrinsic motivation, the goal is the satisfaction of performing the behavior itself. For example, if you studied for an exam solely to get a good grade, your behavior would be activated and directed by extrinsic motivation. If your main goal was to become more knowledgeable, however, you would be intrinsically motivated. Psychologists distinguish between physiological, stimulus, and social motives. Although the boundaries between them are blurry, these distinctions provide a useful way for you to understand the nature of different motives. (See Table 9.1.)

Table 9.1 **Types of Motives**

Type	Definition	Examples
Physiological	Stem from bodily needs necessary for survival	Hunger, sex, thirst
Stimulus	Those in which person seeks to increase stimulation	Exploration, curiosity, contact
Social	Needs shaped by socialization	Achievement, affiliation, power

Physiological Motives

physiological motives—motives that stem from bodily needs necessary for survival

Also called *primary motives*, **physiological motives** are those that stem from bodily needs that must be satisfied for survival. These needs include hunger, thirst, temperature regulation, sex, and the avoidance of pain. With some physiological drives such as hunger and sex, psychological and social factors also play an important role in shaping motivated behavior.

Hunger motivation is based in physiological changes related to food deprivation. Imagine that it is now 7:00 P.M. and you have not eaten since noon. This lack of food results in physiological changes that motivate you to seek food and eat it. One change is the amount of glucose (sugar) in your blood from digested foods. Shortly after your last meal your blood glucose levels were high and decreased your appetite. By 7:00 P.M, however, your glucose levels are pretty low, your hunger increases and you want to eat. Chemicals in your intestines, the degree of stomach distension (stretch), and the taste and texture of food also influence hunger and eating. Animal studies indicate that areas of the brain, particularly the hypothalamus, are also involved in hunger and eating. Presumably, those areas of the brain control your hunger, too.[5]

External cues are known to influence your desire to eat as well. In a classic study, psychologist Stanley Schachter found that compared with

Some obese individuals, like the person shown here, eat in response to external cues as well as hunger cues.

people of normal weight, obese individuals were more *stimulus-bound* and *reactive* than were normal-weight people; that is, they ate more in reaction to the stimulus qualities of food than from hunger. They ate more food when the food looked more attractive, tasted better, or was easier to consume. For instance, they ate more nuts when they were already shelled and ate less Chinese food if they had to use chopsticks. Later research revealed, however, that being responsive to external stimuli is not unique to obese individuals; it is also observed in people of normal weight.[6,7] If you find chopsticks difficult to use, you too might eat less even if you are not overweight.

Social factors, too, can influence hunger. You may have noticed that you are hungrier and eat more than usual when you are in the company of good friends or at a social gathering in which eating is part of the celebration. Timing, too, is important. In this society, it is customary to eat breakfast, lunch, and dinner, and you usually eat your meals at around the same times each day, even if you are not really hungry.

Though *sex* is classified as a physiological motive, it is controlled by a complex interaction of physiological, psychological, and social factors. In the late 1960s, physician William Masters and behavioral scientist Virginia Johnson conducted laboratory studies in which they observed and measured the sexual activities of more than 700 men and women. Their observations of physiological and psychological changes during sexual activity led to a four-stage model of sexual arousal called the **sexual response cycle**.[8,9] The four stages are:

▼

sexual response cycle—four-stage process of sexual arousal

1. *Excitement*—during which sexual arousal is ignited through sexual contact or fantasy. Males experience erection of their penis and females show swelling and lubrication of the vagina.

2. *Plateau*—marked by a peaking of sexual excitement.

3. *Orgasm*—involves involuntary muscle contractions, thrusting of the pelvis, and the ejaculation of semen in males.

4. *Resolution*—a return to preexcitement levels of sexual arousal accompanied by feelings of satisfaction.

Sexual motivation is partially controlled by parts of your brain such as the hypothalamus, limbic system, and the cerebral cortex. Components of sexual arousal such as erection in males and orgasm in males and females involve spinal reflexes (see Chapter 2). The hypothalamus is particularly important in sexual motivation because it is involved in the production of sex hormones.

Sexual motivation in males is correlated with testosterone levels. In general, higher testosterone levels are related to increased sexual desire as well as to the man's ability to develop an erection. The relationship, however, does not appear to be a strong one. Men who have been castrated (had their testicles removed) after puberty report a gradual decline, but not necessarily an elimination of their sexual desire.[10] Moreover, child molesters and rapists, whom you might expect to have abnormally high hormone amounts, actually have average testosterone levels. They do not appear to have an abnormally powerful sexual desire as much as they select socially unacceptable ways to express their sexual desires.[11,12]

Hormones control sexual motivation in women even less than in men, but they are involved nevertheless. Female sexual arousal is somewhat dependent on estrogen. For example, several studies show that women are most likely to initiate sexual activity with a partner during the middle of their menstrual cycle, when estrogen levels are highest.[13,14] Many women report no reduction of sexual desire, however, after removal of their estrogen-producing ovaries. Sexual arousal in women is regulated by testosterone levels, too. Females who take small amounts of testosterone after menopause (the end of their capacity to menstruate) report increased sexual desire and enjoyment.[15]

Are you attracted to a person with long or short hair? To someone who is short or tall, thin or husky? If you think about it for a moment you will realize that sexual motivation is strongly influenced by how attractive you find the other person. Each individual has a certain type of male or female that she or he finds most attractive and who is most likely to arouse sexual desires. Research shows that males are typically attracted by a female's physical characteristics such as overall shape, breasts, legs, and facial features. Although the male's physical characteristics are important to women, many studies indicate that they often are not as important as the man's status, skills, and abilities.[16]

Stimulus Motives

Physiological motives such as hunger, thirst, and sex provoke behaviors necessary to reduce physiological tension. Your behavior, however, is not always motivated by physiological needs. Sometimes you are motivated by a stimulus in the external world because it is fun or because you are bored. **Stimulus motives**—exploration, curiosity, and contact—are those in which you seek to increase stimulation.

stimulus motives—motives in which person seeks to increase stimulation

If you ask a mountain climber why he climbs a mountain, he is likely to tell you he climbs it "because it's there." You have an inborn desire to explore the unknown that is not based on a physiological need. For example, babies are constantly exploring their environment, especially through their senses of vision, taste, and touch. When placed in a new environment, they look around, touch whatever they can reach, and place objects in their mouth.

In addition to the need to explore, animals and humans are curious about their surroundings. For instance, monkeys will learn to solve puzzles without any apparent motivation to satisfy a biological need. The motivation to learn is simply the presence of the puzzle.[17] Shortly after birth, infants prefer complex rather than simple visual stimuli, and as adults we are easily bored by the same repetitive stimuli and seek out stimuli that are more novel and complex. Despite the lure of more money, you might turn down a higher paying job that is dull for work that is more stimulating and challenging.

We have a desire to touch other people and to be touched, hugged, and cuddled. In a classic study by psychologist Harry Harlow, infant rhesus monkeys were separated from their mothers and given access to two "surrogate," or substitute, mothers. One surrogate mother was made of wire and had a bottle of milk from which the infants could nurse. The other was padded with foam rubber and covered with a soft terry cloth. Even though the wire mother provided for the satisfaction of a physiological need, the

In Harlow's studies, infant monkeys preferred a terry cloth mother rather than a wire mother who could provide milk. Harlow interpreted these findings as an indication of a basic desire for contact comfort.

infant monkeys preferred the terry cloth mother and would cling to "her" when they were frightened by a loud noise. Harlow concluded that the attachment shown by the infants demonstrated a basic need for *contact comfort*, which might be as fundamental as the need for food.[18] For ethical reasons, such studies cannot be conducted with human infants; however, we apparently have the same need for contact comfort. Human infants deprived of such contact and attachments are likely to become mistrustful, feel uncomfortable with human contact, and be unable to form lasting relationships.[19] You learned more about the development of attachments in Chapter 8.

Chapter 9 • Motivation and Emotion

Social Motives

Psychologist Henry Murray (1893–1988) identified more than 40 *psychogenic needs*, that is, needs of psychological origin. Although Murray believed that these needs were inborn, he emphasized that they interacted with environmental factors to determine behavior. Because these needs are shaped by society, they often are referred to as **social motives**.[20]

Respond to the following statements about yourself by saying whether you agree or disagree:

► If I do not do something well, I'd rather keep trying to master it rather than do something I'm already good at.

► I enjoy trying to improve my past performance.

► I like to work hard.

If you agree with these statements, you possess some of the characteristics of achievement-motivated individuals. **Achievement motivation** refers to a concern with doing things better and surpassing standards of excellence. As such, achievement motivation is a type of motivation in which the individual seeks out and attempts to master challenges.[21,22]

A prominent feature of individuals with a high *need for achievement* (*n Ach*) is that they prefer challenges that carry moderate risks (see *Issues and Applications: Achievement Motivation and Success in Business*). They are highly motivated to succeed and equally motivated to avoid failure. People with a high n Ach also prefer to determine their own behavior rather than be

social motives—*motives shaped by society*

achievement motivation—*concern with doing things better and surpassing standards of excellence*

Issues and Applications

Achievement Motivation and Success in Business

What do you think of when you see a movie such as *Wall Street*, in which actor Michael Douglas makes important business decisions sitting behind an oak desk? One impression you may have is that of a person with a high need for achievement. Even though high achievement motivation is sometimes associated with executive success, it is more strongly related to success in small business endeavors. In one study, 83 percent of entrepreneurs were previously identified as having a high need for achievement; 79 percent of nonentrepreneurs were low in achievement motivation.[24]

Individuals with a high need for achievement usually choose and are successful in careers they find challenging and in which there is a moderate risk. They like to assume personal responsibility for their decisions and want concrete feedback about their successes and failures. In addition, individuals with a high need for achievement are able to anticipate potential problems and modify their course of action. Because running a small business is challenging, provides concrete

A high n Aff is also related to poor health. Research has shown that when diabetics have their n Aff aroused, they do not assume responsibility for their own care and depend more on others. Consequently, they tend to go off their diets, and doing so leads to an increase in blood sugar levels. Treatment programs designed to decrease n Aff and make individuals less dependent on others result in better health by making individuals take more responsibility for improving their health habits.[27]

The **need for power** (*n Power*) is defined as the motivation to exercise control over events that affect one's life. As one of the most characteristic features of human history, power is at the heart of wars, political struggles, and interpersonal disputes. People with a high n Power seek visibility and like to publicize their own sense of importance. They typically build a group of loyal supporters to help them reach their goals.[28]

People with a strong power motive lean toward careers wherein they can exert their control and demonstrate their leadership qualities. They often become teachers, clergyman, business executives, or assume public office. Psychologist David Winter analyzed the inaugural address of each president and found that many had a high n Power. He also found that a strong power motive was associated with a confrontational foreign policy that sometimes led to war or resulted in the avoidance of war during a crisis. Of all the presidents, Harry S. Truman had the highest n Power. His presidency began with the ending of World War II in 1945, but it also included the entry of the armed forces into the Korean conflict in 1950.[29]

The power motive is related to health and illness as well. In general, increasing power motivation results in better health by enhancing your ability to gain control over your life and improving your health habits. If your n Power is stressed or frustrated, however, high power motivation leads to more illness.[27]

*T*heories of Motivation

Theories of motivation, summarized in Table 9.2, strive to explain the activation and direction of behavior toward a goal. In this section we explore biological and psychological theories of motivation.

Biological Theories

Biological theories of motivation assume that you are motivated by inborn patterns of behavior and biological needs. These theories include instinct theory, sociobiology, and drive theory.

Instinct Theory.
In its early days, psychology's view of motivation was influenced by the British naturalist Charles Darwin's (1809–1882) *theory of evolution*. This view, known as **instinct theory**, holds that physical and psychological traits that increase your chances of survival are passed on to offspring as inherited patterns of behavior. Your instincts motivate you to perform behaviors that increase your chances of survival by

controlled by external forces such as rewards, threats, and social pressures. Their performance worsens when their behavior is under some type of social control. Finally, people with a high n Ach solve problems innovatively, attribute success to their abilities, and persist when faced with failure.[22]

The motivation to do better is also positively correlated with aspects of life other than work and school. In general, people with high achievement motivation have a positive self-image, function well socially, and show good adjustment in their marriages.[22]

High achievement motivation is positively correlated with physical health, too. One study showed that a high need for achievement predicted healthy cardiac functioning in men 30 years after the initial evaluation.[23]

Do you have many friends and acquaintances, socialize a lot, join groups, and often feel that you need to be in the company of others? If so, you may have a strong **need for affiliation** (*n Aff*), expressed in the motivation to seek out others, value their company, and care about them. If you have a high n Aff, being with others can increase your chances of receiving their aid and support and help to buffer some of life's stresses. Isn't it comforting to be able to lean on someone when you have a problem?

On the negative side, though, individuals motivated by affiliative needs are not assertive; they avoid conflicts and usually give in to others' wishes for fear of disapproval and rejection and typically shy away from managerial positions in the business world. Their conformity to others' wishes may actually backfire. People with a very high n Aff often are perceived as "needy," causing others to dislike and reject them.

▼
need for affiliation—
motivation to seek out othe[r]
value their company, and c[are]
about them

feedback in the form of sales and profit figures, and allows for self-determination, it is exactly what people with high achievement motivation are looking for. In contrast, they are less likely to pursue a career such as social work, because even though it may be challenging, immediate concrete feedback is rarely available. The relationship between achievement motivation and entrepreneurial success has also been observed across cultures and in women.[22,25,26]

Though the need for achievement is considered to be a fairly stable motivational trait, studies in several countries have shown that people can be trained to increase achievement motivation. These studies demonstrate that such training can increase productivity among those who run small businesses, especially if the business operators have the freedom to manage the business in their own way.[22]

Having a high need for achievement does not guarantee that you will be a successful entrepreneur, but it appears to be one of the more important ingredients in business success.

Table 9.2 **Theories of Motivation**

Biological Theories	Description
Instinct theory	Behavior is motivated by inborn patterns of behavior.
Sociobiology	Behavior is motivated by interaction of instincts and environment.
Drive theory	Behavior is motivated by need to satisfy biological drives.
Incentive theory	Behavior is motivated by external stimuli.
Arousal theory	Behavior is motivated by desire to maintain a certain level of arousal.
Expectancy value	Behavior is motivated by the expectation of achieving goals and the value assigned to them.
Hierarchy of needs	Behavior is motivated by inborn needs arranged in order of importance.

satisfying biological needs. Thus, hunger stimulates you to obtain and consume food; sexual desire arouses behaviors that help you select a mate and reproduce.[30]

Psychologists extended instinct theory to explain other types of motives as well, such as curiosity and exploration and social motives such as self-assertiveness, sympathy, altruism (unselfishness), jealousy, and parenting. It was not long before one sociologist claimed that we had 5,759 instinctive motives![31,32]

Two basic characteristics of *instincts* are that they are not changed by experience and they are expressed in much the same way by all members of a species. For these reasons, instincts are sometimes called *fixed action patterns*.[33] It is easy to see instinctive behaviors in animals—salmon swim upstream to spawn, spiders spin webs, and birds build nests. But, the existence of instincts in humans is questionable. When was the last time you and your friends spun a web? Consider sexual attraction. Even though your sexual desire may have a genetic basis, the ways in which you seek and attract a sexual partner are determined largely by culture and your individual style. You may be very assertive about your sexual interests and come right out and express them, or you may be more indirect and suggestive.

Sociobiology. Today, instinct theory is reflected in **sociobiology**, which studies the genetic foundations of social behavior according to the principles of evolution. Unlike instinct theory, sociobiology proposes that, although motivation is grounded in your genes, its expression depends on environmental circumstances.[34,35]

Sociobiologists believe that you are motivated to behave in ways that preserve your genes so that they can be passed on to the next generation. For instance, when a mother makes sacrifices and is even willing to give up her life for her child, some say that she did it out of love. According to

sociobiology—study of the genetic foundations of social behavior according to the principles of evolution.

sociobiologists, the motive is not love but "genetic selfishness." Critics of sociobiology argue that, like instinct theory before it, it places too much emphasis on the biological basis of motivation.[36]

Drive Theory. By the 1930s, the popularity of instinct theory waned as psychologists viewed behavior in terms of people's learning experiences. Instinct theory was replaced by **drive theory**, which argues that biological needs motivate you to engage in behaviors that satisfy those needs (see Figure 9.1). In this model, all physiological systems strive to maintain a state of balance, or *homeostasis*. Disruption of homeostasis creates an internal tension that you are motivated to relieve. For instance, a lack of food creates a *need*, which produces a condition of psychological arousal called a **drive**. Your thirst activates a *goal-directed response*, drinking, which satisfies your need for water and reduces the drive. Thus, according to drive theory, you are "pushed" into action by an internal force much in the same way that an engine "drives" a car to accelerate.

Figure 9.1 **Drive Theory of Motivation**

According to the drive theory of motivation, a need produces a condition of psychological arousal, or drive, which activates goal-directed behavior necessary to reduce the drive.

The concept of drive has been an important element of theories of learning (see Chapter 5). Psychologist Clark Hull (1884–1952), saw stimuli as reinforcing because they reduce drives. Without the motivating effects of drive there could be no primary reinforcement and no learning.[37] One of the major shortcomings of drive theory is that it cannot explain motives other than those driven by biological needs. To account for those motives, psychologists have proposed other theories of motivation.

Psychological Theories

Often, there is no apparent biological need that "pushes" you to behave. Can you think of a biological need that motivates you to study hard for an exam, play sports, or listen to music? Perhaps you study for an exam to obtain a high grade and the future benefits that might result—graduating, getting a good job, and making more money. You play sports because you like the competition and want to stay in shape; you listen to music because you enjoy it. To explain these motives, psychologists have offered psychological theories of motivation. Four such theories are incentive theory, arousal theory, cognitive theories, and Maslow's hierarchy of needs.

drive theory—view that biological needs motivate behaviors necessary to satisfy those needs

drive—a condition of psychological arousal

Incentive Theory. According to **incentive theory**, you are motivated by the attractiveness or incentive value of external stimuli. An **incentive** is a stimulus that has a positive or negative value in motivating, or "pulling," behavior. Sometimes you are motivated to seek certain stimuli such as a delicious pie or the fragrance of a rose. At other times you are motivated to avoid painful or unpleasant stimuli, such as the foul odor of spoiled food or the pain caused by touching a hot object. Incentive theory has been important in theories of learning such as instrumental conditioning because it explains how you are motivated to seek rewards and avoid punishments.

Arousal Theory. As you have learned, drive theory claims that you are motivated to reduce the uncomfortable feelings associated with a need state. If you were ever thrilled by riding a roller coaster, bungee jumping, or a loud musical concert, you know that sometimes you seek to increase rather than reduce your arousal levels. Then again, there are times when you feel most comfortable just "hangin' out," lying around, and doing nothing. Such observations have led to **arousal theory**, a model that claims that you are motivated to maintain a preferred level of stimulation.

Arousal theory argues that you have an *optimal level of arousal*, a degree of stimulation with which you feel most comfortable. When stimulation exceeds your optimal level, you are motivated to reduce it; when it falls below, you seek increased stimulation.[38] The relationship between arousal and performance is illustrated in Figure 9.2. The **Yerkes-Dodson law** states that performance generally improves as arousal is increased up to a certain point, then it decreases as arousal increases beyond the optimum level. For example, if your level of arousal was low while taking an exam you would find it difficult to concentrate. As the level of arousal increased, your performance would improve up to a certain point. Increases in arousal beyond that point would lead to decreased performance and a lower grade. If you are one of those students who gets nervous during exams, you know how your grades can suffer.

incentive theory—view that motivation is based on the attractiveness or incentive value of external stimuli

incentive—a stimulus that has a positive or negative value in motivating behavior

arousal theory—model that states that you are motivated to maintain a preferred level of stimulation

Yerkes-Dodson Law—performance increases as arousal increases up to a certain point; increases in arousal beyond that point result in performance decreases

Figure 9.2 **The Yerkes-Dodson Law**

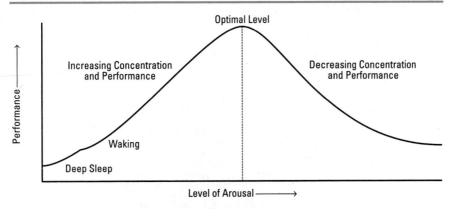

The relationship between arousal and performance. Performance improves with increases in arousal up to a certain point. Increases in arousal beyond that point result in decreased performance.

Chapter 9 • Motivation and Emotion

Research by psychologist Marvin Zuckerman shows that individual differences in preferred levels of arousal are related to a personality trait called *sensation seeking*. Using the *Sensation-Seeking Scale*, Zuckerman has found four dimensions of sensation seeking:

▶ *Thrill and Adventure Seeking*: Enjoyment of high-risk activities such as parachute jumping and driving a motorcycle

▶ *Experience Seeking*: Trying new foods, being hypnotized

▶ *Disinhibition*: Taking drugs, going to wild parties

▶ *Boredom Susceptibility*: Preferring a job that requires a lot of traveling; meeting new and interesting people rather than seeing the same old faces

Zuckerman's research reveals that the motivational differences between high- and low-sensation seekers may have a biological basis in the brain.[39,40,41]

Cognitive Theories. *Cognitive theories* of motivation emphasize the role of mental processes such as thoughts and perceptions in motivation. According to **expectancy-value theory**, behavior is motivated by the expectation of achieving goals and the value assigned to them. If you *value* money and recognition, you are highly motivated to do well at work if you *expect* that your performance will allow you to achieve your goals.[42]

Cognitive theories also stress **attributions**, explanations for the outcomes of behavior. Suppose you perform a task at work successfully. Do you attribute the accomplishment to your skills or to luck? Research on attributions indicates that if you attribute your success to internal factors (skills) rather than to external factors (luck), you will be more motivated to take on other tasks in the future and more likely to perform them well.

Your tendency to attribute outcomes to internal or external factors is a fairly consistent personality characteristic. In other words, you develop an *attributional style*. In addition, internal attributions are positively correlated with good adjustment and negatively correlated with mental problems.[28]

Maslow's Hierarchy of Needs. Psychologist Abraham Maslow (1908–1970) offered a theory that states that we are motivated by innate needs arranged in a hierarchy. The **need hierarchy** is a sequence of

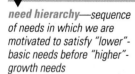

expectancy-value theory—view that behavior is motivated by the expectation of achieving goals and the value assigned to them

attributions—explanations for outcomes of behavior

need hierarchy—sequence of needs in which we are motivated to satisfy "lower"-basic needs before "higher"-growth needs

Figure 9.3 **Maslow's Need Hierarchy**

We are motivated to satisfy "lower" (basic) needs such as physiological and safety needs before we can try to satisfy "higher" (growth) needs such as self-actualization.

needs in which we are motivated to satisfy "lower" *basic needs* before
"higher" *growth needs*. (See Figure 9.3). For example, you must satisfy
basic physiological needs such as the need for food, water, and sex before
you can attempt to satisfy safety and belonging needs. Doesn't this theory
make some sense? What starving person worries about relationships,
achievements, and reaching full potential?

   If you have satisfied your basic needs, you can attend to **self-actualization**, the tendency to reach your full potential. As Maslow put it:

*self-actualization—the
tendency to reach your full
potential*

> **"A** musician must make music, an artist must paint, a poet must write, if he
> is to be ultimately at peace with himself. What a man can be, he must be. He
> must be true to his own nature. This need we may call self-actualization."[43]

   Maslow's need hierarchy is at the core of his theory of personality,
which will be discussed in Chapter 10.

*E*motion

Everyone knows about emotions. You are happy when you get a good grade
in school or when your favorite team wins a game. You feel angry when one
of your possessions is stolen or when somebody cuts you off on the road. You
feel guilty when you do something you are not supposed to do, sad when you
lose a cherished relationship or a good job, and surprised when the unexpected
happens. You can see from these everyday examples that just about every
significant event in your life is flavored by your emotional experiences.

   Emotion is closely tied to motivation. It is one way to communicate
your motivational state to others. As an example, if you are motivated to
succeed and you fail, you become disappointed or sad. When you succeed
you are happy. Try to imagine feeling emotional if nothing mattered, that is,
if you had no motivation. For these reasons, psychologists believe that
without motivation there would be no emotion. Conversely, emotions also
act as motivators of behavior. For instance, feeling guilty motivates you to
repair the harm you may have done to another.[44,45]

   In this section, you will learn about the nature of emotion, how emotion
is expressed and measured, and theories of emotion.

What Is Emotion?

Psychologists have offered many definitions of emotions, but they have
been unable to agree on what it is.[46] **Emotion** is usually defined as a
reaction composed of subjective feelings, cognitive evaluation, physiological changes, and observable behavior. Consider the following situation. You
apply for a job related to your career interests. After two weeks of waiting
for a response, you get a phone call that the job is yours. You are extremely
happy and relieved that the suspense is over (subjective feelings). Perhaps
your happiness stems from the belief that getting the job will bring you

*emotion—reaction composed
of subjective feelings,
cognitive evaluation,
physiological changes, and
observable behavior*

more money and prestige and improve the quality of your life (cognitive evaluation). At the same time, your body feels "charged up" (physiological changes) and you smile, let out a yell, and raise your fist in victory before you let everyone know about your experience (observable behavior).

If you get into a conversation, read a novel, watch a television show or movie, or listen to music, you might become aware of hundreds of words we use to denote emotions. How many emotions are there, and what are they? Research by psychologist Robert Plutchik indicates that there are eight primary emotions: *joy*, *acceptance*, *fear*, *surprise*, *sadness*, *disgust*, *anger*, and *anticipation*.[46] (See Figure 9.4.) The eight primary emotions vary in intensity. For instance, terror is more intense than fear, but apprehension is less intense. The range of your emotions can be widened if you consider mixtures of primary emotions next to each other. For example, the mixture of acceptance and joy yields love. Many mixtures may be beyond the range of your experience, such as the mixture of sadness and joy.

Figure 9.4 **Plutchik's Eight Primary Emotions**

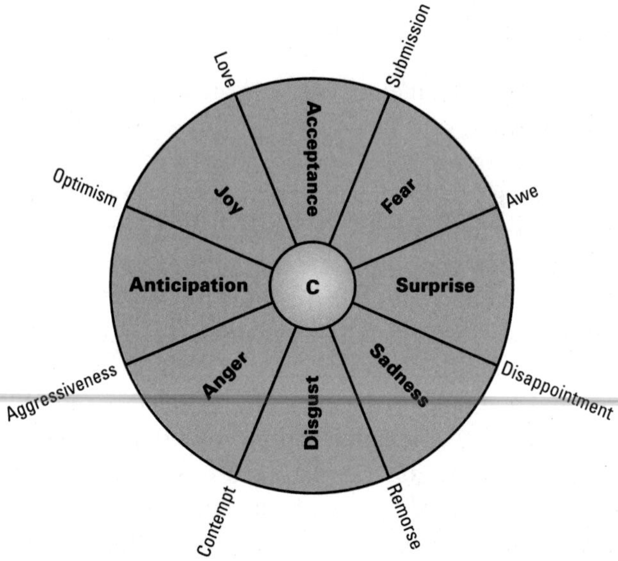

There are 8 primary emotions: joy, acceptance, fear, surprise, sadness, disgust, anger, and anticipation. The range of emotions is widened through mixtures of adjacent primary emotions as shown.

Source: *Emotion: A Psychoevolutionary Synthesis* by Robert Plutchik. Copyright © 1980 by Robert Plutchik. Reprinted by permission of HaperCollins Publishers, Inc.

Another way to catalog emotions has been advanced by psychologist Richard Lazarus, who has identified two major categories of emotions:

1. Emotions resulting from harms, losses, and threats, such as anger, anxiety, fear, guilt, shame, sadness, envy, jealousy, and disgust. These are also called *negative emotions*.

2. Emotions resulting from events that benefit us: happiness, joy, pride, gratitude, and love. These are *positive emotions*.

The Expression and Measurement of Emotion

Emotions are expressed and measured in three basic ways: self-reports of subjective feelings; behavior, especially facial expression; and physiological activity. The most reliable way of understanding emotions is to gain information from all three sources whenever possible.[46,47,48]

If we asked you how you feel emotionally, your response would be a *self-report* of your subjective feelings. The self-report method is probably the most common way of measuring emotions. In research, psychologists usually obtain self-reports by presenting a checklist of mood words, such as *happiness*, *fear*, *sadness*, and *disgust*, and having you numerically rate how you feel right now.

Another way to measure expressed emotion is by observing nonverbal behavior. To this end, body movements, posture, and voice tone have all been evaluated, but the most extensive research in the entire field of emotion has been related to facial expressions of emotion.

Try this little demonstration. Watch a movie or television show without the sound and see if you can identify different emotions on the actors' faces. Research on the facial expression of emotion indicates that you would probably do quite well. In general, your subjective experience of a particular emotion is accompanied by specific changes in your facial muscles. (See *Issues and Applications: Facial Expression and Lying*.) In research, subjects are typically asked to identify specific emotions from photographs or cartoons in which facial expression displays a particular emotion. Numerous studies show that people can accurately recognize emotions such as happiness, fear, and disgust by reading facial expressions.

Psychologists who study emotion believe that facial expression is universal, meaning that facial expressions are similar for humans in different cultures. These similarities are believed to be due to neural circuits for facial expression that have been "programmed" into your brain through the process of evolution. Many elements of emotional expression are culturally determined, however, depending on which emotions a particular culture values and on the unwritten rules that determine which emotions should be expressed and under which conditions. For example, natives of the South Pacific island of Bali fall asleep in reaction to frightening events as a socially approved way of showing fear. Consequently, they are not very good at recognizing fear on other's faces.[49]

The scientific evidence that facial expression is inborn comes from several sources. Different facial expressions can be observed in infants who have not had much of the benefit of observing others. Even children born deaf, blind, and retarded show emotional reactions and corresponding facial expressions similar to those of normal children.[50]

The most persuasive evidence that facial expression has an innate basis comes from cross-cultural studies. Paul Ekman has conducted many studies of facial expression using the *Facial Action Coding System* (FACS), a technique for analyzing distinct facial movements. His studies of college

Facial Expression and Lying

Lying is a common occurrence at home, work, school, and in relationships. Lying is also encountered frequently in police interrogations, courtroom testimony, and in politics. In some cases the stakes are high, such as when a spouse, boyfriend, or girlfriend lies about having an affair, when an employer lies about why you did not get a promotion, or when an elected official tries to conceal some wrongdoing. In other cases, the liar may suffer no more than an embarrassment, as when a family member lies about eating the last brownie. In any case, understanding how lies are displayed in facial expression can be important, especially if you are the one being lied to. With this in mind, the important question is whether you can catch a liar.

Psychological research shows that most people are not very good at catching liars. The average accuracy in detecting a lie is approximately 60 percent. This performance is rather poor when you consider that, if you did nothing more than guess, you would have a 50 percent chance of guessing correctly each time. Research by psychologist Paul Ekman reveals that people who are in careers that require them to be able to detect lying fare no better than the average person. In a study of more than 500 professionals including Secret Service, FBI and CIA agents, police, judges, psychiatrists, and lie detector experts, only Secret Service agents scored above the rate of 50 percent.

Ekman's studies show that individuals who are successful at catching a liar rely on nonverbal cues more than on what the suspected liar is saying. What a person says can easily be rehearsed, but body movements, posture, and voice tone are more difficult to practice. If detecting deceit is important, you should pay attention especially to the person's facial expressions. Careful analysis shows that liars exhibit subtle smiles more often than people who are truthful. In addition, liars are more likely to display slightly higher-pitched tones in their voice. When vocal and facial cues are considered together, research shows that it is possible to catch a liar 86 percent of the time.

There is no foolproof method for catching a liar, but the more nonverbal cues you evaluate, the greater are your chances of detecting deceit. You may be able to increase your lie-catching skills if you focus especially on facial expression and voice tone rather than on the content of the person's vocalizations.[51,52]

students from the United States, Brazil, and Japan indicated that these diverse subjects could accurately recognize emotions from facial expressions. In one study by Ekman, "Stone Age" people from New Guinea were read a simple story in their language and were then shown pictures at the same time. Their task was to pick the picture in which the individual's face showed the emotion described in the story. The results showed high agree-

Happy   **Sad**

Anger   **Disgust**

Ekman's New Guinean subjects were asked to choose the photos, shown here, that indicated the emotions that had previously been described in a story. Ekman interpreted his findings as evidence that facial expression is universal.

ment among adults and children for most emotions, especially happiness, anger, and disgust. American college students also had little trouble identifying facial expression in photographs of New Guineans. Ekman interpreted these findings to mean that particular facial expressions correspond to specific emotions and that facial expression is universal.[53,54,55]

The correspondence between facial expression and emotion is generally accepted in psychology, but controversy revolves around how they are related. Is facial expression a display of what you feel inside or is it a cause of emotional experience? Does smiling reflect a feeling of happiness, or is happiness the result of smiling? Research suggests that both may be correct.

Psychologists Ekman and Carroll Izard, among others support the **facial feedback hypothesis**, which states that specific emotions are determined by the brain's interpretation of muscle feedback from facial expression. According to this view, the perception of a stimulus activates your brain to produce a general pleasant or unpleasant feeling, then the brain signals movements in the facial muscles. Feedback from muscular contractions is

facial feedback hypothesis—view that emotions are determined by the brain's interpretation of muscle feedback from facial expression

Chapter 9 • Motivation and Emotion

sent back to the brain and interpreted whereupon a specific emotion is felt.[56,57] A recent study by Ekman indicates that a certain type of smile can lift your mood.[58] You might be able to demonstrate the facial feedback hypothesis to yourself by raising your cheeks, parting your lips and making the corners of your lips come up. Thus, you do not smile because you are happy; you are happy because you smile.

An interesting twist to the facial feedback hypothesis comes from psychologist Robert Zajonc, who argues that facial contractions alter the blood supply to the brain and thereby change its temperature. Certain facial expressions such as those necessary to say *cheese* lower brain temperature and result in positive feelings. Conversely, the facial expressions involved in saying the word *fur* decrease brain temperature and produce negative

Biography: Paul Ekman

Paul Ekman was born in 1934, the second of two children. His older sister is a psychoanalytic psychologist in New York City. His father was a pediatrician, and his mother was an attorney. Bored with high school, Ekman left home at the age of 15 to enroll at the University of Chicago. Although he never finished high school, he received a bachelor's degree from New York University (NYU) in 1954. While observing group therapy sessions at NYU, Ekman became interested in emotions as they were reflected in patient's facial expressions and body movements. He received his Ph.D. degree in psychology from Adelphi University in New York State in 1958 and was immediately drafted into the army, where he served as chief psychologist at Fort Dix,

New Jersey. In the army, Ekman did research on army stockades and the psychological changes of infantrymen in basic training.

After his stay in the military, Ekman began to study facial expression and body movements more intensively and in

the 1970s, with associate Wallace Friesen, he developed the *Facial Action Coding System* as a way to measure emotions through facial expression. At about the same time, he became interested in facial expression as a method of lie detection, a research topic for which he is internationally known. Paul Ekman has authored many professional articles and books including *Telling Lies: Clues to Deceit in the Marketplace, Marriage, and Politics (1985).* He received the American Psychological Association's Award for Distinguished Scientific Contributions in 1991. Ekman is on the faculty at the University of California–San Francisco, living in San Francisco with his wife, a law professor at Berkeley, and his daughter, Eve.[59]

emotional feelings. This hypothesis may explain how actors are able to experience certain emotions by "acting the part." Although you may consider it odd, Zajonc claims that kissing is pleasurable not because the mouth is a sexually sensitive part of the body, but because it forces breathing through the nose which cools the brain.[60]

The biological basis of emotion lies in the limbic system of the brain (see Chapter 2). However, it is not currently possible to link specific emotions to particular structures in the limbic system, and there are no simple ways to measure limbic system activity during emotional expression. As an alternative, psychologists focus on the activity of the autonomic nervous system (ANS) to measure the physiological expression of emotion. In Chapter 2 you learned that the ANS consists of the sympathetic division, which increases bodily arousal, and the parasympathetic division, which decreases arousal. Emotional reactions are accompanied by easily measured changes in sympathetic activity including heart rate, blood pressure, respiration rate, sweat response, and indirectly, muscle tension. Most studies show that specific emotions do not involve specific patterns of sympathetic activity. In other words, emotions involve generalized ANS arousal. For example, when you are angry or scared, your ANS activity is pretty much the same.

Despite scientific evidence to the contrary, the use of lie detectors is based on the assumption that specific emotions such as guilt are characterized by identifiable patterns of sympathetic arousal. Therefore, distinctive patterns of sympathetic arousal should be useful in detecting a liar during questioning. In a typical lie detector, or *polygraph, test*, the suspect's heart rate, blood pressure, respiration, and skin resistance are monitored. Because polygraph testing is not as accurate as claimed, some psychologists have recommended that measures of brain activity be used as an alternative.[61]

Theories of Emotion

Theories of emotion attempt to identify the different types of emotions and to explain where they come from and how they are expressed. In this section, you will learn about the James-Lange, Cannon-Bard, and cognitive theories of emotion.

The James-Lange and Cannon-Bard Theories

The usual way to think about emotions is that the perception of a situation leads to a feeling of emotion and then bodily changes follow. In other words, if you saw a bear in the woods you would perceive it as a potentially dangerous animal. This perception would give rise to fear, and your body would react with physiological changes such as sweating and increased heart rate.

In the late 1880s, psychologist William James and physiologist Karl G. Lange proposed a theory that countered commonsense beliefs about emotion. Known as the **James-Lange theory**, this model proposed that our interpretation of bodily changes determines emotion. Instead of saying "I

▼

James-Lange Theory (James-Lonn-ga thee-ry)—model that proposes that interpretations of bodily changes determines emotion

run because I'm afraid," the James-Lange theory would say "I'm afraid because I run." Physiologists Walter B. Cannon and Philip Bard rejected the James-Lange theory, arguing that emotions are not the result of our interpretations of physiological arousal. According to the **Cannon-Bard theory**, perception causes brain arousal, which, in turn, causes bodily changes and emotional feeling simultaneously. In this theory, bodily changes and emotional feelings are both consequences of our perceptions.

Cognitive Theories

Cognitive theories focus on the mental processes that shape your emotions in specific situations. Although cognitive theorists hold that your ability to experience emotion is inborn, they emphasize that emotions are determined by how you evaluate the meaning of each situation in which you are involved. Most cognitive theorists believe that these evaluations are largely unconscious.[62]

According to **cognitive labeling theory**, emotion is determined by how we interpret, or label, the physiological changes that occur in certain situations. In a famous experiment by psychologists Stanley Schachter and Jerome Singer, subjects in three experimental groups were given epinephrine (adrenaline) injections and told that they received a vitamin that would affect their vision. One group of subjects was correctly informed about the drug's side-effects, the second group was misinformed, and the third was told nothing. After receiving the injection, subjects were placed in a waiting room to fill out a questionnaire with a "stooge," who was instructed by the experimenters to act happy by throwing paper airplanes in a wastebasket and playing with a Hula Hoop or angry by complaining about the questionnaire and the whole experiment. As predicted, subjects who were misinformed about drug side effects tended to label their physical symptoms according to the situation. Subjects who waited with the happy "stooge" felt happy; subjects who sat with the angry "stooge" were likely to feel angry. Subjects in the informed group attributed their symptoms to the drug.[63]

Psychologist Richard Lazarus explains emotion in terms of appraisals of harm or benefit (cognitive factors), the goals that people strive for (motivational factors), and the person-environment interactions (situations) involved.[64,65] Consider the following example. You are trying to get a high grade in your psychology class and the final exam is scheduled for tomorrow. When you get home from school you realize that you forgot your textbook and notes at school and there is no way to get back in (situation). You appraise the situation as serious because you do not know the material as well as you should and expect that you probably will not perform well on the exam (cognitive). You bang on the table in *anger*, muttering to yourself, "What a jerk! How could I be so stupid to forget the stuff in school." Now your anger activates you to call a friend to see if she can let you look at her notes so that you can prepare for the exam and do well (motivational).

Summary

1. Physiological motives, such as hunger, thirst, and sex, are related to biological needs that must be satisfied for survival. Stimulus motives including exploration, curiosity, manipulation, and contact are those in which the person is motivated to seek stimulation. Social motives such as achievement motivation, the need for affiliation, and the need for power are those shaped by the process of socialization.

2. Hunger is a physiological motive determined by biological factors such as blood glucose levels, intestinal chemicals, stomach distension, the hypothalamus and by external factors such as the attractiveness of the food and eating in the company of others. Sexual motivation is controlled by the hypothalamus, limbic system, and cerebral cortex. The sex hormones, testosterone and estrogen influence sexual desire in males and females, respectively. Sexual motivation is also influenced by physical attractiveness. Males are more attracted to a woman's physical characteristics; women are typically more attracted to a man's status, skills, and abilities.

3. Achievement motivation is defined as a concern with doing better and surpassing standards of excellence. People high in achievement motivation prefer challenges of moderate risk, like to determine their own behavior, and require immediate, concrete feedback about their successes and failures.

4. Instinct theory holds that genetically programmed patterns of behavior increase one's chances of survival. Sociobiology views motivation in terms of the interaction between instincts and the environment. Drive theory argues that we engage in behaviors necessary to satisfy a biological need.

5. Incentive theory claims that we are motivated by external stimuli. Arousal theory states that we seek to maintain an optimum level of arousal. Cognitive theories focus on mental processes in motivation. According to expectancy-value theory, behavior is motivated by the expectation of achieving goals and the value we assign to them. Maslow's need hierarchy view is based on satisfying basic needs before growth needs.

6. Emotion is a reaction to a stimulus. It is composed of subjective feelings, cognitive evaluation, physiological changes, and observable behavior. Plutchik identified eight primary emotions: joy, acceptance, fear, surprise, sadness, disgust, anger, and anticipation. Lazarus categorizes emotions as those that are related to benefit and those related to harm.

7. Emotion is expressed and measured in three ways. When a person reports about her feelings, she is giving a self-report. Psychologists use lists of mood words to monitor self-reports. Behaviors, such as body movements, voice tone, and facial expression also reveal emotions. Emotions are also expressed and measured through changes in autonomic nervous system activity.

8. The James-Lange theory contends that our interpretation of bodily changes determines emotion. The Cannon-Bard theory argues that perception causes brain arousal, which, in turn, causes bodily changes and emotional feelings.

9. Cognitive theories focus on the mental processes that shape emotions in specific situations. Even though cognitive theorists hold that your ability to experience emotion is inborn, they emphasize that emotions are determined by how you evaluate the meaning of each situation in which you are involved.

Questions for Discussion

1. How do physiological, stimulus, and social motives differ? Give examples of each.

2. What determines hunger and sexual motivation?

3. What is achievement motivation, and what are the characteristics of those with a high need for achievement?

4. How do the instinct theory, sociobiology, and the drive theory explain motivation?

5. What are the incentive, arousal, expectancy-value, and need hierarchy theories of motivation?

6. What are the nature and range of emotions?

7. What are the three ways by which emotion is expressed and measured?

8. How do the James-Lange and Cannon-Bard theories explain emotion?

9. How do cognitive theories explain emotion?

Applying Psychology

Have a volunteer classmate practice displaying Plutchik's eight primary emotions: *joy*, *acceptance*, *fear*, *surprise*, *sadness*, *disgust*, *anger*, and *anticipation*. through facial expressions. Without having your classmate announce which emotion is being expressed, see if you can correctly identify each emotion.

Chapter 10

Personality

After completing this chapter, you should be able to:

1. Summarize Freud's theory of personality.

2. Discuss four psychodynamic theories of personality that followed from Freud's theory.

3. Outline Maslow's need theory.

4. Identify the main concepts of Rogers's self theory.

5. Discuss the trait view of personality and compare Allport's theory with the factor theories.

6. Outline the assumptions of behaviorism about personality.

7. Describe the social learning view of personality.

8. Distinguish among the methods of assessing personality.

personality—a stable pattern of behaviors and characteristics that distinguish an individual

psychodynamic (sye-koh-die-nam-ik) view—belief that personality results from conflicting mental forces

Have you ever heard anyone make remarks like these?

▶ "He has absolutely no personality."

▶ "She's got a terrific personality."

▶ "They never agree because of a personality conflict."

Since people often talk about personality, you have certainly heard statements like those. Even though you frequently discuss your own and others' personalities, you probably do so without knowing exactly what you mean by personality. Ask several people what personality is, and you will be surprised by the different answers they give. The variety of opinions about personality is a recurring dilemma for psychologists, too. Most psychologists agree that **personality** is defined as a stable pattern of behaviors and characteristics that distinguish an individual. But, the features, motives, and functions of personality are open to many interpretations (see Table 10.1). As you will learn in this chapter, psychology offers several points of view about the nature of personality.

Table 10.1 Theoretical Views of Personality

Theoretical View	Assumptions about Personality
Psychodynamic	Unconscious motivation Personality structure conflicts
Humanistic	Self-actualization motive Personal freedom and responsibility
Trait	Trait units of personality Objective measurement of traits
Learning	Emphasize learning principles in personality and motivation

The Psychodynamic View

Beginning with the ideas of Sigmund Freud (1856–1939), the **psychodynamic view** describes personality as the result of powerful mental forces in conflict with each other. In this view, your mental life consists mainly of unconscious processes, meaning that you lack conscious awareness and control of them. Dreams, emotions, habits, and impulses are all examples of your unconscious mind's activity. Psychodynamic theory also considers childhood experiences to be critical in personality development. The roots of your personality are set early in life and affect you throughout your teenage and adult years.

Freud's Psychoanalytic Theory

As you learned in Chapter 1, Sigmund Freud developed the psychoanalytic school into a leading perspective in psychology. The core of Freud's *psychoanalytic theory* was a belief that personality has three parts—id, ego, and superego—each regulated by different principles and having unique characteristics.

In Freud's theory, the most powerful part of personality is the **id**, which is controlled by unconscious instinctual drives. These drives, called the *life* and *death instincts*, are expressed mainly through sexual and aggressive impulses, respectively. Freud emphasized the role of sexual energy, or *libido*, in personality. The id works according to the *pleasure principle*, a force that seeks to increase pleasure and decrease discomfort. Your id is the aspect of your personality that is irrational, impulsive, and driven by emotions. Your wishes, dreams, fantasies, and feelings all reflect the id activity known as *primary process thinking* that serves the pleasure principle by expressing and satisfying your unconscious needs. For example, when you are caught up in a pleasant daydream, you are experiencing the id's primary process activity.

Your identity, or sense of self, is determined by your **ego**, the part of personality that controls your rational and conscious mental processes. Adjustment to the real world is a major purpose of the ego, which acts according to the *reality principle*, leading you to cope with the demands of everyday life. In adapting to reality, you rely on your ego's *secondary process thinking*, which includes reasoning, judgment, perception, and memory abilities. By using rational problem solving to overcome a dilemma in your personal life, you are showing the importance of your ego activity.

Have you ever felt ashamed about lying or guilty about neglecting a responsibility? If you have, then you have experienced the action of your **superego**, the part of personality that controls your moral judgment, or *conscience*. Superego evaluates your behavior, thoughts, and feelings according to your own personal morality and defines your sense of right and wrong. The values and standards of the superego originate with your parents' morality, but expand over time to include society's values as well. An important component of superego is your *ego-ideal*, an image of the ideal person you should become. When your behavior falls short of your ideal, guilt and shame result, but when it meets the ideal your self-esteem is lifted.[1]

Satisfying all the demands of your personality is not easy. Freud believed that conflict in personality is unavoidable because the needs of the id, ego, and superego are often incompatible. Suppose that the parts of your personality are involved in a drama in which an employer, parent, or teacher is taking advantage of you and putting you under extreme pressure. The dialogue below indicates how each part might react:

▶ Id: "Kill!"

▶ Ego: "Be reasonable. It's too dangerous to kill anyone."

▶ Superego: "Killing is wrong. You shouldn't do it under any circumstances."

▼

id—part of personality controlled by unconscious instinctual drives and the pleasure principle

▼

ego—part of personality that controls identity, adjustment, and rational processes according to the reality principle

▼

superego—part of personality that controls moral judgment or conscience

What happens when the parts of your personality are at odds with each other? In Freud's view, these conflicts cause anxiety or tension. These forms of emotional distress are relieved by **defense mechanisms**, largely unconscious ego processes for coping with conflict (see Table 10.2). Your defense mechanisms do not necessarily eliminate the underlying conflicts that prompt their use, but they can produce temporary relief from anxiety. Freud believed that the defenses are essential in both mental health and mental disorders (see Chapter 12).[2]

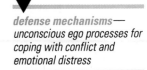

defense mechanisms—unconscious ego processes for coping with conflict and emotional distress

Table 10.2 **Major Ego Defense Mechanisms**

Defense Mechanism	Example
Denial: Refuses to admit the facts of reality.	You will not believe that a friend lied to you.
Displacement: Channels your feelings into substitute outlets or activity.	You "dump" your anger at your parents by being mean to a stranger.
Projection: Places your own unacceptable feelings onto other people.	You blame a family member for your academic failures.
Rationalization: Invents convenient excuses for your behavior.	After being fired, you claim that you wanted to leave your job anyway.
Reaction formation: Turns your feelings into their opposites.	Embarrassed by your attraction to someone, you begin to hate the person.
Regression: Falls back on immature behavior.	When under stress, you become very babyish and dependent.
Repression: Blocks thoughts and feelings from your conscious mind.	You temporarily forget about an ongoing argument with a friend.
Sublimation: Directs urges and feelings into socially acceptable behavior.	You channel your sexual energy into dancing and singing.

Psychoanalytic theory contends that your basic personality structures are set early in life. Freud thought that the first six years of life are critical in development. If serious problems, or *traumas*, arise in those formative years, personality may be permanently impaired. According to Freud, your personality changes through five stages of *psychosexual development*, during which your sexual energy (libido) is focused on specific activities and different developmental challenges must be overcome (see Table 10.3). Developmental problems in any stage may have lasting impact. For example, if you are a chronic fingernail biter or cigarette smoker, you might have an *oral fixation* due to inadequate satisfaction during your oral stage.[3]

Biography: Sigmund Freud

Sigmund Freud, (1856–1939) was born in Moravia (now part of the Czech Republic). He moved during childhood to Vienna, Austria, where he remained until shortly before his death. The oldest of eight children of middle-class parents, Freud was an exceptional student with special talents in science and philosophy. He completed medical training at the University of Vienna in 1881. Early in his career he conducted research on the nervous systems of invertebrates and studied the use of cocaine as an anesthetic. For a few years he even experimented with cocaine and found it to have some beneficial emotional effects, but later recognized its dangers.

In 1885 Freud studied hypnosis in Paris with the famous French psychiatrist Jean-Martin Charcot, and on his return to Vienna he began to practice his new trade. Before long he gave up hypnosis in favor of his own psychoanalytic methods. Initially Freud's psychoanalysis was extremely controversial, and he was widely ridiculed because of his revolutionary ideas. In the early 1900s, However, a small group of students formed around Freud, and soon his psychoanalytic movement was receiving international attention and respect.

It is difficult to overstate Freud's influence on psychology and psychiatry. He is, arguably, the most significant figure in the history of those fields. Although his personality theory is at the heart of the psychoanalytic view, Freud's ideas extended to every aspect of the human experience. Given his larger-than-life reputation, it is easy to overlook Freud's human qualities. He was a devoted family man, and he and his wife, Martha, had six children, the youngest of whom, Anna, also became a famous psychoanalyst. His intellectual courage is evident in his determination to maintain his ideas in the face of intense criticism. Besides his personal strengths Freud also had his share of negative qualities. Despite fame he suffered from depression and self-doubt and was often seen as arrogant and demanding.

In 1938 Freud, a Jew, was forced to leave Vienna after the Nazis took over Austria. The next year at age 83, he died in England as a result of cancer of the jaw from his lifelong habit of smoking cigars. Of his extensive writings, some of the more important works are The *Interpretation of Dreams*, *The Ego and the Id*, *Beyond the Pleasure Principle*, and *The Problem of Anxiety*.[4]

Table 10.3 **Freud's Theory of Psychosexual Development**

Stage	Age (years)	Focus of Libido	Developmental Challenges
Oral	0–2	Eating, nursing	Weaning, teething
Anal	2–4	Defecation	Toilet training
Phallic	4–6	Masturbation	Oedipus and Electra complexes
Latency	6–12	Libido is repressed	Peer relationships
Genital	12–	Sexual behavior	Mature relationships

Freud considered the most significant developmental problem to be the *Oedipus complex* during the phallic stage. At this time, the young boy is sexually attracted to his mother and sees his father as a threatening rival or competitor for her affections. The boy resolves this conflict by identifying with his father, and thus indirectly satisfies his longing for his mother. The parallel in young girls is the *Electra complex*, in which the girl has sexual desires for her father, fears her mother, and eventually identifies with her mother. The same-sex identification at this time strengthens your superego and ego and establishes your gender identity.

An example from Freud's accounts shows how he applied the notion of the Oedipus complex in one case. In the "Little Hans" case, Freud presented a classic analysis of a five-year-old boy who suffered from a fear of horses. Freud interpreted the horse phobia as a symbolic expression of Hans's Oedipus complex. To Freud, the horse was a symbol for Hans's father, and Hans's real (but unconscious) fear was of his father's possible aggression because of Hans's Oedipal longing for his mother.[5]

Although some evidence for Freudian theory has been found in controlled research, critics point out that many of Freud's concepts are scientifically untestable. Nonetheless, psychoanalytic theory was very influential in the fields of personality and abnormal psychology, as you will see in Chapter 12.[6]

Other Psychodynamic Theories

How well do you think Freud explained personality? As important as he was, Freud did not have the last word in psychodynamic theory. Even before his death, his followers had already begun to revise and extend his ideas in new directions. Today, their work continues as the psychodynamic view enters its second century.

Jung's Analytical Psychology. Carl Jung (1875–1961), a Swiss psychiatrist, was attracted to psychoanalysis during the early 1900s and for several years was a close colleague of Freud. Eventually, however, Jung moved away from Freud's ideas and developed his own theory, called

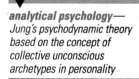

analytical psychology—
Jung's psychodynamic theory based on the concept of collective unconscious archetypes in personality

analytical psychology. The central concept of this theory is the *collective unconscious*, the inborn and universal part of the unconscious mind that is common to everyone. Jung emphasized the unconscious even more than Freud and argued that your personality is based on the inborn structures of your collective unconscious, called *archetypes*. For example, your masculine qualities such as aggressiveness reflect an archetype called the *animus* and your feminine qualities such as emotionality the *anima*. In Jung's view, masculinity and femininity are features of personality based in your collective unconscious, but their expressions are shaped by your culture.[7]

Analytical psychology rejects the Freudian emphasis on sex and aggression drives as the forces behind personality. Instead, a tendency toward *equilibrium*, or balance, in personality is proposed as the motive behind your behavior. Although Jungians point to common themes in mythology, religions, and cultures as evidence of the collective unconscious, many consider Jung's theory to be more philosophical than scientific.

Adler's Individual Psychology.

Another of Freud's early followers, Alfred Adler (1870–1937), offered a psychodynamic theory, called **individual psychology**, that stressed the social dimensions of personality and human development. In Adler's view, your dependency and weakness during infancy and childhood foster feelings of inferiority. Throughout life you are motivated to overcome those inferiority feelings by *striving for superiority*. The characteristic ways in which you strive for superiority define your *style of life* and individual personality. People show this striving in many ways—sports, politics, academics, and social action, to name a few. What is your unique way of striving for superiority?

individual psychology—
Adler's psychodynamic theory emphasizing social dimensions of personality

When someone has extreme feelings of inferiority and is unable to adequately overcome them, an *inferiority complex* may develop, indicated by constant self-doubt, anxiety, and personal insecurity. In Adler's opinion, inferiority complexes are at the root of many mental health and personality problems. Your personality development, for better or worse, is strongly affected by social forces, according to individual psychology. Family influences are especially significant, and Adler was one of the first theorists to address the impact of childrearing practices and family relationships on personality. Adler thought that your position in the family as set by *birth order* had considerable influence on your personality:

▶ *First-Borns*: Parent-oriented, authority-oriented, dominating

▶ *Middle Children*: Peer-oriented, rebellious, nonconforming, sociable

▶ *Last Borns*: Dependent, insecure, pampered[8]

Can you think of anyone whose birth order and personality fit these descriptions? Some research supports the relationship between birth order and personality. But, personality development depends on many factors besides birth order, and birth order does not have as strong an impact as Adler thought.[9]

Interpersonal Theory. Seeking to correct Freud's neglect of the social aspects of human nature, **interpersonal theory** proposes that personality is formed mainly by the interactions and relationships among people.

Psychoanalyst Karen Horney (1885–1952) believed that the underlying force behind the *neurotic personality* was a basic anxiety or insecurity due to disruptions of the early mother-child relationship. Such individuals try to defend against anxiety by three *neurotic strategies*:

▶ *Moving away from people*: Alienation, detachment, social isolation

▶ *Moving toward People*: Conformity, dependency, submissiveness

▶ *Moving against People*: Aggression, hostility, domination[10]

Like Horney, Harry S. Sullivan (1892–1949) also believed that family relationships were crucial in early development. In his view, your personality, or *self-system*, forms as you acquire images of yourself from others. For example, a child who is abused will acquire a negative self-image and develop feelings of self-hatred. Sullivan thought that personality problems come from disturbed parent-child relationships. Perhaps you are able to analyze your own self-system for signs of the images that you acquired in childhood.[11]

Ego Psychology. In Chapter 8, you learned about Erik Erikson's model of psychosocial development. Erikson is a major figure in **ego psychology**, a theory that emphasizes the role of the ego in personality and assumes that your ego is responsible for regulating your mental life and behavior. Erikson's view of development focuses on the formation of an *ego identity* and sees failed ego development as a cause of mental disorders.[12]

Modern ego psychology overlaps with interpersonal theory in many respects. The formation of your ego and its activities such as defense mechanisms is thought to result from your *object relations*, the internalized images of others with whom you identify. For example, if you identified with your kind and gentle mother, you will exhibit similar traits in your own behavior. Your image of her (object relation) has become part of your ego and is reflected in your actions. You can find signs of important early object relations by observing similarities between your own attitudes and behavior and important people in your life such as your parents and grandparents.[6,13]

▼
interpersonal theory—psychodynamic theory of personality as a product of interpersonal relationships

Karen Horney

▼
ego psychology—psychodynamic theory that places the ego at the center of personality and behavior

The Humanistic View

Do you think you are free to control your own destiny? Are you responsible for the consequences of your actions? Is it important for you to be the best you can be? Do you believe that people are basically good? If you answer yes to these questions, your attitudes reflect the humanistic view of personality. *Humanistic psychology* assumes that people have freedom of choice, personal responsibility, a need for self-fulfillment, and an essential goodness. According to this view, personality is also shaped by free and conscious choices, not just by unconscious forces. When you choose personal goals and values and act according to your choices, you are defining yourself as an individual and consequently, you are being responsible for yourself. Humanistic psychology proposes that the most powerful motive behind your behavior is *self-actualization*, or the drive to fulfill your potential. Your development of a healthy personality depends on the opportunities for self-actualization that you experience in your life.

Maslow's Need Theory

need theory—Maslow's theory of personality as a hierarchy of basic and self-actualization needs

What are human needs? The answer to this seemingly simple question was the starting point for Abraham Maslow's (1908–1970) exploration of personality. His **need theory** depicts personality as being focused on the satisfaction of several levels of needs. In Maslow's theory, human needs are organized into a hierarchy, as described in Chapter 9 (see Figure 9.3). The *need hierarchy* indicates that progress from the lower levels (*basic needs*) to the higher levels (*growth needs*) is a sign of psychological growth. According to Maslow's theory, you are able to attend to your higher need levels only after the lower needs have been dealt with. For example, if you are on the brink of starvation (an unfulfilled physiological need), your ability to concern yourself with creativity (a growth need) will be very limited.[14]

Maslow believed that the psychodynamic view offered a narrow image of personality because it emphasized the study of abnormal or unhealthy individuals. In an effort to correct this bias, Maslow conducted a classic study of psychologically well-adjusted individuals, or *self-actualizers*, who were successful, talented people from the arts, sciences, and public life. Among his subjects were people still alive at the time of the study, such as Albert Einstein and Eleanor Roosevelt, as well as historical figures like Abraham Lincoln and Walt Whitman. Maslow found that those self-actualizers shared several important characteristics:[15]

Abraham Maslow

▶ Realistic	▶ Problem-centered
▶ Self-accepting	▶ Need for privacy
▶ Spontaneous	▶ Independence
▶ Open	▶ Democratic values
▶ Nonconforming	▶ Creativity
▶ Fresh outlook	▶ Social interest

Maslow's study examined the lives of truly exceptional individuals, but he believed that many ordinary people may also be self-actualizers. Can you think of anyone who you believe fits the self-actualizer profile?

Rogers's Self Theory

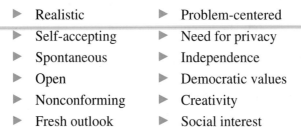

self theory—Rogers's theory of the self-concept and phenomenal field

When you think of your "self" what do you have in mind? Psychologist Carl Rogers (1902–1987) believed that the idea of the *self*, or *self-concept*, was the central feature of personality. In Rogers's **self theory**, personality is a part of your total subjective experience, called your *phenomenal field*. Your self-concept has two aspects: the real self and the ideal self. The *real self* is based on your self-perceptions, that is, how you see yourself at the present time. The hopes, goals, and aspirations that you have for yourself constitute your *ideal self*. When your real self and ideal self are similar, you are in a state of *congruence*, which Rogers believed is essential for your overall psychological well-being.[16]

In self theory, the strongest motive is the *self-actualizing tendency*. When you act to enhance and develop your self-concept, you show signs of self-actualizing. The psychologically healthy individual has what Rogers labeled a **fully functioning personality**, indicated by:

▶ Openness to experiences

▶ Living in the "here and now"

▶ Self-trust

▶ Emotional sensitivity

fully functioning personality—psychologically healthy person who is open, self-trusting, sensitive, and lives in "here and now",

The development of a fully functioning personality requires that your *need for positive regard* is satisfied during childhood. According to Rogers, everyone needs to receive respect and affection (positive regard) in order to acquire a sense of self-worth. Children who get *unconditional positive regard*, love with "no strings attached," experience positive feelings about themselves and develop healthy self-concepts. By contrast, children who experience *conditions of worth* receive positive regard only if they meet the requirements set by parents or authorities. For instance, if you feel loved by your parents only when you obey their commands, you are experiencing conditions of worth. Rogers developed an approach to therapy known as client-centered therapy, which attempts to help people overcome problems in their self-concept, as you will learn in Chapter 12.[17]

The Trait View

If you were asked to describe your best friend's personality, what would you say? Chances are that you would talk about your friend's most outstanding characteristics, for example, kindness, honesty, humor, resourcefulness, and so on. Like this commonsense approach, the *trait view* also describes and explains personality in terms of an individual's **traits**, stable characteristics of behavior, thinking, and emotion. Modern trait psychology seeks to explain personality and individual differences in terms of measurable trait variables.

traits—stable characteristics of behavior, thinking, and emotion that define personality

Allport's Trait Theory

In the 1920s, psychologist Gordon Allport (1897–1967) began the exploration of personality from a trait perspective. For Allport, traits are the enduring characteristics that shape perceptions and behavior. The uniqueness of individual personality was a basic assumption of Allport's theory. Because traits are uniquely organized in everyone, Allport studied personality with an **idiographic approach** that examines the patterns of traits in individuals as expressed in their behavior and personal history.

idiographic (id-ee-oh-graf-ik) approach—Allport's approach to the study of unique trait patterns in individuals

Chapter 10 • Personality

How many traits do you have? The English language has thousands of words that refer to personality traits, as you can see by paging through any dictionary. Allport classified the many kinds of traits according to how broad or general their effects are. The least general is the *secondary trait*, such as a preference for a specific food or clothing. *Central traits* are more influential and important aspects of personality. Your 5–10 most basic characteristics are your central traits. Try to describe your personality as completely as possible in 5–10 words, and you will be summarizing your central traits. The one or two most pervasive motives or dispositions in your personality are your cardinal traits. A *cardinal trait* is an intense drive or passion that affects virtually every aspect of your life. As an example consider Martin Luther King, who devoted his life to the fight for civil rights and equality and whose determination indicates a cardinal trait.[18]

Factor Theories

The study of the individual was Allport's main concern. By contrast, modern trait psychology emphasizes the study of "average" personality by analyzing data from large groups or samples of subjects. The most important method of modern trait theories is *factor analysis*, a statistical procedure to identify the patterns of association among traits. Factor analysis is an elaborate correlational method by which groups of interrelated variables, called *factors*, are revealed. Suppose you measured the traits of aggressiveness, need for power, assertiveness, and dominance in several of your closest friends. By factor analyzing their scores, you would find that those traits are all correlated with each other and define a *personality factor*. Trait researchers hope to uncover the basic structure of human personality by identifying these underlying factors.

Cattell's Factor Theory. Psychologist Raymond Cattell is a pioneer in the application of factor analysis in the study of personality. **Cattell's factor theory** views personality as a composite of 16 factors, called *source traits*, as shown in Figure 10.1. Cattell sees these source traits as the basic units of personality that guide your behavior. Everyone has all 16 source traits, but people differ in the degree to which they are expressed. For example, you may have more warmth than your best friend, but both of you have some degree of that trait.[19]

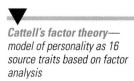

Cattell's factor theory—
model of personality as 16
source traits based on factor
analysis

Like other factor theorists, Cattell relies on objective measurements to support his concepts. His research uses a questionnaire, called the *16 Personality Factor (16 PF) Test*, to measure source traits. Cattell's theory and tests have been applied in many studies of personality, as well as in diagnosing psychological disorders and in screening job applicants.[20] Cattell's critics argue, however, that his theory presents an unnecessarily complex view of personality based on an unreliable test and intricate statistical analyses.[21]

Figure 10.1 A 16PF Profile of a Well-Adjusted Person

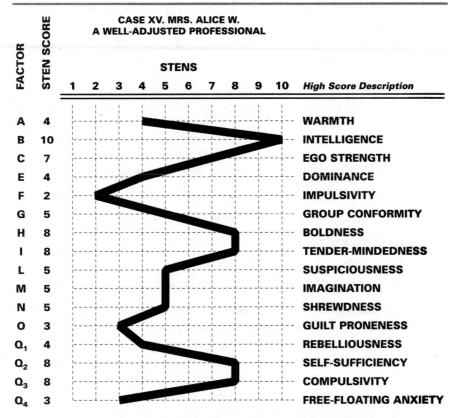

CASE XV. MRS. ALICE W.
A WELL-ADJUSTED PROFESSIONAL

FACTOR	STEN SCORE	STENS	High Score Description
A	4		WARMTH
B	10		INTELLIGENCE
C	7		EGO STRENGTH
E	4		DOMINANCE
F	2		IMPULSIVITY
G	5		GROUP CONFORMITY
H	8		BOLDNESS
I	8		TENDER-MINDEDNESS
L	5		SUSPICIOUSNESS
M	5		IMAGINATION
N	5		SHREWDNESS
O	3		GUILT PRONENESS
Q_1	4		REBELLIOUSNESS
Q_2	8		SELF-SUFFICIENCY
Q_3	8		COMPULSIVITY
Q_4	3		FREE-FLOATING ANXIETY

A personality profile based on results of the 16PF test on Mrs. Alice W., a 39-year-old married nurse. Alice has no history of psychological disturbances and at the time of testing exhibited good adjustment in her work, marriage, and social life. The 16 source traits of Cattell's theory are listed on the right.

Source: Karsen, S., & O'Dell, J. W. (1976). *A Guide to the Clinical Use of the 16PF* (p.148). Champaign, Il: Institute for Personality and Ability Testing.

Eysenck's Type Theory.

British psychologist Hans J. Eysenck's **type theory** describes personality in terms of three broad factors, or dimensions:

▶ *Extraversion-Introversion*: Sociability, activity, impulsiveness, liveliness

▶ *Neuroticism*—Emotional instability, moodiness, tension

▶ *Psychoticism*—Isolation, social alienation, aggressiveness

On the basis of these dimensions, Eysenck proposes *personality types* that describe a wide range of behavior. For example, the *extraverted type* of person is very outgoing, socially active, and assertive, whereas the *introverted type* is quiet, reserved, and thoughtful.[22]

Eysenck and other researchers have found evidence that the basic dimensions of personality and their corresponding personality types are grounded in biology. For example, twin studies show that the dimension of

▼

type theory—Eysenck's theory of personality types based on 3 dimensions of extraversion-introversion, neuroticism, and psychoticism

extraversion-introversion is heritable.[23] Although personality types are strongly affected by heredity and physiology, Eysenck recognizes that the environment also shapes your personality. For instance, an introvert who finds that other people pay little attention to him may become even more socially withdrawn and, thus, strengthen his introversion.

The Five-Factor Model. Personality trait researchers have not reached final agreement on a fundamental question: How many personality factors are there? In addition to Cattell and Eysenck, other trait theorists offer models with varying numbers of factors. In recent years, several researchers have put forth a **five-factor model** that identifies the five most commonly cited personality factors from numerous trait studies.

▼

five factor model—theory of "Big Five" personality factors: extraversion, agreeableness, conscientiousness, emotional stability, and openness

1. *Extraversion*: Socially active, assertive, outgoing, energetic, talkative

2. *Agreeableness*: Likeable, friendly, pleasant, kind, trusting

3. *Conscientiousness*: Dependable, reliable, organized, prudent, thoughtful

4. *Emotional Stability*: Anxious, moody, calm, temperamental, controlled

5. *Openness*: Open to experience, intelligent, creative, imaginative, cultured[24,25]

Although there is still controversy about the exact content of the Big Five, this model holds out promise as a general trait theory that integrates findings from many studies. Tests that measure these factors, such as the *NEO Personality Inventory* (NEO-PI), have been used to predict a variety of behaviors.[26] For instance, an important new area of application for the five-factor model is predicting job performance (see "Issues and Applications: Vocations and Personality").

Issues and Applications

Vocations and Personality

When you imagine your ideal career, what do you see yourself as? A doctor? A social Worker? An engineer? A singer? A business entrepreneur? Thousands of vocational choices are possible, but your own personality will draw you to specific job interests. If you are shy, reserved, and prefer solitary activity, you probably have no desire to become a salesperson. On the other hand, if you are an outgoing and sociable extravert, sales or other people-oriented jobs may be perfect for you.

Psychologists and vocational counselors have examined the role of personality traits in the choice of vocations, as well as in job performance and work satisfaction. Psychologist John Holland offers a useful framework for assessing work interests in terms of your personality. His *Self-Directed Search (SDS)* is a test that identifies six personality types corresponding to vocational preferences and interests. Each type reflects traits that are most adaptive in specific careers.

▶*Realistic Type*: Mechanic, surveyor, electrician, farmer, technician

*T*he Learning View

In Chapter 5, you read about the behavioral and social learning views of learning. As you will learn in this section, those perspectives are also applied to personality. Behaviorism and social learning theory both emphasize the role of learning processes in behavior, but each offers a distinctive model of personality.

Behaviorism

In the area of personality, *behaviorism* insists on the study of objective behavior. B. F. Skinner, the chief figure in modern behaviorism, contended that when you talk about someone's personality you are referring to the person's behavior. For example, if you claim that your cousin Fred has an "aggressive personality," you are just pointing out that Fred exhibits aggressive behavior in many situations.

In Skinner's view, the widely used concepts of personality theory are just labels for your responses. Terms such as *extravert*, *inferiority complex*, and *ego* are names for learned habits, not explanations. Skinner cautioned against confusing those labels for causes. In his opinion, they no more explain behavior than the word *car* explains why an automobile works. To explain your behavior requires an analysis of the forces in your environment that control your responses. The principle of **environmental determinism** claims that your behavior is controlled by your learning environment, not by internal mental forces such as traits and complexes.

▼

environmental determinism—behavioristic concept that behavior is controlled by the learning environment

▶*Investigative Type*: Scientist, researcher, economist, mathematician, academic

▶*Artistic Type*: Actor, musician, decorator, artist, writer, performer

▶*Social Type*: Teacher, social worker, psychologist, minister, counselor

▶*Enterprising Type*: Salesperson, business manager, promoter

▶*Conventional Type*: Clerk, banker, tax analyst, bookkeeper, businessperson[27]

Job satisfaction and performance are affected by the match between your personality and the demands of your work. Like many people, you may not "fit" one particular type but might instead have a combination of types. In addition, specific traits are relevant to occupational success in various jobs. For example, conscientiousness predicts good job performance in many types of work. Of course, numerous variables affect your career choice and work behavior, but by considering your personality traits you can select a rewarding career and improve your chances of achieving satisfaction and success.[28,29]

In the behavioristic view, the habits of personality, like other habits, are acquired and maintained through conditioning. If you are an "extravert," it is because you received considerable reinforcement during your life for extraverted behavior. Personality development depends on your unique history of reinforcement and punishment for specific response patterns and ultimately is a product of your learning environment.[30]

Social Learning Theory

As you have already learned, social learning theory takes a cognitive approach in explaining behavior. Social learning theory defines personality in terms of cognitive *person variables*, including your perceptions, values, plans, and expectations.[31] Albert Bandura, the leading social learning theorist, proposed a model that depicts behavior, person variables, and the environment as having reciprocal cause-and-effect connections. For example, if you have a friendly personality, your social activity influences the people around you, attracting them to you, and changing your environment, which, in turn, affects your subsequent social behavior. In Bandura's model, an understanding of your behavior depends on an analysis of the interactions between your personality (person variables) and environment.[32] (See *Issues and Applications: Personality and Friendships*.)

Bandura examined the role of person variables in his work on **self-efficacy**, the beliefs people have about the effectiveness of their behavior. You have *positive self-efficacy* when you anticipate that your behavior will be successful. If you expect to do well on an exam because you trust your

self-efficacy (eff-uh-kuh-see)—beliefs people have about the effectiveness of their behavior

Issues and Applications

Personality and Friendships

Have you ever heard the sayings "Opposites attract" and "Birds of a feather flock together?" You may even have relationships that support those ideas. Although the sayings contradict each other, both are commonly believed and, in fact, both are supported by research on personality and friendships.

How can two very different people become close? The "opposites attract" relationship is puzzling, but there may be a sound basis for it in personality. Carl Jung believed that we are attracted to people who complement our own personality. In other words, what attracts you to the person is your perception of something in the person's personality that you need, perhaps a quality that you lack. The interlocking needs of two "opposites" may bind them together in a close friendship. For instance, if you have a very dominant personality, you may be attracted to passive or submissive people.

People with similar personalities ("birds of a feather") are often attracted to each other because of a recognition of their shared attitudes, values, and interests. You may find it easy to identify or empathize

knowledge and test-taking skills, you exhibit positive self-efficacy. The expectation of failure, however, indicates *negative self-efficacy*, which unfortunately often creates emotional distress that disrupts behavior and leads to failure. With negative self-efficacy you may lapse into a vicious cycle of expecting failure, failing, and anticipating more failure. Recent studies point to the role of self-efficacy in several mental health problems, such as depression and anxiety.[33]

In the 1950s, social learning theorist Julian Rotter proposed a theory that attempted to predict behavior on the basis of an individual's expectations. Rotter is best known for his concept of **locus-of-control** (LOC), a variable that reflects your beliefs about the forces that control events in your life.[34]

▶ Do you control your own actions?

▶ Are you responsible for your failures?

▶ Can you succeed through hard work?

If you answered yes to those questions, you have an *internal LOC*, indicating your belief that you are responsible for the events in your life. If you believe that forces outside yourself, such as fate or luck, control your destiny, you probably answered no and have an external LOC. People with internal and *external LOC* exhibit different behavior in many areas. For example, internal LOCs take more responsibility for their health and engage in preventive action, such as getting medical checkups, whereas external LOCs are more likely to leave their health to chance.[35]

▼
locus-of-control—person variable that reflects beliefs about the forces controlling events

with someone like yourself. If your personality resembles that of a friend, you will be more likely to share activities, validate each other's thoughts and feelings, and anticipate each other's behavior. As social learning theory suggests, your personality and social environment—including your friends—have mutual cause-and-effect relationships.

The similarity ("birds of a feather") and complementarity ("opposites attract") principles have limits. Very dissimilar people—introverts and extraverts, for example—may repel, rather than attract each other. And, you do not necessarily like everyone who has a personality similar to yours. If you dislike yourself, you almost certainly will not like people who resemble you. Theorists disagree about how to explain these effects, but they recognize that the development of lasting friendships involves both. Similarity is most important early in a friendship when you are just getting to know each other. In a long-term relationship complementarity may be more meaningful. Take a few minutes to examine your most important friendships and see how these principles have affected your own life.[36,37]

People with extreme external locus-of-control perceive events in their lives to be a matter of luck, like a game of roulette.

Assessing Personality

If you find yourself confused by so many different theories of personality, you have a lot of company. Critics often complain that personality psychology has too many theories and not enough facts. Although there is some merit to that complaint, there are plenty of facts about personality. These facts have been obtained mainly by studies that depend on several methods of assessing personality. In this section, you will learn about the major strategies that modern psychologists employ to assess personality. In Chapter 7, you learned about the three requirements for an intelligence test—standardization, reliability, and validity. Those requirements also apply to personality assessment:

▶ *Standardization*: The test has a standard or uniform method for administration and scoring.

▶ *Reliability*: The test results are consistent when given at different times or by different people.

▶ *Validity*: The test accurately measures what it claims to measure and predicts behavior.

Self-Report Tests

A widely used method of personality assessment is the **self-report test** that asks you to respond to a set of questions about your behavior, attitudes, traits, and other characteristics. Self-report tests usually take the form of questionnaires or checklists that subjects complete by themselves. The scope of these tests may be very narrow, focusing on a single trait or behavior, or broad, assessing several different characteristics.

Fundamentals of Psychology

The most popular self-report test is the *Minnesota Multiphasic Personality Inventory* (MMPI), a broad-range test composed of 566 true-false questions that measure 10 traits, as shown in Table 10.4. The focus of the MMPI and its revised version, the MMPI-2, is abnormal personality characteristics. The MMPI tests are based on studies of psychologically disturbed individuals and are used mainly to evaluate mental health problems.[38]

Other comprehensive self-report personality tests have been devised to measure normal traits. Two of the more popular tests of normal personality were mentioned previously: Cattell's 16 Personality Factor (16 PF) Test and the NEO Personality Inventory (NEO-PI).

Table 10.4 **Scales of the MMPI and MMPI-2**

Scale	Characteristics Assessed
Hypochondriasis	Physical complaints; demanding
Depression	Low self-esteem; depressed mood
Hysteria	Dependent; naive; dramatic
Psychopathic deviate	Antisocial; rebellious; impulsive
Masculinity-femininity	Masculine and feminine traits
Paranoia	Suspicious; mistrustful; sullen
Psychasthenia	Worried; anxious; phobic
Schizophrenia	Alienated; detached; bizarre
Hypomania	Energetic; flighty; irritable
Social introversion	Shy; sensitive; overcontrolled

Many single-trait self-report tests have also been constructed to assess individual personality traits. Rotter's *Internal-External Scale* (IE Scale) for measuring locus-of-control is one example of a widely used single-trait test.[34] Among the dozens of others are tests for normal traits, such as the *Coopersmith Self-Esteem Inventory*,[39] and for abnormal traits, such as the *Beck Depression Inventory*.[40]

In general, the most common self-report tests meet the basic requirements of standardization and reliability. However, some widely used tests, such as the 16 PF, have questionable reliability despite their popularity. Self-report tests are open to validity questions because of possible deception. Test takers may lie or distort their answers. Although most tests have built-in checks for deception, they cannot eliminate it altogether. Test-taking subjects are often motivated to provide a favorable impression of themselves, and this *response bias* will distort their answers.[41]

Projective Tests

projective test—personality
test in which subjects interpret
ambiguous stimuli

Unlike self-report tests, which ask clear and direct questions, a **projective test** consists of ambiguous stimuli that subjects are asked to interpret. Projective testing rests on the assumption that your interpretation of the stimulus reveals your underlying, often unconscious, traits, defenses, feelings, and attitudes. Projective tests evolved mainly within the psychodynamic view of personality and reflect many of its assumptions.

The most famous projective test is the *Rorschach (Inkblots) Test*, developed by psychoanalyst Hermann Rorschach in 1921. If you were taking a Rorschach test, you would look at 10 symmetrical inkblots and tell what you see in them (see Figure 10.2 for a sample inkblot). The tester questions the subject about different parts of the stimuli and the associations provided. Several scoring methods for this test are available, and they focus on the content of your answers (what you perceive) as well as their commonness (how usual or unusual).[42]

Figure 10.2 **A Rorschach-like Inkblot**

An inkblot similar to those on the Rorschach test. Subjects are asked to interpret the possible meaning of the inkblot, and their answers are viewed as "projections" of their personalities. What do you see in this picture?

Another widely used projective technique is the *Thematic Apperception Test* (TAT) in which you tell a story about the events depicted in a drawing. In contrast to the Rorschach test, the TAT and other picture-story projectives employ meaningful pictures. For example, in one picture you see a young boy sitting at a table and looking down at a violin on the table.[43]

Although inkblot and picture-story tests are the most common projective tests, several other types of expressive methods are also used. Some projective tests ask subjects to draw pictures of objects or people. In the *Draw-a-Person Test* you draw human figures that are interpreted as expressions of your social perceptions and self-image. For instance, if you draw a large and threatening man you may be revealing a negative perception of male authority figures. A projective strategy commonly used with children involves doll or toy play. By playing with puppets or dolls, a child may express important feelings or memories that are not verbally stated. In evaluations of abused children, for example, play techniques can reveal information that the children are unwilling to talk about.[44]

Given the differences among projective tests, no simple evaluation applies to all of them. The more popular projective tests, the Rorschach, TAT, and Draw-a-Person—are supported by considerable clinical evidence, but many questions remain about their standardization, reliability, and validity. A case in point is the assessment of abused children with the doll play test in which the child may be unintentionally led to express what the tester expects to see. Projective tests typically have more problems of reliability and validity than most self-report tests.

Other Assessment Methods

Although self-report and projective tests are the most commonly employed strategies of personality assessment, other methods are also used. In this section, you will read about two alternative methods: the interview and direct observation.

Have you ever watched a television talk show? If so, you have seen examples of interviewing. In an *interview* to assess personality, the interviewer gathers information about a subject by asking a series of questions in a face-to-face meeting. In a *structured interview*, the interviewer asks you a list of questions in a predetermined order. Structured interviews are preferred for research because they are standardized. However, most interviewers use the *unstructured* (unstandardized) interview, in which questions follow no set order. The goal of an interview is to accumulate facts about the person's background, traits, emotions, habits, social behavior, and beliefs. Provided the subject responds truthfully, interviews can produce valuable insights into personality.[45]

Instead of personality tests and interviews, behaviorists favor *direct observation*, in which trained observers analyze the ongoing behavior of subjects. Behaviorists believe that if you really want to know about people, you should not ask them about themselves, but rather watch what they do. One advantage of direct observation is that it is relatively free from the inferences of the tester. The validity of the observation method is questionable, however, because people who know that they are being observed may not act naturally, and thus the observer will gather biased information.[46]

Summary

1. Freud's psychoanalytic theory proposes that unconscious mental forces govern the three conflicting parts of personality. The id is controlled by instinctual drives and dominated by the pleasure principle. The ego follows the reality principle and uses defense mechanisms to control emotional distress. Morality, conscience, and ego-ideal are features of superego. Psychosexual development has five stages—oral, anal, phallic, latency, and genital—at which problems with lasting effects may arise.

2. Jung's analytical psychology proposes that inborn personality structures called archetypes are based on the collective unconscious. In Adler's individual psychology, striving for superiority is the primary force behind personality and style of life. The social dimension of personality is emphasized in interpersonal theory, as in Horney's concept of neurotic strategies and Sullivan's self-system. Ego psychology emphasizes the central role of ego in regulating personality and development.

3. Maslow's need theory assumes that self-actualization occurs through the satisfaction of basic and growth needs in the need hierarchy. Self-actualizers are people who are psychologically well adjusted and whose behavior focuses on growth needs.

4. In Rogers's self theory, the self-concept is composed of the real self and the ideal self. Congruence between the real self and the ideal self is essential to self-actualization and health. The fully functioning personality is marked by openness to experience, self-trust, and living in the "here and now."

5. The trait view assumes that traits are stable, measurable units of personality. Allport's theory took an idiographic approach to study individuals' cardinal, central, and secondary traits. Cattell's factor theory uses factor analysis to define 16 source traits of personality. Eysenck's theory views extraversion-introversion, neuroticism, and psychoticism as major personality dimensions. The five-factor model specifies extraversion, agreeableness, conscientiousness, emotional stability, and openness as the "Big Five" factors.

6. Behaviorism defines personality in terms of stable habits learned through reinforcement and punishment. Behavior is controlled by the environment according to environmental determinism. Behaviorists warn against confusing personality trait labels with explanations of behavior.

7. Social learning theory describes personality as cognitive person variables that interact with the environment to produce behavior. Self-efficacy refers to expectations for success or failure that influence performance. The locus-of-control concept identifies a person's beliefs about the forces that control events.

8. Self-report tests, such as the MMPI and 16 PF, are objective questionnaires. Projective tests, such as the Rorschach and TAT, require an interpretation of ambiguous stimuli. In structured and unstructured interviews subjects are questioned about themselves. In direct observation, trained observers analyze the behavior of subjects.

Questions for Discussion

1. How did Freud explain personality?

2. What are four psychodynamic views of personality derived from Freud's theory?

3. What is Maslow's need theory? List its components.

4. How does Rogers's self theory describe personality?

5. How do Allport's theory and factor theories explain personality traits?

6. What assumptions does behaviorism make about personality?

7. What is the social learning theory of personality?

8. How do the major methods of assessing personality differ?

Applying Psychology

Studies of Carl Rogers's concept of congruence in personality rely on a method of assessment known as the Q-Sort. In a typical Q-Sort study, subjects describe their personalities by sorting 100 statements into categories ranging from "extremely uncharacteristic of me" to "extremely characteristic of me." First, they describe their real self (how they see themselves at present) and then their ideal self (how they would like to be). Similarities between the real and ideal self ratings for each statement define congruence. You can evaluate your own degree of congruence by adapting the Q-Sort technique into a simple exercise:

1. Take 16 index cards or pieces of paper and write one of these terms on each:

Outgoing	Intelligent	Stable	Assertive
Agreeable	Conscientious	Bold	Tender-minded
Self-sufficient	Imaginative	Shrewd	Apprehensive
Experimental	Suspicious	Open	Controlled

2. Make two card piles, one for traits "Like Me" and one for traits "Unlike Me." Sort the cards twice. First, rate your real self, then your Ideal self.

3. Check the difference between your real self and your ideal self by comparing the traits rated "Like Me" and "Unlike Me" for each aspect of your self-concept. Your real-ideal congruence is reflected in the number of items that match. A high number of matched traits indicates high congruence in your self-concept.

Chapter 11

Psychology and Health

Learning Objectives

After completing this chapter, you should be able to:

1. Describe the nature of stress.

2. Identify the six main sources of stress.

3. Describe the physical effects of stress.

4. Explain the psychological consequences of stress.

5. Define coping and discuss how it is related to health and illness.

6. Explain the relationships among personality, health, and illness.

7. Explain how health and illness depend on cognitive factors.

8. Describe stress management techniques.

9. Discuss the factors in illness prevention and health promotion.

▼
health psychology—application of psychology to the understanding and prevention of illness and the promotion of health

"**I** dreamt I was asleep. It was about midnight and the flood came. My mother tried to get everybody up, but I was the only one who didn't wake up, and she left me there and I drowned.

I was on a ladder and the water started rising. My brother fell. The buildings around us fell. Each building we got to fell."[1]

Those dreams were reported by two young children in Kansas after their homes were swept away by flood waters from the swollen Missouri River in the summer of 1993. Nightmares are common for the survivors of natural catastrophes, like these children and others who suffered through the Midwest floods. You may never have been ravaged by a flood or some other traumatic event, but you experience stress in your everyday life nonetheless. You simply may not have realized that stress can eventually take its toll and negatively affect your physical and mental health, your productivity at school and work, and the quality of your relationships.

Today, psychologists believe that health and illness depend on the interaction of psychological, social, and biological factors, meaning that stress is determined by how you think, your relationships, and the way your body functions. This position is reflected in the field of **health psychology**, which applies psychological knowledge and principles to the understanding of health and illness, the prevention of illness, and the promotion of health.[2,3]

As you study this chapter you will learn about the nature of stress and its physical and psychological effects, as well as how psychology can help in the prevention and treatment of stress-related problems.

The Nature of Stress

Though stress is common, psychologists disagree on how to define it. In this section you will learn about different ways of viewing stress and where it comes from.

What Is Stress?

You find out that the final exams for two of your most difficult courses are scheduled on the same day. As you prepare for the exams, you realize that there is a lot of information to study and that you are not well prepared. In the days before the exams, you become tense, irritable, and worried. You snap at your friends and family for the littlest things and dwell on how bad it will be if you "blow" the exams. You also have some trouble falling asleep and your appetite is not as good as usual. You are under *stress*. Whether it involves taking an exam, being "chewed out" at work, driving in bumper-to-bumper traffic, or just putting up with little daily "hassles," stress is an unpleasant yet unavoidable part of life.

Stress is an unpleasant yet unavoidable part of life.

What do psychologists mean when they talk about stress? Many definitions of stress have been offered, but there is no general agreement on what it is. Some experts define stress as the physical and psychological effects that stimuli or situations have on you. Applying this definition to the example above, stress would be defined in terms of your experience of tension, irritability, worry, and impaired appetite and sleep. Another way to define stress is according to the **stressor**, the stimulus or event that distresses you. One example of a stressor is any positive or negative life change such as going on a vacation or failing an exam. According to this idea, anything that results in a change in the circumstances of your everyday life is stressful.

Cognitive explanations of stress emphasize your beliefs about whether a particular event is important for your well-being. **Stress** is a relationship between a person and the environment that is appraised by the person as threatening to his or her well-being.[3] In general, events you consider to be negative, threatening, uncontrollable, or unpredictable are most likely to be stressful for you.[4] This view of stress also implies that what is stressful for you may not be stressful for someone else. In the earlier example, someone who was well-prepared for the exams or who did not care about the results would be unlikely to perceive the situation as threatening and therefore, probably would not experience much stress. If you look at it in this way, you realize that stress is not a simple matter of the stressor or your reaction to it.

▼
stressor—the stimulus or event that distresses a person.

▼
stress—a relationship between a person and the environment that is appraised as threatening to well-being

The Sources of Stress

There are many sources of stress. You hear stories every day about unfortunate people who have been victimized by catastrophic events such as floods, earthquakes, wars, and traumatic experiences such as sexual abuse, financial ruin, or the death of a loved one. Such events, though terrible, typically are not your main sources of stress. Your daily life is filled with stress in school, at work, and in your relationships (see *Issues and Applications: Stress at Work*).

Issues and Applications

Stress at Work

A nationwide survey in 1991 indicated that nearly 46 percent of American workers claimed that their jobs were stressful, and almost 27 percent felt that work was the single most stressful part of their lives. When you consider that more than 70 percent experienced stress-related physical and mental conditions, you can begin to understand just how stressful work can be. Work stress is something you should be concerned about because even if you are not working yet, you eventually will spend at least one-third of your life on the job.[5]

Psychologists have identified three principal sources of stress at work. The first is the condition of the physical environment—for example, air temperature, light, noise, space, and safety factors. The second involves how the job is organized and managed. These sources of stress include issues such as promotion policies, the flexibility of work hours, pay and benefits, and job security. The third area of stress deals with interpersonal relationships including supervisory and staff relations and the toleration of discrimination and harassment.[6]

Work-related stress can result in psychological problems such as anxiety and depression and dangerous behaviors such as substance abuse and violence. For example, job stress has been blamed, in part, for incidents in which postal employees returned to their jobs to shoot fellow workers and supervisors. Medical problems, such as heart disease, headaches, restless sleep, high blood pressure, and ulcers, are also related to work stress. Stress reactions are often worse for women because of the unique stressors they experience—discrimination, stereotyping, sexual harassment, and work-home conflicts. The cost of job stress is high for the business or organization too, because low worker morale, absenteeism, high personnel turnover, co-worker conflicts, and drug and alcohol abuse lead to low productivity.[7,8]

Although you may never have a stress-free job, psychologists have been involved in finding remedies for work stress. One approach involves changing aspects of the work environment to make it less stressful. Another is the development of stress management programs designed to help people cope with specific job-related stressors.

Change.   Are you the kind of person who does not mind, or even enjoys, changes in your life? Like most people, you probably prefer some order and predictability in your life and so any change is stressful for you. Imagine going to a different school every year and having to make new friends and adjust to new teachers. You probably would find those circumstances stressful. The *Social Readjustment Rating Scale* (SRRS), shown in Table 11.1, was constructed by researchers Thomas Holmes and Richard Rahe to measure stress as changes in life that people must adjust to.[9] In the SRRS, each life event is given a number indicating the life change's impact. For example, "being fired at work" is assigned a value of 47, indicating that most people consider this event to be more stressful than a "change in schools," which has a value of 20. To take the SRRS, you pick those life events that you experienced in the last year, then add them up to derive a total score. Holmes and Rahe found that higher SRRS scores were usually associated with an increased likelihood of developing a physical illness within the next couple of years.

Table 11.1 **The Social Readjustment Rating Scale**

Life Event	Life-Change Units	Life Event	Life-Change Units	Life Event	Life-Change Units
Death of a spouse	100	Change to a different line of work	36	Revision of personal habits	24
Divorce	73	Change in the number of arguments with a spouse	35	Trouble with boss	23
Marital separation	65	Mortgage over $10,000	31	Change in work hours or conditions	20
Jail term	63	Foreclosure of a mortgage or loan	30	Change in residence	20
Death of a close family member	63	Change in responsibilities at work	29	Change in schools	20
Personal injury or illness	53	Son or daughter leaving home	29	Change in recreation	19
Marriage	50	Trouble with in-laws	29	Change in church activities	19
Being fired at work	47	Outstanding personal achievement	28	Change in social activities	18
Marital reconciliation	45	Wife beginning or stopping work	26	Mortgage or loan less than $10,000	17
Retirement	45	Beginning or ending school	26	Change in sleep habits	16
Change in the health of a family member	44	Change in living conditions	25	Change in number of family get-togethers	15
Pregnancy	40			Change in eating habits	5
Sexual difficulties	39			Vacation	13
Gain of a new family member	39			Christmas	12
Business readjustment	39			Minor violations of the law	11
Change in financial status	38				
Death of a close friend	37				

Source: From Holmes, T. H., and Rahe, R. H. (1967). The social readjustment rating scale. Journal of Psychosomatic Research, 11, 213–218.

Hassles, Pressure, and Frustration.   You might be saying to yourself, "I've had no major life changes, but I'm still stressed out." According to psychologist Richard Lazarus, that may be because *hassles*, that is, petty annoyances, frustrations, and irritations are a major source of stress in everyday life, too. Although hassles may be defined as petty annoyances, they can have a significant effect on your health. Studies have found that daily hassles were associated with health problems such as the flu, headaches, and backaches.[10,11]

To see if you are hassled, answer the following questions:

▶ Are you annoyed by unexpected company?

▶ Do you have too many things to do and not enough time to do them?

▶ Are you bothered by noise?

▶ Do you owe some money?

▶ Do you get annoyed with people at work or school?

▶ Do traffic jams drive you crazy?

If you answered yes to most of those questions, you are probably hassled. Lazarus claims that major events are stressful because of the hassles that follow them. For example, even though losing your job may be stressful in itself, its effects are like ripples that spread when you throw a rock in the water. Now you may have to borrow some money, perhaps put up with some ridicule from friends or family, and spend time looking through the classified ads and going on interviews when you would rather be doing anything else.

Pressure, the feeling of being strongly influenced or forced to do something, is another source of stress. You probably have been told many times that if you want to get ahead in life, you have to get a good education. If you accept that notion, you are certainly under pressure to obtain good grades. Work is no different. If you want a rewarding job you will be driven to compete with other qualified people who want the same job that you do. Once you get the job you are under pressure to perform well or find yourself on the unemployment line. Of course, pressure is not confined to school and work. If you are involved in athletics, there is pressure to win. If you are a musician, you are under pressure to perform well.

You are about to drive to work, school, or a friend's house and your car will not start no matter what you try. This is an example of another source of stress, *frustration*, which results when you are blocked from reaching a goal. Personal losses, such as the death of a loved one, the breakup of a relationship, or the loss of income, are other common causes of frustration. Finally, if you have ever been discriminated against because of your sex, sexual orientation, religion, race, or body weight, you know how frustrating it can be and how angry you can get.

Conflict. One of the most common sources of stress is *conflict*, the clashing of feelings or interests. Consider a situation in which you are in a "rocky" relationship. On one hand you are in love, but on the other you realize that you are often miserable when you are with the other person. You get into a big fight and break up for a few days, but the more you stay away the more you feel the need to call and get together again. At first you hesitate to call because you remember how miserable you were when you

Chapter 11 • *Psychology and Health*

were together. You go back and forth between making the call and deciding to never call again before you come to a final decision.

In an **approach-avoidance conflict** like the one just described, you are attracted to the pleasant features of a stimulus and motivated to avoid the same stimulus because of its unpleasant features. Whether you ultimately approach or avoid will depend on the strength of the two motives, so that if your love exceeds your misery you probably will call (see Figure 11.1). If you decide that your misery is stronger than your love for the other person, you may decide to break off the relationship permanently. Can you think of other approach-avoidance conflicts you have experienced?

Figure 11.1 **Approach-Avoidance Conflict**

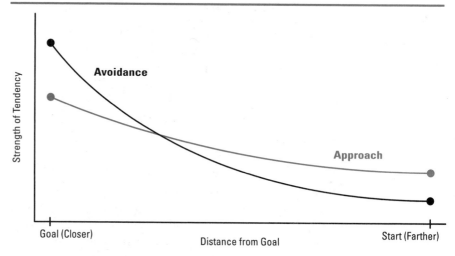

In an approach-avoidance conflict, your tendency to approach a goal increases as you near it. Because of its negative features, your tendency to avoid the same goal also increases as you get closer to it.

In the movie *The Firm*, the character played by Tom Cruise joins a law firm and quickly suspects that they are conducting business illegally. He is approached by FBI agents who tell him that the firm is connected with the Mafia and that they want him to gather incriminating files. Of course if the firm finds out that he is squealing to the FBI, they will have him killed, so he refuses to cooperate at first. The FBI agent reminds Cruise that if he doesn't cooperate, he will eventually be arrested for participating in the firm's illegitimate dealings. Clearly, Cruise is in a "no-win" situation much like being given the choice of fighting a shark or a tiger. This is an example of an **avoidance-avoidance conflict**, one in which you are faced with two negative choices that motivate you to escape from both of them. Though Tom Cruise eventually made a decision, in many avoidance-avoidance situations, you are unable to escape either choice, and that inability to escape is what is stressful.

In an **approach-approach conflict** you must decide between two desirable goals. How would you like to be offered two very attractive jobs

---

approach-avoidance conflict—*conflict that comes from being attracted to the positive features of a stimulus and the motivation to avoid the same stimulus because of its negative features*

avoidance-avoidance conflict—*conflict involving the motivation to escape from two negative choices*

approach-approach conflict—*conflict that comes from having to decide between two desirable goals*

that promise you big money, a luxury car, and the house of your choice? Isn't this a problem you would like to have? Think again. Although you probably cannot lose either way, making this decision can result in some sleepless nights.

Traumatic Experiences.   Although they are beyond the realm of experience for many, traumatic experiences are usually a powerful source of stress for those victimized. Natural catastrophes such as earthquakes, floods, hurricanes, and tornadoes and events such as combat, terrorist attacks, and sexual abuse can strike an emotional blow with long-lasting psychological effects.

How Stress Affects You

Stress can affect you in many ways besides creating an annoyance. One of the most serious consequences of stress is that it can make you physically ill. In addition, stress can lead to psychological difficulties and affect your emotions and behavior. In this section you will learn about what psychologists have discovered about the effects of stress on physical and psychological health.

Physical Effects

In 1929 biologist Walter Cannon (1871–1945) proposed that all biological systems strive to maintain homeostasis in which body functions are balanced and work at their best. A good example of homeostasis is the regulation of your body temperature. Regardless of the external temperature, your body adjusts its temperature so that it is maintained at around 98.6 degrees Fahrenheit. According to Cannon's **emergency theory**, stress disrupts homeostasis and activates the sympathetic division of the autonomic nervous system. These physiological changes, known as "fight or flight" reactions, prepare you to cope with the stressor by confronting or avoiding it. If you succeed, your body returns to a condition of homeostasis.

Physiologist Hans Selye proposed the **general adaptation syndrome** (GAS), a three-stage model that describes your body's reactions to stress (see Table 11.2).

▼

emergency theory—model that states that stress disrupts homeostasis and activates the sympathetic division of the autonomic nervous system

▼

general adaptation syndrome—a three-stage model that describes the body's reactions to stress

Table 11.2 The General Adaptation Syndrome

Stage	Features
Alarm	Initial reaction to stressor; mobilization, sympathetic nervous system arousal
Resistance	Physiological changes take place in the hypothalamus and endocrine system to help cope with the stressor
Exhaustion	Failure to cope results in organ breakdown

The *alarm* stage is marked by increased sympathetic nervous system arousal that includes sweating, elevated blood pressure and heart rate, and dry mouth. If you do not adequately cope with the problem, your body enters the *resistance* stage. During this stage, physiological changes involving the hypothalamus and endocrine system are triggered to help you cope with the stressor. If the stress is prolonged and you cannot cope with it, a body organ or system may "break down" and you will suffer a physical symptom or disease. Organ breakdown identifies the *exhaustion* stage.

Stress and the Immune System. One consequence of reaching the exhaustion stage is that you may be susceptible to infection.

Biography: Hans H. Selye

Hans Hugo Selye, 1907–1982) was one of the great pioneers of stress research. His concept of stress described in his general adaptation syndrome (GAS) had a powerful influence on our understanding of stress and how it affects our bodies.

The son of a physician, Selye was born in Vienna, Austria, and was raised near Budapest, Hungary. He received his M.D. degree from the German University in Prague, now in the Czech republic, in 1929 and a Doctor of Science degree from McGill University in Montreal in 1942. While at McGill, he began to develop his concept of the GAS. Later, he became director of the Institute of Medicine at the University of Montreal. At the Institute, assisted by a team of prominent researchers from around the world, he continued his research on stress and refined the general adaptation syndrome model.

Selye admitted that he owed much of his productivity as a researcher to the high standard of excellence set by his family. As a child he was taught to detest quitting and being mediocre. As an example, he recalls that when he was nine years old his father bought him an Arabian pony. One day while he was riding, the horse jumped and Selye fell off and broke his arm. As soon as his father set the arm in a cast, he commanded Selye to get right back on lest he would always be afraid to ride.

Remarkably, Hans Selye authored more than 1,600 scientific articles and some famous books, including *Stress without Distress*, *The Stress of Life*, and *Stress in Health and Disease*. Selye also received more than 80 medals and prizes and 17 honorary degrees.[12]

Have you ever wondered why you are more likely to feel sick after a period of stress than when you are relaxed? Although you may believe that one thing has nothing to do with the other, the possibility that mental events might contribute to infectious disease has received increasing scientific support.

In recent years, researchers have discovered a link between stress and the **immune system**, bodily mechanisms that identify and eliminate foreign materials such as viruses and bacteria. Your immune system accomplishes this task through specialized cells, called *antibodies*, that are released into the blood (see color plate 11.1). *Chronic* (long-lasting) *stress*, like that from loneliness, the death of a loved one, witnessing fights between divorcing parents, unemployment, and prolonged marital problems, interferes with immune function and makes you more susceptible to disease. Prolonged marital conflict results in impaired immune function in both men and women, but its effects on women are more pronounced.[13] *Acute stress* (stress associated with a single event), such as sleep deprivation and taking exams, can also negatively affect immune functioning.[14,15]

A relationship also exists between stress, impaired immune function, and viral infections such as colds and influenza and diseases such as cancer. This does not mean that stress is the primary cause of those conditions. Rather, it appears that stress, by weakening the immune system, increases your susceptibility to viruses that you would ordinarily be able to resist.

Psychosomatic Disorders. Stress can result in a **psychosomatic disorder**, a physical (*somatic*) symptom or disease caused, in part, by psychological (*psycho*) factors. In other words, a psychosomatic disorder is stress-related inasmuch as your thoughts, feelings, and behavior help to produce it. Though many physical disorders are believed to have a psychosomatic basis, psychologists have focused much of their attention on several serious conditions outlined in Table 11.3.

▼
immune system—bodily mechanisms that identify and eliminate foreign materials

▼
psychosomatic (sy-koh-so-ma-tik) disorder—a physical symptom or disease caused in part by psychological factors

Table 11.3 **Types of Psychosomatic Disorders**

Disorder	Description
Coronary artery disease	Narrowing of coronary arteries
Hypertension	High blood pressure
Ulcers	An open sore in the gastrointestinal tract
Arthritis	A chronic joint disease with stiffness and swelling
Migraine	Headache on one side of the head
Tension headache	Dull aches from muscle tension
Asthma	Respiratory disorder involving breathing difficulty

Psychological Effects

Besides having detrimental effects on your physical health, stress can result in unpleasant emotional reactions such as anger, depression, and anxiety. In extreme cases these reactions develop as symptoms of mental disorders (see Chapter 12).

Earlier in this chapter you learned that one source of stress is frustration. The **frustration-aggression hypothesis** states that frustration leads to aggression.[16] According to this idea, when you are blocked from reaching a goal you become frustrated, lose your patience, and become angry and aggressive. Sometimes you lash out directly against the obstacle. Consider a situation in which someone cuts in front of you on the cafeteria line and then invites several friends to join him. This act may lead to some angry words and, possibly, a physical confrontation. In other situations, you may relieve your frustration through indirect aggression. Rather than confront your teacher about giving you a poor grade on a term paper, you might "bad-mouth" him to your classmates instead. Despite its commonsense ring, the frustration-aggression hypothesis is not a comprehensive explanation for aggression. Research shows that frustration is not the only cause of aggression, and aggression is certainly not an automatic consequence of frustration.[17]

Psychologists have found a link between stress and *depression*, marked by feelings of sadness and a loss of the ability to experience pleasure. A prominent feature of depression is **learned helplessness**, a state in which individuals believe they cannot control unpleasant events and therefore give up trying to control their lives. Because depression also involves a lack of motivation and energy as well as concentration problems, it is very difficult for a depressed person to perform well in school and work and meet everyday responsibilities, such as relating to family and friends.[18] Depression can also weaken your immune system.[19]

The stress associated with depression can make you more depressed and interfere with your ability to get better. In one study, depressed subjects who did not respond to treatment were those who had experienced severe stress just before or during the treatment period.[20]

Another consequence of stress is *burnout*, a condition of emotional exhaustion, feelings of detachment, and reduced personal accomplishment.[21,22] Burnout is often a feature of depression. "Burned out" people have little energy, feel unable to control their lives, and have little motivation to work, especially in contact with others. Burnout can occur in anyone who works hard. You can even get burned out by studying too long and hard. Doctors, therapists, teachers, nurses, and other individuals who work with other people are most likely to burn out, especially if they feel that they have tried their hardest without much to show for it. In one study, nurses who experienced burnout were likely to perceive themselves as having little job control and to have a sense of failure and helplessness.[23]

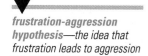

frustration-aggression hypothesis—the idea that frustration leads to aggression

learned helplessness—a state in which a depressed person believes he cannot control unpleasant events

One consequence of too much stress is job burnout, in which a person feels there is too much to do and too much pressure.

Individuals who suffer traumatic experiences, like the children discussed at the beginning of this chapter, experience *anxiety*. Some of the more prominent features of anxiety are intense worry, fear, avoidance of anxiety-producing stimuli, and arousal of the sympathetic nervous system. In some cases, the anxiety accompanies other symptoms as part of a mental disorder. For example, **posttraumatic stress disorder** (PTSD) is identified by anxiety, concentration problems, and reexperiencing the event in vivid nightmares and "flashbacks." Furthermore, traumatized individuals are often riddled with guilt that they survived while others died.[24]

Many studies show that the stress associated with traumatic experiences has damaging emotional effects. For example, college students in the San Francisco Bay area reported frequent nightmares about earthquakes in the three-week period following the 1989 earthquake that killed 62 people.[25] No doubt many survivors, relatives, and recue personnel involved in the Oklahoma City bombing, which killed 167 people on April 19, 1995, will also experience symptoms of PTSD. A study by the Centers for Disease Control in Atlanta showed that approximately 15 percent of Vietnam war veterans had had PTSD at some time since their service.[26] Furthermore, the effects of PTSD spread to other family members. Vietnam veterans with PTSD reported more marital problems, more problems in raising their children, and more violent behavior than veterans without PTSD.[27] Many victims of sexual abuse have PTSD too. They also suffer personality disturbances and problems with security and trust in their relationships. As a result, they are often unable to form meaningful and lasting relationships.[28]

posttraumatic stress disorder—a mental disorder identified by anxiety, concentration problems, and reexperiences of the traumatic event

The Psychology of Health and Illness

Thus far you have learned what stress is and how it can affect your physical and emotional health. In this section you will explore how psychological factors such as coping, personality, and cognitive factors (thoughts) are related to health and illness.

Coping

You have learned that a critical factor in stress is *appraisal*—your judgment that a situation is threatening to your well-being. Once you have appraised a situation as threatening, you will be motivated to deal, or cope, with it in order to reduce the threat. **Coping** is defined as attempts you make to manage situations you appraise as threatening.[29] In general, stronger coping abilities make you more resistant to the effects of stress and promote your health, as illustrated in Figure 11.2.[2,30,31] Consider the example described earlier, in which you had to take two final examinations on the same day (a sobering thought). If you care about your grades, you might be overwhelmed with stress if you are not prepared, have poor study habits, or cannot find a way to catch the flu on exam day. In this situation you do not have what it takes to cope. By contrast, you would probably experience only minimal stress if you coped by preparing well in advance, employing your best study skills, and staying relaxed during the exams.

coping—attempts to manage situations appraised as threatening

Figure 11.2 **Coping, Health, and Illness**

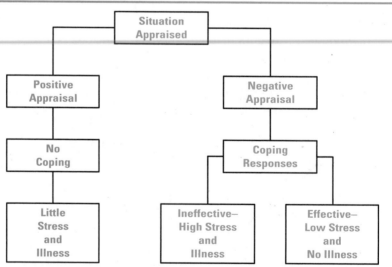

When you appraise a situation as a positive, coping is unnecessary and there is little stress and illness. By contrast, when you appraise a situation as negative, you must cope with it. If you cope effectively you will minimize stress and illness. Ineffective coping efforts may lead to high stress and illness.

Coping Strategies. There are three basic ways to cope with stress.

▶ *Problem-focused coping* involves direct efforts to change a stressful situation. You can accomplish this by altering, removing, or avoiding the stressor.

▶ *Emotion-focused coping* is characterized by attempts to relieve the unpleasant feelings associated with the stressful situation through relaxation or engaging in a pleasurable activity.

▶ Perception-focused coping means reappraising a situation so that you perceive it as less threatening.

To see how these coping strategies work, imagine that you are upset because someone to whom you are attracted shows no interest in you. Understandably you feel rejected, unattractive, and insignificant. You could cope with the rejection by changing the way you dress (problem-focused coping), or you could do more fun things to lift your spirits (emotion-focused coping). If all else fails, you might attempt to reappraise the situation by convincing yourself that you are an attractive, worthy person and he or she is the one that stands to lose (perception-focused coping).

Research on coping suggests that the strategy that will be most effective in protecting you against stress depends on the nature of the stressor and the resources, or "tools," available to you. In general, problem-focused coping works best when you are faced with stressors you can control, such as exams or certain job-related duties. When you are confronted with uncontrollable stressors, such as a catastrophe or the death of a loved one, emotion-focused coping is most effective. Psychologists also distinguish between coping strategies that involve coping through avoidance, and those that involve taking an active role, confronting the problem head-on. Avoidance works best in managing short-term threats, but direct confrontation is better suited for threats that persist. Individuals who have good personal coping skills and help from the environment, like friends and family, rely on active coping more than avoidance.[3]

Social Support.   **Social support** is defined as the functions performed for a distressed individual by others.[29,32] The beneficial effects of social support have been well documented. People with strong social support show better psychological adjustment to stressful events, recover more quickly from illnesses, and have a lower chance of dying from physical diseases than do people without social support.[3] Psychologists believe that social support provides you with a stable social role that allows you to fit in, and thereby increases your self-esteem and gives you confidence in controlling and mastering events in your life. It also serves as a buffer, or softens, the effects of stress by having others assume some of the responsibility for your welfare.

Social support comes in many forms. Friends or relatives might help alleviate the effects of stress by providing you with emotional support, or comfort, during difficult times. A hug, a pat on the back, or a kiss may not

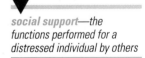

social support—the functions performed for a distressed individual by others

Chapter 11 • Psychology and Health

solve your problem, but it can make you feel better. Others may also provide direct assistance or information and advice you can use to attack the problem directly. At other times, others can support you by helping you reinterpret a situation so that you might perceive it as less stressful. If you have ever had a parent or a good friend help you look at a problem in a different way, you realize how useful this kind of social support can be.[3]

By buffering the effects of stress, social support leads to better psychological adjustment and reduces your chances of developing or continuing an illness

Unfortunately, social support can also work against you. Consider that substance abuse among teenagers is often encouraged and reinforced by the peer pressure of friends. Family members and friends, powerful sources of social support, can also leave you more distressed than ever through their overinvolvement. When they worry too much about you, are overprotective, or bend over backward to help, they actually reduce your sense of control and mastery, making you less able to cope.

Physical and psychological disorders are more prevalent in communities in which social ties are weak or lacking than in those with strong ties. Changes in employment, migration, aging, death, and serious marital problems can disrupt your social ties with family, friends, neighbors, classmates, and co-workers and diminish the benefits of the social support they provide. For example, psychologist Janice Kiecolt-Glaser has discovered that unhappily married people report poorer mental and physical health than do individuals who are happily married or divorced. In general, marital problems seem to affect women more than men. Women with marital problems experience more depression and alcohol problems and have a weaker immune system. In conclusion, social support can protect you against the effects of stress, but it can become a source of stress when inappropriately provided.[33,34]

Personality

For centuries, philosophers and scientists have speculated about the role of personality characteristics in the development of disease. In the 1930s and 1940s, psychoanalyst Franz Alexander (1891–1964) proposed that specific personality types were associated with specific illnesses, but his ideas never received much scientific support. Modern researchers have found that certain personality types are associated with health and illness. The **disease-prone personality** consists of a general negative emotional style marked by depression, anxiety, and hostility. It has been associated with psychosomatic disorders such as coronary artery disease, headaches, bronchial asthma, and peptic ulcers.[35] Researchers have also found a link between a *repressed personality style* and cancer. The person with a repressed personality is passive, has difficulty expressing emotions, and is very defensive. These individuals avoid social situations that they believe might be threatening and thoughts that might create emotional conflict or embarrassment.[2,3]

disease-prone personality—characteristics of depression, anxiety, and hostility; associated with psychosomatic disorders

In the late 1950s, cardiologists Raymond Rosenman and Meyer Friedman noticed a set of behaviors and personality characteristics typical of their patients with coronary heart disease (CHD). They called it the **Type A behavior pattern** (TABP), identified by competitive striving for achievement, easily aroused hostility, aggressiveness, and time urgency. Type A individuals are extremely competitive and base much of their self-esteem on their accomplishments. Because of their competitiveness, they are always under pressure to do more in less time. For Type A individuals there are never enough hours in a day. They are easily angered and irritable and express their anger in vigorous speech and forceful body movements. Some of the questions used to assess the existence of the TABP are listed below.[36,37,38]

Type A behavior pattern—characteristics of competitive striving for achievement, hostility, and time urgency; associated with heart disease

▶ Does your job carry heavy responsibility?

▶ When you are angry or upset, do people around you know it? How do you show it?

▶ Is there competition on your job? Do you enjoy it?

▶ Do you have children? When they were around the ages of 6 or 8, did you ever play competitive games like checkers or monopoly with them?

▶ Do you eat or walk rapidly? After you've finished eating, do you sit around the table and chat or do you just get going?

▶ How do you feel about waiting in line at the bank, supermarket, or post office?

Since the work of Rosenman and Friedman, research has suggested that the most important component of the TABF in predicting CHD is the **hostility complex**, expressed as frequent anger and irritation at small things.[39,40,41,42,43] Apparently, anger leads to CHD by causing "wear and tear" on the walls of coronary arteries and decreasing the pumping efficiency of the heart. The moral of this story is that when you get angry, do not hold it in. You should vent your anger by being assertive rather than aggressive. Instead of just letting it out, you should express it in a way that will lead to a resolution of the problem.[44]

hostility complex—traits of anger and irritability; associated with heart disease

Despite their appeal and their correlation with CHD, the final word on the TABP and hostility complex is not in. Not all studies show them to be clear predictors of coronary disease. Furthermore, the assessment methods used to detect TABP and hostility have been criticized as invalid instruments. Finally, most of the research correlating TABP and the hostility complex with disease has been conducted with white, middle-class, white-collar American men to the neglect of women and ethnic minorities. Although the TABP is found in many women and ethnic minorities as well, its relationship to coronary heart disease in those groups has not been studied.[45]

Health psychologists have also studied personality characteristics related to the promotion of health. The **Type B personality** is just the opposite of the Type A. Type B individuals are not so competitive and are not easily angered or pressured by time. Another personality variable that seems to buffer the effects of stress is **hardiness**, which consists of commitment, control, and challenge.[46] Hardy individuals approach tasks and situations with a sense of purpose and the firm belief that they can control what happens to them. Unlike people who shudder at the thought of change, hardy individuals enjoy challenge and the possible change in life circumstances that may come with it.[2]

Some psychologists believe that the buffering effects of hardiness may be due to the optimism of hardy people. If you are an optimist, you are always looking at the bright side of things and constantly trying to make the best out of situations. Hardy people believe they are in control. Pessimists,

▼

Type B personality—lack of competitiveness, anger, and time urgency; associated with health promotion

▼

hardiness—traits of commitment, control, and challenge; related to health promotion

Issues and Applications

Stress-Inoculation Training

How would you like to get an injection that will make you immune to stress, like getting vaccinated against polio or smallpox? Even though you know that is impossible, there are methods you can use to help you cope better and make your stress reactions more tolerable. One such method is *stress-inoculation training*. Originally used in coping with anxiety, it is also useful in dealing with anger and other stress-related problems.[49,50]

Stress-inoculation training involves three basic steps. The first is *cognitive preparation*, in which you mentally prepare yourself for a potentially stressful event. In the second step, *skill acquisition*, you learn specific coping skills that you test in the third step, *application practice*.

For example, to cope with anger, you can keep a diary in which you track the situations that typically make you angry. Pay particular attention to how you appraise the events that lead to anger. In this way you will begin to understand how your thoughts affect your feelings. Next, learn skills that will help you cope with your anger. Practice some type of relaxation exercise regularly and learn to modify your thoughts. For

Fundamentals of Psychology

by contrast, tend to view situations in a negative light, expect failure, and usually get it. Compared with pessimists, optimists show a lesser physiological response to stress and faster recovery from certain illnesses.[47]

Cognitive Factors

You learned early in this chapter that events you consider to be negative, threatening, uncontrollable, or unpredictable are most likely to be stressful for you. Thus, stress is ultimately a personal matter tied to your cognitive activities. Coping with stress depends partly on your belief that you can control events that have an impact on your mental and physical health. The ability to control your life is related to improved physical and emotional health. On the other hand, a lack of control leads to feelings of hopelessness, helplessness, tension, unhappiness, and possibly physical illness.[8]

Over time, you develop an *attributional style*, a consistent way of explaining responsibility for your condition. If you believe that you are responsible for and can control your own health and welfare, you will be motivated to cope with stressful situations and increase the chances that you will succeed. Inasmuch as you believe that the situation is too much for your coping abilities and that you are unable to control what happens, you will be less likely to cope effectively. Say you feel distressed about new duties assigned to you at work. Are you upset because the job is truly stressful? Perhaps. It is more likely, however, that you will have a stress reaction because you do not believe you have been adequately trained, you

example, you probably get angry because you take things to heart. Step back for a minute and try to stop taking things so personally. The most important cognitive technique you can develop is to use self-instructions—directions you give yourself privately. Imagine that someone passes an uncomplimentary remark. You say to yourself, "This could be very difficult, but I know I can handle it. All I have to do is cool off and take it easy, and I won't have to get into a fight. Take a deep breath and stay cool. I know he's trying to provoke me, but I won't show him that he's getting to me." After the conflict is resolved you could say to yourself, "I did okay. I resolved the problem without fists. It's over now so don't think about it anymore. It will only make me aggravated again."

After you have mentally practiced coping with stress, you are ready to apply your skills in real-life situations. If things do not work well at first you can go back and make corrections. Remember that stress-inoculation training will not make your life stress-free, but it can result in a noticeable difference in how you react to tough situations.

believe the job is too tough, or both. Unless your job is a monumental task—solving the Balkan crisis, perhaps—your response to the new job duties will depend largely on your perceptions about the nature of the task and your beliefs about your ability to handle it. You can see that not only stress is a cognitive matter, but so is your ability to cope with it.

Stress Management and the Promotion of Health

Managing stress involves the use of techniques designed to reduce bodily arousal. Individuals who learn how to relax, modify their thoughts, and change their lifestyle can develop coping strategies that lead to a sense of psychological control (see *Issues and Applications: Stress-Inoculation Training*). To this end, **behavioral medicine** integrates principles of behavior and therapy with knowledge and techniques from medicine in the treatment of medical disorders.[2] The promotion of health involves educating people about the risky behaviors linked with the development of illness and training them to adopt a healthy lifestyle.[3,51]

Stress Management Techniques

Stress management refers to techniques designed to reduce the bodily arousal associated with stress. It includes procedures for relaxation and cognitive methods for altering thoughts. Stress management techniques have proved effective in the treatment of stress-related disorders such as migraine and tension headaches, hypertension, asthma, and gastrointestinal (stomach and intestinal) disorders.[52,53,54]

Muscle relaxation has subjects contract and relax major muscle groups. Typically, the person sits or reclines comfortably and alternately relaxes and tenses her muscles, beginning with her face then progressively working down to her torso and legs. Throughout the procedure, the person is instructed to become aware of the difference between tension and relaxation. The routine is practiced at home for 15 or 20 minutes a day. Muscle relaxation is a simple procedure you can try yourself without professional assistance.

Guided imagery techniques reduce bodily arousal by having the individual imagine pleasurable sensory experiences. Think of something pleasurable such as a lake, beach, a beautiful mountain scene, or whatever you enjoy. Focus on how you experience it through your senses of sight, hearing, taste, smell, and touch, and in a few minutes you might feel as if you are really there and quite relaxed. Hypnosis and meditation (discussed in Chapter 4) are also frequently used in stress management.

One of the most popular stress management techniques is **biofeedback**, a procedure that "feeds back" to the person information about bodily functioning that is usually not noticed. If you were hooked up to a biofeedback machine, tones or colored lights would signal changes in arousal so

behavioral medicine—use of principles of behavior and medical knowledge and techniques in the treatment of medical disorders

stress management—techniques designed to reduce the bodily arousal associated with stress

biofeedback—a procedure that "feeds back" to the person information about bodily functioning that is usually not noticed

that you could learn to control your physiological reactions to stress. In a standard biofeedback program, the individual learns to control muscle tension, skin temperature, and skin resistance (the degree to which your skin conducts electrical currents).

By signaling changes in body arousal, biofeedback helps individuals, like the person shown here, control their physiological reactions to stress.

Cognitive approaches to stress management emphasize changing the way people think about events. One way to do this is to reinterpret the significance of stressors. For example, when facing an upcoming exam you might once have moaned, "If I fail this exam I think I'll die." Of course, nobody ever died because they failed an exam! Once you realize that, although failing an exam is not fun, it certainly is not a catastrophe, you can put the exam in its proper perspective and react to it less dramatically. Another cognitive method is distraction. The next time you experience pain, see if you can dull it by concentrating on something else. It does not matter what it is as long as you can concentrate.

Besides relaxation and lifestyle changes, changing attitudes is an important element in the psychological treatment of stress.[45] For example, therapists can challenge the irrational beliefs of Type A individuals that their self-esteem depends so heavily on their accomplishments. They can also help people reinterpret delays, such as getting stuck in traffic, as events that do not signal the end of the world.

Preventing Illness and Promoting Health

In 1993, Americans spent nearly a trillion dollars on health care. If predictions about increases in HIV infection that causes AIDS are correct, the amount of money we spend on health care is bound to skyrocket even more.

Chapter 11 • Psychology and Health

Since the early 1900s, in the United States the incidence of infectious diseases such as influenza, measles, and polio has declined. During the same time span, however, lung cancer, heart disease, drug and alcohol abuse, and injuries and deaths from automobile accidents have increased dramatically. These facts are particularly interesting to psychologists because the latter problems could be prevented by changing people's behavior. For example, it has been estimated that 25 percent of all cancer deaths and 350,000 premature deaths from heart attack could be prevented each year by altering one risk factor—smoking. Furthermore, the incidence of certain cancers, stroke, and heart attack would decrease in men 35 to 55 years old if they reduced their weight by just 10 percent.[3,55,56]

The prevention of illness requires that the factors that put you at risk are identified and that you are aware of them. Then, you must learn to change these risky behaviors. We have already noted several risk factors in the process of describing the nature and effects of stress. Characteristics such as Type A behavior pattern, poor coping skills, lack of social support, and negative appraisal are just a few. Cigarette smoking and the excessive use of drugs, alcohol, and food are known to be major factors that increase your risk for developing cancer, cardiovascular disease, hypertension, liver damage, and more. You may also recall from Chapter 8 that excessive use of alcohol by pregnant women can lead to a devastating condition in the newborn called *fetal alcohol syndrome*. If these were not enough, you cannot forget about the dire consequences of unsafe sexual behavior in the age of AIDS and other sexually transmitted diseases.[2,3,51]

What can be done? Research shows that individual and public health education can promote good health by providing people with the knowledge they need about prevention. Health promotion can be accomplished through community-based educational programs, public service media announcements, and school-based programs with which you are probably quite familiar. Another way to approach prevention and health promotion is to create environmental barriers. An example would be limiting the hours of operation of liquor stores and having a minimum age for the purchase of cigarettes and alcohol.[2,3,51]

To a degree, however, adopting a healthy lifestyle is a matter of personal decision. No matter how many times you are told to stay away from drugs, practice safe sex, or exercise, you may ignore the advice. You realize that even with environmental barriers, you can find a way to get drugs and alcohol if you want to. Influenced by peer and other pressures, the desire for immediate satisfaction, and your personality, you may not adhere to the lifestyle that will make you healthy. How many "risky" things have you done in the last few months?[46]

If health psychology is to succeed in preventing illness and promoting health, it must not only identify risk factors, it must also find a way to influence people to change.

Summary

1. Stress is sometimes defined in terms of the effects that situations have on you. It can also be defined in terms of the stressor, the stimulus that produces stress. Cognitive psychologists emphasize beliefs about whether a situation is important for well-being. In this view, stress is seen as a relationship between the person and the environment that is appraised by the person as threatening to well-being.

2. Change in one's life circumstances is a source of stress for many people. Stress is also caused by hassles, or petty annoyances, and pressure. Frustration, or being blocked from reaching a goal, is a common source of stress. Stress can result from conflict, the clashing of feelings or interests. People who have experienced a catastrophe or some other trauma suffer from extreme stress.

3. Stress produces arousal of the autonomic nervous system and changes in the functioning of the hypothalamus and endocrine and immune systems. These physiological changes can result in psychosomatic disorders such as coronary artery disease, hypertension, headaches, peptic ulcers, bronchial asthma, and rheumatoid arthritis. Some people under stress experience a weakened immune system, which makes them more susceptible to viral and bacterial infections.

4. Stress can result in anger and aggression when the person is frustrated. Stress also leads to depression, marked by sadness, guilt, feelings of worthlessness, loss of pleasure, crying spells, sleep disturbance, loss of appetite, and weight loss. Depressed people experience a state of learned helplessness in which they believe they cannot control unpleasant events. Burnout, another emotional consequence of stress involves emotional exhaustion, feelings of detachment, and a reduced sense of personal accomplishment. People who have been traumatized often experience posttraumatic stress disorder, marked by anxiety, depression, and reexperiences of the traumatic event.

5. Coping is defined as attempts you make to manage a situation that you appraise as threatening to your well-being. In general, people with good coping skills are more resistant to stress. Those with poor coping abilities are at risk to develop stress-related disorders.

6. The disease-prone personality identified by depression, anxiety, and hostility is a personality type associated with disease in general. The Type A behavior pattern, involving competitiveness,

anger, and time urgency, is associated with coronary heart disease. The hostility complex, marked by anger and irritation at small things, is the component of the Type A behavior pattern most predictive of coronary heart disease. Hardiness, involving traits of commitment, control, and challenge, is related to physical health. The Type B personality, also related to physical health, is the opposite of the Type A.

7. How you appraise situations that are important for your well-being determine whether you will be affected by stress. Coping depends on your belief that you can control these situations. Control is related to improved mental and physical health. You develop an attributional style that determines whether you will attempt to cope, and if you do, how successful you will be.

8. Stress management techniques include muscle relaxation, guided imagery, hypnosis, meditation, and biofeedback. In muscle relaxation, you alternately contract and relax major muscle groups. With guided imagery, you imagine a pleasant scene. With hypnosis and meditation you reduce bodily arousal by focusing on something nonstressful. Biofeedback involves feeding back information about aspects of bodily functioning that usually are not noticed.

9. Illness prevention involves identifying psychological factors that place people at risk for developing illnesses and training them to modify their thoughts and behaviors. Health promotion involves the elimination of unhealthy habits and the adoption of a healthy lifestyle.

Questions for Discussion

1. What is the nature of stress?

2. What are the sources of stress?

3. What are the physical effects of stress?

4. How does stress affect people psychologically?

5. What is coping and how is it related to health and illness?

6. How are personality, health, and illness related?

7. How are cognitive factors related to health and illness?

8. What are some stress management techniques?

9. What are the factors related to illness prevention and health promotion?

Stress-inoculation training is a method designed to help people manage their stress. You learned in this chapter that stress-inoculation training involves three steps: cognitive preparation, skill acquisition, and application practice.

Think of a situation in the last few weeks that was stressful for you, especially one that you might encounter often, such as arguing with a friend, family member, or boss or taking an exam. Your job is to apply the stress-inoculation training model to your stressful situation. Remember that the first step is to mentally prepare for the stress. After you have done that, develop some specific stress-reduction methods. Now you are ready to apply your skills to a real-life situation.

Chapter 12

Abnormal Psychology and Therapy

After completing this chapter, you should be able to:

1. Summarize prescientific views of abnormal behavior.

2. List four definitions of abnormal behavior.

3. Identify the anxiety, somatoform, and dissociative disorders.

4. Distinguish between substance abuse and dependence.

5. Outline the mood disorders.

6. Describe the main features of schizophrenia.

7. Summarize the personality disorders.

8. Outline the psychotherapies for mental disorders.

9. Describe biological therapies for mental disorders.

In 1992 Jeffrey Dahmer was convicted by a Milwaukee court for the brutal murders and mutilation of 15 people. The chilling details of his crimes leave no doubt that Dahmer's behavior was abnormal. As one police officer put it, "He talks about killing people just as if it's like pouring a glass of water." In spite of the clear abnormality of Dahmer's behavior, however, he was not judged insane and was sentenced to life in prison instead where he was murdered by another inmate.

What does the word *abnormal* mean to you? Is it a term you would use to describe the extreme actions of Jeffrey Dahmer, the behavior of a person talking to imaginary people, or the drug use of a friend? Perhaps your idea of abnormal can be extended to that of a person who is always "down in the dumps," nervous, or simply unable to get his life together. In fact, all of these behaviors might be considered abnormal, depending on how you define the term.

In this chapter you will study the field of *abnormal psychology*—the scientific study of abnormal behavior and mental disorders. In reading this chapter you will discover how psychologists define abnormal behavior, learn that abnormal behavior may be classified as a mental disorder, and recognize that abnormal psychology is also concerned with therapies for mental disorders.

What Is Abnormal Behavior?

Though you probably know abnormal behavior when you see it, there is no definition of abnormal that is accepted by all psychologists. Furthermore, views of abnormal behavior have changed throughout history. In this section we trace definitions of abnormal behavior leading up to modern views.

Historical Views

Abnormal behavior is probably as old as the human race, and we know that since ancient times people have tried to understand and treat it. Before the scientific revolution, the most accepted views of abnormal behavior were based on the religious beliefs of each culture.

The dominant prescientific view was *supernaturalism*, the belief that behavior is controlled by gods, demons, spirits, and magic. Individuals who behaved abnormally were thought to be possessed by demons or evil spirits and, because of this, exorcisms, magic rituals, and witch hunts were often used to remove evil spirits. Supernaturalism still exists today in many cultures in which religious and magical healing rituals are used.

The late 1800s marked the beginning of *psychiatry*, a branch of medicine concerned with the diagnosis and treatment of mental disorders. Encouraged by findings that some psychological problems were due to brain infections and other physical disturbances, the early psychiatrists believed that abnormal behavior had biological causes and could be treated medically.

During this period, a psychological view of abnormal behavior also emerged. Psychologists and some psychiatrists, such as Freud, promoted the view that abnormal behavior was due to problems in thinking, emotions, learning, and personality. The late 1890s also saw the development of *clinical psychology*, which studies the causes and treatments of abnormal behavior. The views of psychiatry and clinical psychology were combined with other influences resulting in models of abnormal behavior that are still influential today. These models are described in Table 12.1.

Table 12.1 **Models of Abnormal Behavior**

Model	Assumed Causes of Abnormal Behavior
Behavioral	Faulty learning experiences
Biological	Biochemical, neurological, and genetic causes
Cognitive	Faulty patterns of thinking and problem solving
Humanistic	Problems in making choices, personal responsibility, and personal growth
Psychodynamic	Internal mental conflicts involving drives, emotions, and personality
Sociocultural	Social problems such as discrimination and poverty

The actions of serial killer Jeffrey Dahmer, shown here, represent an extreme example of abnormal behavior.

abnormal behavior— *behavior that is either uncommon, or violates social norms, or is distressing or maladaptive*

Modern Views

Today, normal and abnormal behavior are viewed in terms of levels of psychological adjustment. Imagine normality and abnormality as points on a yardstick. On one end you find extremely abnormal behaviors such as that of Jeffrey Dahmer. On the other there are normal behaviors, such as studying for an exam, going to work, or helping a friend solve a personal problem. Between those two points are numerous behaviors that are not clearly normal or abnormal. Thus, the boundaries between normal and abnormal are not absolute. Instead, how normal and abnormal are defined depends on where you set the boundaries. There are four main definitions of **abnormal behavior**:

1. Abnormal behavior is a statistical deviation.

2. Abnormal behavior is a violation of social norms.

3. Abnormal behavior is maladaptive behavior.

4. Abnormal behavior causes personal distress.

According to the *statistical deviation* definition, abnormal behavior is rare or uncommon. Can you paint like Rembrandt, play basketball like Shaquille O'Neill, or perform on stage like Madonna? Don't feel bad if you cannot—

few people can. Because their behavior is statistically rare, it would be considered abnormal according to this definition. But do you think it is reasonable to equate unusual talent with abnormality? Most psychologists do not.

Abnormal behavior can also be defined as a violation of *social norms*—a society's rules of conduct. Though your behavior falls outside the social norm, it is not necessarily abnormal. For example, you may not be in the habit of eating insects, but in some countries, you would violate the social norm if you did not! You can see that, because they vary from culture to culture, social norms cannot be used as exclusive ways of defining abnormality. You might be amazed that even though Dahmer's behavior would be considered abnormal according to this standard, he was not judged legally insane (see *Issues and Applications: Insanity and the Law*).

Issues and Applications

Insanity and the Law

You are watching the news on television, reading a newspaper or magazine, or listening to the radio and you find out about a terrible crime to which the accused pleads not guilty by reason of insanity. Remarkably, despite the judgment that the behavior was clearly abnormal, you learn that the defendant was not ruled insane. You probably shake your head and mumble to yourself, "How can they say that this guy is not insane?" The answer to this question lies in the fact that legal definitions of insanity are not based on science or on the views of the general public.

Legal insanity depends on judgments about the person's mental state at the time of the crime. According to the *M'Naughten rule*, a person is insane if at the time of the crime the individual suffered from a mental defect so that he or she could not understand the nature of the act or could not tell right from wrong. Another standard is the *ALI*, or *Brawner, rule* proposed by the American Law Institute. Like the M'Naughten rule, the ALI rule states that a person is insane if he could not understand the wrongfulness of the crime or could not control himself by reason of a mental disease. The ALI rule adds, however, that committing a crime is not in itself proof of a mental disease. One problem with both the M'Naughten and ALI rules is that the psychologist or psychiatrist must determine in the present what a person's mental state was at some time in the past. That is a tall order!

Because psychologists are often asked to give expert testimony about insanity, the American Psychological Association (APA) has taken a position on the insanity defense. The APA contends that there is not enough scientific evidence to prove that psychologists can judge a person's mental state as the law requires.[1] Though you might think that the insanity defense is common, it is actually used in fewer than 2 percent of murder trials and it is rarely successful, as in Dahmer's case.[1] The legal view of insanity just goes to show that there is no universal definition of abnormality.

Chapter 12 • Abnormal Psychology and Therapy

Many psychologists contend that it is most useful to define abnormal as *maladaptive behavior*, that is, behavior that interferes with your ability to meet or cope with everyday responsibilities such as school, work, and relationships. Even if you have some problems in dealing with everyday responsibilities, your behavior is maladaptive only if you fail to successfully cope with them.

Finally, abnormal behavior is that which causes you *personal distress*. If you experience guilt, shame, anxiety, fear, or other unpleasant emotions as a result of your actions or thoughts, then your behavior is abnormal according to this standard. Personal distress is not always a reliable gauge of abnormality, however, because some individuals do not experience painful emotions no matter how they behave. Consider Dahmer's cold unemotional reaction to killing. Furthermore, many painful emotions that you might experience are normal reactions to life events such the death of a loved one or a low grade in an exam.

In conclusion, you should remember that there are several ways to define abnormality and that none of them is totally satisfactory. These definitions should be used as imperfect guidelines that can be used to observe and evaluate behavior.

Abnormal Behavior and Mental Disorders

▼
mental disorder—abnormal behavior associated with suffering, pain, death, or disability

Besides defining abnormal behavior, psychology and psychiatry have also contributed to its classification. When abnormal behavior is associated with suffering, pain, death, or disability, it is known as a **mental disorder**.[2] On the basis of this definition, it has been estimated that approximately 32 percent of Americans will suffer from a mental disorder in their lifetimes.[3] (See Figure 12.1.)

▼
Diagnostic and Statistical Manual of Mental Disorders-Fourth Edition—a system for classifying mental disorders

Today, the most popular system for classifying mental disorders is the **Diagnostic and Statistical Manual of Mental Disorders–Fourth Edition** (DSM-IV), proposed by the American Psychiatric Association.[2] The DSM-IV is a descriptive diagnostic system, meaning that it classifies mental disorders, not people, according to their predominant abnormal behaviors. In this section you will learn about some of the major mental disorders.

Anxiety, Somatoform, and Dissociative Disorders

The anxiety, somatoform, and dissociative disorders are a group of conditions formerly called *neuroses*, a term used by Freud to indicate a mental disorder caused by repressed childhood conflicts. In the DSM-IV, they represent distinct categories.

Anxiety Disorders.
The *anxiety disorders* are one of the most common types of mental disorder in the United States today and are especially prevalent in women. In fact, the chances that you will have an

Figure 12.1 **The Prevalence of Mental Disorders in the United States**

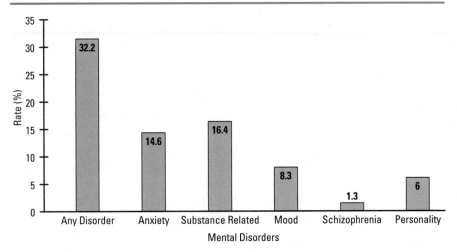

The percentage of the U.S. population, 18 years of age and older, that suffer from mental disorders. These estimates are pased on 18,571 individuals from five cities: New Haven, CT; Baltimore, MD; St. Louis, MO; Durham, NC; and Los Angeles, CA.

Source: Reiger, D.A., et al. (1988) "One month prevalence of mental disorders in the United States" *Archives* of *General Psychiatry, 45*, p. 977-993

anxiety disorder at some time in your life is approximately 15 percent.[3] Worry, fear, apprehension, tension, and physiological arousal are common experiences of anxiety, but the mere presence of anxiety does not mean that you have an anxiety disorder. You have an **anxiety disorder** only if your anxiety and related thoughts, feelings, and behaviors interfere with your normal functioning. You have already learned about one type of anxiety disorder, *posttraumatic stress disorder* in Chapter 11. Other anxiety disorders include generalized anxiety disorder, panic disorders, phobias, and obsessive-compulsive disorder.

The most common anxiety disorder is **generalized anxiety disorder** (GAD) in which there is excessive worry about several things such as finances, school, or work performance. Individuals with GAD are tense, restless, and keyed up much of the time. They have trouble concentrating and have difficulty falling and staying asleep.

Panic disorders are marked by frequent and unexpected *panic attacks*, which usually reach their peak in about 10 minutes. During the panic attack, you may break out into a sweat, tremble, and feel chest pains, heart palpitations (irregular heartbeats), and nausea. Many individuals feel faint, have sensations of choking, and think they are going to lose control, go crazy, or die. Fortunately, the symptoms of panic are not as dangerous as they feel.

If you know someone with a **phobia disorder**, you recognize that the person has excessive and unreasonable fears and is strongly motivated to avoid a certain type of object, activity, or situation. Some phobic individuals are afraid of a specific type of object or activity, such as animals, blood, flying or heights. Others suffer from *agoraphobia*, the fear of being in

anxiety disorder—a mental disorder involving anxiety and related thoughts, feelings, and behaviors that interfere with normal functioning

generalized anxiety disorder—an anxiety disorder involving excessive worry about several things

panic disorders—an anxiety disorder marked by frequent, unexpected panic attacks

phobia disorder—an anxiety disorder involving excessive and unreasonable fears and avoidance

situations or places from which the person believes that escape might be difficult or embarrassing. Agoraphobic individuals have difficulty leaving their home, traveling, or being in crowded places without company. Individuals suffering from *social anxiety disorder* (social phobia) have an intense fear of situations in which they are exposed to unfamiliar people or possible evaluation by others. Because they are afraid of being embarrassed and rejected, people with social phobia have difficulty speaking around others, eating in public, or using public restrooms. It is obvious that social anxiety disorder can seriously affect your social functioning.

Either obsessions or compulsions are the main features of **obsessive-compulsive disorder** (OCD). An *obsession* is a recurrent thought, impulse, or image that causes anxiety such as the impulse to harm someone or the thought that you will catch a germ and spread it to your family. A *compulsion* is a behavior or ritual that is performed over and over and in the same way each time. Common compulsions include checking, washing, counting, and touching.

> "Keith was plagued by several obsessions. One thought that popped into his head hundreds of times a day was that his tears were dirty. Anxiety-provoking as it was, Keith was able to deal with his obsession for a while, but eventually he couldn't resist the urge to cleanse his tears by repeatedly pouring scalding water on his face (author's file, Perrotto)."

Both biological and psychological factors cause anxiety disorders. A higher than average rate of anxiety disorders among close relatives of the affected person suggests that there is an inherited tendency toward developing an anxiety disorder. Abnormal functioning of neurotransmitters such as GABA, norepinephrine, and serotonin also indicate a biological basis for anxiety disorders.

Experiences in childhood and adolescence are involved in the development of anxiety disorders, too. Psychodynamic psychologists view anxiety as an indication of repressed childhood conflict. According to behaviorists, anxiety and avoidance are the result of maladaptive learning. You may recall that Little Albert, discussed in Chapter 5, was conditioned to fear white rats. Because avoiding the situation reduces your anxiety, your avoidance is reinforced.

Somatoform Disorders.

A physical symptom that suggests a physical disorder for which no medical basis can be found is the essential feature of a **somatoform disorder**. Two of the best known somatoform disorders are conversion disorder and hypochondriasis. **Conversion disorder** involves one or more symptoms usually affecting voluntary movement or sensory function. For example, a person with conversion disorder might be unable to move a limb or to speak or may experience periods of deafness or blindness. In **hypochondriasis** there is excessive fear of having a serious illness because the person misinterprets bodily symptoms. For instance, the hypochondriac might misinterpret a simple tension headache as a sign of a brain tumor.

---

obsessive-compulsive disorder—an anxiety disorder involving obsessions or compulsions

somatoform (soh-matt-oh-form) disorders—mental disorders in which a physical symptom suggests a physical disorder for which no medical basis can be found.

conversion disorder—a somatoform disorder that involves symptoms affecting voluntary movement or sensory function

hypochondriasis (hi-poh-konn-dry-uh-sis)—a somatoform disorder involving an excessive fear of having a serious illness

Very little is known about the causes of somatoform disorders. The most influential views have been psychodynamic theories that explain somatoform disorders in terms of repressed conflicts that arise in the form of physical disability.

Dissociative Disorders. *Dissociation* is a mental state in which aspects of your mind are "split off" from consciousness. In **dissociative disorders**, a sudden alteration of consciousness, memory, or identity causes serious disturbances in the person's functioning.

The most serious and fascinating dissociative disorder is **dissociative identity disorder** (formerly called *multiple personality disorder*) characterized by two or more distinct identities or personalities. Usually, each personality has little or no knowledge of the other personalities so that the person may have no memory of what he did for hours or days at a time. Once considered rare, dissociative identity disorder is now believed to be far more prevalent than previously thought, especially among adults who were victims of childhood physical and sexual abuse.[4]

▼
dissociative disorders—mental disorders involving a sudden alteration of consciousness, memory, or identity

▼
dissociative identity disorder—a dissociative disorder characterized by two or more distinct personalities

People with dissociative identity disorder have two or more distinct personalities. Chris Sizemore, the real "Eve" in The Three Faces of Eve, exhibited 22 different personalities.

"Sexually abused as a child by her older sister and father, Dara developed four distinct personalities to cope with her trauma. One personality was homicidal and suicidal. Another was sexually promiscuous. A third personality was addicted to heroin and hated sex, and the fourth was an ordinary, caring person who just went to work and came home at night. Needless to say, Dara's life was in disarray because she would switch personalities suddenly and had no recollection of her behavior (author's file, Perrotto)."

Substance-Related Disorders

The use of drugs for medicinal, spiritual, and recreational purposes is nothing new. You learned in Chapter 4 that people have used psychoactive drugs at least since the beginning of recorded history. You also learned that most adults and teenagers have used a drug for nonmedical purposes at least once. Does this mean that most people have a drug problem? Definitely not. Experts estimate that approximately 19 percent of people in the United States have a significant drug problem and that two-thirds of them involve alcohol.[5] Drug problems are more commonly diagnosed in men than in women.

The diagnosis of a **substance-related disorder** in the DSM-IV requires a maladaptive pattern of drug use leading to distress or significant impairment of everyday functioning. The repeated abuse of drugs in *substance abuse* results in a failure to meet major obligations at work, school, and in relationships. The person's work performance may decline, he or she may be excessively absent from school, and may argue with family members or friends. Worse, the individual might continue to use drugs in situations in which doing so is physically hazardous—for example driving or operating a machine while intoxicated. Repeated drug-related legal problems, such as being arrested for disorderly conduct, stealing, or possession of drugs are also typical consequences of substance abuse.

Sadly, many individuals who abuse drugs eventually cross over the line into a condition of *substance dependence*, popularly known as *addiction*. The two outstanding indications of substance dependence are tolerance and withdrawal. If the person needs increasingly larger amounts of the drug to get the desired effects or gets a reduced effect from the same amount of the drug, that person shows drug tolerance. Once the individual develops a tolerance and stops using the drug, he or she may experience unpleasant psychological and physical reactions called drug withdrawal. If you ever saw someone guzzle a drink to stop the "shakes," you have witnessed withdrawal. Other signs of substance dependence include taking more of the drug than intended, an inability to cut down or stop using the drug, and spending much time trying to get the drug.

*"**A**fter several months of using heroin, Robert needed more of it to get high. Depending on the quality of the heroin, he would get itchy all over, feel aches and pains, and become agitated 6-8 hours after his last injection. Emotionally, he felt miserable. Though he would resist at first, Robert's withdrawal symptoms eventually led him to use more heroin. These facts made it clear that Robert's substance abuse had escalated into substance dependence (author's file, Perrotto)."*

Most of the research on the causes of substance-related disorders has been with alcoholism. Evidently, alcoholism has a modest hereditary basis, especially for males. The most convincing proof comes from adoption studies in which children of alcoholic parents have a higher than average rate of alcoholism even when they are raised by adoptive, nonalcoholic parents.[6,7] Psychological factors are involved as well. Though no distinct *addictive* or *alcoholic personality* has been found, childhood aggressiveness, rebelliousness, antisocial behavior, and poor impulse control are fairly good predictors of substance-related disorders later in life. Peer pressure, family problems, poverty, unemployment, and other social stressors are also associated with an increased risk of developing a substance-related disorder.[8]

Mood Disorders

Mood is a term you use to describe your feelings at some point in time. Your mood normally varies from situation to situation. In general, you are happy when you gain something, such as money or a good grade, and you are sad when you lose something, such as a friend or a job, or fail at something. Those mood variations are quite normal. Some people, however, show mood disturbances that affect their everyday functioning. Their moods are excessively high or low for too long a period of time. In these cases the person is in the throes of a **mood disorder**, defined by episodes of depression or mania or an alternation of the two.

Depression is the most common type of mood disturbance. It affects about 15 percent of Americans.[3] Because it is so prevalent, chances are that you or someone you know has experienced depression at some time. One of the most severe forms of depression is called **major depressive disorder**, marked by one or more major depressive episodes. During the episode, the person feels sad and loses interest in most things. He feels worthless and guilty, has trouble concentrating, and may consider suicide. Many depressed people experience appetite problems, sleep disturbances, and fatigue as well.

Some people have **bipolar disorder**, formerly called manic depression, in which their mood alternates between periods of depression and an abnormal mood elevation. During the abnormal mood elevation, called a *manic episode*, the individual feels great, does not require much sleep, talks too much, and is easily distracted. He will also get involved in a variety of activities and may impulsively start business ventures that are doomed to failure because they were poorly planned. Manic individuals are risk takers; they often abuse drugs, drive recklessly, or go on uncontrolled sex sprees.

"During his most recent manic episode, Joe started an auto repair business and a taxi service to go along with his full-time job. At first, things went well because Joe did not need much sleep, but it wasn't long before his energy reservoir dried up. Within a few weeks, his businesses failed and he lost his regular job because he was too fatigued to get to work on time. (author's file, Perotto)"

On the positive side, however, bipolar disorder has been associated with creativity. Many creative people, including author Edgar Allan Poe and painter Vincent van Gogh, were believed to have suffered from bipolar disorder, which may have contributed to their artistic creativity.

The fact that mood disorders, especially bipolar disorder, run in families suggests a hereditary basis. Having a close relative with bipolar disorder increases your chances of having it by a factor of nearly six.[9] One popular

▼
mood disorder—a mental disorder involving episodes of depression or mania, or an alternation of the two

▼
major depressive disorder—a mood disorder marked by major depressive episodes

▼
bipolar disorder—a mood disorder in which mood alternates between periods of depression and mania

It is thought that many creative individuals, including Edgar Allen Poe, shown here, suffered from bipolar disorder.

biochemical explanation, the *catecholamine hypothesis* states that depression and mania are due to abnormal functioning of the neurotransmitter norepinephrine.[10] Abnormalities in serotonin and other neurotransmitters are apparently involved in causing mood disorders as well.

One prominent psychological explanation for mood disorders is the cognitive theory of psychiatrist Aaron Beck. According to this view, depression is caused by faulty thinking, especially the expectation of failure.[11] When you expect to fail you develop a distorted view of yourself and your abilities, which ensures failure and leads to depression. Many psychologists view depression in terms of *learned helplessness*, which you learned about in Chapter 11.[12] According to this view, you become depressed when you believe that you are unable to control what happens to you.

Schizophrenia

When a person cannot distinguish between reality and fantasy, he or she is suffering from a *psychosis*. One type of psychosis is **schizophrenia**, marked by severe problems in judgment and reasoning, emotions, perceptions, and behavior. Afflicting nearly 1 percent of Americans, schizophrenia causes great impairment in its victims because it affects all aspects of their mental life.[2]

Schizophrenics have a *thought disorder*, meaning that their judgment and reasoning abilities are disturbed. If you were to listen to the speech of a schizophrenic, you would notice that it does not make much sense. These confused and incoherent thoughts are called *loose associations*. Schizophrenic individuals also show their disturbed thinking in *delusions*, false beliefs that the person maintains in the absence of any evidence for them.

"**J**oan told her therapist that she was kidnapped by the police, who placed tiny transmitters under her skin. Then the signals were sent to hummingbirds and bumble bees, who relayed the messages back to the police. In this way, she believed, the police always knew what she was thinking (author's file, Perrotto)."

Schizophrenics have severe perceptual disturbances, such as *hallucinations*, that are false perceptions without a basis in reality. Because the schizophrenic is out of touch with reality, he or she often acts on the hallucinations. For example in 1977 the "Son of Sam," David Berkowitz, followed commands from his neighbor's dog to shoot people. Auditory hallucinations (hearing voices) are the most common. Many experts have proposed that auditory hallucinations are perceptions that schizophrenics do not recognize as their own thoughts. It is as if the person were silently talking to her or himself. This notion has been supported by recent findings that show that during a hallucination, areas of the left hemisphere involved in speaking are activated.[13] Though commands to kill or hurt people do occur and are commonly portrayed in the movies and other media, most schizophrenics are not violent, and the voices usually provide an insulting commentary or command them to do something ridiculous.

"Gary believed that God sent him commands through radio receivers implanted in the fillings in his teeth. One day God told Gary to stand outside the United Nations building to offer solutions for world peace. Because Gary truly believed that the command came from God, he obeyed (author's file, Culkin)."

Many schizophrenics lack normal emotional expression. Sometimes their emotions are flat or blunted, meaning that they are unemotional in situations in which most people would be emotionally expressive. At other times, they exhibit strong emotions for no apparent reason. And at other times, they express inappropriate emotions. For example, rather than cry upon hearing of the death of a friend, the schizophrenic might laugh. In general, schizophrenics have motivational problems as well. They lack interest in most things and are unable to muster the motivation to reach whatever goals they may have set. Schizophrenic individuals show disturbed behavior. They are usually withdrawn and socially isolated and spend a lot of time muttering to themselves. Some show weird, purposeless behaviors such as walking in circles or holding a strange posture for long periods of time.

No two schizophrenics display the same symptoms exactly; there are variations from person to person that reflect the different types of schizophrenia outlined in Table 12.2.

Table 12.2 **Types of Schizophrenia**

Type	Main Features
Catatonic	Movement disturbances such as stupor, excitement, and negativism (the refusal to move)
Disorganized	Incoherent speech, loose associations, irrational thinking, disorganized behavior
Paranoid	Delusions and hallucinations that reflect fears of being harmed or controlled and beliefs of having extraordinary abilities
Undifferentiated	Mixture of symptoms that do not fit the other types

Though many psychological explanations have been proposed, most experts think that schizophrenia is a biological disorder. As do the mood disorders, schizophrenia appears to have a strong hereditary basis. One of the most unusual and unfortunate examples comes from the Genains, four genetically identical sisters who were diagnosed as schizophrenic in the 1950s. Apparently, the hereditary source of their schizophrenia was Mr. Genain, who had paranoid symptoms, severe emotional disturbances, and drank excessively. Mr. Genain's mother had been hospitalized for a "nervous breakdown," and other relatives had psychological problems.[14]

Abnormal neurotransmitter activity is involved in schizophrenia as well. According to the *dopamine hypothesis*, schizophrenia is caused by abnormal dopamine activity in the brain.[15] Dopamine activity does not tell the whole story, however, because many schizophrenics have brain damage

The Genain sisters were genetically identical quadruplets, each of whom was diagnosed with schizophrenia. Their case is often cited in support of a hereditary basis for schizophrenia.

involving the frontal lobes and areas of the limbic system (see color plate 12.1). An integrated view is the *diathesis-stress hypothesis*, which holds that schizophrenia is caused by a combination of genetic factors (diathesis) and environmental stress such as poverty, urban crowding, and prenatal exposure to viral infection.[16]

Personality Disorders

personality disorder— mental disorder characterized by maladaptive, inflexible, and distressing personality traits

A mental disorder characterized by maladaptive, inflexible, and distressing personality traits is a **personality disorder**. Because these personality traits are viewed as "the way I am" rather than a problem that needs a remedy, people with personality disorders get themselves in trouble over and over again. Nowhere is this tendency more apparent than in their interpersonal relationships. People with personality disorders have great difficulty relating to other people, including friends, spouses, and bosses. Furthermore, personality disorders are strongly associated with other mental disorders such as anxiety, substance-related, mood, and psychotic disorders.[17]

paranoid personality disorder— a disorder with maladaptive traits of distrust, suspiciousness, fear, and jealousy

The DSM-IV categorizes personality disorders into three main types: eccentric, dramatic, and anxious. *Eccentric* disorders are identified by odd or withdrawn behavior. An example is **paranoid personality disorder**, in which the individual displays maladaptive traits of distrust, suspiciousness, fear, and jealousy. Individuals with this disorder do not trust people and are suspicious of their motives. They are afraid to confide in others for fear that they will be betrayed. Paranoid people are extremely jealous as well. For example, a police officer with paranoid personality disorder routinely checked his wife's undergarments for "evidence" that she had slept with another man (author's file, Perrotto). Unlike paranoid schizophrenics, however, people with paranoid personality disorder do not experience delusions and hallucinations.

The *dramatic disorders* are defined by dramatic, emotional, or erratic behavior. The most widely studied personality disorder is **antisocial personality disorder**, characterized by a history of antisocial behavior such as lying, fighting, stealing, delinquency, and cruelty. People with this mental disorder have little regard for the rights, feelings, or property of others, and they coldly manipulate or harm others without showing any remorse or shame for their deeds. As you might suspect, people with antisocial personality disorder engage in criminal behavior, drug abuse, and violence. Serial killers, like Jeffrey Dahmer, or Joel Rifkin, are often portrayed as *psychopaths*, people with an extreme form of antisocial personality disorder.

Unstable mood, self-image, and relationships as well as impulsive, self-defeating behavior define the **borderline personality disorder**. People with this condition move between the extremes of emotion. One minute they seem unusually happy, and the next they may be depressed or angry. Their depression or anger often triggers impulsive behaviors such as drug abuse, binge eating, suicide attempts, or unrestrained sexual activity. Borderline individuals are confused about who they are and show uncertainty about their goals, attitudes, and values. For example, in the span of four therapy sessions Rhonda, a 40-year-old woman, told her therapist that she wanted to go to law school, become a computer programmer, and become a manicurist. A week later she had abandoned all of her ideas (author's file, Perrotto). Disturbed interpersonal relationships are the rule for individuals with borderline personality disorder because they are needy people who go back and forth between feelings of intense love and hate.

The *anxious* disorders involve anxious, fearful, or inhibited behavior. The most common anxious disorder among psychiatric patients is **dependent personality disorder**, marked by excessive dependency on others and an inability to make important decisions.

> "**M**ark was a 30-year-old college graduate who was working as a low-paid clerical worker when he entered therapy. He rarely complained at work even though he was never given responsibilities he knew he could handle. Because he feared that she would divorce him and her father would withhold his financial support, Mark rarely challenged his wife, who told him how to spend his money, what clothes to wear, and which TV programs to watch. Mark's therapy ended when his wife commanded him to stop seeing his therapist (author's file, Perrotto)."

Table 12.3 summarizes the types of mental disorders.

antisocial personality disorder—a disorder characterized by antisocial behavior

borderline personality disorder—a disorder marked by unstable mood, self-image, and relationships as well as impulsive, self-defeating behavior

dependent personality disorder—a disorder marked by excessive dependency on others and an inability to make important decisions

Table 12.3 Types of Mental Disorders

Mental Disorder	Main Features
Anxiety disorders	Overwhelming anxiety and related thoughts, feelings, and behaviors that interfere with normal functioning
Somatoform disorders	Physical symptoms that suggest a physical disorder but for which no medical basis can be found

Table 12.3 **Types of Mental Disorders** (continued)

Mental Disorder	Main Features
Dissociative disorders	Alteration of consciousness, identity, or memory
Substance-related disorders	Maladaptive pattern of drug use
Mood disorders	Episodes of mania or depression or an alternation of the two
Schizophrenia	Severe problems in judgment, reasoning, emotions, perceptions, and behavior
Personality disorders	Maladaptive, inflexible, and distressing personality traits

*T*reatments for Mental Disorders

Treatments for mental disorders have come a long way since the crude and inhumane treatments of the past. Mental health professionals today have many techniques at their disposal to help individuals relieve their symptoms and function better in their everyday lives. The prevention of mental disorders is also a concern of psychologists. (See *Issues and Applications, The Prevention and Treatment of Mental Disorders in the Workplace*.) In this section you will learn about some of the psychological and biological therapies used in clinical practice today.

Issues and Applications

The Prevention and Treatment of Mental Disorders in the Workplace

Consider these facts:

▶ Mental disorders are most common during the prime working years of 25 to 44.

▶ Nearly 1 in 10 U.S. workers is suffering from depression, at a cost to business of $27 billion a year.

▶ Mental disorders are the most common reason for disability among people who receive disability benefits.

▶ Mental disorders have accounted for a dramatic increase in Worker's Compensation payments since 1980. By the year 2000, they are expected to reach $90 billion.

▶ The cost of mental disorders in terms of treatment, employment, and productivity has been estimated at between $50 and $100 billion.[18]

Psychological Therapies

One approach to the treatment of mental disorders that is based on psychological principles and methods is known as **psychotherapy**. Psychotherapy comes in many forms. Some forms are designed to deal directly with the individual's problems in thinking, emotions, and behavior. In other cases, psychotherapy tries to remedy problems by altering the interpersonal basis of abnormal behavior. Such therapies are conducted with couples, families, or groups. The major psychotherapies are the focus of this section.

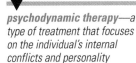

psychotherapy—the treatment of mental disorders based on psychological principles and methods

Psychodynamic Therapy.

A type of treatment that focuses on the individual's internal conflicts and personality is called **psychodynamic therapy**. In general, psychodynamic therapy is a long-term, intensive process in which repressed childhood memories and conflicts are uncovered. By gaining insight into his or her conflicts, the individual learns to work through them, leading to a more adult, stable personality and better functioning in everyday life.

psychodynamic therapy—a type of treatment that focuses on the individual's internal conflicts and personality

The original psychodynamic therapy was *psychoanalysis*, pioneered by Sigmund Freud and his colleague Josef Breuer (1842–1925). The cornerstones of psychoanalytic technique are the "golden rule" of *free association* and the "royal road to the unconscious," *dream interpretation*. If you were in psychoanalysis, your analyst would ask you to lie on a couch and free associate, that is, say whatever came into your mind no matter how silly, unpleasant, or irrelevant you thought it was. You would also be asked to

---

These sobering statistics should convince you that mental disorders represent a serious health problem that can affect not only your social and academic life, but your ability to work too. In response to these facts, psychologists and other health professionals have labored to find solutions. One promising solution is prevention. *Primary prevention* concerns measures designed to eliminate or reduce mental health risks in the workplace. *Secondary prevention* involves teaching workers new skills that they can use to deal with unavoidable problems in the workplace. When primary and secondary prevention fail, psychological therapy can be used to alleviate suffering. This stage is known as *tertiary prevention*. Though primary prevention is the most desirable, workers usually begin at the stage of secondary prevention.[19]

The treatment of mental disorders in the workplace has been accomplished through Employee Assistance Programs (EAPs). Originally, EAPs were designed to offer tertiary prevention for problem drinkers, but more recently, EAPs have expanded to cover a variety of mental disorders and have moved slowly toward primary prevention.[20]

Psychoanalysis, the original psychodynamic therapy, was pioneered by Sigmund Freud and his colleague, Josef Brewer, pictured here.

▼

behavior therapy—an approach to treatment based on the application of learning principles

report your dreams. From this raw material the analyst would interpret your communications as reflections of your repressed childhood conflicts.

While free associating or reporting a dream, you may show *resistance*— the inability or unwillingness to talk about certain memories for defensive reasons. For example, in the midst of recalling a painful childhood experience you might want to change the topic. As you got in touch with your past you might also shift feelings, anger or disappointment, perhaps, about a parent onto your analyst in a process called *transference*. By analyzing your resistance and transference, the analyst would discover the unconscious sources of your present difficulties and help you work through them.

Since Freud, psychodynamic therapy has been revised in many ways. One important revision has been to make the therapy much shorter in duration. By directly confronting the person's defenses and provoking strong emotional reactions, the analyst can sometimes cut to the core of a problem more rapidly.

Behavior Therapy. **Behavior therapy** is an approach to the treatment of abnormal behavior based on the application of learning principles described in Chapter 5. Instead of searching for the unconscious sources of your problems, behavior therapy attempts to replace maladaptive behaviors with more adaptive ones. Behavior therapy includes exposure therapy, aversion therapy, reinforcement techniques, and modeling.[21]

Exposure therapy refers to procedures to extinguish maladaptive behaviors by exposing the individual to feared stimuli. One procedure based on classical conditioning is *systematic desensitization*, developed by psychiatrist Joseph Wolpe in the 1950s for the treatment of phobias and other anxiety problems. While relaxed, the person is asked to imagine or is actually exposed to stimuli that provoke anxiety. The level or intensity of exposure is gradually increased until the anxiety is reduced. The stimuli that provoke the least anxiety are presented first, followed by those that elicit the most anxiety. By contrast, *flooding* involves direct exposure to intensely frightening stimuli until fear reactions are reduced. The distinction between systematic desensitization and flooding is like the difference between overcoming your fear of water by slowly moving from shallow to deeper water and jumping into the deep end immediately.

You may recall from Chapter 5 that you can be conditioned to have unpleasant emotional reactions to stimuli or situations. In *aversion therapy*, maladaptive behavior is eliminated by associating it with something painful or unpleasant such as an electrical shock or a nausea-producing chemical. Aversion therapy has been used with some success for the control of dangerous or undesirable habits such as substance abuse, self-mutilation, nailbiting, and pulling out hair. In aversion therapy for alcohol problems, the person drinks an alcoholic beverage containing a chemical that makes him vomit, while focusing on the visual, taste, smell, and tactile qualities of the drink. By associating the sensory qualities of the drink with nausea and vomiting, the person will, it is hoped, become averse to drinking.

In contrast to exposure and aversion procedures, which are designed to extinguish undesirable behaviors, *reinforcement techniques* are used to strengthen desirable behaviors. For example, *shaping* can be used to encourage depressed or schizophrenic individuals to socialize and communicate better. Also, shaping is often an important component of treatment for anxiety disorders. By being rewarded for approaching situations they fear, phobic individuals can learn to overcome their problem. Reinforcement can help individuals learn basic skills, too. For instance, many psychiatric hospitals use structured reinforcement programs to help schizophrenics with self-care, such as good personal hygiene, and social skills, such as asserting oneself in social situations. Reinforcement techniques are also helpful in teaching assertive behavior to people with dependent personality disorder and in helping borderline individuals control their impulsive behavior.

Based on social learning theory, *modeling* involves learning more effective behavior by observing the adaptive behavior of others—therapists, family members, or friends, for example. Modeling techniques have been used successfully in the treatment of many problems including anxiety, phobias, depression, and interpersonal problems.

Cognitive Therapy.

If you consulted a cognitive therapist about a problem, she would tell you that your difficulties stem from the way you think. **Cognitive therapy** refers to procedures used to correct the faulty beliefs and thought patterns responsible for abnormal behavior. Two important cognitive approaches to treatment are psychologist Albert Ellis's rational-emotive therapy and psychiatrist Aaron Beck's cognitive therapy.

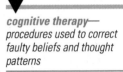

cognitive therapy—procedures used to correct faulty beliefs and thought patterns

In *rational-emotive therapy* (RET) the individual learns to identify, confront, and eliminate irrational thoughts.[22] Do you believe that:

► You must be perfect in everything you do?

► It is horrible when things do not go the way you'd like them to?

► Your misery is caused by outside forces such as people and events?

► If something is dangerous you should be terribly upset by it?

► You ought to avoid rather than face problems?

► You should be loved by everyone?

If you answered yes to most of these questions you would have irrational thoughts, according to Ellis. If you went into RET you would be taught to identify such irrational beliefs and to face their irrationality. Then you would be taught how to change those beliefs through logical persuasion and argument. In short, RET helps distressed individuals look at themselves more realistically by removing the "shoulds," "oughts," and "musts" from their thinking.

Like Ellis, Beck believes that emotional problems are related to faulty thinking. Unpleasant emotions do not come from events, but rather from negative thoughts that automatically pop into your head when you are in particular situations.[11] In cognitive therapy you are taught to identify the negative automatic thoughts and to ask yourself, "What is the evidence for these beliefs? What are their consequences? Are there other ways to interpret the situation?" The following hypothetical dialogue illustrates negative thinking and how the cognitive therapist helps to change it by challenging the irrational thoughts.

Client: **I'm fed up. Everything I do ends in failure.**

Therapist: **Everything?**

Client: **Yeah. Everything.**

Therapist: **Last week you told me that your boss complimented you on your performance and that you are being considered for a promotion. I would hardly call that failure.**

Client: **Well I guess you're right but...**

Therapist: **But what? Either everything is a failure or it isn't. I realize that your recent problems have had an impact on you, but perhaps you are focusing too much on the negative and minimizing your accomplishments."**

Beck's cognitive therapy was originally designed for the treatment of depression, but has since been applied to anxiety disorders, personality disorders, and many other abnormal behaviors.

Client-Centered Therapy.

In Chapter 10, you learned about Carl Rogers's *self theory*. He also developed an important type of psychotherapy. Rogers's **client-centered therapy** (also called *person-centered therapy*) involves the therapist's attitudes of unconditional positive regard, empathy (being in touch with the feelings of others), and honesty to help clients accept themselves. Rather than give advice and direction or probe your unconscious conflicts, client-centered therapists let individuals explore their current feelings and values and make their own decisions about how to behave. In client-centered therapy, you would talk about your problems while the therapist listened carefully. The therapist would not challenge or criticize your feelings. Instead she would restate them in a way that would show that she respects, understands, and cares for you as a person. In this way, you would eventually become more congruent, that is, come to accept yourself for who you are.[23]

▼
client-centered therapy—a type of psychotherapy that uses the therapist's attitudes of unconditional positive regard and empathy to help clients accept themselves

Group, Family, and Couples Therapy.

Over the years, psychotherapy has expanded to include approaches that involve more than one person at a time. Group, family, and couples therapy focus on identifying and resolving the interpersonal conflicts that give rise to individual problems and dissatisfactions.

Group therapy involves a small group of individuals who get together to discuss their problems under the guidance of a group leader. Some groups have a particular focus such as alcoholism, depression, or schizophrenia; others emphasize a life issue such as assertiveness, personal growth, or women's issues.

Biography: Carl Rogers

For his contributions to personality theory, psychotherapy, and psychology in general, Carl Rogers (1902–1987) is truly one of the most important figures in the history of psychology. In the 1940s, Rogers was accused of "destroying the unity of psychoanalysis" because he developed a completely new method of psychotherapy. Thanks to his pioneering efforts, we have many forms of psychotherapy today.

Rogers was born in Illinois as the middle child in a large, close-knit, religious family. Growing up in the suburbs and then on a farm, Rogers never drank, smoked, danced, played cards, went to the movies, or showed any sexual interest. Rogers's interest in science—the study of moths—led him to the University of Wisconsin, but as a sophomore his interests turned to religion. He entered the Union Theological Seminary in New York City where he prepared to become a minister. His concern for people eventually influenced him to transfer to Teachers College of Columbia University, where he received his doctorate in clinical and educational psychology in 1931. Working at universities and guidance clinics thereafter, Rogers formed his self theory of personality and client-centered therapy. In 1964 he moved to California where he began to work with normal individuals struggling to improve their human relations. In 1968 Rogers and some colleagues formed the Center for the Studies of the Person in La Jolla.

Carl Rogers received many honors, including the American Psychological Association's (APA) awards for Distinguished Scientific Contribution and Distinguished Professional Contribution. He also served as the president of the APA in 1946 and 1947. He authored many books, including *Counseling and Psychotherapy* (1942), *Client-Centered Therapy* (1951), and *On Becoming a Person* (1961).[24,25,26]

Family therapy is designed to uncover and change the maladaptive family relationships that cause abnormal behavior in family members. Regardless of which family member is expressing abnormal behavior, family therapy insists that all individuals share some responsibility for change. The goals of *couples*, or *marital therapy* are to help partners understand the nature of their interactions and to assist them in developing more constructive and satisfying ways of relating to each other. Typically, partners attend therapy sessions together. The different types of psychotherapy are summarized in Table 12.4.

Table 12.4 Types of Psychotherapy

Types	Main Features
Psychodynamic therapy	Focuses on internal conflicts and personality
Behavior therapy	Applies learning principles to change maladaptive behavior
Cognitive therapy	Corrects faulty beliefs and thought patterns
Client-centered therapy	Helps people gain self-acceptance through therapist's unconditional positive regard, empathy, and honesty
Group, family, and couples therapy	Resolves interpersonal problems that contribute to the individual's problems

An Evaluation of Psychotherapy. Many clinical studies indicate that psychotherapy is effective for the treatment of many mental disorders.[27] Though it may not be a "cure," psychotherapy certainly provides the majority of individuals with some relief from symptoms and helps them to function better in their everyday lives. Which therapies work best for particular mental disorders and which patient characteristics best predict success in therapy are questions that psychologists are still trying to answer.

Biological Therapies

Though psychotherapy works for the majority of individuals with mental disorders, many require some type of biological treatment. In some cases, the most effective treatment involves a combination of psychotherapy and biological therapy. In this section you will learn about the major biological treatments—drug therapy and electroconvulsive therapy.

Drug Therapy. The modern use of drugs for the treatment of mental disorders began in the 1950s with the introduction of chemicals to alter thinking, emotions, and behavior. Although their precise mechanisms of action are not fully understood, the drugs apparently work by altering the neurotransmitters involved in the symptoms. These drugs are categorized into three types: antianxiety, antidepressant, and antipsychotic drugs.

Antianxiety drugs, such as Valium, Ativan, and Xanax, control symptoms of anxiety, panic, fear, and tension. They also help individuals relax, sleep better, and focus on their tasks.[28] *Antidepressant drugs*, such as Prozac, Tofranil, and Pamelor, elevate your mood and activate depressed individuals so that they can experience more positive feelings about themselves and their lives.[29] Although not an antidepressant, lithium is successful in the treatment of bipolar disorder. Finally, *antipsychotic drugs*, such as Thorazine, Haldol, and Clozaril, help reduce the impact of hallucinations and delusions on schizophrenic patients. Because of these drugs, many schizophrenic individuals have been able to lead active lives outside the hospital.[30]

electroconvulsive therapy—biological therapy involving the use of small electrical currents applied to the patient's head

Electroconvulsive Therapy. Commonly known as "shock treatment," **electroconvulsive therapy** (ECT) involves the use of small electrical currents applied to the patient's head, producing seizure

Fundamentals of Psychology

activity. How ECT produces its therapeutic effects is unknown, but it certainly helps many depressed people feel better and overcome their suicidal tendencies. Usually, ECT is used after psychotherapy and antidepressants have failed. Even though you may be aware of media depictions of ECT as barbaric and inhumane, most research indicates that it is relatively safe when applied properly.[31] The late concert pianist Vladimir Horowitz underwent ECT in 1973 and subsequently played Beethoven and Mozart concertos without memory problems often attributed to the procedure.

An Evaluation Of Biological Therapies.   Biological therapies involving the use of drugs and ECT generally work well in reducing many of the symptoms of mental disorders. Like psychotherapy, though, biological therapies do not solve problems by themselves and do not work for all people. In addition, drugs and ECT can produce troublesome and sometimes serious side effects. For example, there is a risk of substance dependence with the use of antianxiety drugs. Antidepressants often make people drowsy and give them dry mouth and constipation. Neurological problems such as abnormalities in movement are a common result of antipsychotic drug use. With ECT, memory impairment and confusion occures in many cases, and may last for a few days after treatment. The side effects notwithstanding, biological therapies hold an important place in the battle against mental disorders.

Summary

1. The dominant prescientific view of abnormal behavior was supernaturalism, the belief that behavior is controlled by gods, demons, spirits, and magic. In this view, people who behaved abnormally were thought to be possessed by demons or evil spirits.

2. There are four ways to define abnormal behavior. According to the statistical deviation definition, abnormal behavior is rare or uncommon. Another view is that behavior that violates the social norm is abnormal. Behavior that interferes with your ability to meet everyday responsibilities is maladaptive. Finally, behavior that causes personal distress is abnormal.

3. Anxiety disorders involve anxiety and related thoughts, feelings, and behaviors that interfere with normal functioning. With somatoform disorders, there are physical symptoms that suggest physical illness in the absence of a medical cause. Dissociative disorders are marked by sudden alterations in consciousness, memory, or identity.

4. Substance abuse involves repeated drug use that affects the person's ability to meet major obligations. Substance abuse is also indicated by continued drug use in situations in which it is

physically hazardous and drug-related legal problems. Substance dependence is marked by tolerance, withdrawal, taking more of the drug than intended, an inability to stop or cut down, and spending a lot of time getting the drug.

5. Mood disorders are characterized by periods of depression or mania or an alternation of the two. If the disorder involves only periods of depression, the diagnosis is major depressive disorder. People with bipolar disorder experience alternating periods of depression and mania.

6. Schizophrenia is a psychosis marked by serious problems in judgment, reasoning, emotions, perceptions, and behavior. Schizophrenics have loose associations, delusions, hallucinations, and flat or blunted emotions. Schizophrenics lack interest and motivation and often show weird, purposeless behaviors.

7. Maladaptive, inflexible, and distressing personality traits characterize the personality disorders. The eccentric personality disorders involve odd or withdrawn behavior. The dramatic types are marked by emotional or erratic behavior, and the anxious disorders are characterized by anxious, fearful, or inhibited behaviors.

8. Psychodynamic therapy focuses on internal conflicts and personality. Behavior therapy strives to change maladaptive behavior through the application of learning principles. Cognitive therapy refers to procedures used to correct the faulty beliefs and thought patterns that underlie abnormal behavior. Client-centered therapy involves the therapist's use of unconditional positive regard, empathy, and honesty to help clients accept themselves. Group, family, and couples therapies focus on resolving the interpersonal conflicts that give rise to abnormal behavior.

9. The main biological therapies are drug therapy and electroconvulsive therapy. Antianxiety drugs alleviate symptoms of anxiety. Antidepressants elevate mood and energize people. Antipsychotic drugs help reduce hallucinations and delusions in schizophrenic patients. Electroconvulsive therapy, used in the treatment of depression, involves the application of small electrical currents to the patient's head.

Questions for Discussion

1. How was abnormal behavior viewed before the scientific revolution?

2. What are the four definitions of abnormal behavior?

3. What are the main features of the anxiety, somatoform, and dissociative disorders?

4. How does the DSM-IV distinguish between substance abuse and dependence?

5. What are the characteristics of the mood disorders?

6. What are the main features of schizophrenia?

7. How are the personality disorders identified?

8. What types of psychotherapies are used for mental disorders?

9. What biological therapies are used in the treatment of mental disorders?

Applying Psychology

Though you may not have a mental disorder, you probably have a bothersome behavior or bad habit you would like to control or get rid of. Good news! Many of the therapeutic techniques used to treat mental disorders can be adapted to solve other problem behaviors too. Here's what you can do:

Step 1: Identify the behavior you would like to control. It might overeating, nailbiting, smoking, or spending too much money, to name a few.

Step 2: Construct a diary in which you keep a record of the occurrence of the problem behavior. Make a column for each of the following: Time of Day, Location (where are you?), Companion(s) (who are you with?), Activity (what are you doing?), Feelings (how do you feel?). After recording your diary each day for a week or two, you should start to notice a pattern, that is the circumstances in which you are most likely to perform the problem behavior.

Step 3: Think about what preceded the behavior. Were you bored, upset, angry? If you can discover what events preceded the behavior, you might be able to prevent the behavior by preventing the event that usually precedes it. For example, you could do something to keep yourself from getting bored.

Step 4: List the positive and negative consequences of performing the behavior. If the behavior is really a problem you should find more negative than positive consequences. Remind yourself of the negatives each time you get the urge to perform the behavior.

Of course, no method of self-control is foolproof, but after practicing these techniques for a while you may be better able to control your problem behavior.

Chapter 12 • Abnormal Psychology and Therapy

Chapter 13

Psychology of Social Behavior

1. Describe the processes that affect how people perceive one another.

2. Discuss the principles that influence how people explain each other's behavior.

3. Explain how attitudes form, change, and influence behavior.

4. Describe the nature and causes of prejudice and discrimination.

5. Define conformity and discuss the factors that influence it.

6. Identify the causes and consequences of obedience and compliance.

7. Discuss the effects of social facilitation and social loafing.

8. Explain the nature and development of social affiliation.

9. Summarize the factors that influence helping behavior.

10. Define aggression and explain its causes.

11. Identify the processes that characterize group behavior.

social psychology—the scientific study of social behavior

social cognition—thinking about other people and the causes of their behavior

A small cult, called the Seekers, predicted that the world would end on a specific day and that they would be saved from destruction by rescuers from outer space. When doomsday passed without incident, cult members were initially distressed and puzzled. In the coming weeks, however, they did not give up their belief. Instead, their conviction about the end of the world was strengthened, and they increased their efforts to convert others to their point of view.[1]

The behavior of this end-of-the-world cult might lead you to ask some important questions:

▶ How do people develop such unusual beliefs?

▶ Why are disproved attitudes strengthened?

▶ What gives groups their influence over people?

Those questions touch on several fundamental problems in **social psychology**, the scientific study of social behavior. Consider for a moment how much of your life involves social behavior and the impact that social forces have on you. Clearly, the social dimension of your life is one of its most prominent aspects. In this chapter, you will learn about the many factors that shape your behavior as a social being.

Social Cognition

In studying **social cognition**, you will learn about the processes that people use in thinking about one another and how that thinking influences social behavior. Social cognition research investigates how you perceive the characteristics of other people and how you explain the causes of their behavior.

Perceiving Other People

When you meet someone for the first time, what affects your perception of that person? Appearance? Clothing? Accent? You perceive different aspects of others depending on the setting, the individual's characteristics, and your own beliefs.

Studies of *impression formation* find that your perceptions are strongly shaped by the first information you receive. Suppose that the first time you meet someone in class she is cruelly making fun of another student. If your initial perception of that classmate is negative, you may continue to have a negative opinion even though later you obtain positive information about that person. The lasting impact of first impressions is known as the *primacy effect* in person perception. In a classic experiment on the primacy effect, social psychologist Solomon Asch provided subjects with a list of adjectives describing a hypothetical person and asked them to give their impression of that person. When positive adjectives were given first and negative ones last, subjects had more favorable impressions than when the negative traits were given first and positive ones last.[2]

Impressions are influenced not only by the order in which information is received, but also by the importance of the information. You do not consider all information equally in impression formation. Your impression of a person would probably be shaped more by knowing that he did volunteer work at a hospital than that he liked ice cream. How important a trait is in your overall impression depends largely on your own ideas about human personality. According to *schema theory*, your impressions are controlled by your beliefs, or schemas, about how human behavior and traits are connected. For example, you may think that a hospital volunteer is caring and unselfish, and, as a result, that assumption produces a favorable impression. What schemas do you use most when judging someone's personality?[3]

Physical attractiveness is a powerful determinant of impressions for many people. An attractive person is usually judged as more sociable, warm, mentally healthy, and dominant than an unattractive person. In our society attractiveness is perceived as a sign of status, and attractive people are often assumed to be much better than the average person. According to the *halo effect*, this favorable impression colors your perception of the attractive person's mental and social characteristics. When your positive impressions of attractive people carry over to your judgments about their other attributes, you are showing the halo effect.[4]

Attractive people are often perceived as having other favorable qualities simply on the basis of their physical appearance.

Interestingly, there is some truth to the "beautiful-is-good" assumption. Attractive people tend to be more popular and socially competent than unattractive people; however, they also tend to be more vain and self-conscious.[5,6] Many misconceptions about attractive people may be due to the influence of television and films in which leading characters are often attractive, successful, intelligent, and powerful. In some cases, the effects of the "beautiful-is-good" belief may be socially harmful. For example, attractive "baby-faced" criminals are given lighter sentences than less attractive criminals for comparable crimes.[7]

Nonverbal communication also affects your person perceptions. In social interactions you receive and send numerous signals in the form of "body language," especially in gestures, movements, and facial expressions. How you read others' body language will influence your ideas about them. As you learned in Chapter 9, basic emotions such as fear and sadness have universally recognizable facial expressions. Other nonverbal signals, too, such as your tone of voice, convey widely understood emotional meanings. Many other nonverbal behaviors provide impressions about emotion, personality, and attitudes. But, culture shapes the meanings of those signals.

If someone touches your hand while speaking to you, your impression will depend on your cultural background. Northern Europeans often see the toucher as violating their personal space, while Mediterranean, Arabic, and African people tend to perceive touch as a sign of closeness or trust.[8]

Explaining People's Behavior

When you think about other people, your perceptions reflect not only impressions about what they do, but also your ideas as to why they behave as they do. People naturally try to understand one another's actions, especially if those actions are disturbing or unusual. Your explanations, or *attributions*, influence your feelings and beliefs about others as well as your behavior toward them. **Attribution theory** is an explanation of how people judge the causes of behavior. Your attributions are complex judgments that address three questions about the causes of behavior:

▶ Is the cause *internal* (in the person) or *external* (in the environment)?

▶ Is the cause *stable* (present all or most of the time) or *unstable* (rarely present)?

▶ Is the cause *controllable* (under the person's control) or *uncontrollable* (not under the person's control)?[9]

Psychologist Harold Kelley believes that people make attributions in everyday life, as if they were "naive scientists," by observing associations between behavior and other available information. Kelley's *covariation model* points to three kinds of information that people use in explaining behavior: distinctiveness, consensus, and consistency.[10] You judge a behavior's *distinctiveness* by how usual or unusual it is for the person observed. *Consensus* information refers to your evaluation of how likely it is that other people would act in the same way. When you consider how the person behaves in other situations, you are judging the *consistency* of the person's actions. Imagine a student named Mark who bursts out laughing in the middle of a history class. You might ask yourself whether he has ever done that before in this class (distinctiveness), whether other people are also laughing (consensus), and whether he has laughter outbursts in his other classes (consistency). If his behavior is distinctive and consistent, but lacks consensus, you will probably attribute it to internal causes. What might be the causes of Mark's laughter?

Your attributions shape your feelings and attitudes about other people and influence how you respond to them. Judgments about the controllability of behavior are critical in this regard. When you perceive someone's behavior as controllable, you assume that the person is responsible for the behavior. On the other hand, when behavior is judged as uncontrollable, no responsibility is assigned. Suppose you encounter a beggar who asks you for a dollar. If you judge his condition to be the result of a controllable problem, such as a drug habit, you might not be sympathetic and give him the money. However, if you attribute his begging to an uncontrollable factor, such as losing his job or being ill, you might be more inclined to help out. Many social controversies today reflect differences in attributions about

attribution theory—explanation of how people judge the causes of behavior

behavior. For example, people who see poverty as due to laziness are opposed to public assistance for the needy, whereas those who view poverty as a general social problem are more supportive of programs to aid the poor.[11]

Because attributions have a significant impact on individual and societal behavior, it is important to realize that attributions are not necessarily correct. Attribution theory describes only what people believe to be the causes of other's behavior. These judgments are often inaccurate because they reflect several types of **attribution bias** on the part of the perceiver that distort his or her judgment. Table 13.1 summarizes the major sources of bias in social attributions.[12]

▼
attribution bias—biases that distort judgments about the causes of behavior

Table 13.1 **Bias in Social Attributions**

Bias	Description
False consensus bias:	The assumption that other people share your beliefs, attitudes, and habits
Fundamental attribution error:	The tendency to attribute others' behavior to internal causes and your own behavior to external causes
Just-world assumption:	The belief that people get what they deserve—for better or worse
Self-serving bias:	The tendency to attribute your own failures to external causes and successes to internal causes

*A*ttitudes

▼
attitude—pattern of beliefs, feelings, and response tendencies organized around a topic

Since the 1930s the study of attitudes has occupied a central place in social psychology. An **attitude** is a pattern of beliefs, feelings, and response tendencies organized around some topic. For example, your attitude toward the death penalty might include a belief ("I think it is necessary to control crime"), a feeling ("I am glad that murderers are severely punished"), and a response tendency ("I would vote for any candidate who supports the death penalty"). Attitudes serve a few basic purposes in your life. They express your personal values, satisfy your psychological needs, and aid your social adjustment. In the above example, support for the death penalty might reflect your belief in "law and order" (*value expression*), increase your sense of personal security (*need satisfaction*), and enable you to conform with your friends' similar attitudes (*social adjustment*).[13]

Social psychologists have been interested in attitudes mainly because they assume that attitudes exert great influence on behavior. Surprisingly, studies of the *attitude-behavior link* give inconsistent results. Your attitudes certainly affect your behavior, but the extent to which they do so is open to question.[14] A classic demonstration of attitude-behavior inconsistency is found in a 1934 study in which a white researcher named LaPiere toured the United States with a young Chinese couple. During their trip they stayed at many hotels and ate at many restaurants. They were refused service only

290

Fundamentals of Psychology

once, but after their tour they wrote to the businesses asking if Chinese guests were accepted. Over 90 percent of the replies said no![15]

Since the LaPiere study, debate over the link between attitudes and behavior has continued. Today, researchers recognize that this link is influenced by several variables, including situational factors, social norms, the strength of the attitude, and the relevance of the attitude to the action. For example, a hotel owner who claims to discriminate against Chinese people might not refuse service to a well-dressed Chinese couple because of the presence of their white friend or the norms about treating customers politely. A modified attitude-behavior link is proposed by the *planned action model*, in which both attitudes and social norms affect your intentions, which then predict behavior. Attitudes will influence your behavior, but only by shaping your intention to act in a specific manner.[16] (See Figure 13.1.)

Figure 13.1 **The Planned Action Model**

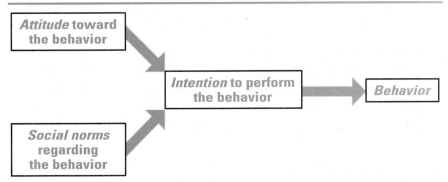

The planned action model depicts the relationship between attitudes, social norms, intentions, and behavior. Your attitude about performing a behavior and your perception of the social norms that apply in a situation determine your intention to perform the behavior. The attitude-behavior link is an indirect one that is affected by social norms and intentions.

Source: Ajzen, I. (1985). *From Intentions to Actions: A Theory of Planned Action.* In J. Kuhl and J. Beckman (eds.). *Action Control: From Cognition to Behavior.* New York: Springer.

Forming and Changing Attitudes

Everyone develops attitudes. Some attitudes are short-lived, and some persist for a lifetime. Consider how your own attitudes have evolved since childhood, and you will recognize the complexity of attitude formation. Many basic attitudes are acquired through learning experiences involving reinforcement and imitation. In childhood your attitudes are established by exposure to your parents and other role models with whom you identify and from whom you receive social reinforcement for attitudes. Attitude learning does not end in childhood, but continues throughout your life as a result of both your personal relationships and more general social forces.

Many of your attitudes result from *persuasive communication* from your social environment. The effect of communications on attitudes depends on features of the message and the recipient of the message. You are most likely to be persuaded to favor an attitude when the source of the message is believable, trustworthy, and attractive. Can you think of any instances when you have been persuaded by commercials or advertisements presented by people who have those characteristics? The recipient of the message also matters in attitude change. Your attitude is more likely to change if you pay attention to the persuasive message and comprehend it fully. How well the message fits with your prior attitudes also affects your acceptance of it. For example, you would be more likely to change your toothpaste than your religion in response to a persuasive message. Personality, too, determines attitude change, and people with low self-esteem are more easily persuaded to change their attitudes than are those with high self-esteem.[17]

Have you ever been bothered because you have two attitudes that are inconsistent? Most people have some inconsistency in their ideas and beliefs. You may, for instance, have a prejudice against one ethnic or racial group, but also believe in social equality. When your beliefs or attitudes are in conflict, you are in a state of **cognitive dissonance**. Tension results from cognitive dissonance. The end-of-the-world Seekers cult mentioned at the beginning of this chapter provides an example of one strategy for reducing dissonance: After their doomsday prophecy failed, cult members doubled their efforts to convince others (and perhaps themselves) that their belief was correct. You can lessen cognitive dissonance by altering one or both of the conflicting attitudes.[18]

Another cognitive mechanism in attitude change is described in **self-perception theory**, which explains attitude formation and change as the result of how you perceive your own behavior.[19] For example, if you give money to a charity you may perceive yourself as a kind or generous individual who helps others. When you are persuaded by someone to perform a behavior, you may change your attitudes as a result, especially if your initial attitudes were not well defined. In a study of attitudes about environmental issues, students with initially weak pro-environment attitudes rated themselves as having stronger pro-environment attitudes after being encouraged to recall instances of their own pro-environment actions, such as recycling cans.[20]

Prejudice and Discrimination

Ethnic warfare, racism, religious conflicts, sexism, bias crimes, and other exhibitions of prejudice and discrimination in modern life are hard to miss. In a multiracial, multiethnic society such as the United States, prejudice and discrimination are urgent social concerns. They are not exclusively American dilemmas, however, as numerous international conflicts show. **Prejudice** is a negative attitude toward members of a social group on the basis of their characteristics, such as race, religion, or sexual orientation. **Discrimination** refers to a harmful or unfair behavior toward a group as a result of prejudice.

The roots of prejudice and discrimination are very complex. Psychologist Gordon Allport (whose personality theory you encountered in Chapter 10) described several causes of prejudice.[21] Historical causes, often based on long standing group conflicts, foster many prejudices. For example, the

cognitive dissonance —
state of tension due to conflicting beliefs or attitudes

self-perception theory—
view that attitudes form and change as a result of perceiving your own behavior

prejudice—negative attitude toward members of a social group

discrimination—harmful or unfair behavior toward a group as a result of prejudice

Fundamentals of Psychology

antagonism in South Africa between the black majority and white minority has a deep historical basis. Like rigid social traditions, sociocultural forces, such as racial segregation and unfair employment practices, also can promote divisive attitudes among groups (see *Issues and Applications: Employment Discrimination*). Competition for scarce jobs or housing in urban areas can spark tensions and hatred between racial or ethnic communities. At the individual level, these attitudes and behaviors have powerful psychological causes involving beliefs, emotions, and personality.

Issues and Applications

Employment Discrimination

HELP WANTED: NO COLORED NEED APPLY

Imagine reading a job ad with a statement like that! Not so long ago, such flagrantly prejudiced employment advertisements were commonplace. Many groups besides African Americans were also the victims: Chinese, Jews, Catholics, and women. Today, although discriminatory practices are illegal and less common than in the past, employment discrimination appears in many more subtle, but equally unfair, ways. Certainly racism still makes African Americans a main target of job discrimination, but many other forms of prejudice and stereotyping also creep into the world of work: sexism, ageism, homophobia, as well as prejudices against physically challenged and obese individuals.

Evidence of employment discrimination against various groups is found in hiring, salary, and promotion practices. Discriminatory hiring practices "filter out" unwanted candidates and "channel" others into select job categories. The unequal racial distribution of jobs in the United States has been described as "occupational apartheid".[26] Even after being hired, many people experience salary discrimination, receiving unequal pay for equal work. The wage gap between men and women and between blacks and whites for comparable jobs is clear: Men tend to make more than women and whites more than blacks. Even within ethnic groups, discrimination on the basis of arbitrary "racial" features is present. A study of Mexican American workers found that light-skinned workers were paid more than dark-skinned workers for comparable jobs.[27] In terms of job advancement, the "glass ceiling" for women and other minorities is well documented by the relative absence of those groups from high-level managerial positions.[28] Stereotypes about their abilities and traits increase the chances that minorities will be passed over for promotions.

Progress has been made in changing employment discrimination since the 1960s. Today, you are more likely to find racial, ethnic, and gender integration in your workplace than you were thirty years ago. As a result you need to become more attuned to people who are different from you. Becoming aware of and challenging discrimination at work will help you to promote a larger goal of social equality.

At the heart of individuals' prejudices and discrimination are **stereotypes**, general beliefs about the typical characteristics of some group. Stereotypes are usually unfavorable attitudes that categorize people in highly simplistic ways. How many of these stereotypes have you heard?

▶ "Orientals are inscrutable." ▶ "Blacks are dumb."

▶ "Fat people are lazy." ▶ "Jews are cheap."

▶ "Gays are perverted." ▶ "Whites are racists."

Prejudice and discrimination fuel many conflicts among groups in modern society

Like other cognitive schemas, stereotypes guide your perceptions, memory, and behavior. If you have a stereotype of some group, you are more likely to notice and remember occasions when your beliefs were supported than when they were not. People with stereotypical beliefs are unlikely to interact with those about whom they have the stereotype, and thus their beliefs will not be challenged. Studies show that stereotypes weaken when people have close contact with members of the group to whom their beliefs refer. When members of different groups cooperate in the interest of a common goal, their stereotypes are likely to diminish, and conflict among group members also declines.[22,23]

Emotional factors further shape the development and expression of prejudice and discrimination. An individual who is angry or unhappy may displace that emotional distress onto a stereotyped group by a process called *scapegoating*. The scapegoat, or target of the prejudice, is unfairly blamed and mistreated by the prejudiced individual. An extreme case of scapegoating was found in Germany during the Nazi regime, when Jews were targeted as the cause of the country's economic problems and marked for extermination. In more recent times, minority groups in the United States have been blamed for social ills, such as crime. Scapegoating is certainly not restricted to any one nation or group, as attacks on foreign workers and immigrants in European countries have shown.

Prompted by the Nazi phenomenon, studies of anti-Semitism found that such powerful racism was related to a personality type with very rigid, conventional values and a strong need to submit to authority. The attitude of **authoritarianism** is reflected in strong conformity to the norms of one's own group (in-group) and hostility to members of other groups (out-groups).[24] Examples of authoritarianism today are found in members of many racial supremacist groups, such as neo-Nazis and some skinhead groups. These attitudes help to bind group members together and foster conflicts with members of out-groups.

Social Influence

Part of what it means to be a social being is that you are constantly affected by other people, and they in turn are influenced by you. *Social influence* is sometimes quite subtle—as when you automatically accept a decision made by your friends—and in other instances very obvious—for example, when you are forced into action by an authority figure. In this section you will examine several aspects of social influence in the forms of conformity, obedience, compliance, social facilitation, and social loafing.

Conformity

Before reading any further, try to recall how many times in the past month you have "gone along with" the ideas or actions of your peers. In remembering those episodes you are considering examples of **conformity**, a decision to act in ways that resemble others' behavior. All societies depend on some degree of conformity to social norms, and your social adjustment reflects your willingness to conform to those norms. Too much conformity however, may produce harmful consequences, such as when you get caught up with the "wrong crowd" or squelch your individual beliefs for the sake of "fitting in."

Suppose that you volunteered for an experiment on visual perception in which you were asked to judge the length of a line by comparing it with some other lines and that, before your turn, three other people gave the same, obviously wrong, judgment of the line's length. What would your answer be? In the 1950s, social psychologist Solomon Asch conducted a classic study of conformity in which subjects were confronted with that situation (see Figure 13.2).[25]

Figure 13.2 **Stimuli in the Asch Conformity Experiment**

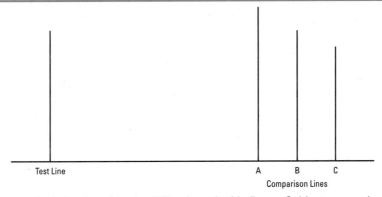

Asch tested conformity with stimuli like those in this figure. Subjects were shown the test line on the left and asked to judge which of the three comparison lines on the right was most similar to it in length

The subjects of this study did not know it, but the other people were giving wrong answers intentionally, as part of the experiment. You may be surprised to learn that nearly half of the subjects conformed and gave the wrong answer. Later research supported the conformity effect and identified three factors in a situation that affect conformity:

▶ *Group Unanimity*: When all group members give the wrong answer conformity increases, but even one dissenter decreases conformity.

▶ *Group Cohesiveness*: When members are strongly committed to the group, conformity increases.

▶ *Group Size*: The larger the group, the more conformity. (In a group of five or more members conformity levels off.).[12]

As you probably have observed with your own acquaintances, conformity depends on the person as well as on the situation. What makes one person conform, while another does not? The motives to conform are mainly two desires: to be right and to be liked. When you are confronted with a discrepancy between your own and others' ideas, you may question your own judgment and go along with the others to be correct. In conformity studies including difficult or ambiguous tasks, subjects are not certain of their answers and are highly likely to conform. Fear of disapproval or of being perceived unfavorably also plays a role. Subjects with low self-esteem and a high need for approval are most likely to conform, even when the others are clearly incorrect.[12,29] Extreme examples of conformity are found in the behavior of some cults, as discussed in *Issues and Applications: The Power of Cults.*

Obedience and Compliance

In contrast to conformity, the social behaviors of obedience and compliance do not involve voluntarily chosen actions. If you exhibit obedience or compliance, you do not necessarily want to do what is asked or demanded of you, but you do it nonetheless.

Obedience refers to submission to a demand by an another, such as an authority figure. Like conformity, obedience is sometimes a necessary part of social life. The preservation of any society depends on its members' willingness to submit to the demands of authority. But, authorities do not

obedience—submission to a demand by another person

Issues and Application

The Power of Cults

Outside of Waco, Texas in March of 1993, a standoff between federal authorities and followers of David Koresh's Branch Davidian cult of Seventh Day Adventists turned into a bloody confrontation in which dozens of cult members were killed.

Shortly after the murder of a U.S. congressman and four others who investigated charges that Jim Jones held people against their wills, Jones and more than 900 members of his People's Temple committed suicide by drinking poison in Jonestown, Guyana, in 1978.

Although these examples of group behavior are remarkable because of their horrendous consequences, the cults of David Koresh and Jim Jones are just two instances of a widespread phenomenon of cultism. The United States, with its history of religious tolerance, seems to produce an enormous variety of cults. An estimated 2,500 cults of different sizes, with a combined total of between 2 and 3 million members, are found in this country alone. In some ways, cults are no different from other religious or political groups who share a common set of beliefs. But, cults also have unique characteristics that distinguish them from more traditional groups and that give them the potential for

Fundamentals of Psychology

always make reasonable demands, and blind obedience can lead to horrifying results. Consider, for example, the chilling defense of Nazi war criminal Adolf Eichmann that he was "only following orders" when overseeing the mass exterminations of European Jews. Numerous examples of the dangers of blind obedience are found in many other groups as well, such as the military and cults. What negative examples of obedience to authority have you heard of recently?

In 1963, social psychologist Stanley Milgram ran an experiment on obedience that was as controversial as it was important.[30] Milgram told his subjects that they were "teachers" in a study of learning and would have to punish mistakes in the "learners" by giving them a series of increasingly powerful electrical shocks. Although the subjects were not actually shocking the "learner," they believed that they were. Subjects did not realize that the true intent of the study was to measure their obedience to the experimenter's commands. How many people do you guess would be willing to go all the way to a shock level marked "450 Volts Danger: Severe Shock"? Before the study, Milgram had asked mental health professionals how many people might obey, and they had guessed that about 1 or 2 percent, a small deviant minority, would. In fact, nearly 66 percent, two-thirds, of the subjects went "all the way."

As you learned in Chapter 1, Milgram's study generated a storm of debate over ethical issues. His subjects had been deceived and exposed to a manipulation that many found very disturbing. In the aftermath of the Milgram study, psychology began to develop stricter rules about how experiments should be conducted. Nevertheless, Milgram's findings were

more deviant behavior. Studies of cults find several features that set them apart from other social groups:

▶ Extreme consensus of beliefs, conformity with group norms, and cohesiveness of group members

▶ Extreme isolation of the group from "out-groups" and a belief in the group's specialness

▶ Strong and charismatic leader whose authority is fully and unconditionally accepted

▶ Control mechanisms to regulate group members, such as constant indoctrination, or "brainwashing"

Clearly, not all cults are destructive, for example the Hare Krishnas are a benign group, and many serve very positive purposes for their members. Nevertheless, instances of violent and self-destructive behavior by some cults raise important questions about the need to monitor cult members to prevent unfortunate episodes in the future.[31,32]

significant. Ordinary people will obey an order to harm a stranger simply because an authority tells them to do so. Subsequent research indicated that the likelihood of obedience was affected by several factors:

▶ *Closeness of the Victim*: When the victim is remote, as in another room, obedience increases.

▶ *Status of the Authority*: The higher in power or status authorities are perceived to be, the higher the level of obedience.

▶ *Setting*: When the study is held in a high-prestige setting, such as a university, obedience increases.[12]

Biography: **Stanley Milgram**

Best known for his work on obedience, social psychologist Stanley Milgram (1933–1984) was also an influential theorist and researcher in the areas of urban psychology and aggression. Milgram was born in New York City and raised in the Bronx. His father, a baker, and mother were immigrants from Eastern Europe. After graduating from Queens College of the City University of New York with a bachelor's degree in political science, Milgram attended Harvard University, where he received his doctorate in psychology in 1960. He taught at Yale and Harvard for a few years and in 1967 came to the Graduate Center of the City University of New York, where he remained until his death.

At Harvard, Milgram studied under two of the most important American social psychologists, Gordon Allport and Solomon Asch. His interest in Asch's conformity investigations led him to explore the forces that promote obedience to authority. In 1963, at the age of 30, Milgram conducted his now-classic obedience study. In the aftermath of that research came enormous controversy over both the findings and the ethics of the study. The study stimulated other research on obedience, confirming Milgram's results, as well as the development of stricter ethical principles regarding the use of deception in psychological experiments.

Milgram's attention moved from obedience to other important issues. He conducted research on the effects of television violence on real-life aggression and arrived at a controversial conclusion that there was little relationship between them. In the 1970s he directed his efforts at understanding the psychology of urban life and proposed his concept of "overload" in city dwellers, who withdraw from one another to escape the constant intense stimulation of city living. At the age of 51, Stanley Milgram died of a heart attack.[33]

Of course, not all of Milgram's subjects obeyed to the fullest. Many refused to continue when they felt the learner was suffering or endangered. A critical element in obedience or disobedience was the subject's feeling of responsibility for the victim. Although they were upset by their actions and asked to stop, many subjects continued administering shocks when assured that the experimenter was responsible for the consequences. Milgram's results suggest that you are most likely to obey an authority's demand when you forfeit your own responsibility and assign it to the authority.[34]

As Milgram showed, people are quite willing to submit to the commands of authority figures. In many instances, however, people give in to requests, even when the person making the request has no real authority. Have you ever donated money to a collector for a charity or done a favor for a stranger? You probably have responded to similar requests on any number of occasions. At those times you were exhibiting **compliance**, or following a request by another person. Researchers have identified a few techniques to increase compliance, as well as the variables that influence it.

compliance—following a request by another person

The *foot-in-the-door technique* is one method of gaining compliance with a large request by first obtaining compliance with a small request. Suppose you want to borrow your friend's new car (large request), but you think she will probably turn you down. You could try the foot-in-the-door technique and first ask her to lend you a dollar (small request). Research shows that if she complies with the small request, your friend is more likely to give in to the larger one too.[35]

What if you turned it around and asked for a large favor first? The *door-in-the-face technique* does just that, and, oddly enough, by making an initial large request you can increase compliance with a later small one. Studies indicate that after subjects refuse to comply with a large request (that is, they slam the door in your face), the chance of their complying with a second smaller request improves. So, if you really just want to borrow a dollar from your friend, try asking first to borrow her car, and when she turns you down you will have a better chance at getting the loan.[36]

As you might guess, the foot-in-the-door and door-in-the-face techniques do not always work, nor do they increase compliance by everyone. The degree of compliance is affected by several variables. Compliance is increased when subjects expect positive consequences for compliance and negative consequences for refusal. For example, if your friend thinks you will be mad at her for turning down your request, she might comply more easily. If she expects a powerfully negative effect from refusing you, she may feel coerced into compliance. The norms for compliance in the situation also make a difference. Social norms may support compliance in one setting and undermine it in others. If you attend a school-sponsored dance at which you are asked to donate money to the school's student activity fund, the norm in that situation points to compliance. By contrast, if a stranger interrupts you in the library and asks you for money, you probably will refuse, because the norm for behavior in that situation does not support compliance.[37]

Although their methods differ, the two compliance techniques may both work for similar reasons. According to self-perception theory, your perceptions of your behavior can change your attitudes. In foot-in-the-door situations, your compliance with a small request may lead you to see yourself as someone who is willing to comply, thus increasing your subsequent compliance to the larger request. After refusing a large request in the door-in-the-face situation, you may see yourself as uncooperative or unhelpful, an unfavorable self-perception, and be motivated to give in to a later small request to change that view. Of course, compliance has its limits, and when you perceive your freedom or personal control as being threatened, you are likely to refuse most requests.[12]

Social Facilitation and Social Loafing

In examining obedience and compliance you saw how the intentional commands and requests of other people can influence your behavior. Sometimes, the mere presence of other people affects your behavior, too, without any effort on their part. In the late 1890s, psychologist Norman Triplett observed that bicyclists seemed to perform better when they competed against one another than when they rode alone. He described this effect as **social facilitation**, an improvement in behavior or performance due to the presence of other people. By testing children's skill in winding fishing line while alone and in groups, Triplett demonstrated the social facilitation effect.[38] Many other researchers since Triplett have tested this effect and found inconsistent results. In some instances the presence of others helps, and in other instances it harms performance. The mixed findings might be due to the influence of other people on your arousal and attention.[39]

Social psychologist Robert Zajonc proposed that the presence of others increases arousal, and the increase in arousal interferes with performance of complex tasks but helps on simple familiar tasks.[40] In addition, the presence of others may impair your attention to the task by distracting you from what you are trying to accomplish.[41] Imagine that you are performing a simple task, such as riding an exercise bicycle. You might be able to pedal faster in front of an audience because of an increase in your overall arousal level. What if you were trying to make three-point baskets in front of a capacity crowd at Madison Square Garden? You would probably do worse than if you were alone because your high arousal state would inhibit this complex action and you would be distracted by the crowd.

Whereas social facilitation shows a positive impact of others on behavior, **social loafing** indicates that the presence of others can result in a loss of motivation and performance. When there are other people around, you can "hide in the crowd" and actually do less than you would if you were alone. Social loafing is sometimes present in job settings where a group is working on a common project. Because there are other people involved, you might be

Studies of social loafing show that people tend to work less diligently when they are in a group than when they are alone.

willing to "slack off" and do less than your fair share. Studies find that social loafing is most likely when people feel anonymous in the group or believe that they will not be held personally accountable for the group's performance.[42,43]

Social Interaction

If you are like most people, you spend most of your waking life involved in activities with others. Your social relations not only occupy your time, but also provide a framework for your behavior and overall psychological adjustment. Social psychologists are concerned with the interactions among people. In this section you will examine their findings in four areas: affiliation, helping, aggression, and group behavior.

Affiliation

As you learned in Chapter 9, *affiliation* is a basic social motive. People are social animals who by their nature seek out relationships with one another. Throughout life your friendships and intimate relationships provide an invaluable social support network that is essential for your overall psychological adjustment.

Think about your best friends for a moment. What forces have brought and kept you together? Research has identified some general factors in friendship formation that you may recognize in your own experience. As common sense suggests, you are most likely to befriend someone whose life overlaps with your own. Someone who lives near you, works with you, or is in your class is likely to become your friend simply because of familiarity or closeness. Studies show that repeated exposure to people increases their attractiveness.[44]

How strongly you are attracted to someone is obviously influenced by more than just how often you see that person. The perceived attractiveness of people depends on their physical attributes as well as society's norms regarding beauty. Although cultural differences about attractiveness do exist, some similar judgments have been found in many cultures. In general, a youthful appearance is perceived as more attractive, especially for women, and the appearance of dominance and maturity is considered attractive for men.[45]

The old saying "like attracts like" suggests that a similar degree of attractiveness is an important element in relationships, and research shows that this saying has some truth. You are more likely to become involved with someone whom you perceive to be as attractive as yourself than with someone whom you judge as more or less attractive than yourself. When one party is much less attractive, he or she usually possesses another characteristic, such as a great sense of humor, that compensates for it. The *matching effect* goes well beyond just physical attractiveness to include similarity of attitudes, beliefs, and needs as well. Friendships are closer and more lasting when friends have psychological characteristics in common.[12,46]

Attractiveness and similarity are important in forming your relationships, but they are probably not enough to keep those relationships alive. You have undoubtedly met many people whom you found attractive and similar to yourself, but you did not develop lasting relationships with them. According to **social exchange theory**, relationships are maintained by reinforcements that are exchanged by those involved. In deciding to continue or discontinue your relationships with others you evaluate the relative rewards that you expect and the costs to you. When the rewards outweigh the costs, you are inclined to preserve the relationship. For example, if your friend has a great sense of humor (reward) but always depends on you for transportation (cost), your willingness to continue the friendship depends on how much you value his humor over the hassle of driving him around.[47]

Relationships depend on *reciprocity*, the mutual exchange of rewards and costs. Relationships in which both friends receive relatively equal rewards and costs are most likely to persist. An imbalance or inequity in the exchange undermines the relationship. For instance, if your friend feels that you are getting more from the relationship than he is, and your driving services are not worth his having to listen to you complain about driving, then he may withdraw from the relationship.[48]

Friendships may evolve into more intimate relationships depending on the *self-disclosure* that takes place by both parties. Intimate friends share their feelings, beliefs, and values more freely and completely with each other than do casual friends, and their self-disclosure promotes much closer bonding. How much you are willing to disclose to another depends largely on how much you trust that person. Trust and self-disclosure tend to feed one another. The more trusting you are the more you reveal yourself, and the more friends reveal themselves to each other the more trust they share.[49]

Romantic relationships are perhaps the most intimate of all social affiliations. Oddly, social psychologists have only recently paid much attention to love and romance. Two kinds of love relationships have been

social exchange theory— *view that relationships are maintained by an exchange of reinforcements and costs*

identified: passionate and companionate. Relationships of *passionate love* are characterized by intense mutual emotional arousal and attachment, romantic or erotic interactions, and highly idealized perceptions of the loved one. When you "fall in love" with someone, you place the person at the center of your emotional life and see him or her as perfect, or nearly so. Passion, however, does not last forever, and over time the intensity of the romance diminishes. By contrast, *companionate love* is slower to develop but more lasting. In long-term romantic relationships, companionate love depends on mutual trust, tolerance, and practical considerations, such as a willingness to help and support each other.[50]

Romantic relationships are significant aspects of social life and are based on complex emotional and psychological factors.

Helping Behavior

What would you do if you heard someone outside your home screaming for help in the middle of the night? You probably think that you would call the police or go out to assist the person, and perhaps you would. One night in 1964 in a middle-class neighborhood in Queens, New York, 38 people listened for a half-hour to their neighbor Kitty Genovese cry for help as she was being viciously attacked outside her apartment building. Not one person called for or offered help until after she was dead. The murder of Kitty Genovese caused a public outcry against the apparent indifference of people to those in need of help and stimulated many researchers to examine the reasons that people give, or fail to give, help.

Helping is a kind of *prosocial behavior*, that is, an action performed to benefit another person. Many forms of helping can be identified. You may might help because you expect a reward or praise for helping or because everyone else is helping and you want to conform. In those circumstances, helping is shaped by some clear motives. Often, however, people help others when there is no obvious advantage to them for helping. This type of

altruism (al-true-iz-um)—
helping due to a desire to help
without hope of reward

helping, called **altruism**, is the result of a desire to help without hope of any reward. Social psychologists have concentrated mainly on altruistic helping and found it to be influenced by characteristics of the helper and the helping situation.

Who is most likely to help another person? Several factors play a role in determining your helpfulness. You are more likely to give help if you are in a good mood than a bad mood. In addition, you will be likeliest to help when you have no doubt that help is needed and you empathize with the person. Another critical element in your willingness to give help is your belief in your ability to be helpful. For example, if you witnessed a car accident in which someone was injured, your giving help would depend on the amount of confidence you had in your first-aid skills. Although there are no specific personality traits of all help givers, many have a sense of personal responsibility to others and a strong need for approval.[12]

Aspects of the situation also affect the chances that help will be given. Victims who are attractive and familiar will receive help more often than unattractive and strange people. The strongest situational variable, however, is the number of potential helpers. You might suppose that more help would come in the presence of more people, but in fact just the opposite is true. The **bystander effect** indicates that help is less likely to be given by any one person when there are more bystanders present. People are more likely to help when no one else is available to give help. As the neighbors of Kitty Genovese later confessed, they thought someone else must surely have called for help.[51,52]

bystander effect—helping is
less likely when several
bystanders are present

Social norms stress the importance of helping other people. From childhood, most people are taught to be sympathetic to others and to help those in need. As you learned in Chapter 9, some theorists even believe that altruism may have a genetic basis in our species. Why then, do individuals decide not to help? One important reason is the *diffusion of responsibility* that results from the presence of a group. When more potential helpers are present, each individual feels less personal responsibility for helping, as was true for Kitty Genovese's neighbors. But, even when potential helpers feel personal responsibility, they will not help if they think that the costs to themselves are too high or if they do not actually know how to help. For example, if you saw a knife-wielding assailant attacking someone, you might want to help, but you might avoid doing so because of the potential danger to yourself.

Aggression

You need look no further than the headlines of today's paper to realize that aggression is a serious social problem. There is no escaping the accounts of murder, rape, child abuse, family violence, warfare, and other types of aggressive behavior. Although it takes many forms, **aggression** is behavior that involves intentional harm directed at another person. The roots of aggression lie in biology, society, and the psychological makeup of individuals.

aggression—behavior that
directs intentional harm at
another person

According to *instinct theory*, aggression is an inborn drive like hunger and sex. In his psychoanalytic theory, Freud argued that aggression results from the death instinct, an inborn urge for destruction. Biologist Konrad Lorenz also proposed that aggressive drives are a natural part of our animal heritage.[53] Support for the biological view comes from studies that find aggression to be a heritable trait, especially in males. One of the most consistent gender differences is the male's greater aggressiveness, which may reflect a genetic and hormonal basis. Male sex hormones are related to overall aggressiveness in both sexes. In addition, studies indicate that sex hormones affect brain development differently in males and females, suggesting a possible neurological basis for aggression.[54]

One problem with instinct theory is obvious: Not everyone is aggressive. Alternatives to instinct theory propose that aggression is not an inborn drive, but a result of environmental factors and learning. As you learned in Chapter 11, the *frustration-aggression hypothesis* views aggression as a reaction to being frustrated in seeking goals. The escalation of violent crime among impoverished urban youths may give evidence of this theory. When their hope for the future is limited, they may take out their frustrations in antisocial destructive ways.

The frustration-aggression hypothesis is not a general explanation of all aggression. Frustration does not always cause aggression, and in fact, aggression does not always follow frustration. Social psychologist Leonard Berkowitz modified the frustration-aggression hypothesis to include not just frustrating events, but other aversive events and external aggression cues in the situation.[55] In his model, frustration may lead to aggression if it causes anger and if there are provocative cues for aggression, such as a weapon, in the person's environment. Stimuli, such as guns and knives, that are clearly associated with aggression can prompt aggressive behavior in someone who otherwise would not act aggressively. In addition to such stimuli, other factors that increase feelings of anger can also increase aggressiveness. For example, people are more inclined toward aggression when they are uncomfortably hot and when under the influence of alcohol.

Berkowitz's research indicates that learned associations to environmental cues can provoke aggression. Other learning processes also influence aggressive behavior. Aggression is often strongly reinforced if it reduces feelings of tension or anger, or if it produces positive consequences for the aggressor, such as gaining power over someone. According to *social learning theory*, observational learning is also behind the development of aggression. When children observe an aggressive adult who is rewarded, they are likely to imitate similar aggression.[56] The social learning view of aggression has been well supported. As you read in Chapter 5, television and film violence have an impact on real-life aggression in children (see *Issues and Applications: The Effects of the Media on Children's Behavior*, page 116). Exposure to violence in the media reduces inhibitions against aggression and desensitizes the viewer to violent acts.[57]

Portrayals of violence in the media may influence the expression of real-life aggression.

Even more than exposure to televised violence, exposure to real-life violence provokes aggression. Children who are raised in families with violent interactions between parents or siblings are more prone to aggressive behavior than other children. Aggression is especially prevalent among children who have been the direct victims of violence. Children who are physically abused are more inclined to aggressive antisocial behavior than are nonabused children. Regrettably, a *cycle of violence* often emerges in families, in which abused children grow up to be abusive parents.[58]

Besides the biological and psychological roots of aggression in the individual, the social situation in which aggression unfolds also has a role. Studies of mob violence indicate that people are sometimes more inclined toward aggression when they are in a crowd than when they are alone. The **deindividuation model** proposes that in a group you are more likely to show aggression because you give up your individuality to the group, substituting the group's values for your own. When you are part of a crowd, you are relatively anonymous and are not as likely to feel personal responsibility for the aggression. Deindividuation involves forces like those at work in the bystander effect and in conformity.[59]

Group Behavior

As you have learned in previous parts of this chapter, people behave differently when they belong to a group than when they act as individuals. Like most people, you probably belong to several social groups and, consequently, are familiar with the results of group interactions on your attitudes and actions. In this last section, you will examine some of the more common phenomena of group behavior.

Have you ever noticed that when you act as a part of a group you become more daring than when you are by yourself? Perhaps you have

deindividuation (dee-*in-di-vid-you*-**ay**-*shun*) **model**— view that aggression is more likely in a group because of a loss of individuality

experienced this effect with your friends when you have talked each other into doing something that individually you are all reluctant to do. Psychologists who study group behavior have labeled this tendency the *risky shift effect*, meaning that groups often make riskier decisions than the individual group members would make alone. The unfortunate consequences of the risky shift may have been demonstrated by several fatal copy-cat incidents provoked by the film *The Program*, in which teenagers lay in the middle of a busy highway to prove their courage.

Actually, the risky shift effect is just one example of a more general phenomenon known as **group polarization**, in which group members' opinions become more extreme after a group discussion. For instance, during a discussion of political attitudes, group members tend to express more polarized or extreme positions than they originally held. Group polarization is affected by the persuasion of other members and by the comparison of members' opinions. If you were in a group political discussion, you might be inclined to express more extreme views to conform with others' similar opinions and to distinguish yourself clearly from those whose opinions differ from your own.[60]

> **group polarization**—group members' opinions become more extreme following group discussion

The decision-making process in groups may be adversely influenced by a phenomenon called *groupthink*. Not only do groups make riskier and more extreme decisions, but they also sometimes make much worse decisions than individuals would. Group members often struggle to maintain agreement or consensus among themselves, even when disagreement would be more productive. Social psychologist Irving Janis has studied groupthink in different settings and attributes some famous, disastrous decisions to it. For instance, Janis believes that the groupthink effect was instrumental in the Kennedy administration's decision to help Cuban exiles invade their homeland, leading to the Bay of Pigs fiasco in 1962. Groupthink results when groups members are isolated from contrasting opinions, convinced of their own correctness, and pressured to conform. The tragic conflicts between extremist cults and authorities in recent years may show the regrettable result of groupthink among cult members.[61]

You may get the impression that groups are more trouble than they are worth, but that is far from true. Despite some of the problems found in group behavior, groups have a valuable place in your social life. According to **social identity theory**, your identification with groups and their activity defines many of your characteristics as a social being and also shapes your self-concept.[62] Consider your own experiences as a group member: You are a member of a family group, peer group, ethnic group, racial group, religious group, and probably other groups as well. Your identification with these *reference groups* gives you a foundation for much of your social behavior. Social psychology is only just beginning to appreciate the importance of this social diversity for individual functioning.

> **social identity theory**—view that identification with social groups defines identity and behavior

Summary

1. Person perception starts with impression formation, which is affected by the perceiver's own beliefs as well as information about others, such as their physical attractiveness. Nonverbal communication through body language, facial expressions, and voice also shape impression formation.

2. Attribution theory explains judgments about the causes of actions in terms of internal or external origins, stability, and controllability. In the covariation model, a behavior's distinctiveness, consensus, and consistency are the basis of attributions. Attribution is influenced by biases including the fundamental attribution error, false consensus bias, just-world assumption, and self-serving bias.

3. Conditioning and observational learning influence attitude development and change. Persuasive messages and their sources also shape attitudes, as do features of the recipient. Attitudes change because of cognitive dissonance and self-perception processes. Attitude-behavior consistency is mediated by both intentions and social norms.

4. Prejudice and discrimination result from historical, social, and individual factors. Stereotypes support prejudice, discrimination, and scapegoating. The attitude of authoritarianism is a personality trait of the prejudiced individual.

5. A decision to act in ways that resemble the behavior of others is conformity. Conformity is affected by characteristics of the situation, such as group unanimity, cohesiveness, and size. The motives to be approved and to be correct also affect conformity.

6. Obedience to authority is supported by social norms and variables in the obedience situation, such as the victim's closeness, status of authorities, and setting prestige. Compliance depends on expectations regarding compliance and noncompliance as well as on the social norms in the situation. Foot-in-the-door and door-in-the-face techniques for compliance involve self-perception mechanisms.

7. In social facilitation, the individual performs better in the presence of others than when alone, but the presence of others may inhibit complex task performance. In social loafing, the presence of others inhibits performance by reducing individual accountability for the outcome.

8. Affiliation is a motive that leads to friendships and love. Attraction between people depends on their familiarity, attractiveness, and similarity. In social exchange theory, relationships rely on the exchange of reinforcements and costs. Intimate relationships involve self-disclosure, reciprocity, and passionate and companionate love.

Fundamentals of Psychology

9. Helping behavior is affected by the potential helper's mood, competence, empathy, perception of need, and feeling of responsibility. Social norms and the number of potential helpers also influence helping. When more potential helpers are present, each is less likely to help.

10. Aggression is an intentional act of harm. Instinct theory proposes an innate biological basis for aggression. In frustration-aggression hypothesis, goal frustration and aversive events cause aggression. Aggression is socially learned by observation of aggressive models. Deindividuation of group members also promotes aggression.

11. Group decision making is often more extreme or riskier than individual decision making. Consensus seeking among group members can produce faulty groupthink decisions. Social identity theory views the identification with a reference group as a framework for social behavior and self-concept.

Questions for Discussion

1. What processes influence person perception?

2. How do people make attributions about others' behavior?

3. What influences the formation and change of attitudes and the link between attitudes and behavior?

4. What are prejudice and discrimination? What causes them?

5. What is conformity? Why do people conform?

6. What are the causes and consequences of obedience and compliance?

7. How do social facilitation and social loafing affect behavior?

8. Why does social affiliation occur?

9. What factors influence helping behavior?

10. What is aggression and how is it caused?

11. What processes characterize group behavior?

Applying Psychology

Stereotyping of people who belong to different groups is the basis for prejudice and discrimination in our society. To evaluate the role of stereotyping in your own life, write some of your ideas about how the social group or groups to which you belong are stereotyped. Discuss how these stereotypes have influenced your interactions with people from your own and other groups.

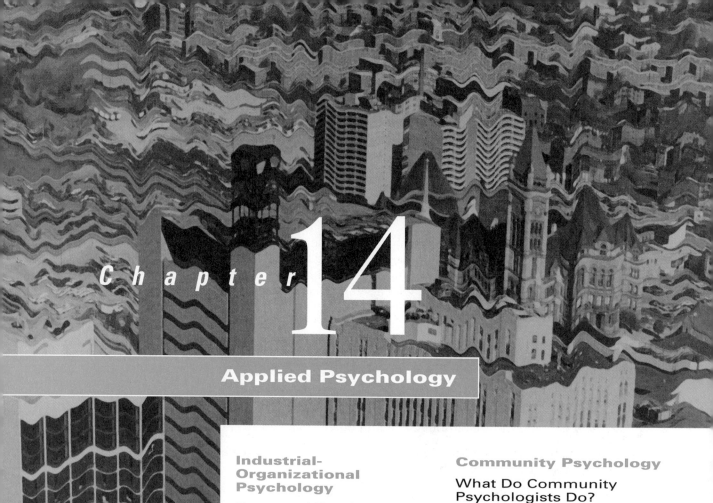

Chapter 14

Applied Psychology

Learning Objectives

After completing this chapter, you should be able to:

1. Outline the important elements of personnel selection, placement, and training.

2. Identify the factors that increase work motivation.

3. Describe the factors associated with job satisfaction.

4. Discuss how technology and social change influence human performance on the job.

5. Describe the effects of noise, violations of personal space, and overcrowding on human behavior.

6. Summarize the goals and methods of community psychology.

7. Discuss the role of community psychology in the prevention of AIDS.

8. Identify the characteristics of homeless people and explain how they affect solutions to the problem of homelessness.

9. Define consumer, forensic, educational, and sports psychology.

▼

applied psychology—the application of psychological methods and knowledge to solve practical problems

▼

industrial-organizational psychology—a kind of applied psychology concerned with human behavior in the workplace

▼

personnel psychology—the branch of industrial-organizational psychology concerned with the selection, placement, and training of employees

On July 19, 1989, a DC-10 crashed in a fireball during an emergency landing at Sioux City, Iowa. Crew members and 184 passengers survived, but 112 died.

You might be wondering what psychology has to do with a plane crash. You have now learned many of the principles of psychology and have seen how they apply to a variety of human concerns—controlling dreams, childrearing, improving thinking skills, intelligence, memory, health promotion, and the treatment of mental disorders, to name a few. These are examples of **applied psychology**, which uses psychological methods and knowledge to solve practical problems. In this chapter, you will examine industrial-organizational, engineering, environmental, community, consumer, forensic, educational, and sports psychology. You will also learn about what psychology has to do with a plane crash.

*I*ndustrial-Organizational Psychology

When you consider businesses, corporations, or industries, you probably think about their success in developing and marketing their products or services. All enterprises, however, are only as good as the people who work in them. How successful do you think a company would be if it hired people with poor job skills, placed them in the wrong positions, trained them inadequately, and then added insult to injury by putting workers and managers in dismal working conditions? **Industrial-organizational psychology** (I-O psychology) is a kind of applied psychology concerned with human behavior in the workplace. As such, I-O psychology applies principles from topics in psychology, including learning, testing, problem solving, motivation, and social psychology, to the selection and training of workers, worker motivation, and job satisfaction. The ultimate goal is to help organizations operate more efficiently.

Personnel Psychology

Imagine that you are running a company and must hire new employees. How will you go about it? Will you hire anyone who seems qualified, or will you be more selective in your choices? I-O psychologists are often faced with this type of problem, and, in response, they have developed techniques for predicting job performance. The branch of I-O psychology concerned with the selection, placement, and training of employees is known as **personnel psychology**.

Selection and Placement. Personnel psychologists use many methods to select and place employees, as outlined in Table 14.1. The most commonly used method is the *interview*, in which the interviewer asks specific questions and evaluates your responses with an eye toward your technical abilities, work motivation, and interpersonal skills. When you go for your next job interview you might be interested to know that successful applicants are typically given longer interviews and talk more than unsuccessful ones.[1]

The work interview is the most commonly used method of personnel selection and placement. In a typical interview, like the one shown here, the interviewer evaluates your technical abilities, motivation, and interpersonal skills.

The use of *biodata* (biographical data) in job interviews is based on the assumption that the best way to predict your future job performance is to look at your past performance. On a job application you might be questioned about your job history, family background, financial situation, and health as well as your attitudes, values, and preferences. Bear in mind that according to antidiscrimination laws, the questions that an employer asks you must be job-related. According to federal laws, questions about your race, religion, sexual orientation, age, or disability cannot be used by an employer to make a decision to hire you.[2]

Some employers may ask you to take a *psychological test* for selection or placement purposes. The most commonly used are ability and aptitude tests that tap your cognitive abilities or specific talents.[3]

Many studies indicate that general cognitive ability, or intelligence, is the best predictor of job performance. One study, for example showed that intelligence test scores of high school sophomores accurately predicted their job success 11 years later.[4] The use of interest tests is based on the assumption that one good predictor of your job performance is that your interests are similar to those of successful employees. For example, if you were applying for a sales job, the personnel psychologist would want to see if

Table 14.1 Techniques of Personnel Selection and Placement

Technique	Description
Interview	You answer questions that are evaluated by the interviewer
Biodata	You provide information about job history and other personal information
Psychological tests	You take tests of ability, aptitude, interest, or personality
Work sample	You perform a task that is similar to what the job requires
Letter of recommendation	Your previous supervisor answers questions about your job performance

your interest profile matched that of the typical successful salesperson. The *Strong-Campbell Interest Inventory* and the *Kuder Occupational Interest Survey* are two commonly used interest tests. If your advisor or guidance counselor ever gave you a test to help you decide on a career, it was probably one of those.

Personality tests are sometimes used in personnel selection to determine whether your personality is likely to be an aid or a detriment for a particular job. In general, personality tests are not as good as ability tests in predicting job success, but tests such as the *16 PF* (see Chapter 10), however, can be helpful in selecting people for a wide variety of occupations including sales personnel and clerical workers. Projective tests such as the *Thematic Apperception Test* have been helpful in predicting managerial success.

Many jobs that require clerical or mechanical skills ask for *work samples* to help in selection and placement. For example, you may be asked to type a letter if you are applying for a secretarial job or to operate a machine for a mechanical job. Finally, some studies show that the best predictors of job performance are *letters of recommendation*, especially if your previous supervisor is questioned specifically about behaviors related to job performance.

Assume that you have been working in a particular position in a company. At some point your employer will conduct a **job analysis** as a method to evaluate whether you are doing your job as well as you are supposed to. A job analysis involves three parts:

▼

job analysis—a method of evaluating whether workers are doing their job as well as they are supposed to.

1. A job description, which specifies the activities and duties of the job
2. The job specification, which indicates the job skills and knowledge required
3. The job environment, which describes the physical and social environment and work conditions—shifts, pay, benefits, and so on

Information about job performance can come from several sources, including observations of your job activities, interviewing your supervisors and fellow employees, and having you keep a job diary. Besides the possibility that your supervisors and fellow employees may have personal likes and dislikes about you, their ratings in one area of your work may be influenced by your performance in another area. For example, your mechanical skills may overshadow the fact that your paperwork leaves a lot to be desired.

Training. No matter how skillful an employer is in selecting and placing job applicants, they must be adequately trained to do well. Although the need for training may be obvious to you, only 27 percent of companies surveyed in one study had specific training procedures.[5]

needs analysis—an organizational method to determine the need for training

A critical aspect of training is a **needs analysis**, in which the organization determines who needs training and what type of training is needed. Because our economy and the characteristics of our population are always changing, needs analyses are very important. Experts project that as we approach the twenty-first century the workforce will consist of more older and more female workers and that nine out of ten new jobs will be service-oriented. This means that you probably will doing "people work," dealing directly with customers and clients. At the same time, your job will involve technological advances in office or factory automation involving robots and computer-assisted manufacturing. Your job will also require more cognitive activities. For example, executives at the Mazda plant in Michigan expect their employees to work in teams, rotate jobs, understand how their tasks fit into the entire manufacturing process, troubleshoot problems, explain them to others, suggest improvements, and write detailed charts and memos. These demands are a far cry from jobs in the past, which rarely taxed your mental abilities.[6]

Many contemporary workers, like those at the Mazda plant shown here, are expected to work in teams.

Needs analyses must also address the training of undereducated youths, many of whom are from cultural groups that have not yet blended into the workforce. They also must address the training of the small percentage of women, African Americans, Hispanics, and Asians in high management positions.[7,8,9]

Personnel training applies many of the learning and motivational principles you learned about in Chapters 5, and 9. Positive reinforcers such as praise, recognition, money, and prizes are used liberally, and the cognitive skills that lead to mastery are emphasized.[10] The hope is that trainees eventually will be guided by the desire to do well (intrinsic motivation) as they develop a sense of mastery. Research also shows that your motivation increases when the material to be learned is made meaningful to you; when you receive immediate, concrete feedback about your training; and when you are given many chances to practice what you have learned.[10] One of the worst ways to be trained is for your boss to give you instructions and then leave you "swinging in the wind," so to speak.

Training can be accomplished either on the job or off the job. *On-the-job training* is the most widely used and includes apprenticeships, internships, and coaching by a mentor or supervisor. On-the-job training gives you hands-on experience, which tends to increase job satisfaction, but it often is unsystematic and includes the risk that the trainer is not much more knowledgeable than the trainee. If you have ever been frustrated because you were skilled enough to train your trainer, you know what we mean. With *off-the-job* techniques you learn from a professional trainer who helps you focus on specific job skills. This training uses lectures, audio-visual presentations, and programmed instruction, in which you teach yourself material that is broken down into units from the simple to the more complex. Business schools, consulting firms, and the armed services routinely use computer-assisted instruction, business games or combat games, for instance, in which job activities are simulated.[11] Behavior-modeling techniques, in which trainees observe the skilled behavior of a model, are effective in teaching concrete skills such as operating equipment or assembling a machine. They are also used in training interpersonal and leadership skills required of managers.[10,12]

Organizational Behavior

Another important aspect of psychology in the workplace is **organizational behavior**, which is concerned with issues such as worker motivation, satisfaction, and leadership.

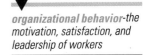

organizational behavior-the motivation, satisfaction, and leadership of workers

Job Motivation and Satisfaction.

How well you do on the job is affected by your motivation. Because there is a limited supply of qualified workers and people are changing jobs and careers at a rapid pace, I-O psychologists have become concerned with developing and retaining the people they already have. For these reasons, the study of motivation in the workplace has become one of the hottest topics in I-O psychology.

Many theories of work motivation have been proposed, and from them I-O psychologists have applied strategies to improve work performance. There are two main types of work motivation theories. One type focuses on external sources, or "handles," that organizations use to motivate behavior. The other type of motivation theory emphasizes internal factors, such as expectancies and attitudes.[13,14] There are several specific theories within each type (see Table 14.2).

Table 14.2 Theories of Work Motivation

Theory	Description
Goal theory:	You will perform better if goals are defined as challenging, specific, meaningful, and attractive. Employers should set clear and meaningful objectives and supply performance feedback.
Incentive-reward theory:	You are motivated to perform behaviors that result in positive consequences such as good pay, recognition, having some authority, time off, and working with friendly, cooperative fellow employees.
Motive-need theory:	You are motivated by needs to seek or avoid certain stimuli. Motivation is accomplished by matching personnel to specific jobs and through formal motivational training programs in achievement, power, and personal growth.
Attitude theory	You will perform best when you have favorable attitudes toward your job.
Attribution/self-efficacy theory:	Your motivation improves when you believe that job success is related to your abilities and efforts.
Equity theory:	The need for fair treatment motivates you. Pay and promotions should be related to your ability and seniority.
Expectancy-value theory:	Your motivation is highest when you expect that your efforts will lead to good performance and valued outcomes.

Are you satisfied with your job? If not, you are not alone. Though precise statistics are not available, surveys indicate that many Americans are dissatisfied with their jobs.[13] Inasmuch as job satisfaction is related to performance, it is the most studied job attitude in I-O psychology.

What determines job satisfaction? Ask all your friends, and they probably will tell you that the main factors are the nature of the job and the working conditions. Think about it. How could you be satisfied with a boring, low-paying job, working in a dismal atmosphere, with little chance for advancement?

Certainly, job satisfaction is strongly associated with the work itself. In general, your satisfaction increases when you get a chance to use your skills and control the work pace and when the tasks involve some variety. Pay, benefits, job security, and opportunities for promotion are also critical factors. In terms of the work environment, you are bound to like your job if you have a fair, considerate supervisor, and if you work with others who have values similar to yours. The conditions of the physical environment are important, too, but research generally indicates that this factor is not as important as the other variables mentioned.[13,14]

Research in I-O psychology indicates that worker characteristics are important factors as well.[14] In general, satisfaction increases with increases in age, occupational status, and education, though the reasons are unclear.

Fundamentals of Psychology

In other words, older, white-collar workers with more education are more likely to be satisfied with their jobs than are younger, blue-collar workers with little education. Intelligence, is not consistently related to job satisfaction. Some research suggests that you are likely to be dissatisfied with your job if its requirements simply do not match your intellectual abilities.[13,14] Race is another factor. At all occupational levels, nonwhites are twice as likely as whites to express dissatisfaction with their jobs.[13,14]

A hotly debated, but unresolved, issue in I-O psychology is whether job satisfaction is largely determined by the personality makeup of the individual. Evidence for this idea comes from research that shows that negative emotional reactions to work are relatively stable over time and among jobs.[14] In other words, you will probably be dissatisfied with almost any job if you generally have a negative outlook about work and life.

Research on gender differences in job satisfaction has yielded inconclusive results. Some studies suggest that women are generally more satisfied than men, and other studies have found women to be more dissatisfied, possibly because many women feel exploited in the workplace.[13,14] They tend to be employed in lower-level jobs and are usually paid less than men for doing comparable work.[13,14] Interpersonal factors, including sexual harassment, may also contribute to dissatisfaction among female workers (see *Issues and Applications: Sexual Harassment in the Workplace*).

Leadership.   It should come as no surprise to you that the success of any business or organization depends on strong leadership and responsive followers. Accordingly, I-O psychologists have been studying leadership and suggesting methods to improve it. Historically, leaders were viewed as headstrong individuals with special traits, and followers were seen as people who obediently followed their leader's commands. If you have ever held a job in which you were "bossed around" from task to task with nothing to say about it, however, you know how this kind of leadership can ruin your motivation, satisfaction, and productivity.

Do you think you would be more motivated and satisfied with a job in which you could offer your opinions and participate in decision making? Today, the prevailing view of effective leadership has shifted away from that of a person with special traits and exclusive power toward two-way influence and power sharing, which can be accomplished in several ways. At the lowest level of power sharing, the manager or supervisor allows participation in management by asking you and your co-workers for your opinions or suggestions. Another method of power sharing involves the formation of **quality circles**, groups of employees who get together regularly to deal with work-related tasks and who present their conclusions to management. These can be effective ways to share power if some of your input is used by the supervisor to make important decisions. Otherwise, you will probably become discouraged, believing that your participation is nothing but a sham.[8]

The best leadership approach is to delegate or distribute power. With this method, managers allow workers to make certain decisions on their

quality circles—groups of employees who get together regularly to deal with work-related issues

Sexual Harassment of Women in the Workplace

In the most publicized case of sexual harassment, attorney Anita Hill accused U.S. Supreme Court Justice nominee Clarence Thomas of sexual harassment. Did you think that Thomas was guilty of the charge? Well, no matter how you answered you would have plenty of company. I-O psychologists are concerned about sexual harassment because its stressful effects may work against work motivation, job satisfaction, productivity, and career development. Because it is an important issue in businesses and organizations today, you should be concerned, too.

Sexual harassment is defined as any unwanted sexually oriented behavior—whether or not it interferes with job performance or creates psychological harm. Examples of sexual harassment include unwelcome sexual advances; requests for sexual favors; and explicit sexual comments, jokes, or gestures. As clear as this definition may seem to you, men and women often disagree about what makes up harassment. For example, men rarely complain of sexual harassment, possibly because they are likely to be flattered rather than offended by a woman's sexual advances. Furthermore, many men misinterpret a woman's friendliness as flirting.

Between 30 and 50 percent of women have been sexually harassed. Feelings of power on the part of the harasser and powerlessness in the victim and ideas about sex roles are the most common reasons cited for sexual harassment. Though sexual harassment usually involves an employee's harassing a co-worker of equal rank, the most severe cases involve a man in power harassing a lower ranking, unmarried woman. The attitude of some men that women are primarily sexual partners may also contribute.

What can be done to prevent sexual harassment? I-O psychologists recommend several measures. First, personnel selection should be designed to detect potential harassers. Second, education and training should be provided to help men "think like a woman" so they can become sensitive to unacceptable behaviors. Third, work settings should be geared to encourage more equality for men and women. Even though these measures may not eliminate sexual harassment, they may help to reduce its frequency.[15,16,17]

▼
self-managed work teams—groups of workers who are responsible for assigning jobs to members, solving production problems, and selecting and training new members

own, depending on the workers' capabilities. A good example is **self-managed work teams** that are responsible for assigning jobs to members, solving production problems, and selecting and training new members under the guidance of an external leader who acts as a consultant or coordinator.[8]

Engineering and Environmental Psychology

What do working in a noisy factory and living in a crowded city have in common? They are examples of how factors outside you can affect your ability to function in life and work. Your job performance does not depend on your abilities, personality, and motivation alone. Features of the work environment, such as noise, light, temperature, and your work schedule, can affect your performance. So can the kinds of tasks you must perform. Experts say that your job will become increasingly more complex than before and will require more mental work needed to deal with technological advances.[14] Outside your job, environmental factors including noise, violations of personal space, and overcrowding can affect the quality of your life. In this section you will study two areas of applied psychology that are concerned with these issues: engineering and environmental psychology.

Engineering Psychology

Picture yourself working at a job that requires that you read information displayed on a video monitor. The room is noisy, hot and stuffy, and dimly lit, and your co-workers are packed around you like sardines in a can. To make matters worse, you rarely get a break when you are supposed to, your schedule never changes, and it is tough to get a day off when you need it. How well do you think you could perform in these work conditions? Matters such as these are the concern of **engineering psychology**, which involves the application of scientific knowledge about people to the design of machines, systems, and environments. Also called *human factors psychology* or *ergonomics*, engineering psychology seeks to provide knowledge concerning your capacity to process and retrieve information and thereby make systems safer, more efficient, more accurate, and more "user-friendly."[18]

▼

engineering psychology—application of scientific knowledge about people to the design of machines, systems, and environments

You can get a good idea about the focus of engineering psychology by sitting behind the wheel of a car and working the controls. Are they conveniently placed and easy to use, or do you get frustrated with or angry at the way they are designed? Are the displays and gauges easy to read, or do they make you feel inadequate and only a trained astronaut could figure them out? Whether you are operating a car, factory machine, a sophisticated fighter jet, or a VCR, engineering psychologists strive to design them with human, that is, psychological factors in mind.

Like psychology in general, engineering psychology is driven by several forces. One force is technology. As you know, technology continues to advance at a rapid pace, particularly with regard to computer hardware and software and the use of robots and other types of automation. This means that you will have more and more interactions with technology in your everyday life and work. Because machines can do more, do it much faster than ever, and you are no longer faced with the knobs and dials of the past, the cognitive demands placed on you, the operator, will increase, too.

As computer hardware and software, the use of robots, and other technology advances rapidly, the cognitive demands placed on you at work will increase.

Engineering psychologists strive to determine how to best display information to the operator so that cognitive capabilities are not overloaded. This means that display designs should consider your perceptual abilities and limitations.[19] Some clues about how to make displays easier for operators to deal with have been provided. A good display is coded so that it is easy to detect and to distinguish from other codes. It should also be meaningful and standardized.[20] A good example is a traffic light. At all intersections with traffic lights red means stop and green means go. Can you think of other examples of displays in your everyday life that meet these criteria?

Sadly, our performance capacities are sometimes no match for innovations in technology, resulting in system failure from human error. We have become painfully aware of this mismatch in light of nuclear power plant and aircraft disasters, like the one mentioned at the beginning of the chapter, and other accidents as well. In these cases, the disaster stemmed from a combination of human error and mechanical failure.[21]

Social change, too, is a driving force in engineering psychology. Our population is getting older and more diverse in terms of gender and ethnicity, and educational levels are declining. In this light, engineering psychologists are predicting a shortage in talent that must be considered in training the workforce to deal with advances in technology.[21]

Environmental Psychology

▼

environmental psychology—studies the relationships between the physical environment and behavior

Environmental psychology studies the relationships between the physical environment and behavior.[22] Environmental psychologists are interested in factors that can affect the quality of life, such as noise, personal space, and overcrowding. Ideally, the knowledge gained from environmental psychology can be used to design work and living environments wherein people can be productive and reach their personal goals.

To function well in any environment you must know and adapt to it. Of course, knowing the environment is a process whereby you perceive and evaluate its elements in terms of your capacity to cope with them. You may recall from Chapter 11 that you will experience stress if you believe that a situation is threatening to you. Certain elements of your environment can affect your performance and the quality of your life because you perceive them as unpleasant and threatening.[23]

Noise.　Unless you live and work in a meadow where most sounds come from singing birds, babbling brooks, and the rustling of trees, you are probably bombarded by disturbing noise from cars and buses, jets, lawn mowers, and other machinery. Keep in mind that loud sounds are not necessarily noisy. Consider a live performance of your favorite music group. Though the live music is louder than the sounds coming from the vehicles on a busy street, you would say that the street is noisier because the sounds are unpleasant. Research shows that noise can affect job performance when it is unpredictable and uncontrollable.[22,23] This adverse effect is especially noticeable when a person is subjected to high-frequency noises while involved in a complex task that requires careful attention. Noise can affect your social life, too. People who reside in noisy neighborhoods are likely to be more aggressive and to encounter more social problems than are individuals who reside in quieter neighborhoods.

Personal Space and Overcrowding.　The next time you are conversing with someone, notice whether you feel a little uncomfortable. If you do, it may be because that person has entered your **personal space**, an imaginary "bubble" or area surrounding you that you stake as your own. When someone invades your personal space you feel stressed, and this feeling can affect your ability to communicate effectively.

　　Personal space varies from person to person and also depends on ethnic background, the degree of interpersonal attraction, and other aspects of the situation.[24] According to anthropologist Edward Hall, most people have a personal space of about one-and-a-half to four feet, but these figures can increase or decrease depending on the circumstances (see Table 14.3).[25] For example, your personal space would lessen if you were interacting with a boyfriend or girlfriend, and it probably would expand in dealing with a stranger. Imagine how edgy you would feel if a door-to-door salesperson was right in your face. Gender and cultural differences in personal space have also been noted, but they are influenced by the situation as well. Women generally have a smaller personal space than men, but they have a larger space when they are interacting with strange men. One study showed that Venezuelans generally sat closer together than Japanese people, but their personal space was influenced by language. Venezuelans sat closer if they were speaking Spanish but farther apart if they were speaking English.[26]

▼

personal space—an area surrounding you that you stake as your own

Table 14.3 **Interpersonal Distance**

Intimate	Direct contact to 6–16 inches: private activities
Personal	1.5–2.5 feet: husband and wife standing in public
Social	4–7 feet: business transactions, conversation
Public	25 feet or more: public speaking

Source:　*Adapted from Hall, E. T., and Hall, M. T. (1971). The sounds of silence. In P. Whitten & D. E. K. Hunter (Eds.). Anthropology: Current perspectives (125–130). Boston: Little, Brown.*

Chapter 14 • Applied Psychology

Studies in environmental psychology show that individuals who are exposed to a high density of people, or *overcrowding*, are more physiologically aroused and report more negative emotions than people who live and work in less crowded conditions.[22] Thus, living in a crowded city or household may cause problems for you. If you ever felt as if you were ready to get away from the mobs and live alone in the mountains or on a tropical isle, you have scientific support for your feelings.

Environmental psychologists are concerned about the effects of the environment on behavior. They have learned that children in overcrowded classrooms, like the one pictured here, are likely to have perceptual, language, and social problems.

The psychological effects of overcrowding are worst if you have little control over it and when there is minimal cooperation in the situation. Overcrowding, for example, is a major problem in prisons, where generally uncooperative inmates are confined involuntarily.[22] Many prison riots involving injuries, murders, and the taking of hostages have been blamed on overcrowding. Overcrowding creates difficulties in college dormitory life, too. One study showed that the negative psychological effects of overcrowding were strongest for students in tripled rooms who had stormy interpersonal relationships with their roommates.[23] Finally, overcrowding and the associated noise has been shown to have negative effects on children's perceptual and cognitive development and social behavior. Compared with children in less densely populated schools, children in overcrowded schools have more visual and auditory discrimination problems, language and reading difficulties, they socialize less, and are more likely to be verbally and physically abusive toward others.[22] Though these studies do not prove a direct cause-and-effect connection between overcrowding and psychological problems, they nevertheless indicate a relationship that psychologists should continue to investigate.

Community Psychology

In the early 1960s, President Kennedy concluded that psychological distress was linked to cultural and educational deprivation and that doing something about such harsh environmental conditions would help to prevent mental illness. This conclusion led to a policy of **deinstitutionalization**, which involved moving mental patients out of overcrowded mental hospitals so that they could be treated using resources in the community. The community mental health movement was born.

Today, **community psychology** studies the effects of social and environmental factors on behavior and applies this knowledge to promote the well-being of individuals in the population. As an outgrowth of clinical and social psychology as well as sociology and anthropology, community psychology is concerned with how detrimental environmental conditions can affect behavior and the education of community members in practices they can use to combat these conditions. Unlike clinical psychologists, who diagnose and treat mental disorders, community psychologists emphasize the importance of prevention to solve many types of problems besides mental disorders. Table 14.4 outlines some of the approaches used by community psychologists to promote well-being. In this section you will examine the types of problems addressed by community psychologists and the approaches they use.[27,28,29]

▼

deinstitutionalization—a policy of moving mental patients out of overcrowded mental hospitals

▼

community psychology— studies the effects of social and environmental factors on behavior and applies this knowledge to promote the well-being of individuals in the population

Table 14.3 **Community Psychology Approaches to Promote Well-being**

Approach	Description
Competence building	Individuals learn personal and social skills
Empowerment	Individuals get stronger and cope better when they develop a sense of control over their lives
Self-help	People cope with problems through involvement in groups of people with similar problems
Social support	People fight stress and solve problems through meaningful social interactions

Source: Adapted from E.L. Gesten & L.A. Jason (1987). Social and Community Interventions. *Annual Review of Psychology, 38, 427-460.*

What Do Community Psychologists Do?

Other than working in the area of mental health, what do you think you would be doing if you were a community psychologist? The interests of community psychologists are too numerous to describe here: For example, they are involved in promoting recycling, increasing inoculation rates among preschoolers, and planning for disaster and crisis response. After a plane crash, like the one described at the beginning of the chapter, psychologists are called to help people cope with their trauma. Community psychologists are involved in designing projects to reduce the risk of heart disease, to educate adolescents to refuse alcohol and cigarettes, and to prevent teenage pregnancy. Finally, they also influence public policy related to these community concerns by participating in the political process.[28]

If you already think that community psychologists are busy individuals, consider that their interests have expanded in recent years to cover many other problems of modern society. Important issues such as violence against women and children, the war on drugs, and violence in the inner cities also lie in the domain of community psychology (see *Issues and Applications: Youth Violence*). In this section you will study how community psychology has been involved in the war against two major problems: AIDS and homelessness.

The Prevention of AIDS

Few diseases strike more fear in the hearts of people than **acquired immune deficiency syndrome** (AIDS), an immune system disease that kills its victims by making them more susceptible to life-threatening infections. In the United States nearly 300,000 cases of AIDS had been reported by 1993, and the number of infected people who do not yet have symptoms is probably more than a million.[30] Those numbers should be cause for concern to you because AIDS is the second leading cause of death in men between the ages of 18 and 45 and the sixth leading cause of death for women in the same age bracket.[31]

Issues and Applications

Youth Violence

In the 1991 movie *Boyz n the Hood*, Doughboy said, "Can't we have one night where there ain't no problem...nobody gets shot?" Two weeks later he was murdered. Sadly, these words reflect the fact that violence and bloodshed have become a part of everyday life for many youths in America today, and there does not appear to be any letup in sight. If you are like many teenagers and young adults today, it is likely that you have been in a fight within the last year and you may fear for your safety.

Signs of violence are all around you. Surveys show, for example, that 1 in 5 high school students bring a weapon to school and 1 in 20 say they carry a gun. Is it any wonder that homicide is the second leading cause of death among children and adolescents in the United States and that the risk is highest for people between the ages of 15 and 24? Although homicide knows no race or age, statistics show that African American youths are most vulnerable. Homicide is the leading cause of death for both male and female African Americans between the ages of 15 and 34, and the rates are rising for those between 15 and 19 years

Community psychology's involvement in the fight against AIDS is based on the fact that, although AIDS is caused by HIV (human immunodeficiency virus) infection, it is transmitted by behavior. Intravenous drug use and unsafe sex with an infected person are the most common behaviors associated with getting AIDS. Because neither a vaccine nor cure is available (and a vaccine would probably be only 60–80 percent effective), the only way to stem the spread of AIDS is through prevention. Psychologists have been involved in many programs designed to educate people about risky behaviors. One community-based program that focused on gay and bisexual men in San Francisco was so successful in reducing the number of new AIDS cases that it is now being used in other areas of the country. AIDS-prevention programs are also being adapted to minority communities under the leadership of psychologists like Hortensia Amaro.[32,33,34]

Despite the efforts of psychologists, AIDS remains an urgent problem. One difficulty that community psychologists face is that many people underestimate their own personal risk of getting AIDS. For example, if you are heterosexual you might not be motivated to change your sexual practices because you mistakenly believe that you can get AIDS only through homosexual activity. Furthermore, many individuals believe that recreational drug use poses little risk of HIV infection, but, in fact, some research hints at a relationship between drug and alcohol abuse and HIV infection. Though the association has not been confirmed, substance use may lower your inhibitions and thereby increase your chances of engaging in unsafe sexual behavior such not using protection during intercourse.[32,33,34,35]

of age. In the typical case, the young adult from an inner city, low-income family is shot by an African American friend or acquaintance as retaliation or revenge for some misdeed. In fact, more than 90 percent of slain African Americans were killed by other African Americans.

The prevention of youth violence depends on understanding its causes, but, unfortunately, psychologists and other community-minded people have not been able to provide satisfactory explanations. Contrary to what you might think, neither racial discrimination nor economic deprivation is sufficient to account for violence in African Americans and other youths. In fact, most youths are not violent at all. Though media portrayals may suggest that drug and alcohol use and gang activities are the chief causes, research shows that they account for only a small proportion of youth violence. The most sensible approach for now is to teach general communication, problem solving, and social skills designed to help youths find alternative ways to cope with conflicts. With African American and other minorities, prevention programs should be tailored to the unique characteristics of their culture.[36]

Chapter 14 • Applied Psychology

Biography: Hortensia Amaro

Hortensia de los Angeles Amaro is one of the most important figures in the development of AIDS-prevention programs in ethnic minority communities. As a researcher and founder of the Latino Health Council, the Latino Health Network, and the Multicultural AIDS Coalition, she has had a major impact on AIDS public policy.

Hortensia Amaro was born in 1950 in Camaguey, Cuba, and lived there for 10 years until she emigrated to Miami after Fidel Castro took power. Because Miami was a hostile place for Cubans at the time, she moved to Los Angeles with her family and attended elementary school there. Upon entering school she was given an IQ test in English, a language she did not know, and by junior high school she was placed in a class for slow learners. At her parents' insistence she was retested, did well, and was placed in a college preparatory class. At that

time the usual practice was to place Hispanics in noncollege-type courses. She considers her enrollment in a college prep class to be one of the most important events in her career.

In 1975 Amaro received her bachelor's degree in psychology from UCLA, then continued her graduate work there in developmental psychology. While in graduate school she began conducting research on substance abuse in women, which ac-

quainted her with community psychology. In 1983 Amaro moved to Boston, where she became assistant professor of social and behavioral sciences at the Boston University School of Public Health and assistant professor of pediatrics at the Boston University School of Medicine.

Amaro's interest in AIDS was the result of her younger brother's diagnosis. Painfully aware of the impact of AIDS in the African American and Hispanic communities, she developed a community-based prevention program for drug-addicted women. Eventually the federally funded program, involving more than 600 women, provided drug treatment, counseling, and other support services. Besides her research and community program development, Hortensia Amaro has testified at several House and Senate briefings about substance abuse and AIDS. In 1992, she won the APA Award for Distinguished Contribution to Psychology in the Public Interest.[37]

Psychologists now recommend several approaches to AIDS prevention. How many of them are you already familiar with?

▶ Educate people about AIDS risk factors.

▶ Help individuals more accurately appraise their personal risk.

▶ Train people in the cognitive and behavioral skills necessary to change faulty behavior and reinforce behavior change.

▶ Try to modify social norms so that safe sex becomes more acceptable among community members.

▶ Mass market the message about AIDS through print, radio, and television[35]

Homelessness

The U.S. government estimates that nearly 600,000 people in this country do not have a permanent place to live, but advocates of the homeless insist that the actual figure is probably more than 3 million. You may have encountered homeless people in your everyday life, and you might find it hard to imagine how there can be so many "down-and-out" people in the richest country in the world. Before we can attack the problem of homelessness, it is necessary to know who the homeless are. Community psychologists have focused most of their efforts on characterizing homeless people.

The media and advocates of the homeless portray them as "typical Americans" who have suffered a stroke of bad luck because of hard economic conditions and uncaring government policies. We are told that these are otherwise hard-working people who have lost their jobs or simply cannot find affordable housing. Indeed, many homeless individuals fit this picture. Unfortunately, however, solving homelessness is not a simple matter of changing government policies to ensure more jobs and affordable housing because not all homeless individuals are just unlucky.[38]

About one-third of homeless people, especially homeless men, have serious alcohol or drug problems, and another third have mental disorders such as schizophrenia, mood disorders, and personality disorders. (See Figure 14.1.) Worse yet is the fact that many homeless people have substance-related problems and mental disorders at the same time, and more than one-third have been in jail, often for serious crimes. You might have heard of Larry Hogue, who has become a national symbol of the mentally ill, drug-addicted, homeless population. Referred to as the "Wild Man of 96th Street" by the media, Hogue has been in and out of jails and mental hospitals for years for terrorizing people in New York City and possession of crack cocaine.

Many homeless people have other characteristics that argue against the notion that they are "typical Americans." Compared with people with a home, homeless people are less likely to have completed high school, have fewer occupational skills, had more childhood behavior problems, and were more likely to have come from problem families. To complicate matters, homeless people have more health problems such as liver damage, brain damage, lung disease, and AIDS. They also are more likely to get into fights, traffic accidents, and prostitution.[39,40]

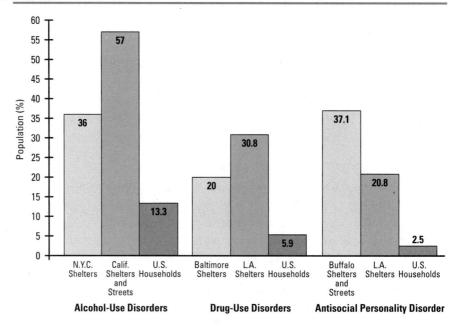

Figure 14.1 Prevalence of Alcohol and Drug Use and Mental Disorders among the U.S. Homeless

The percentage of various U.S. populations who have alcohol or drug problems or antisocial personality disorders. Compared with U.S. households, these problems are more prevalent among the homeless population.

Source: Fisher, P. J. & Breakey, W. R. (1990). "The epidemiology of alcohol, drug, and mental disorders among homeless persons." *American Psychologist, 46,* p. 1115–1128

As we learn more about the homeless we discover that a growing segment, more than 30 percent, are women and children. The typical profile of a homeless woman is that of an under-35-year-old mother from an ethnic minority group who never completed high school and has been homeless before.[41] Homeless children are dealt an especially severe blow, suffering from hunger, poor nutrition, anxiety, depression, behavior problems, and educational underachievement.[42]

Another growing portion of the homeless population in the United States is youths. Some experts estimate that there are 1.5 million homeless youths, and that 4 percent of them are infected with HIV. Most are white, but in large U.S. cities more are likely to be African American. If you are wondering how these individuals became homeless, there are three typical routes. Many homeless youths are "runaways," kids who left home to escape from abuse or neglect. Others, called "throwaways," are those who were put out of their homes by parents for various reasons. The remaining homeless youths are those without families who lack basic shelter. They are called "street youths."[43]

Now that you see that there are many different kinds of homeless people with a variety of needs and problems, you can begin to understand that there is no easy solution to homelessness. Whether the mental, drug, and other problems are the causes of homelessness, or consequences as many have argued, they tell us nevertheless that many obstacles must be overcome.[44] Clearly, the solution to homelessness will require comprehensive changes in governmental, economic and social policies to ensure affordable housing. This solution will not be enough, however. Community psychologists and others must reach out to provide evaluation, treatment, and rehabilitation services for those with mental disorders and drug and alcohol addiction, and medical services, occupational training, and educational programs must be provided to help the growing number of homeless children.[29]

Other Areas of Applied Psychology

Besides the areas that you have already studied, the principles and methods of psychology have also been applied to matters such as consumer behavior, legal concerns, education, and sports.

Consumer Psychology

What goes through your mind when you buy a particular product? Why do you prefer one brand of cola over another or a certain type of jeans or sneakers? Do you sometimes buy an item because it is wrapped in an attractive package? Does sex sell cars? No doubt your buying preferences are determined partly by the quality of the product. For example, you might like Coke more than Pepsi because you feel it tastes better. Psychological research reveals, however, that there is more to your buying decisions than you might imagine. Issues such as these are the concern of **consumer psychology**, which applies psychological methods and principles to the study of consumer behavior. The knowledge derived from consumer psychology research is important not only because it sheds light on another aspect of human behavior, but also because it is useful to companies in developing marketing strategies.[45]

▼
consumer psychology—the application of psychological methods and principles to the study of consumer behavior

Forensic Psychology

You probably have seen television shows and movies in which the police consult with a psychologist to develop a psychological profile of a ruthless serial killer who is still on the loose. This is one example of **forensic psychology**, which involves the application of psychological research or assessment information to legal issues. Clinical psychologists with an interest in legal matters are the best known forensic psychologists. They are involved in matters such as evaluating a person's competency to stand trial, insanity determinations, jury selection, child custody evaluations, and many other kinds of legal proceedings in which knowledge about human behavior is important. Lawyers, judges, and juries then decide the worth of the information supplied by the forensic psychologist.[46,47]

▼
forensic psychology—the application of psychological research or assessment information to legal issues

Educational Psychology

Educational psychology is concerned with the application of psychological principles and methods to teaching and learning. Educational psychologists, for example, develop instructional methods that allow them to present knowledge in an understandable manner. They also explore new ways to motivate children and teach them strategies to help them learn and retain information and perfect skills. The SQ3R method of textbook instruction you learned about in Chapter 6 is an example of how educational psychologists have applied the principles of learning and memory research. Educational psychologists are also involved in classroom management—creating a classroom environment that is conducive to learning for everyone involved.

Sports Psychology

No matter which sport you play, you probably at some time hit a slump in which you could not seem to do anything right despite your skills. As the slump continued, you might have started talking negatively to yourself and even have expected to fail. Less than perfect performance can be a real problem for high-caliber amateur athletes who may have a medal at stake. For professional athletes, sub-par performance not only means failure but can also make the difference in securing a multimillion dollar contract. How many times have you seen a professional miss a field goal, strike out, or miss an important free throw only to see the person cut from the team? To deal with the mental factors in athletic performance, many teams take advantage of sports psychology, which applies psychological methods and principles to athletic performance. **Sports psychologists** are concerned with issues such as how to help athletes visualize success, think positively, focus on their task, and improve teamwork.

Summary

1. Personnel selection and placement involve the use of interviews, biodata, psychological tests, work samples, and letters of recommendation. A job analysis is a method used to evaluate whether an employee is performing as expected. Needs analyses are conducted to determine the need for training. Personnel training involves the application of learning and motivational principles and can be conducted on or off the job.

2. You are motivated to perform behaviors that result in positive consequences, and you will perform better if goals are defined as difficult, specific, meaningful, and attractive, if you are treated fairly, and when you have favorable attitudes toward your job. Your motivation is highest when you expect that your efforts will lead to good performance and valued outcomes. Motivation improves if you believe that job success is related to your abilities and efforts.

3. Job satisfaction increases when people can use their skills and control their work pace and when the tasks involve some variety, the supervisor is fair, and co-workers have similar values. Job satisfaction increases with increases in age, occupational level, and education. A negative outlook about work and life is associated with job dissatisfaction.

4. Engineering psychologists strive to figure out how to best display information to the operator so that cognitive capabilities are not overloaded. Social change must be considered in training the workforce to deal with advances in technology. Engineering psychologists must consider the facts that our population is getting older and more diverse in terms of gender and ethnicity and educational levels are declining.

5. Noise can affect your job performance when it is unpredictable and uncontrollable and can lead to aggression and social problems. When your personal space is invaded you feel uncomfortable, and your ability to communicate effectively can be affected. Overcrowding often results in increased physiological arousal and negative emotions. The psychological effects are worst if you have little control and if there is minimal cooperation.

6. Community psychology studies the effects of social and environmental factors on behavior and applies this knowledge to promote the well-being of individuals in the population. It is concerned with how detrimental environmental conditions can affect behavior and in educating community members in practices they can use to combat these conditions. Community psychologists emphasize the importance of primary prevention to solve many types of problems and use methods that will build competence, provide social support, empower individuals, and provide opportunities for self-help.

7. Community psychology's involvement in the fight against AIDS is focused on stemming the spread of AIDS through prevention. Psychologists recommend education about AIDS risk factors, helping people appraise their personal risk, training in the cognitive and behavioral skills necessary to change faulty behavior and reinforce behavior change, the modification of social norms toward acceptance of safe sex practices, and media marketing of the message about AIDS.

8. One-third of homeless people have serious substance-related problems, another third have mental disorders, and many have combined problems. Homeless people are less likely to have completed high school, have fewer occupational skills, had more childhood behavior problems, were more likely to have come from problem families, and have more health problems. Women, children and youths are a growing segment of the homeless population. These characteristics call for changes in governmental social and economic policies as well as specialized services.

9. Consumer psychology applies psychological methods and principles to the study of consumer behavior. Forensic psychology involves the application of psychological research or assessment information to legal issues. Educational psychology is concerned with the application of psychological principles and methods to teaching and learning. Sports psychology applies psychological methods and principles to athletic performance.

Questions for Discussion

1. What are the important elements of personnel selection, placement, and training?

2. What factors increase work motivation?

3. What factors are associated with job satisfaction?

4. How do technology and social change influence human performance on the job?

5. What are the effects of noise, violations of personal space, and overcrowding on human behavior?

6. What are the goals and methods of community psychology?

7. What is the role of community psychology in the prevention of AIDS?

8. What are the characteristics of homeless people, and how do they affect solutions to the problem?

9. How are consumer, forensic, educational, and sports psychology defined?

Fundamentals of Psychology

Applying Psychology

In this chapter, you learned that job satisfaction increases if:

▶ You can use your skills

▶ You can control the work pace

▶ The tasks involve some variety

▶ You have a fair supervisor

▶ You work with others who have values similar to yours

▶ You have a positive outlook about work and life in general.

Even if you have only a part-time job, evaluate your job satisfaction according to these six criteria on a scale from 1 to 10. One means you are totally dissatisfied, 10 means you are completely satisfied. If your total score is less than 43, you probably are dissatisfied enough with your job to see if you can do anything to make improvements. If this is the case, what can you do to improve your job satisfaction?

References

Chapter 1

1. American Psychological Association (1986). *Careers in psychology*. Washington, DC: American Psychological Association.

2. Woods, P. J. (Ed.) with Wilkinson, C.S. (1987). *Is psychology the major for you? Planning for your undergraduate years*. Washington, DC: APA.

3. Wertheimer, M. (1970). *A brief history of psychology*. New York: Holt

4. Fancher, R. E. (1979). *Pioneers of psychology*. New York: Norton.

5. Denmark, F., Russo, N. F., Frieze, I. H., & Sechzer, J. A. (1988). Guidelines for avoiding sexism in psychological research. *American Psychologist, 43*, 582-585.

6. Gannon, L., Luchetta, T., Rhodes, K., Pardie, L., & Gegrist, D. (1992). Sex bias in psychological research: Progress or complacency? *American Psychologist, 47*, 389-396.

7. Graham, S. (1992). Most of the subjects were white and middle class: Trends in published research on African Americans in selected APA journals, 1970-1989. *American Psychologist, 47*, 629-639.

8. Mowen, J. C. (1989). Consumer psychology. In W. L. Gregory & W. J. Burroughs (Eds.), *Intro-duction to applied psychology*. Glenview, IL: Scott Foresman.

9. Gross, M. (1978). *The psychological society*. New York: Random House.

10. Rosenthal, R. & Jacobson, L. V. (1968). *Pygmalion in the classroom: Teacher expectation and pupils' intellectual development*. New York: Holt

11. Milgram, S. (1963). Behavioral study of obedience. *Journal of Abnormal and Social Psychology, 67*, 371-378.

12. American Psychological Association (1992). Ethical principles of psychologists and code of conduct. *American Psychologist, 47*, 1597-1611.

Chapter 2

1. Milner, B. (1966). Amnesia following operation of the temporal lobes. In C.W.M. Whitty & D.L. Zangwill (Eds.), *Amnesia*. London: Butterworth.

2. Fischbach, G. D. (1992). Mind and brain. *Scientific American, September*, 48-57.

3. Widner, H., Tetrud, J., Rehncrona, S., Snow, B., Brundin, P., Gustavii, B., Bjorkland, A., Lindvall, O., Langston, J. W. (1992). Bilateral fetal mesencephalic grafting in two patients with Parkinsonism induced by 1-Methyl-4-Phenyl-1,2,3,6-Tetrahydropyridine (MPTP). *New England Journal of Medicine, 327*, 1556-1563.

4. Olds, J. & Milner, P. (1954). Positive reinforcement produced by electrical stimulation of septal area and other regions of rat brain. *Journal of Comparative and Physiological Psychology, 47*, 419-427.

5. Valenstein, E. S. (1980). Rationale and surgical procedures. In E. S. Valenstein (Ed.), *The psychosurgery debate*. San Francisco: W.H. Freeman

6. Levinthal, C. F. (1990). *Introduction to physiological psychology, (3rd ed.)*. Englewood Cliffs, NJ: Prentice-Hall.

7. Kalat, J. W. (1992). *Biological psychology, (4th ed.)*. Belmont CA: Wadsworth.

8. Stuss, D. T. & Benson, D. F. (1984). Neuropsychological studies of the frontal lobes. *Psychological Bulletin, 95*, 3-28.

9. Rosenzweig, M. R. & Leiman, A. I. (1989). *Physiological psychology, (2nd ed.)*. New York: Random House.

10. Bloom, F. E. and Lazerson, A. (1988). *Brain, mind, and behavior*. New York: Freeman.

11. Sperry, R. W. (1964). The great cerebral commissures. *Scientific American, 210,* 42-52.

12. Gazzaniga, M. S. (1970). *The bisected brain.* New York: Appleton-Century-Crofts.

13. Sperry, R. W. (1974). Lateral specialization in the surgically separated hemispheres. In F. Schmitt & F. Worden (Eds.), *The neurosciences: Third study program.* Cambridge, MA: MIT press, 5-19.

14. The Corporation for Public Broadcasting (1988). Annenberg CPB Project. *The Brain.* Author.

15. Wasson, T. (Ed.) (1987). Roger Sperry. In T. Wasson, (Ed.). *Nobel prize winners: An H. W. Wilson biographical dictionary.* New York: H.W. Wilson, 997-1000.

16. Springer, S. P. (1989). Educating the two sides of the brain. *American Educator,* Spring, 32-37.

17. Levy, J. (1983). Language, cognition, and the right hemisphere. *American Psychologist, 38,* 538-541.

18. Shapiro, B.E. & Danly, M. (1985). The role of the right hemisphere in the control of speech prosody in propositional and affective contexts. *Brain and Language, 25,* 19-36.

19. Levy, J. (1982). Handwriting posture and cerebral organization: How are they related? *Psychological Bulletin, 91,* 589-608.

20. Satz, P. (1979). A test of some models of hemispheric speech organization in the left-and right-handed. *Science, 203,* 1131-1133.

21. Vaid, J. (1983). Bilingualism and brain lateralization. In S. J. Segalowitz (Ed.), *Language functions and brain organization.* New York: Academic Press, 315-339.

22. Kimura, D. (1992). Sex differences in the brain. *Scientific American, September,* 119-125.

23. Frankenhauser, M. (1979). Psychoneuroendocrine approaches to the study of emotion as related to stress and coping. *Current theory and research in motivation, 26,* 123-162.

24. Gitlin, M. J. & Pasnau, R. O. (1989). Psychiatric syndromes linked to reproductive functions in women: A review of the current knowledge. *American Journal of Psychiatry, 146,* 1413-1422.

25. Plomin, R. (1989). Environment and genes. Determinants of behavior. *American Psychologist, 44,* 105-111.

26. Plomin, R. (1990). The role of inheritance in behavior. *Science, 248,* 183-188.

Chapter 3

1. Keller, H., *The Story of My Life, Garden City,* NY: Doubleday, 1954, p. 102.

2. Engen, T. (1971). Psychophysics I. Discrimination and detection. In J. W. Kling & L. A. Riggs (Eds.), *Woodworth and Schlossberg's Experimental Psychology, 3rd ed.* New York: Holt.

3. Green, D. M. & Swets, J. A. (1966). *Signal detection theory and psychophysics.* New York: Wiley.

4. Swets, J. A. (1992). The science of choosing the right decision threshold in high-stakes diagnostics. *American Psychologist, 47,* 522-532.

5. Key, B. W. (1973). *Subliminal seduction.* Englewood Cliffs, NJ: Prentice-Hall.

6. Pratkanis, A. R. & Greenwald, A. G. (1988). Recent perspectives on unconscious processing: Still no marketing applications. *Psychology and Marketing, 5,* 337-353.

7. Bornstein, R. F. (1989). Subliminal techniques as propaganda tools: Review and critique. *Journal of Mind and Behavior, 10,* 231-262.

8. McConnell, J. V., Cutter, R. L., & McNeal, E. L. (1958). Subliminal stimulation: An overview. *American Psychologist, 13,* 229-242.

9. Greenwald, A. G., Spangenberg, E. R., Pratkanis, A. R., & Eskenazi, J. (1991). Double-blind tests of subliminal self-help audio tapes. *Psychological Science*, *2*, 119-122.

10. Hardaway, R. A. (1990). Subliminally activated symbiotic fantasies: Facts and artifacts. *Psychological Bulletin*, *107*, 177-195.

11. Vokey, J. R. & Read, J. D. (1985). Subliminal messages: Between the devil and the media. *American Psychologist*, *40*, 1231-1239.

12. Kihlstrom, J. F. (1987). The cognitive unconscious. *Science*, *237*, 1445-1452.

13. Fernandez, E. & Turk, D. C. (1992). Sensory and affective components of pain: Separation and synthesis. *American Psychologist*, *112*, 205-217.

14. Livingstone, M. S., Rosen, G. D., Drislane, F. W., & Galaburda, A. M. (1991). Physiological and anatomical evidence for a magnocellular defect in developmental dyslexia. *Proceedings of the national Academy of Sciences USA*, *88*, 7943-7947.

15. Lehmkuhle, S., Garzia, R. P., Turner, L., Hash, T., & Baro, J. A. (1993). A defective visual pathway in children with reading disability. *The New England Journal of Medicine*, *238*, 989-996.

16. Hubel, D. H. & Wiesel, T. N. (1979). Brain mechanisms of vision. *Scientific American*, March, *241*, 150-162.

17. Zeki, S. (1992). The visual image in mind and brain. *Scientific American*, September, *267*, 69-76.

18. Boynton, R. M. (1988). Color vision. *Annual Review of Psychology*, *39*, 69-100.

19. Wasson, T. (1987). *Nobel prize winners*. New York: H. W. Wilson

20. Hurvich, L. (1981). *Color vision*. Sunderland, Mass.: Sinauer.

21. Land, E. H. (1986). Recent advances in retinex theory. *Vision Research*, *26*, 7-21.

22. Rock, I. (1984). *Perception*. New York: Scientific American Books.

23. Rock, I. & Palmer, S. (1990). The legacy of Gestalt psychology. *Scientific American*, December, 84-91.

24. Kanizsa, G. (1976). Subjective contours. *Scientific American*, *234*, 48-52.

25. Kaufman, L. (1974). *Sight and mind: An introduction to perception*. New York: Oxford University Press.

26. Sekuler, R. & Blake, R. (1990). *Perception, 2nd ed.*, New York: McGraw Hill.

27. Moore, B. C. J. (1977). *Introduction to the psychology of hearing*. Baltimore: University Park

28. Middlebrooks, J. C. (1991). Sound localization by human listeners. *Annual Review of Psychology*, *42*, 135-159.

29. Melzack, R. & Wall, P. D. (1965). Pain mechanisms: A new theory. *Science*, *150*, 971-979.

30. Kalat, J. (1992). *Biological psychology*. Belmont, Calif.: Wadsworth.

31. Melzack, R. (1992). Phantom limbs. *Scientific American*, April, *266*, 120-126.

32. Freedman, D. H. (1993). In the realm of the chemical. *Discover*, June, 1993, 69-76.

33. Birchall, A. (1990). A whiff of happiness. *New Scientist*, August 25, 1990, 44-47.

34. On the scent of a better day at work. *New Scientist*, March 2, 1991, 18.

35. Engen, T. (1991). *Odor sensation and memory*. New York: Praeger.

36. Richardson, J. T. E. & Zucco, G. M. (1989). Cognition and olfaction: A review. *Psychological Bulletin*, *105*, 352-360.

37. Porter, R. H., Balogh, R. D., Cernoch, J. M., & Franchi, C. (1986). Recognition of kin through char-acteristic body odors. *Chemical Senses*, *11*, 389-395.

38. McBurney, D. H. & Gent, J. F. (1979). On the nature of taste qualities. *Psychological Bulletin, 86*, 151-167.

39. Institute of Food Technologists. Office of Scientific Public Affairs (1989). Food flavors. *Food Technology*, December 1989, 99-106.

40. Beauchamp, G. K. (1990). Research in chemosensation related to flavor and fragrance perception. *Food Technology*, January, 1990, 98-100.

Chapter 4

1. Luce, G. C. (1965). *Research on sleep and dreams*. Bethesda, MD: National Institute of Mental Health.

2. Aserinsky, E. & Kleitman, N. (1955). Two types of ocular motility occurring in sleep. *Journal of Applied Physiology, 8*, 1-10.

3. Hobson, J. A. (1989). *Sleep*. New York: Scientific American Library.

4. Wallace, B. & Fisher, L. E. (1991). *Consciousness and behavior*. Boston: Allyn and Bacon.

5. Babkoff, H., Caspy, T., Mikulincer, M., & Sing, H. C. (1991). Monotonic and rhythmic influences: A challenge for sleep deprivation research. *Psychological Bulletin, 109*, 411-428.

6. Horne, J. A. (1988). *Why we sleep*. Oxford: Oxford University Press.

7. Rechtschaffen, A., Gilliland, M. A., Bergmann, B. M., & Winter, J. B. (1983). Physiological correlates of prolonged sleep deprivation in rats. *Science, 221*, 182-184.

8. Crick, F. & Mitchison, G. (1983). The function of dream sleep. *Nature, 304*, 111-114.

9. Winson, J. (1990). The meaning of dreams. *Scientific American*, November 1990, 86-96.

10. Freud, S. (1900). *The interpretation of dreams*. London: Hogarth.

11. Freud, S. (1950). Fragment of an analysis of a case of hysteria (1905). In J. Strachey (Ed.), *The standard edition of the complete psychological works*. London: Hogarth.

12. Jung, C. G. (1964). *Man and his symbols*. New York: Dell.

13. Cartwright, R. (1990). A network model of dreams. In R. R. Bootzin, J. F. Kihlstrom, & D. L. Schachter (Eds.), *Sleep and cognition*. Washington, DC: American Psychological Association.

14. Cartwright, R. & Lamberg, L. (1992). *Crisis dreaming*. New York: Harper Collins.

15. Hobson, J. A. (1988). *The dreaming brain*. New York: Basic Books.

16. Foulkes, D. (1982). *Children's dreams*. New York: Wiley.

17. Hall, C. S. (1966). *The meaning of dreams*. New York: McGraw Hill.

18. LaBerge, S. (1986). *Lucid dreaming*. New York: Ballantine.

19. Hauri, P. J. (1985). Primary sleep disorders and insomnia. In T. Riley (Ed.), *Clinical aspects of sleep and sleep disturbance*. Boston: Butterworth.

20. Hales, P. (1986). *The complete book of sleep*. Reading, MA: Addison Wesley.

21. Hartmann, E. (1984). *The nightmare*. New York: Basic Books.

22. American Psychiatric Association (1987). *Diagnostic and statistical manual of mental disorders, 3rd edition, revised*. Washington, DC: American Psychiatric Association.

23. Hilgard, E. R. (1979). Divided consciousness in hypnosis: The implications of the hidden observer. In E. Fromm & R. E. Shor (Eds.), *Hypnosis: Developments in research and new perspectives*. Chicago: Aldine.

24. Kihlstrom, J. F. (1985). Hypnosis. *Annual Review of Psychology, 36*, 385-418.

25. Gilligan, S. G. (1987). *Therapeutic trances: The cooperation principle in Ericksonian hypnotherapy*. New York: Brunner/Mazel.

26. Sarbin, T. R. & Coe, W. C. (1972). *Hypnosis: A social psychological analysis of influence communication.* New York: Holt.

27. Barber, T. X. (1979). Suggested ("hypnotic") behavior: The trance paradigm versus an alternative paradigm. In E. Fromm & R. E. Shor (Eds.), *Hypnosis: Developments in research and new perspectives.* Chicago: Aldine.

28. Hilgard, E. R. (1965). *Hypnotic susceptibility.* New York: Harcourt, Brace, World.

29. Hilgard, E. R. & Hilgard, J. R. (1983). *Hypnosis in the relief of pain.* Los Altos, CA: Kaufmann.

30. Rieser, M. & Nielson, M. (1980). Investigative hypnosis: A developing specialty. *American Journal of Clinical Hypnosis, 23,* 75-83.

31. Orne, M. (1986). The validity of memories obtained in hypnosis. In B. Zilbergeld, M. G. Edelstein, & D. L. Araoz (Eds.), *Hypnosis: Questions and answers.* New York: Norton.

32. Whitehorse, W. G., Dinges, D. F., Orne, E. C., & Orne, M. T. (1988). Hypnotic hypermnesia: Enhanced memory accessibility or report bias? J*ournal of Abnormal Psychology, 97,* 289-295.

33. Dowd, E. T. & Healy, J. M. (Eds.) (1986). *Case studies in hypnotherapy.* New York: Guilford.

34. Barber, T. X. (1970). *LSD, marihuana, yoga, and hypnosis.* Chicago: Aldine.

35. Marlatt, G. A. & Rohsenow, D. J. (1981). The "think-drink" effect. *Psychology Today,* December 1981, 60-69.

36. Watson, D. L. & Tharp, R. G. (1993). *Self-directed behavior: Self-modification for personal adjustment.* Pacific Grove, CA: Brooks/Cole.

37. Benson, H. (1984). *Beyond the relaxation response.* New York: Times Books.

38. Ray, O. & Ksir, C. (1987). *Drugs, society, and human behavior.* St. Louis: Mosby.

39. Hamilton, L. W. & Timmons, C. R. (1990). *Principles of behavioral pharmacology.* Englewood Cliffs, NJ: Prentice Hall.

40. Nace, E. P. & Isbell, P. G. (1991). Alcohol. In R. J. Frances & S. I. Miller (Eds.), *Clinical textbook of addictive disorders.* New York: Guilford.

41. DuPont R. L. & Saylor, K. E. (1991). Sedatives/hypnotics and benzodiazepines. In R. J. Frances & S. I. Miller (Eds.), *Clinical textbook of addictive disorders.* New York: Guilford.

42. Gawin, F. H. (1991). Cocaine addiction: Psychology and neurophysiology. *Science, 251,* 1580-1586.

43. Thomason, H. H. & Dilts, S. L. (1991). Opioids. In R. J. Frances & S. I. Miller (Eds.), *Clinical textbook of addictive disorders.* New York: Guilford.

44. Gust, S. W., Walsh, J. M., Thomas, L. B., & Crouch, D. J. (1990). *Drugs in the workplace: Research and evaluation data, vol. II.* Rockville, MD: NIDA.

44. Cohen, S. (1989). The hallucinogens. In T. B. Karasu (Ed.), *Treatment of psychiatric disorders.* Washington, DC: American Psychiatric Press.

45. Hoffman, A. (1971). LSD discoverer disputes "chance" factor in finding. *Psychiatric News, 6,* 23-26.

46. Millman, R. B. (1989). Cannabis use and dependence. In T. B. Karasu (Ed.), *Treatment of psychiatric disorders.* Washington, DC: American Psychiatric Press.

Chapter 5

1. Hilgard, E. R. & Bower, G. H. (1975). *Theories of learning.* Englewood Cliffs, NJ: Prentice Hall.

2. Rachlin, H. (1992). *Introduction to modern behaviorism, (3rd ed.).* New York: Freeman.

3. Bernstein, I. L. & Borson, S. (1986). Learned food aversion: A component of anorexia syndromes. *Psychological Review, 93,* 462-472.

4. Stewart, J., de Wit, H., & Eikelboom, R. (1984). Role of unconditioned and conditioned drug effects in the self-administration of opiates and stimulants. *Psychological Review, 91,* 251-268.

5. Rescorla, R. A. (1988). Pavlovian conditioning: Its not what you think it is. *American Psychologist, 43,* 151-160.

6. Domjam, M. (1987). Animal Learning comes of age. *American Psychologist, 42,* 546-554.

7. Kamin, L. J. (1968). Attention-like processes in classical conditioning. In M. R. Jones (Ed.). *Miami symposium on the prediction of behavior: Aversive stimuli* (pp. 9-32). Coral Gables, FL: University of Miami Press.

8. Skinner, B. F. (1990). Can psychology be a science of mind? *American Psychologist, 45,* 1206-1210.

9. Dinsmoor, J. A. (1992). Setting the record straight: The social views of B. F. Skinner. *American Psychologist, 47,* 1454-1463.

10. Delprato, D. J., & Midgley, B. D. (1992). Some fundamentals of B. F. Skinner's behaviorism. *American Psychologist, 47,* 1507-1520.

11. Smith, L. D. (1992). On prediction and control. *American Psychologist, 47,* 216-223.

12. Lattal, K. A. (1992). B. F. Skinner and psychology: Introduction to the special issue. *American Psychologist, 47,* 1269-1272.

13. Hall, C. S. & Lindzey, G. (1985). Operant reinforcement theory: B. F. Skinner. In C. S. Hall and G. Lindzey (Eds.). *Introduction to theories of personality,* New York: Wiley.

14. Holland, J. G. (1992). B. F. Skinner. *American Psychologist, 47,* 665-667.

15. Fancher, R. E. (1979). *Pioneers of psychology.* New York: Norton.

16. Offerman, L. R. & Gowing, M. K. (1990). Organizations of the future: Changes and challenges. *American Psychologist, 45,* 95-108.

17. Baron, R. A. (1988). Negative effects of destructive criticism: Impact on conflict, self-efficacy, and task performance. *Journal of Applied Psychology, 73,* 199-207.

18. Katzell, R. A. & Thompson, D. E. (1990). Work motivation: Theory and practice. *American Psychologist, 45,* 144-153.

19. Turnage, J. J. (1990). The challenge of new workplace technology for psychology. *American Psychologist, 45,* 171-178.

20. Schlinger, H. D. (1992). Theory in behavior analysis: An application to child development. *American Psychologist, 47,* 1396-1410.

21. Rohles, F. H. (1992). Orbital bar pressing: A historical note on Skinner and chimpanzees in space. *American Psychologist, 47,* 1531-1533.

22. Steinberg, E. R. (1991). *Teaching computers to teach.* Hillsdale, NJ: Erlbaum.

23. Comunidad los Horcones, (1989). Walden Two and social change: The application of behavior analysis to cultural design (S. D. Roberts, Trans.). *Behavior Analysis and Social Action, 7,* 35-41.

24. Fishman, S. (1993). The town B. F. Skinner boxed. In K. G. Duffy (Ed.). Annual editions: *Psychology.* Guilford, CT: Dushkin.

25. Greenwood, C. R., Carta, J. J., Hart, B., Kamps, D., Terry, B., Arreaga-Mayer, C., Atwater, J., Walker, D., Risley, T., & Delquadri, J. C. (1992). Out of the laboratory and into the community: 26 years of applied behavior analysis at the Juniper Gardens children's project. *American Psychologist, 47,* 1464-1474.

26. Bandura, A., Ross, D., & Ross, S. A. (1963). Imitation of film-mediated aggressive models. *Journal of Abnormal and Social Psychology, 67,* 527-534.

27. Myer, H. H. & Raich, M. S. (1983). An objective evaluation of a behavior modeling training program. *Personnel Psychology, 36*, 755-762.

28. Wood, W., Wong, F. Y., & Chachere, J. G. (1991). Effects of media violence on viewer's aggression in unconstrained social interaction. *Psychological Bulletin, 109*, 371-383.

Chapter 6

1. Loftus, E. F. & Ketcham, K. (1991). *Witness for the defense.* New York: St. Martin's Press.

2. Broadbent, D. E. (1958). *Perception and communication.* New York: Pergamon.

3. Atkinson, R. C. & Shiffrin, R. M. (1968). Human memory: A proposed system and its control processes. In W. K. Spence & J. T. Spence (Eds.), *The psychology of learning and motivation: Advances in research and theory.* New York: Academic.

4. Cowan, N. (1988). Evolving conceptions of memory storage, selective attention, and their mutual constraints with the human information processing system. *Psychological Bulletin, 104*, 163-191.

5. Sperling, G. (1960). The information available in brief visual presentations. *Psychological Monographs, 74* (Whole No. 498), 1-29.

6. Long, G. M. (1980). Iconic memory: A review and critique of the study of short-term visual storage. *Psychological Bulletin, 88*, 785-820.

7. Haber, R. N. (1983). The impending demise of the icon: A critique of the concept of iconic storage in visual information processing. *The Behavioral and Brain Sciences, 6*, 1-54.

8. Best, J. B. (1986). *Cognitive psychology.* St. Paul, MN: West.

9. Klatzky, R. (1980). *Human memory: Structures and processes.* San Francisco: Freeman.

10. Baddeley, A. (1986). *Working memory.* New York: Oxford

11. Neisser, U. (1967). *Cognitive psychology.* New York: Appleton-Century-Crofts.

12. Norman, D. A. (1968). Toward a theory of memory and attention. *Psychological Review, 75*, 522-536.

13. Triesman, A. M. (1969). Strategies and models of selective attention. *Psychological Review, 76*, 282-299.

14. Cherry, C. (1966). *On human communication: A review, a survey, and a criticism (2 ed.)*, Cambridge, MA: MIT Press

15. Kahneman, D. (1973). *Attention and effort.* Englewood Cliffs NJ: Prentice Hall.

16. Johnston, W. A. & Dark, V. J. (1986). Selective attention. *Annual Review of Psychology, 37*, 43-75.

17. Peterson, L. R. & Peterson, M. J. (1959). Short-term retention of individual verbal items. *Journal of Experimental Psychology, 58*, 193-198.

18. Miller, G. A. (1956). The magical number seven, plus or minus two: Some limits on our capacity for processing information. *Psychological Review, 63*, 81-97.

19. Greene, R. L. (1987). Effects of maintenance rehearsal on human memory. *Psychological Bulletin, 102*, 403-413.

20. Craik, F. I. M. & Lockhart, R. S. (1972). Levels of processing: A framework for memory research. *Journal of Verbal Learning and Verbal Behavior, 11*, 671-684.

21. Loftus, E. F. (1980). *Memory.* Reading, MA: Addison-Wesley.

22. Loftus, E. F. & Loftus, G. R. (1980). On the permanence of stored information in the human brain. *American Psychologist, 35*, 409-420.

23. Anderson, J. R. (1976). *Language, memory, and thought.* Hillsdale, NJ: Erlbaum.

24. Chang, T. M. (1986). Semantic memory: Facts and models. *Psychological Bulletin, 99*, 199-220.

25. Tulving, E. (1985). How many memory systems are there? *American Psychologist, 40*, 385-398.

26. Brown, R. & Kulik, J. (1977). Flashbulb memories. *Cognition, 5*, 73-79.

27. McGaugh, J. L. (1990). Significance and remembrance: The role of neuro-modulatory systems. *Psychological Science, 1*, 15-25.

28. Bohannon, J. N., III (1988). Flashbulb memories for the space shuttle disaster: A tale of two theories. *Cognition, 29*, 179-196.

29. Neisser, U. & Harsch, N. (1992). Phantom flash-bulbs: False recollections of hearing the news about Challenger. In E. Winograd & U. Neisser (Eds.), *Affect and accuracy in recall: Studies of "flashbulb memories."* New York: Cambridge

30. Roediger, H. L. (1990). Implicit memory: Reten-tion without remember-ing. *American Psycholo-gist, 45*, 1043-1056.

31. Schacter, D. L. (1992). Understanding implicit memory: A cognitive neurosciences approach. *American Psychologist, 47*, 559-569.

32. Squire, L. R., Knowlton, B., & Musen, G. (1993). The structure and organi-zation of memory. *Annual Review of Psychology, 44*, 453-495.

33. Tulving, E. & Schacter, D. L. (1990). Priming and human memory systems. *Science, 247*, 301-306.

34. Jacoby, L. L., Woloshyn, V., & Kelley, C. M. (1989). Becoming famous without being recognized: Uncon-scious influences of memory produced by dividing attention. *Journal of Experimental Psychol-ogy: General, 118*, 115-125.

35. Durkin, K. (1989). Implicit memory and language acquisition. In S. Lewan-dowsky, J. C. Dunn, & S. Kirsner (Eds.), *Implicit memory: Theoretical issues.* Hillsdale, NJ: Erlbaum.

36. Craik, F. I. M. (1979). Human memory. *Annual Review of Psychology, 30*, 63-102.

37. Marschark, M., Richman, C. L., Yuille, J. C., & Hunt, R. R. (1987). The role of imagery in memory: On shared and distinctive information. *Psychologi-cal Bulletin, 102*, 28-41.

38. Paivio, A. (1986). *Mental representations: A dual coding approach.* New York: Oxford

39. Bartlett, F. C. (1932). Remembering: *A study in experimental and social psychology.* Oxford: Cambridge

40. Alba, J. W. & Hasher, L. (1983). Is memory sche-matic? *Psychological Bulletin, 93*, 201-231.

41. Loftus, E. F. (1979). *Eyewitness testimony.* Cambridge MA: Harvard.

42. Wells, G. L. (1993). What do we know about eyewit-ness identification? *Amer-ican Psychologist, 48*, 553-571.

43. Ceci, S. J. & Bruck, M. (1993). Suggestibility of the child witness: A historical review and synthesis. *Psychological Bulletin, 113*, 403-409.

44. McCauley, R. N. (1988). Walking in our own footsteps: Autobiographi-cal memory and recon-struction. In U. Neisser & E. Winograd (Eds.), *Remembering reconsid-ered: Ecological and traditional approaches to the study of memory.* New York: Cambridge

45. McCloskey, M. & Zaragoza, M. (1985). Misleading postevent information and memory for events: Arguments and evidence against memory impair-ment hypotheses. *Journal of Experimental Psychol-ogy: General, 114*, 1-16.

46. Loftus, E. F. & Palmer, J. C. (1974). Reconstruction of automobile destruction: An example of interaction between language and memory. *Journal of Verbal Learning and Verbal Behavior, 13*, 585-589.

47. Tulving, E. & Thompson, D. M. (1973). Encoding specificity and retrieval processes in episodic memory. *Journal of Experimental Psychology: Learning, Memory, and Cognition, 8*, 336-342.

48. Godden, D. R. & Baddeley, A. D. (1975). Context-dependent memory in two natural environments: On land and underwater. *British Journal of Psychology*, *66*, 325-331.

49. Bower, G. H. (1981). Mood and memory. *American Psychologist*, *36*, 129-148.

50. Blaney, P. H. (1986). Affect and memory: A review. *Psychological Bulletin*, *99*, 229-246.

51. Bahrick, H. P. (1984). Semantic memory content in permastore: Fifty years of memory for Spanish learned in school. *Journal of Experimental Psychology: General*, *113*, 1-29.

52. Solso, R. L. (1991). *Cognitive psychology (3rd ed.)*. Boston: Allyn & Bacon.

53. Haber, R. N. (1980). Eidetic images are not just imaginary. *Psychology Today*, *14*, 72-82.

54. Underwood, B. J. (1957). Interference and forgetting. *Psychological Review*, *64*, 49-60.

55. Shiffrin, R. M. & Cook, J. R. (1978). Short-term forgetting of item and order information. *Journal of Verbal Learning and Verbal Behavior*, *17*, 189-218.

56. Mensink, G.-J. & Raaijmakers, J. G. W. (1988). A model for interference and forgetting. *Psychological Review*, *95*, 434-455.

57. Fowler, M. J., Sullivan, M. J., & Ekstrand, B. R. (1973). Sleep and memory. *Science*, *179*, 302-304.

58. Brown, A. S. (1991). A review of the tip-of-the-tongue experience. *Psychological Bulletin*, *109*, 204-223.

59. Loftus, E. F. (1993). The reality of repressed memories. *American Psychologist*, *48*, 518-537.

60. Wetzler, S. E. & Sweeney, J. A. (1986). Childhood amnesia. In D. C. Rubin (Ed.), *Autobiographical memory*. New York: Cambridge.

61. Holmes, D. (1990). The evidence for repression: An examination of sixty years of research. In J. Singer (Ed.), *Repression and dissociation: Implications for personality theory, psychopathology, and health*. Chicago: University of Chicago.

62. Milner, B. R. (1970). Memory and medial temporal regions of the brain. In K. H. Pribram & D. E. Broadbent (Eds.), *Biology of memory*. Orlando FL: Academic.

63. Lashley, K. (1950). In search of the engram. *Symposia of the Society of Experimental Biology*, *4*, 454-482.

64. Goldman-Rakic, P. S. (1992). Working memory and the mind. *Scientific American*, September, 1992, 111-117.

65. Squire, L. R. (1987). *Memory and the brain*. New York: Oxford.

66. Mishkin, M. & Appenzeller, T. (1987). The anatomy of memory. *Scientific American*, *256*, 80-89.

67. Thompson, R. F. (1988). The neural basis of basic associative learning of discrete behavioral responses. *Trends in Neurosciences*, *11*, 152-155.

68. Hebb, D. O. (1949). *The organization of behavior*. New York: Wiley.

69. Alkon, D. (1989). Memory storage and neural systems. *Scientific American*, *258*, 42-50.

70. Rosenzweig, M. R. & Leiman, A. L. (1989). *Physiological psychology, 2nd ed.* New York: Random House.

71. Kandel, E. R. & Hawkins, R. D. (1992). The biological basis of learning and individuality. *Scientific American*, September, 1992, 79-86.

72. Cotman, C. W. & Lynch, G. S. (1989). The neurobiology of learning and memory. *Cognition*, *33*, 201-241.

73. Lynch, G. S. (1986). *Synapses, circuits, and the beginning of memory*. Cambridge MA: MIT Press.

74. Kalat, J. W. (1992). *Biological psychology, 4th ed.* Belmont CA: Wadsworth.

Chapter 7

1. Sternberg, R. J. (1988). *The triarchic mind*. New York: Viking.

2. Oden, G. C. (1987). Concept, knowledge, and thought. *Annual Review of Psychology, 38*, 203-207.

3. Holyoak, K. J. & Spellman, B. A. (1993). Thinking. *Annual review of Psychology, 44*, 265-315.

4. Stenning, K. & Oberlander, J. (1992). *A cognitive theory of graphical and linguistic reasoning: Logic and implementation*. Research Paper HCRC/RP-20, Human Community Research Center, University of Edinburgh.

5. Finke, R. A. (1990). *Creative imagery: Discoveries and inventions in visualization*. Hillsdale, NJ: Erlbaum.

6. Shepard, R. N. & Meltzer, J. (1971). Mental rotation of three-dimensional objects. *Science, 171*, 701-703.

7. Dunker, K. (1945). *Psychological Monographs, 58* (whole no. 70), 5.

8. Isenberg, D. Managerial thinking: An inquiry into how senior managers think. Unpublished manuscript.

9. Kotter, J. (1982). *The general managers*. New York: Free Press.

10. Streufert, S. & Swezey, R. W. (1986). Complexity, managers, and organiza-tions. Orlando, Fl: Academic Press.

11. Osborn, A. F. (1963). *Applied imagination*, 3rd ed., New York: Charles Scribner's Sons.

12. Winters, A. A. & Milton, S. F. (1982). *The creative connection*. New York: Fairchild.

13. Rice, M. L. (1989). Children's language acquisition. *American Psychologist, 44*, 149-156.

14. Chomsky, N. (1957). *Syntactic structures*. The Hague: Mouton.

15. Chomsky, N. (1964). A transformational approach to syntax. In J. A. Fodor and J. J. Katz, eds., *The structure of language: Readings in the philosophy of language*. Englewood Cliffs, NJ: Prentice-Hall.

16. Gardner, H. (1985). *The mind's new science*. New York: Basic Books.

17. Rosch, E. (1973). Natural categories. *Cognitive Psychology, 4*, 328-350.

18. Weinberg, R. A. (1989). Intelligence and IQ. *American Psychologist, 44*, 98-104.

19. Snyderman M. & Rothman, S. (1987). Survey of expert opinion on intelligence and aptitude testing. *American Psychologist, 42*, 137-144.

20. Guilford, J. P. (1967). *The nature of human intelligence*. New York: McGraw-Hill.

21. Gardner, H. (1983). *Frames of mind: The theory of multiple intelligences*. New York: Basic Books.

22. American Psychological Association, (1982). Robert J. Sternberg. *American Psychologist, 37*, 74-78.

23. Matarzzo, J. D. (1992). Psychologist testing in the 21st century. *American Psychologist, 47*, 1007-1018.

24. Cravens, H. (1992). A scientific project locked in time. *American Psychologist, 47*, 183-189.

25. Anastasi, A. (1988). *Psychological testing* (6th ed.). New York: Macmillan.

26. Graham, J. R. & Lilly, R. S. (1984). *Psychological testing*. Englewood Cliffs, NJ: Prentice-Hall.

27. Delaney, E. & Hopkins, T. (1987). *Stanford-Binet intelligence scale-Examiner's handbook: An expanded guide for fourth edition users*. Chicago: Riverside.

28. Wechsler, D. (1981). *Wechsler adult intelligence scale* (rev.). New York: Psychological Corporation.

29. Frederikson, N. (1986). Toward a broader conception of human intelligence. *American Psychologist, 41*, 445-452.

30. Cattell, R. B. (1949). *The culture-free intelligence test*. Champaign, Il: Institute for Personality and Ability Testing.

31. Sternberg, R. J. (1984). How can we teach intelligence? In B. L. Slife and J. Rubinstein, (Eds.) *Taking sides (7th ed.).* 146-156, Guilford, CT: Dushkin.

32. Hernstein, R. J., Nickerson, R. S., deSanchez, M., & Swets, J. (1986). Teaching thinking skills. *American Psychologist, 41,* 1279-1289.

33. Bransford, J., Sherwood, R., Vye, N. & Rieser, J. (1986). Teaching thinking skills and problem solving. *American Psychologist, 41,* 1078-1089.

34. Horowitz, F. D. & O'Brien, M. (1986). Gifted and talented children. *American Psychologist, 41,* 1147- 1152.

35. Turkheimer, E. (1991). Individual and group differences in adoption studies of IQ. *Psychological Bulletin, 110,* 392-405.

36. Plomin, R. (1989). Environment and genes. Determinants of behavior. *American Psychologist, 44,* 105-111.

37. Plomin, R. (1990). The role of inheritance in behavior. *Science, 248,* 183-188.

38. Bouchard, T. J., Lykken, D. T., McGue, M., Segal, N., & Tellegen, A. (1990). Sources of human psychological differences: The Minnesota study of twins reared apart. *Science 250,* 223-228.

39. Bouchard, T. J., & McGue, M. (1981). Familial studies of intelligence: A review. *Science 212,* 1055-1059.

40. Bouchard, T. J. & Segal, N. L. Environment and IQ. (1985). In B. B. Wolman, (Ed.). *Handbook of intelligence: Theories, measurements, and applications.* New York: Wiley.

41. Scarr, S. & Weinberg, R. A. (1976). IQ test performance of black children adopted by white families. *American Psychologist, 31,* 726-739.

Chapter 8

1. Dorris, M. (1989). *The broken cord. New York*: Harper & Row.

2. Santrock, J. W. (1992). *Life-span development,* 4th ed. Dubuque, IA: W. C. Brown.

3. Kopp, C. B. & Kaler, S. R. (1989). Risk in infancy: Origins and implications. *American Psychologist, 44,* 224-230.

4. Lozoff, B. (1989). Nutrition and behavior. *American Psychologist, 44,* 231-236.

5. Barr, H. M., Streissguth, A. P., Darby, B. L., & Sampson, P. D. (1990). Prenatal exposure to alcohol, caffeine, tobacco, and aspirin. *Developmental Psychology, 26,* 339-348.

6. Adler, T. (1992). Prenatal cocaine exposure has subtle, serious effects. *APA Monitor,* November 1992, 17.

7. Meredith, H. (1987). Variations in body stockiness among and within ethnic groups at ages from birth to adulthood. In H. Reese (Ed.), *Advances in child development and behavior, vol. 20.* New York: Academic.

8. Fontana, V. J. (1985). Child maltreatment and battered child syndromes. In H. I. Kaplan & B. J. Sadock (Eds.), *Comprehensive textbook of psychiatry,* IV, *vol. 2.* Baltimore: Williams & Wilkins.

9. Shatz, C. J. (1992). The developing brain. *Scientific American,* September 1992, 61-67.

10. Gormly, A. V. & Brodzinsky, D. M. (1993). *Lifespan human development, 5th ed.* New York: Harcourt Brace Jovanovich.

11. *National Children and Youth Fitness Study* (1984). Washington, DC: U.S. Public Health Service.

12. Meltzoff, A. N. (1988). Imitation of televised models by infants. *Child Development, 59,* 1221-1229.

13. Fantz, R. L., Fagan, J. F., & Miranda, S. B. (1975). Early visual selectivity. In L. B. Cohen & P. Salapatek (Eds.), *Infant perception: From sensation to cognition, vol. 1.* New York: Academic

14. Gibson, E. J. & Walk, R. D. (1960). The visual cliff. *Scientific American, 202*, 64-71.

15. Piaget, J. (1970). Piaget's theory. In P. Mussen (Ed.), *Carmichael's manual of child psychology, vol. 1.* New York: Wiley

16. Phillips, J. L. (1969). *Origins of intellect: Piaget's theory.* San Francisco: Freeman.

17. Flavell, J. H. (1992). Cognitive development: Past, present, and future. *Developmental Psychology, 28*, 998-1005.

18. Siegler, R. S. (1989). Mechanisms of cognitive development. *Annual Review of Psychology, 40*, 353-379.

19. Whitehurst, G. J., Falco, F. L., Lonigan, C., Fischel, J. E., DeBaryshe, B. D., Valdez-Menichacha, M. C., & Caulfield, M. (1988). Accelerating language development through picture-book reading. *Developmental Psychology, 24*, 552-558.

20. Kohlberg, L. (1976). Moral stages and moralization: The cognitive developmental approach. In J. Lickona (Ed.), *Moral development and behavior.* New York: Holt

21. Snarey, J. R. (1985). Cross-cultural universality of social-moral development: A critical review of Kohlbergian research. *Psychological Bulletin, 97*, 202-233.

22. Gilligan, C. (1982). *In a different voice: Psychological theory and women's development.* Cambridge, MA: Harvard

23. Erikson, E. H. (1963). *Childhood and society.* New York: Norton

24. Chess, S. & Thomas, A. (1977). Temperamental individuality from childhood to adolescence. *Journal of Child Psychiatry, 16*, 218-226.

25. Kagan, J. (1989). Temperamental contributions to social behavior. *American Psychologist, 44*, 668-674.

26. Kagan, J. & Snidman, N. (1991). Temperamental factors in human development. *American Psychologist, 46*, 856-862.

27. Ainsworth, M. D. S. (1984). Attachment. In N. S. Endler & J. McV. Hunt (Eds.), *Personality and the behavioral disorders, vol. 1, 2nd ed.* New York: Wiley.

28. Hartup, W. W. (1989). Social relationships and their developmental significance. *American Psychologist, 44*, 120-126.

29. Lewis, M. (1990). Self knowledge and social development in early life. In L. A. Perrin (Ed.), *Handbook of personality: Theory and research.* New York: Guilford.

30. Wylie, R. C. (1979). *The self concept, vol. 2,* revised. Lincoln, NE: University of Nebraska

31. Coopersmith, S. (1967). *The antecedents of self-esteem.* San Francisco: Freeman.

32. American Association of University Women (1991). *Shortchanging girls, shortchanging America.* Washington, DC: AAUW.

33. Baumrind, D. (1978). Parental disciplinary patterns and social competence in children. *Youth and Society, 9*, 239-276.

34. Jacklin, C. G. (1989). Female and male: Issues of gender. *American Psychologist, 44*, 127-133.

35. Maccoby, E. E. (1990). Gender and relationships: A developmental account. *American Psychologist, 45*, 513-520.

36. Bem, S. L. (1985). Androgyny and gender schema theory: A conceptual and empirical integration. In T. B. Sonderegger (Ed.), *Nebraska symposium on motivation: Psychology of gender.* Lincoln, NE: University of Nebraska.

37. Lytton, H. & Romney, D. M. (1991). Parents' differential socialization of boys and girls: A meta-analysis. *Psychological Bulletin, 109*, 267-296.

38. Chumlea, W. C. (1982). Physical growth in adolescence. In B. Wolman (Ed.), *Handbook of developmental psychology.* Englewood Cliffs, NJ: Prentice Hall.

39. Phinney, V., Jensen, L., Olson, J., & Cundrick, R. (1990). The relationship between early development and psychosocial behaviors in adolescent females. *Adolescence, 25*, 322-332.

40. Sommers, R. & Blyth, D. (1987). *Moving into adolescence: The impact of pubertal change in school context.* New York: deGruyter.

41. Buchanan, C. M., Eccles, J. S., & Becker, J. B. (1992). Are adolescents the victims of raging hormones: Evidence for activational effects of hormones on mood and behavior at adolescence. *Psychological Bulletin, 111*, 62-107.

42. Erikson, E. H. (1968). *Identity: Youth and crisis.* New York: Norton.

43. Marcia, J. E. (1980). Identity in adolescence. In J. Adelson (Ed.), *Handbook of adolescent psychology.* New York: Wiley.

44. Peterson, A. (1988). Adolescent development. *Annual Review of Psychology, 39*, 583-607.

45. Phinney, J. S. (1990). Ethnic identity in adolescents and adults: Review of research. *Psychological Bulletin, 108*, 499-514.

46. Waldman, S. & Springer, K. (1992). Too old, too fast? *Newsweek*, November 16, 1992, 80-88.

47. Gottfredson, D. (1985). Youth employment, crime, and schooling: A longitudinal study of a national sample. *Developmental Psychology, 21*, 419-432.

48. Greenberger, E., Steinberg, L., & Vaux, A. (1981). Adolescents who work: Health and behavioral consequences of job stress. *Developmental Psychology, 17*, 691-703.

49. Elkind, D. (1984). *All grown up and no place to go: Teenagers in crisis.* Reading, MA: Addison Wesley.

50. Collins, W. A. & Gunnar, M. R. (1990). Social and personality development. *Annual Review of Psychology, 41*, 387-416.

51. Newman, P. R. (1982). The peer group. In B. B. Wolman (Ed.), *Handbook of developmental psychology.* Englewood Cliffs, NJ: Prentice Hall.

52. Elkind, D. (1978). Understanding the young adolescent. *Adolescence, 13*, 127-134.

53. Hoffereth, S. & Hayes, C. (Eds.) (1987). *Risking the future: Adolescent sexuality, pregnancy, and child bearing*, vol. 2. Washington, DC: National Academy of Sciences.

54. Levinson, D. J. (1986). A conception of adult development. *American Psychologist, 41*, 3-13.

55. Schulz, R. & Ewen, R. B. (1988). *Adult development and aging: Myths and emerging realities.* New York: Macmillan.

56. Selkoe, D. J. (1992). Aging brain, aging mind. *Scientific American*, September 1992, 134-143.

57. Costa, P. T. & McCrae, R. R. (1989). Personality continuity and the changes of adult life. In M. Storandt & G. R. VandenBos (Eds.), *The adult years: Continuity and change.* Washington, DC: American Psychological Association.

58. Vaillant, G. E. (1977). *Adaptation to life.* Boston: Little Brown.

59. Neugarten, B. L. (1977). Personality and aging. In J. E. Birren & K. W. Schaie (Eds.), *Handbook of the psychology of aging.* New York: van Nostrand Reinhold.

60. Gilligan, C., Lyons, N. P., & Hammer, T. J. (Eds.) (1990). *Making connections: The relational worlds of adolescent girls at Emma Willard School.* New York: Plenum.

61. Havighurst, R. J. (1974). *Developmental tasks and education.* New York: McKay.

62. Glick, P. (1989). The family life cycle and social change. *Family Relations, 38*, 123-129.

63. Hetherington, E. M., Hagen, M. S., & Anderson, E. R. (1989). Marital transitions: A child's perspective. *American Psychologist, 44*, 303-312.

64. Rice, R. W. (1984). Organizational work and the overall quality of life. In S. Oskamp (Ed.), *Applied social psychology annual (vol. 5)*. Beverly Hills, CA: Sage.

65. Scarr, S., Phillips, D., & McCartney, K. (1989). Working mothers and their families. *American Psychologist, 44*, 1402-1409.

66. Mathews, K. A. & Rodin, J. (1989). Women's changing work roles: Impact on health, family, and public policy. *American Psychologist, 44*, 1389-1393.

67. Kubler-Ross, E. (1969). *On death and dying.* New York: Macmillan.

68. Kastenbaum, R. & Costa, P. T. (1977). Psychological perspectives on death. *Annual Review of Psychology, 28*, 225-241.

Chapter 9

1. Spitzer, R. L., Skodol, A. E., Gibbon, M., & Williams, J. B. W. (1983). *Psychopathology: A case book.* New York: McGraw-Hill.

2. Levin, J. & Fox, J. A. (1985). *Mass murder: America's growing menace.* New York: Plenum.

3. Norris, J. (1988). *Serial killers: The growing menace.* New York: Doubleday.

4. Kleinginna, P. R. & Kleinginna, A. M. (1981). A categorized list of motivation definitions with a suggestion for a consensual definition. *Motivation and Emotion, 5*, 263-291.

5. Kalat, J. W. (1992). *Biological Psychology* (4th ed.) Belmont, CA: Wadsworth.

6. Schachter, S., Friedman, L, & Handler, J. (1974). Who eats with chopsticks? In S. Schachter & J. Rodin (Eds.), *Obese humans and rats.* Washington, DC: Erlbaum.

7. Striegel-Moore, R. Rodin, J. (1986). The influence of psychological variables in obesity. In K. D. Brownell & P. J. Foreyt (Eds.), *Handbook of eating disorders,* 99-121. New York: Basic Books.

8. Masters, W. H. & Johnson, V. E. (1966). *Human sexual response.* Boston: Little, Brown.

9. Masters, W. H. & Johnson, V. E. (1970). *Human sexual inadequacy.* Boston: Little, Brown.

10. Carani, C., Zini, D., Della Casa, L., Ghizzani, A., & Marrama, P. (1990). Effects of androgen treatment in impotent men with normal and low levels of free testosterone. *Archives of Sexual Behavior, 19*, 223-234.

11. Lang, R. A., Flor-Henry, P., & Frenzel, R. R. (1990). Sex hormone profiles in pedophilic and incestuous men. *Archives of Sex Research, 3*, 59-74.

12. Earls, C. M. (1988). Aberrant sexual arousal in sexual offenders. *Annals of the New York Academy of Sciences, 528*, 41-48.

13. Udry, J. R. & Morris, N. M. (1968). Distribution of coitus in the menstrual cycle. *Nature, 220*, 593-596.

14. Adams, D. B., Gold, A. R., & Burt, A. D. (1978). Rise in female-initiated sexual activity at ovulation and its suppression by oral contraceptives. *New England Journal of Medicine, 229*, 1145-1150.

15. Sherwin, B. B. (1988). A comparative analysis of the role of androgen in human male and female sexual behavior: Behavioral specificity, critical thresholds, and sensitivity. *Psychobiology, 16*, 416-425.

16. Buck, R. (1988). *Human motivation and emotion.* New York: Wiley.

17. Harlow, H. F. (1953). Mice, monkey, men, and motives. *Psychology Reviews, 60*, 23-32.

18. Harlow, H. F. (1958). The nature of love. *American Psychologist, 13*, 673-685.

19. Magid, K. (1988). *High risk: children without a conscience.* New York: Bantam.

20. Murray, H. A. (1938). *Explorations in personality: A clinical and experimental study of fifty men of college age.* New York: Oxford University Press.

21. McClelland, D. C., Atkinson, J. W., Clark, R. A., & Lowell, E. L. (1953). *The achievement motive.* New York: Appleton-Century-Crofts.

22. Koestner, R., & McClelland, D. C. (1990). Perspectives on competence motivation. In L. A. Pervin, (Ed.). *Handbook of personality,* 527-548. *Theory and research.* New York: Guilford.

23. McClelland, D. C. (1979). Inhibited power motivation and high blood pressure in men. *Journal of Abnormal Psychology, 88,* 182-190.

24. McClelland, D. C. (1965). N Achievement and entrepreneurship: A longitudinal study. *Journal of Personality and Social Psychology, 1,* 389-392.

25. Burger, J. M. (1990). *Personality* (2nd ed.). Belmont, CA: Wadsworth.

26. Jenkins, S. R. (1987). Need for achievement and women's careers over 14 years: Evidence for occupational structure effect. *Journal of Personality and Social Psychology, 53,* 922-932.

27. McClelland, D. C. (1989). Motivational factors in health and disease. *American Psychologist, 44,* 675-683.

28. Phares, E. J. (1991). *Introduction to Personality (3rd ed.).* New York: HarperCollins.

29. Winter, D. G. (1987). Leader appeal, leader performance, and the motive profiles of leaders and followers: A study of American presidents and elections. *Journal of Personality and Social Psychology, 52,* 196-202.

30. Darwin, C. (1859).*On the origin of species by means of natural selection.* London: J. Murray.

31. James. W. (1980). *Principles of psychology.* New York: Holt.

32. McDougall, W. (1908). *Social Psychology.* New York: G. P. Putnam's Sons.

33. Lorenz, K. (1971). *Studies in animal and human behavior, (vol. 1 & 2).* R. Martin (Transl.) London: Metheun.

34. Leak, G. K. & Christopher, S. B. (1982). Freudian psychoanalysis and sociobiology. *American Psychologist, 37,* 31, 3-322.

35. Crawford, C. B. & Anderson, J. L. (1989). Sociobiology. An environmentalist discipline? *American Psychologist, 44,* 1449-1459.

36. Hamilton, W. D. (1978). The genetical evolution of social behavior. In A. L. Caplan (Ed.). *The sociobiology debate,* 191-209. New York: Harper & Row.

37. Hilgard, E. R. & Bower, G. H. (1975). *Theories of learning.* Englewood Cliffs, NJ: Prentice-Hall.

38. Hebb, D. O. (1955). Drives and the C.N.S. (conceptual nervous system). *Psychological Review, 62,* 243-253.

39. Zuckerman, M. (1979). Sensation seeking: Beyond the optimal level of arousal. Hillsdale, NJ: Lawrence Erlbaum Associates.

40. Zuckerman, M. (1984). Experience and desire: A new format for the sensation seeking scales. *Journal of Behavioral Assessment, 6,* 101-114.

41. Zuckerman, M., Ballenger, J., Jimerson, D. Murphy, D., & Post, R. (1983). A correlational test in humans of the biological models of sensation seeking, impulsivity, and anxiety. In M. Zuckerman (Ed.), *Biological basis of sensation seeking, impulsivity, and anxiety.* Hillsdale, NJ: Erlbaum.

42. Rotter, J. B. (1954). *Social learning and clinical psychology.* Englewood Cliffs, NJ: Prentice-Hall.

43. Maslow, A. H. (1970). *Motivation and personality.* New York: Harper & Row.

44. Weiner, B. (1989). *Human motivation.* Hillsdale, NJ: Erlbaum.

45. Petri, H. L. (1991). *Motivation. Theory, research, and applications.* Belmont, CA: Wadsworth.

46. Plutchik, R. (1980). *Emotion: A psychoevolutionary synthesis*. New York: Harper & Row.

47. Plutchik, R. & Kellerman, H. (1989). *Emotion: Theory, research, and experience (vol. 4)*, San Diego: Academic Press.

48. Oatley, K. & Jenkins, J. M. (1992). Human emotions: Function and dysfunction. *Annual Review of Psychology, 43*, 55-85.

49. Mesquita, B. & Frijda, N. H. (1992). Cultural variations in emotion: A review. *Psychological Bulletin, 112*, 179-204.

50. Eibl-Eibesfeldt, I. (1973). The expressive behavior of the deaf-and-blind-born. In M. von Cranach and I. Vine (Eds.), *Social communication and movement*. New York: Academic Press.

51. Ekman, P. (1985). *Telling lies: Clues to deceit in the marketplace, marriage, and politics*. New York: Norton.

52. Ekman, P. & O'Sullivan, M. (1991). Who can catch a liar? *American Psychologist, 46*, 913-920.

53. Ekman, P. & Friesen, W. V. (1969). Nonverbal leakage and clues to deception. *Psychiatry, 32*, 88-105.

54. Ekman, P. (1993). Facial expression and emotion. *American Psychologist, 48*, 384-392.

55. Ekman, P. & Friesen, W. V. (1971). Constants across cultures in face and emotion. *Journal of Personality and Social Psychology, 17*, 124-129.

56. Izard, C. E. (1990). Facial expressions and the regulation of emotions. *Journal of Personality and Social Psychology, 58*, 487-498.

57. Adelmann, P. K. & Zajonc, R. B. (1989). Facial efference and the experience of emotion. *Annual Review of Psychology, 40*, 249-280.

58. Goleman, D. (1993). One smile (only one) can lift mood. *New York Times*, October 11, C11.

59. American Psychological Association. (1992). Paul Ekman. *American Psychologist, 47*, 470-471.

60. Zajonc, R. (1990). The face as window and machine for the emotions. *LSA magazine, 14*, 17-21.

61. Bashore, T. R. & Rapp, P. E. (1993). Are there alternatives to traditional polygraph procedures? *Psychological Bulletin, 113*, 3-22.

62. Frijda, N. H. (1988). The laws of emotion. *American Psychologist, 43*, 349-358.

63. Schachter, S. & Singer, J. (1962). Cognitive, Social, and Physiological determinants of emotional state. *Psychological Review, 69*, 379-399.

64. Lazarus, R. S. (1991). Progress on a cognitive-motivational-relational theory of emotion. *American Psychologist, 46*, 819-834.

65. Smith, C. A., & Lazarus, R. S. (1990). Emotion and adaptation. In L. A. Pervin, (Ed.). *Handbook of personality. Theory and research*. New York: Guilford.

Chapter 10

1. Freud, S. (1949). *An outline of psychoanalysis*. New York: Norton.

2. Freud, S. (1936). *The problem of anxiety*. New York: Norton.

3. Freud, S. (1953). *Three essays on sexuality. In Standard Edition, vol. 7*. London: Hogarth Press.

4. Clark, R. W. (1980). *Freud: The man and the cause. A biography*. New York: Random House.

5. Freud, S. (1959). *Analysis of a phobia in a five year old boy. In Collected papers, vol. 3*. New York: Basic.

6. Westen, D. (1990). Psychoanalytic approaches to personality. In L. A. Pervin (Ed.), *Handbook of personality theory and research*. New York: Guilford.

7. Jung, C. G. (1982). *Contributions to analytical psychology*. New York: Harcourt Brace Jovanovich.

8. Adler, A. (1927). *Understanding human nature*. New York: Greenberg.

9. Ernst, C. & Angst, J. (1983). *Birth order: Its influence on personality*. Berlin: Springer-Verlag.

10. Horney, K. (1937). *The neurotic personality of our time*. New York: Norton.

11. Sullivan, H. S. (1953). *The interpersonal theory of psychiatry*. New York: Norton.

12. Erikson, E. H. (1963). *Childhood and society, 2nd ed*. New York: Norton.

13. Blanck, G. & Blanck, R. (1974). *Ego psychology: Theory and practice*. New York: Columbia University Press.

14. Maslow, A. H. (1970). *Motivation and personality, 2nd ed*. New York: Harper.

15. Maslow, A. H. (1950). *Self-actualizing people: A study of psychological health. Personality symposia: Symposium #1 on values*. New York: Grune and Stratton.

16. Rogers, C. R. (1959). A theory of therapy, personality, and interpersonal relationships, as developed in the client-centered framework. In S. Koch (Ed.), *Psychology: A study of a science, vol. 3*. New York: McGraw Hill.

17. Rogers, C. R. (1961). *On becoming a person*. Boston: Houghton Mifflin.

18. Allport, G. W. (1937). *Personality: A psychological interpretation*. New York: Holt.

19. Cattell, R. B. (1966). *The scientific analysis of personality*. Chicago: Aldine.

20. Cattell, R. B., Eber, H. W., & Tatsuoka, M. M. (1970). *Handbook for the 16 PF*. Champaign, IL: Institute for Personality and Ability Testing.

21. Goldberg, L. R. (1981). Language and individual differences: the search for universals in personality lexicons. In L. Wheeler (Ed.), *Review of personality and social psychology*. Beverly Hills, CA: Sage.

22. Eysenck, H. J. (1982). *Personality, genetics, and behavior*. New York: Springer-Verlag.

23. Eysenck, H. J. (1990). Biological dimensions of personality. In L. A. Pervin (Ed.), *Handbook of personality theory and research*. New York: Guilford.

24. Digman, J. M. (1990). Personality structure: Emergence of the five-factor model, *Annual Review of Psychology, 41*, 417-440.

25. Goldberg, L. R. (1993). The structure of phenotypic personality traits. *American Psychologist, 48*, 26-34.

26. Costa, P. T. Jr. & McCrae, R. R. (1985). *The NEO Personality Inventory manual*. Odessa, FL: Psychological Assessment Resources.

27. Holland, J. L. (1979). *The self-directed search professional manual*. Palo Alto, CA: Consulting Psychologists Press.

28. Costa, P. T. Jr., McCrae, R. R., & Holland, J. L. (1984). Personality and vocational interests in an adult sample. *Journal of Applied Psychology, 69*, 390-400.

29. O'Reilly, C. A. III (1990). Organizational behavior: Where we've been, where we're going. *Annual Review of Psychology, 42*, 427-458.

30. Skinner, B. F. (1974). About behaviorism. New York: Knopf.

31. Mischel, W. (1990). Personality dispositions revisited and revised: A view after three decades. In L. A. Pervin (Ed.), *Handbook of personality theory and research*. New York: Guilford.

32. Bandura, A. (1989). Human agency in social cognitive theory. *American Psychologist, 44*, 1175-1184.

33. Bandura, A. (1977). Self-efficacy: Toward a unifying theory of behavioral change. *Psychological Review, 84*, 191-215.

34. Rotter, J. B. (1990). Internal versus external control of reinforcement: A case history of a variable. *American Psychologist, 45*, 489-493.

35. Strickland, B. R. (1989). Internal-external control expectancies: From contingency to creativity. *American Psychologist, 44*, 1-12.

36. Brigham, J. C. (1986). *Social psychology*. Boston: Little Brown.

37. Perlman, D. & Fehr, B. (1986). Theories of friendship: The analysis of interpersonal attraction. In V. J. Derlega & B. A. Winstead (Eds.), *Friendship and social interaction*. New York: Springer-Verlag.

38. Butcher, J. N. (1989). *MMPI-2 user's guide*. Minneapolis: National Computer Systems.

39. Coopersmith, S. (1967). *The antecedents of self-esteem*. San Francisco: Freeman.

40. Beck, A. T. (1978). *Depression inventory*. Philadelphia: Center for Cognitive Therapy.

41. Anastasi, A. (1988). *Psychological testing, 6th ed*. New York: Macmillan.

42. Exner, J. E. Jr. (1986). *The Rorschach: A comprehensive system, vol. 1. Basic foundations. 2nd ed*. New York: Wiley.

43. Murray, H. A. (1943). *Thematic apperception test manual*. Cambridge, MA: Harvard University Press.

44. Wheeler, J. R. & Berliner, L. (1988). Treating the effects of sexual abuse on children. In G. E. Wyatt & G. J. Powell (Eds.), *Lasting effects of child sexual abuse*. Newbury Park, CA: Sage.

45. Pope, B. (1983). The initial interview. In C. E. Walker (Ed.), *The handbook of clinical psychology: Theory, research, and practice, vol. 1*. Homewood, IL: Dow Jones Irwin.

46. Bellack, A. S. & Hersen, M. (1988). *Behavioral assessment: A practical handbook, 3rd ed*. New York: Pergamon.

Chapter 11

1. Wilkerson, I. (1993, August 20). Back to school bearing tales of the flood. *New York Times*, pp. A1, A18.

2. Rodin, J. & Salovey, P. (1989). Health psychology. *Annual Review of Psychology, 40*, 533-579.

3. Lazarus, R. S. & Folkman, S. (1984). *Stress, appraisal, and coping*. New York: Springer.

4. Taylor, S. E. (1990). Health psychology. *American Psychologist, 45*, 40-50.

5. Quick, J. C., Murphy. L. R., Hurrell, Jr., J. J. & Orman, D. (1992). The value of work, the risk of distress, and the power of prevention. In J. C. Quick, L. R. Murphy, and J. J. Hurrell, Jr. (Eds.), *Stress & well-being at work*, pp. 3-13. Washington, DC: American Psychological Association.

6. MacLennan, B. W. (1992). Stressor reduction: An organizational alternative to individual stress management. In J. C. Quick, L. R. Murphy, and J. J. Hurrell, Jr. (Eds.), *Stress & well-being at work*, pp. 79-95. Washington, DC: American Psychological Association.

7. Jones, J. W. & Boye, M. W. (1992). Job stress and employee counterproductivity. In J. C. Quick, L. R. Murphy, and J. J. Hurrell, Jr. (Eds.), *Stress & well-being at work*, p. 239-251. Washington, DC: American Psychological Association.

8. Guastello, S. J. (1992). Accidents and stress-related health disorders among bus operators. In J. C. Quick, L. R. Murphy, and J. J. Hurrell, Jr. (Eds.), *Stress & well-being at work*. Washington, DC: American Psychological Association.

9. Holmes, T. H. & Rahe, R. H. (1967). The social readjustment rating scale. *Journal of Psychosomatic Research, 11*, 213-218.

10. Lazarus, R. S. (1981). Little hassles can be hazardous to your health. *Psychology Today, 15*, 58-62.

11. Lazarus, R. S., DeLongis, A., Folkman, S., & Gruen, R. (1985). Stress and adaptational outcomes. *American Psychologist, 40*, 770-779.

12. Malmo, R. B. (1986). Obituary: Hans Hugo Selye. *American Psychologist, 41*, 92-93.

13. Adler, T. (1993). Men and women affected by stress equally. *The APA Monitor, July*, Washington, DC: American Psychological Association, pp. 8-9.

14. O'Leary, A. (1990). Stress, emotion, and human immune function. *Psychological Bulletin, 108*, 363-382.

15. Kiecolt-Glaser, J. K. & Glaser, R. (1992). Psychoneuroimmunology: Can psychological interventions modulate immunity? *Journal of Consulting and Clinical Psychology, 60*, 569-575.

16. Dollard, J., Doob, L., Miller, N. E., Mowrer, O. H., & Sears, R. R. (1939). *Frustration and aggression*. New Haven, CT: Yale University Press.

17. Burger, J. M. (1990). *Personality, 2nd Edition*. Belmont, CA: Wadsworth.

18. Hammen, C., Davila, J., Brown, G., Ellicott, A. & Gitlin, M. (1992). Psychiatric history and stress: Predictors of severity of unipolar depression. *Journal of Abnormal Psychology, 101*, 45-52.

19. Weisse, C. S. (1992). Depression and immunocompetence: A review of the literature. *Psychological Bulletin, 111*, 475-489.

20. Monroe, S. M., Kupfler, D. J., & Frank, E. (1992). Life stress and treatment course of recurrent depression. *Journal of Consulting and Clinical Psychology, 60*, 718-724.

21. Freudenberger, H. J. (1980). *Burnout: How to beat the high cost of success*. New York: Bantam.

22. Maslach, C. (1982). *Burnout: The cost of caring*. Englewood Cliffs, NJ: Prentice-Hall.

23. Glass, D. C., McKnight, J. D. & Valdimarsdottir, H. (1993). Depression, burnout and perceptions of control in hospital nurses. *Journal of Consulting and Clinical Psychology, 61*, 147-155.

24. Task Force on the DSM-IV, (1993). *DSM-IV draft criteria*. Washington, DC: American Psychiatric Association.

25. Wood, J. M., Bootzin, R. R., Rosenhan, D., Nolen-Hoeksema, S., & Jourden, F. (1992). Effects of the 1989 San Francisco earthquake on frequency and content of nightmares. *Journal of Abnormal Psychology, 101*, 219-224.

26. Roberts, L. (1988). Vietnam's psychological toll. *Science, 241*, 159-161.

27. Jordan, B. K., Marmar, C. R., Fairbank, J. A., Schengler, W. E., Kulka, R. A., Hough, R. L. & Weiss, D. S. (1992). Problems in families of male Vietnam veterans with posttraumatic stress disorder. *Journal of Consulting and Clinical Psychology, 60*, 916-926.

28. Cole, P. M., & Putnam, F. W. (1992). Effect of incest on self and social functioning: A developmental psychopathology perspective. *Journal of Consulting and Clinical Psychology, 60*, 174-184.

29. Thoits, P. A. (1986). Social support as coping assistance. *Journal of Consulting and Clinical Psychology, 54*, 416-423.

30. Folkman, S., Lazarus, R. S., Gruen, R. J., & DeLongis, A. (1986). Appraisal, coping, health status, and psychological symptoms. *Journal of Personality and Social Psychology, 50*, 571-579.

31. Roth, S., and Cohen, L. J. (1986). Approach, avoidance, and coping with stress. *American Psychologist, 41*, 813-819.

32. Cohen, S. & Syme, S. L. (1985). *Social support and health*. New York: Academic Press.

33. Kiecolt-Glaser, J. K., Fisher, L. D., Ogrocki, P., Stout, J. C., Speicher, C. E., & Glaser, R. (1987). Marital quality, marital disruption, and immune function. *Psychosomatic Medicine, 49*, 13-34.

34. Kiecolt-Glaser, J. K., Kennedy, S., Malkoff, S., Fisher, L., Speicher, C. E., & Glaser, R. (1988). Marital discord and immunity in males. *Psychosomatic Medicine, 50*, 213-229.

35. Friedman, H. S., & Booth-Kewley, S. (1987). The disease-prone personality: A metaanalytic view of the construct. *American Psychologist, 42*, 539-555.

36. Friedman, M. & Rosenman, R. H. (1974). *Type-A behavior and your heart*. New York: Knopf.

37. Friedman, H. S., & Booth-Kewley, S. (1988). Validity of the type-A construct: A reprise. *Psychological Bulletin, 104*, 381-384.

38. Rosenman, R. H. (1978). The interview method of assessment of the coronary-prone behavior pattern. In T. M. Dembroski, S. M. Weiss, J. L. Shields, S. G. Haynes, & M. Feinleib (Eds.), *Coronary-prone behavior*, pp. 55-69. New York: Springer-Verlag.

39. Mathews, K. A. (1982). Psychological perspectives on the Type-A behavior pattern. *Psychological Bulletin, 91,* 293-323.

40. Mathews, K. A. (1988). Coronary heart disease and Type-A behaviors: Update on an alternative to the Booth-Kewley and Friedman quantitative review. *Psychological Bulletin, 104,* 373-380.

41. Mathews, K. A., & Haynes, S. G. (1986). Type-A behavior pattern and coronary risk: Update and critical evaluation. *American Journal of Epidemiology, 123,* 923-960.

42. Williams, R. B., & Barefoot, J. C. (1988). The emerging role of the hostility complex. In B. K. Houston & C. R. Snyder (Eds.), *Type-A behavior pattern: Research, theory, and prevention,* pp. 189-211. New York: Wiley.

43. Wright, L. (1988). Type-A behavior and coronary artery disease: Quest for the active ingredients and elusive mechanism. *American Psychologist, 43,* 2-14.

44. Goleman, D. (1992 September 2). Study documents how anger can impair heart function. *New York Times.*

45. Thorenson, C. E., & Powell, L. H. (1992). Type A behavior pattern: New perspectives on theory, assessment, and intervention. *Journal of Consulting and Clinical Psychology, 60,* 595-604.

46. Kobasa, S. C. (1982). The hardy personality: Toward a social psychology of stress and health. In G. S. Sanders and J. Suls (Eds.), *Social psychcology of health and illness.* Hillsdale, NJ: Erlbaum.

47. Peterson, C., Seligman, M. E. P., & Vaillant, G. E. (1988). Pessimistic explanatory style is a risk factor for physical illness. A thirty-five-year longitudinal study. *Journal of Personality and Social Psychology, 55,* 23-27.

48. Peterson, C. & Seligman, M. E. P. (1987). Explanatory style and illness. *Journal of Personality, 55,* 237-265.

49. Novaco, R. W. (1978). Anger and coping with stress. In J. P. Foreyt and D. P. Rathjen (Eds.), *Cognitive behavior therapy. Research and Application,* pp. 135-174. New York: Plenum.

50. Meichenbaum, D. (1985). *Stress inoculation training: A clinical guidebook.* New York: Pergamon Press.

51. Jeffrey, R. W. (1989). Risk behaviors and health. *American Psychologist, 44,* 1194-1202.

52. Blanchard, E. B. (1992). Psychological treatment of benign headache disorders. *Journal of Consulting and Clinical Psychology, 60,* 537-551.

53. Lehrer, P. M., Sargunaraj, D., & Hochron, S. (1992). Psychological approaches to the treatment of asthma. *Journal of Consulting and Clinical Psychology, 60,* 639-643.

54. Whitehead, W. E. (1992). Behavioral medicine approaches to gastrointestinal disorders. *Journal of Consulting and Clinical Psychology, 60,* 605-612.

55. American Heart Association (1988). *Cigarette smoking and cardiovascular disease: Special report for the public.* Dallas, TX: American Heart Association.

56. American Heart Association (1984). *Exercise and your heart.* Dallas, TX: American Heart Association.

Chapter 12

1. Roger, R. (1987). APA's position on the insanity defense: Empiricism versus emotionalism. *American Psychologist, 42,* 846-848

2. American Psychiatric Association (1994). *Diagnostic and statistical manual of mental disorders (4th ed.).* Washington, DC: Author.

3. Regier, D. A., Boyd, J. H., Burke, J. D. Jr., Rae, D. S., Myers, J. K., Kramer, M., Robins, L. N., George, L. K., Karno, M., & Locke, B. Z. (1988). One month prevalence of mental disorders in the United States. *Archives of General Psychiatry, 45*, 977-993.

4. Dunn, G. E. (1992). Multiple personality disorder: A new challenge for psychology. *Professional Psychology: Research and Practice, 23*, 18-23.

5. Smith, W. (1989). *A profile of health and disease in America: Mental illness and substance abuse.* New York: Facts on File.

6. Cadoret, R. J., & Gath, A. (1978). Inheritance of Alcoholism in adoptees. *British Journal of Psychiatry, 132*, 252-258.

7. Goodwin, D. W. (1985). Alcoholosm & Genetics. *Archives of General Psychiatry, 42*, 171-174

8. Shedler, J., & Block, J. (1990). Adolescent drug use and psychological health: A longitudinal inquiry. *American Psychologist, 45*, 612-630.

9. Rice, J., Reich, T., Andreasen, N. C., Endicott, J., Van Eerdwegh, M., Fishman, R., Hirschfeld, R. M. A., & Klerman, G. L. (1987). The familial transmission of bipolar illness. *Archives of General Psychiatry, 44*, 441-447.

10. Schildkraut, J. J., Green, A. I., & Mooney, J. J. (1985). Affective disorders: Biochemical aspects. In H. I., Kaplan & B. J. Sadock (Eds.) *Comprehensive textbook of Psychiatry, (V, IV).* Baltimore: Williams & Wilkins.

11. Beck, A. T. (1991). Cognitive Therapy: A 30-year perspective. *American Psychologist, 46*: 368-375.

12. Maier, S. F. & Seligman, M. E. P. (1976). Learned helplessness: Theory and evidence. *Journal of Experimental Psychology: General, 105*, 3-46.

13. Goleman, D. (1993). Scientists trace voices in schizophrenia. *The New York Times*, September 22, C12.

14. Mirsky, A. F., & Quinn, D. W. (1988). The Genain quadruplets. *Schizophrenia Bulletin 14,* 595-612.

15. Heritch, A. J. (1990). Evidence for reduced and dysregulated turnover of dopamine in schizophrenia. *Schizophrenia Bulletin, 16*, 605-615.

16. Rosenthal, D. H. (1970). *Genetic theory and abnormal behavior.* New York: McGraw-Hill

17. Koenigsberg, H. W., Kaplan, R. D., Gilmore, N. M., & Cooper, A. M. (1985). The relationship between syndrome and personality disorder in DSM-III: Experience with 2,642 patients. *American Journal of Psychiatry, 142*, 207-212.

18. Millar, J. D. (1992). Public enlightment and mental health in the workplace. In G. Puryear Keita & S. L. Sauter, (Eds.), *Work and well-being.* Washington, DC: American Psychological Association.

19. Quick, J. C. (1992). Health promotion, education, and treatment. In G. Puryear Keita & S. L. Sauter, (Eds.), *Work and well-being.* Washington, DC: American Psychological Association.

20. Sauter, S., Murphy, L. R., & Hurrell, Jr., J. H. (1992). Prevention of work-related psychological disorders. In G. Puryear Keita & S. L. Sauter, (Eds.), *Work and well-being.* Washington, DC: American Psychological Association.

21. Rimm, D. C., & Masters, J. C. (1979). *Behavior therapy: Techniques and empirical Findings (2nd ed.).* New York: Academic Press.

22. Ellis, A., & Dryden, W. (1987). *The practice of rational-emotive therapy.* New York: Springer.

23. Rogers, C. R., & Sanford, R. C. (1985). Chant-Centered Therapy. In H. I. Kaplan & B. J. Sadock (Eds). *Comprehensive texbook of Psychiatry, (5th ed.).* Baltimore: Williams & Wilkins.

24. American Psychological Association (1988). Carl Rogers. *American Psychologist*, *43*, 127-128. Washington, DC: Author.

25. Prochaska, J. O. (1984). *Systems of psychotherapy, (2nd ed.).* Chicago: Dorsey Press.

26. Hall, C. S. & Lindzey. G. (1985). *Theories of personality*. New York: Wiley.

27. Kazdin, A. E. (1986). Comparitive outcome studies of psychotherapy: Methodological issues and strategies. *Journal of Consulting & Clinical Psychology, 54*, 95-105.

28. Gorman, J. M., & Davis, J. M. (1989). Antianxiety drugs. In H. I. Kaplan & B. J. Sadock (Eds.). *Comprehensive textbook of psychiatry (5th ed.).* Baltimore: Williams & Wilkins.

29. Davis, J. M. & Glassman, A. H. (1989). Antidepressant drugs. In H. I. Kaplan & B. J. Sadock (Eds.). *Comprehensive Textbook of Psychiatry (5th ed.).* Baltimore: Williams & Wilkins.

30. Davis, J. M., Barter, J. T., & Kane, J. M. (1989). Antipsychotic drugs. In H. I. Kaplan & B. J. Sadock (Eds.). *Comprehensive Textbook of Psychiatry (5th ed.).* Baltimore: Williams & Wilkins.

31. National Institutes of Health Consensus Development Conference Statement (1985). Electro-convulsive Therapy. *Consensus Development Conference Statement*, p. 5.

Chapter 13

1. Festinger, L., Riecken, H. W., & Schachter, S. (1956). *When prophecy fails*. Minneapolis: University of Minnesota Press.

2. Asch, S. E. (1946). Forming impressions of personality. *Journal of Abnormal and Social Psychology, 41*, 258-290.

3. Fiske, S. T. & Taylor, S. E. (1991). *Social cognition, 2nd ed.* New York: McGraw Hill.

4. Dion, K. K., Berscheid, E., & Walster, E. (1972). What is beautiful is good. *Journal of Personality and Social Psychology, 24*, 285-290.

5. Eagly, A. H., Ashmore, R. D., Makhijani, M. G., & Longo, L. C. (1991). What is beautiful is good, but...:A meta-analytic review of research on the physical attractiveness stereotype. *Psychological Bulletin, 110*, 109-128.

6. Feingold, A. (1992). Good-looking people are not what we think. *Psychological Bulletin, 111*, 304-341.

7. Berry, D. S., Zeibrowitz-McArthur, L. (1988). What's in a face? Facial maturity and the attribution of legal responsibility. Personality and Social Psychology Bulletin, *14*, 23-33.

8. Hall, E. T. (1966). *The hidden dimension*. New York: Doubleday.

9. Weiner, B. (1986). *An attributional theory of motivation and emotion*. New York: Springer-Verlag.

10. Kelley, H. H. (1967). Atribution theory in social psychology. In D. Levine (Ed.), *Nebraska symposium on motivation, 1967, vol. 15*. Lincoln, NE: University of Nebraska Press.

11. Weiner, B. (1993). On sin versus sickness: A theory of perceived responsibility and social motivation. *American Psychologist, 48*, 957-965.

12. Sears, D. O., Peplau, L. A., & Taylor, S. E. (1991). *Social psychology, 7th ed.* Engle-wood Cliffs, NJ: Prentice Hall.

13. Olson, J. M. & Zanna, M. P. (1993). Attitudes and attitude change. *Annual Review of Psychology, 44*, 117-154.

14. Ajzen, I. & Fishbein, M. (1977). Attitude-behavior relations: A theoretical analysis and review of empirical research. *Psychological Bulletin, 84*, 888-918.

15. LaPiere, R. T. (1934). Attitudes vs. actions. *Social Forces, 13*, 230-237.

16. Ajzen, I. (1985). From intentions to actions: A theory of planned action. In J. Kuhl & J. Beckman (Eds.), *Action control: From cognition to behavior*. New York: Springer.

17. McGuire, W. J. (1985). Attitudes and attitude change. In G. Lindzey & E. Aronson (Eds.), *Handbook of social psychology, 3rd ed., vol. 2*. New York: Random House.

18. Festinger, L. (1957). *A theory of cognitive dissonance*. Evanston, IL: Row, Peterson.

19. Bem, D. J. (1972). Self-perception theory. In L. Berkowitz (Ed.), *Advances in experimental social psychology, vol. 6*. New York: Academic.

20. Chaiken, S. & Baldwin, M. W. (1981). Affective-cognitive consistency and the effect of salient behavioral information on the self-perception of attitudes. *Journal of Personality and Social Psychology, 41*, 1-12.

21. Allport, G. W. (1954). *The nature of prejudice*. Garden City, NY: Doubleday.

22. Cook, S. W. (1984). Cooperative interaction in multi-ethnic contexts. In N. Miller & M. Brewer (Eds.), *Groups in contact: The psychology of desegregation*. New York: Academic.

23. Slavin, R. (1983). When does cooperative learning increase student achievement? *Psychological Bulletin, 94*, 429-443.

24. Adorno, T. W., Frenkel-Brunswik, E., Levenson, D. J., & Sanford, R. N. (1950). The authoritarian personality. New York: Harper & Row.

25. Asch, S. (1955). Opinions and social pressure. *Scientific American, 19*, 31-35.

26. Steinberg, S. (1991). Occupational apartheid. *Nation*, December 9, 1991, 744-746.

27. Murguia, E. & Telles, E. E. (1990). Phenotypic discrimination and income differences among Mexican-Americans. *Social Science Quarterly, 71*, 682-696.

28. Committee on Labor and Human Resources. Subcommittee on Employment and Productivity (1991). *Women and the workplace: the glass ceiling*. Washington, DC: U.S. Government Printing Office.

29. Campbell, J. D. & Fairey, P. J. (1989). Informational and normative routes to conformity: The effect of faction size as a function of norm extremity and attention to the stimulus. *Journal of Personality and Social Psychology, 57*, 457-468.

30. Milgram, S. (1963). Behavioral study of obedience. *Journal of Abnormal and Social Psychology, 67*, 371-378.

31. Osherow, N. (1984). Making sense of the nonsensical: An analysis of Jonestown. In E. Aronson (Ed.), *Readings about the social animal, 4th ed*. New York: Freeman.

32. Galanter, M. (Ed.) (1989). *Cults and new religious movements: A report of the American Psychiatric Association*. Washington, DC: American Psychiatric Association.

33. *Current Bibliography* (1979). Stanley Milgram. 256-261. New York: Witson.

34. Milgram, S. (1974). Obedience to authority: An experimental view. New York: Harper & Row.

35. Freedman, J. L. & Fraser, S. C. (1966). Compliance without pressure: The foot-in-the-door technique. *Journal of Personality and Social Psychology, 4*, 195-202.

36. Cialdini, R. B., Vincent, J. E., Lewis, S. K., Catalan, J., Wheeler, D., & Darby, B. L. (1975). Reciprocal concessions procedure for inducing compliance: The door-in-the-face technique. *Journal of Personality and Social Psychology, 31*, 206-215.

37. Cialdini, R. B. (1985). *Influence: Science and practice*. Glenview, IL: Scott Foresman.

38. Triplett, N. (1898). The dynamogenic factors in pacemaking and competition. *American Journal of Psychology, 9*, 507-533.

39. Guerin, B. (1986). Mere presence effects in humans: A review. *Journal of Experimental Social Psychology, 22,* 38-77.

40. Zajonc, R. B. (1965). Social facilitation. *Science, 149,* 269-274.

41. Baron, R. S. (1986). Distraction-conflict theory: Progress and problems. In L. Berkowitz (Ed.), *Advances in experimental social psychology, vol. 20.* New York: Academic.

42. Latane, B., Williams, K., & Harkins, S. (1979). Many hands make light the work: The causes and consequences of social loafing. *Journal of Personality and Social Psychology, 37,* 822-832.

43. Harkins, S. G. & Szymanski, K. (1989). Social loafing and group evaluation. *Journal of Personality and Social Psychology, 56,* 934-941.

44. Bornstein, R. F. (1989). Exposure and affect: Overview and meta-analysis of research 1968-1987. *Psychological Bulletin, 106,* 265-289.

45. Buss, D. M. (1989). Sex differences in human mate preferences: Evolutionary hypothesis tested in 37 cultures. *Behavioral and Brain Sciences, 12,* 1-49.

46. Feingold, A. (1988). Matching for attractiveness in romantic partners and same-sex friends: A meta-analysis and theo- retical critique. *Psychological Bulletin, 104,* 226-235.

47. Kelley, H. H. & Thibaut, J. W. (1978). *Interpersonal relations: A theory of interdependence.* New York: Wiley.

48. Walster, E., Walster, G. W., & Berscheid, E. (1978). *Equity: Theory and research.* Boston: Allyn & Bacon.

49. Brehm, S. S. (1986). *Intimate relationships, 2nd ed.* Boston: McGraw Hill.

50. Hatfield, E. (1988). Passionate and companionate love. In R. J. Sternberg & M. L. Barnes (Eds.), *The psychology of love.* New Haven, CT: Yale University Press.

51. Latane, B. & Darley, J. (1970). *The unresponsive bystander: Why doesn't he help?* Englewood Cliffs, NJ: Prentice Hall.

52. Latane, B. & Nida, S. (1981). Ten years of research on group size and helping. *Psychological Bulletin, 89,* 308-324.

53. Lorenz, K. (1969). *On aggression.* New York: Bantam.

54. Kalat, J. W. (1992). *Biological psychology, 4th ed.* Belmont, CA: Wadsworth.

55. Berkowitz, L. (1989). Frustration-aggression hypothesis: Examination and reformulation. *Psychological Bulletin, 106,* 59-73.

56. Bandura, A., Ross, D., & Ross, S. A. (1961). Transmission of aggression through imitation of aggressive models. *Journal of Abnormal and Social Psychology, 63,* 575-582.

57. Freedman, J. L. (1988). Television violence and aggression: What the evidence shows. In S. Oskamp (Ed.), *Television as a social issue.* Newbury Park, CA: Sage.

58. Malinowsky-Rummell, R. & Hansen, D. J. (1993). Long-term consequences of childhood physical abuse. *Psychological Bulletin, 114,* 68-79.

59. Zimbardo, P. G. (1970). The human choice: individuation, reason and order versus deindividuation, impulse and chaos. In N. J. Arnold & D. Levine (Eds.), *Nebraska symposium on motivation, 1969.* Lincoln, NE: University of Nebraska Press.

60. Isenberg, D. J. (1986). Group polarization: A critical review and meta-analysis. *Journal of Personality and Social Psychology, 50,* 1141-1151.

61. Janis, I. L. (1982). *Groupthink: Psychological studies of policy decisions and fiascoes, 2nd ed.* Boston: Houghton Mifflin.

62. Hogg, M. A. & Abrams, D. (1988). *Social identifications: A social psychology of intergroup relations and group processes.* New York: Routledge.

Chapter 14

1. Tullar, W. L. (1989). Relational control in the employment interview. *Journal of Applied Psychology, 75*, 13-20.

2. Schmidt, F. L., Ones, D. S., & Hunter, J. E. (1992). Personnel selection. *Annual Review of Psychology, 43*, 627-670.

3. Anastasi, A. (1989). Ability testing in the 1980s and beyond: Some major trends. *Public Personnel Management Journal, 18*, 471-484.

4. Austin, J. T., & Hanisch, K. A. (1990). Occupational attainment as a function of abilities and interests: A longitudinal analysis using project TALENT data. *Journal of Applied Psychology, 42*, 583-596.

5. Saari, L. M., Johnson, T. R., Mclaughlin, S. D., & Zimmerle, D. M. (1988). A survey of management training and education practices in U.S. companies. *Personnel Psychology, 41*, 731-743.

6. Vobejda, B. (1987 October, 12). The new cutting edge in factories. *Washington Post*, p. A14.

7. Goldstein, I. L., & Gilliam, P. (1990). Training systems in the year 2000. *American Psychologist, 45*, 134-143.

8. Turnage, J. J. (1990). The challenge of new workplace technology for psychology. *American Psychologist, 45*, 171-178.

9. Morrison, A. M., & Von Glinow, M. (1990). Women and minorities in management. *American Psychologist, 45*, 200-208.

10. Tannenbaum, S. I., & Yukl, G. (1992). Training and development in work organizations. *Annual Review of Psychology, 43*, 399-441.

11. Faria, A. J. (1989). Business gaming: Current usage levels. *Journal of Management Development, 8*, 59-65.

12. Thornton, G. C., & Cleveland, J. N. (1990). Developing managerial talent through simulation. *American Psychologist, 45*, 190-199.

13. Katzell, R. A., & Thompson, D. E. (1990). Work motivation: Theory and practice. *American Psychologist, 45*, 144-153.

14. O'Reilly, C. A. (1991). Organizational behavior: Where we've been and where we're going. *Annual Review of Psychology, 42*, 427-458.

15. Riger, S. (1991). Gender dilemmas in sexual harassment policies and procedures. *American Psychologist, 46*, 497-505.

16. Adler, T. Sexual harassment at work hurts victim, organization. The APA Monitor, 24, 25-26.

17. Fitzgerald, L. F. (1993). Sexual harassment. *American Psychologist, 48*, 1070-1076.

18. Howell, W. C., Colle, H. A., Kantowitz, B. H., & Weiner, E. L. (1987). Guidlines for education and training in engineering psychology. *American Psychologist, 42*, 602-604.

19. Gopher, D., & Kimchi, R. (1989). Engineering psychology. *Annual Review of Psychology, 40*, 431-455.

20. McCormick, E. G., & Ilgen, D. (1985). *Industrial and organizational psychology, 8th ed.* Englewood Cliffs, NJ: Prentice-Hall.

21. Howell, W. C. (1993). Engineering psychology. *Annual Review of Psychology, 44*, 231-263.

22. Holahan, C. J. (1986). Environmental psychology. *Annual Review of Psychology, 37*, 381-407.

23. Saegert, S., & Winkel, G. (1990). Environmental psychology. *Annual Review of Psychology, 41*, 441-477.

24. Gifford, R. (1982). Projected interpersonal distance and orientation choices: Personality, sex, and social situation. *Psychology Quarterly, 45*, 145-152.

25. Hall, E. T., & Hall, M. R. (1971). The sounds of silence. In P. Whitten & D. E. K. Hunter, (Eds.). *Anthropology: Contemporary perspectives.* Boston: Little, Brown, 125-130.

26. Sussman, N. M., & Rosenfeld, H. M. (1982). Influence of culture, language, and sex on conversational distance. *Journal of Personality and Social Psychology, 42*, 66-74.

27. Heller, K., Price, R. H., Reinharz, S., Riger, S. & Wandersman, A. (1984). *Psychology and community change, 2nd ed.,* Pacific Grove, CA: Brooks/Cole.

28. Gesten, E. L., & Jason, L. A. (1987). Social and community interventions. *Annual Review of Psychology, 38*, 427-460.

29. Levine, M., Toro, P. A., & Perkins, D. V. (1993). Social and community interventions. *Annual Review of Psychology*, 525-558.

30. Centers for Disease Control and Public Health Service. *(1993, April) HIV/ AIDS surveillance.* Atlanta, GA: Centers for Disease Control.

31. Kelly, J. A., Murphy, D. A., Sikkema, K. J., & Kalichman, S. C. (1993). Psychological interventions to prevent HIV infection are urgently needed. *American Psychologist, 48*, 1023-1034.

32. Morin, S. F. (1988). AIDS: The challenge to psychology. *American Psychologist, 43*, 838-842.

33. Landers, S. (1988). Latinos combat AIDS. *The APA Monitor, 19*, 42.

34. Youngstrom, N. (1993). Without behavioral science, war on AIDS can't be won. *The APA Monitor, 24*, 25.

35. Leigh, B. C., & Stall, R. (1993). Substance use and risky sexual behavior for exposure to HIV: Issues in methodology, interpretation, and prevention. *American Psychologist, 48*, 1046-1055.

36. Hammond, W. R., & Yung, B. (1993). Psychology's role in the public health response to assaultive violence among young African-American men. *American Psychologist, 48*, 142-154.

37. American Psychological Association. (1993). Hortensia Amaro. *American Psychologist, 48*, 364-367.

38. Kondratas, A. (1991). Ending homelessness. *American Psychologist, 46*, 1226-1231.

39. Fisher, P. J., & Breakey, W. R. (1991). The epidemiology of alcohol, drug, and mental disorders among homeless persons. *American Psychologist, 46*, 1115-1128.

40. McCarty, D., Argeriou, M., Huebner, R. B., & Lubran, B. (1991). Alcoholism, drug abuse, and the homeless. *American Psychologist, 46*, 1139-1148.

41. Milburn, N., & D'Ercole, A. (1991). Homeless women: Moving toward a comprehensive model. *American Psychologist, 46*, 1161-1169.

42. Rafferty, Y., & Shinn, M. (1991). The impact of homelessness on children. *American Psychologist, 46*, 1170-1179.

43. Rotheram, M. J., Coopman, C., & Ehrhardt, A. A. (1991). Homeless youths and HIV infection. *American Psychologist, 46*, 1188-1197.

44. Cohen, C. I., & Thompson, K. S. (1992). Homeless mental ill or mentally ill homeless? *American Journal of Psychiatry, 149*, 816-823.

45. Cohen, J. B., & Chakravarti, D. (1990). Consumer psychology. *Annual Review of Psychology, 41*, 243-288.

46. Grisso, T. (1987). The economic and scientific future of forensic psychologist assessment. *American Psychologist, 42*, 831-839.

47. Melton, G. B., & Limber, S. (1989). Psychologist's involvement in cases of maltreatment: Limits of role and expertise. *American Psychologist, 44*, 1225-1233.

Glossary

abnormal behavior—behavior that is either uncommon, or violates social norms, or is distressing, or maladaptive

achievement motivation—a concern with doing things better and surpassing standards of excellence

acquired immune deficiency syndrome (AIDS)—an immune system disease that kills its victims by making them more susceptible to life-threatening infections

acquisition (ack-kwi-zi-shun)—the strengthening of a conditioned response by repeated pairings of the conditioned and unconditioned stimuli

activation-synthesis theory—a biological view of dreams as the result of brain arousal in REM sleep

addiction—a condition of drug dependence, with physical need, drug tolerance, and withdrawal

aggression—behavior that directs intentional harm at another person

alcohol—a depressant drug produced by fermenting sugar

algorithm—a formula for solving a problem

altruism (al-true-i-zum)—helping due to a desire to help without hope of reward

analytical psychology—Carl Jung's psychodynamic theory based on the concept of collective unconscious archetypes in personality

antisocial personality disorder—a disorder characterized by antisocial behavior

anxiety disorder—a mental disorder involving anxiety and related thoughts, feelings, and behaviors that interfere with normal functioning

applied psychology—the application of psychological methods and knowledge to solve practical problems

approach-approach conflict—a conflict that comes from having to decide between two desirable goals

approach-avoidance conflict—a conflict that comes from being attracted to the positive features of a stimulus and the motivation to avoid the same stimulus because of its negative features

arousal theory—a model that states that you are motivated to maintain a preferred level of stimulation

attitude—a pattern of beliefs, feelings, and response tendencies organized around a topic

attribution bias—a bias that distorts judgments about the causes of behavior

attributions—explanations for the outcomes of behavior

attribution theory—a theory that explains how people judge the causes of behavior

authoritarianism (aw-thor-i-tair-ee-an-i-zum)—an attitude consisting of conventional values, need to submit to authority, conformity to in-group values, and hostility to out-groups

autonomic nervous system—the division of the peripheral nervous system that regulates internal organs

avoidance-avoidance conflict—a conflict that arises from the motivation to escape from two negative choices

behavioral medicine—the use of the principles of behavior and medical knowledge and techniques in the treatment of medical disorders

behavior genetics—the study of the hereditary basis of behavior

behaviorism—school of psychology that uses objective methods to study observable behavior

behavior therapy—an approach to the treatment of abnormal behavior; based on the application of learning principles

binocular cues—distance and depth cues that are available only when both eyes work together

biofeedback—a stress mana-gement procedure that "feeds back" to the person information about bodily functioning that is usually not noticed

bipolar disorder—a mood disorder in which mood alternates between periods of depression and mania

body senses—the senses of body movement, position, and balance

borderline personality disorder—a disorder marked by unstable mood, self-image, and relationships as well as impulsive, self-defeating behavior

brain—the main part of the central nervous system; a complex structure consisting of 100 billion neurons

bystander effect—the phenomenon that help is less likely to be given when several bystanders are present

Cannon-Bard theory—view of emotion that perception causes brain arousal, which results in bodily changes and emotional feeling

case study—a research method involving in-depth investigation of an individual or group

Cattell's factor theory—a model of personality as 16 source traits; derived from factor analysis

central nervous system—the brain and spinal cord

cerebellum (se-ruh-bel-lum)—a hindbrain structure involved in movement and memory

cerebral cortex—the outer covering of the cerebrum; responsible for higher mental functions

chemical senses—the senses of taste and smell

chunking—an STM process that organizes information into larger, meaningful items

classical conditioning—a kind of learning in which a new stimulus comes to produce a reflexive response by its association with a stimulus that naturally triggers the reflex

client-centered therapy—a type of psychotherapy developed by Carl Rogers that uses the therapist's attitudes of unconditional positive regard and empathy to help clients accept themselves

cochlea—an organ in the inner ear containing the basilar membrane and hair cell receptors

cognitive dissonance—a state of tension caused by the presence of conflicting beliefs or attitudes

cognitive labeling theory—a view that emotion is determined by how physiological changes are interpreted

cognitive learning—a theory of learning concerned with unobservable mental activity

cognitive therapy—psychotherapy procedures used to correct faulty beliefs and thought patterns

community psychology—branch of psychology that studies the effects of social and environmental factors on behavior and applies this knowledge to promote the well-being of individuals in the population

compliance—the following of a request made by another person

concept—an idea that represents a group of things or events that have features in common

concrete operations stage—stage of cognitive development marked by conservation and concrete reality-based logic

conditioned response—the reflexive response to the conditioned stimulus

conditioned stimulus—a neutral stimulus that eventually elicits a reflexive response after repeated pairings with an unconditioned stimulus

cones—visual receptor cells that respond to color and high light intensity

conformity—a decision to act in ways that resemble the behavior of other people

consciousness—a state of mental awareness

consolidation hypothesis—the view that memory is based on the formation of reverberating neural circuits in the brain

consumer psychology—a branch of psychology concerned with the application of psychological methods and principles to the study of consumer behavior

continuous reinforcement schedule—a reinforcement method in which each correct response is reinforced

control group—subjects in an experiment who are not manipulated; basis of comparison for evaluation of the effect of the independent variable on the experimental group

conversion disorder—a somatoform disorder that involves symptoms affecting voluntary movement or sensory function

coping—attempts made to manage situations appraised as threatening

corpus callosum (cor-puss kall-oh-summ)—a bundle of axons that connects the cerebral hemispheres

correlational research—a method that describes the statistical associations, or correlations, between variables

creativity—the ability to solve problems in unique ways

critical period—a time during which the individual is most ready for developmental change and is sensitive to environmental events

cue-dependent memory—a memory phenomenon in which recollection is influenced by cues in the situation or in the person's emotional state

decay theory—the view that forgetting results from the gradual weakening of unused memories over time

defense mechanisms—unconscious ego processes for coping with conflict and emotional distress

deindividuation (dee-in-di-vid-you-ay-shun) model—view that a person is more likely to be aggressive when in a group than when alone because of a loss of individuality

deinstitutionalization—a policy of moving mental patients out of overcrowded mental hospitals

dependent personality disorder—a disorder marked by excessive dependency on others and an inability to make important decisions

dependent variable—the experiment variable that is observed for changes after a manipulation; assumed to be the effect of the independent variable

depth-of-processing model—a theory that explains long-term memory strength in terms of encoding processes

depressant—a type of drug that slows or suppresses nervous system activity

Diagnostic and Statistical Manual of Mental Disorders–Fourth Edition—a system for classifying mental disorders; developed by the American Psychiatric Association

discrimination—harmful or unfair behavior toward a group as a result of prejudice

disease-prone personality—characteristics of depression, anxiety, and hostility; associated with psychosomatic disorders

dissociative disorders—mental disorders that involve a sudden alteration of consciousness, memory, or identity

dissociative identity disorder—a disorder characterized by two or more distinct personalities

drive—a condition of psychological arousal

drive theory—a view that biological needs motivate behaviors necessary to satisfy those needs

educational psychology—a branch of psychology concerned with the application of psychological principles and methods to teaching and learning

ego—the part of personality that controls identity, adjustment, and rational processes according to the reality principle

ego psychology—a psychodynamic theory that places the ego at the center of personality and behavior

elaborative rehearsal—a memory strategy of associating new information with familiar facts

electroconvulsive therapy—a biological therapy for depression involving the application of small electrical currents to the patient's head

emergency theory—a model that states that stress disrupts homeostasis and activates the sympathetic division of the autonomic nervous system

emotion—a reaction composed of subjective feelings, cognitive evaluation, physiological changes, and observable behavior

endocrine system—a collection of glands that secrete hormones

engineering psychology—a branch of psychology concerned with the application of scientific knowledge about people to the design of machines, systems, and environments

engram—the physical form or trace of memory in the brain

environmental determinism—a behavioristic assumption that behavior is controlled by the learning environment

environmental psychology—a branch of psychology that studies the relationships between the physical environment and behavior

episodic (epp-e-sod-ik) memory—memory for personal, autobiographical facts

ethical principles—guidelines that protect the rights and dignity of research subjects

ethnic identity—identity based on an awareness of and attitudes about one's cultural or racial group

expectancy-value theory—a view that behavior is motivated by the expectation of achieving goals and the value assigned to them

experiment—a research method that examines the cause-and-effect relationships between variables through controlled manipulations

experimental group—subjects in an experiment who are manipulated in terms of the independent variable

extinction—the weakening and elimination of a conditioned response

extraneous (ex-tray-nee-us) variables—experimental factors in addition to the independent variable that affect the dependent variable

facial feedback hypothesis—a view that emotions are determined by the brain's interpretation of muscle feedback from facial expression

failure-to-thrive—disorder of delayed physical growth due to abuse or neglect

feature detectors—cortical neurons that respond to specific features of visual stimuli

fetal alcohol syndrome—a condition of brain damage and mental retardation due to prenatal exposure to alcohol

five-factor model—the theory of the "Big Five" factors of personality: extraversion, agreeableness, conscientiousness, emotional stability, and openness

forensic psychology—a branch of psychology concerned with the application of psychological research or assessment information to legal issues

forgetting—the failure to remember because of one or more problems in the memory processes of encoding, storage, and retrieval

formal operations stage—a stage of cognitive development, characterized by abstract thinking and reasoning

fovea (foh-vee-ah)—a small, cone-packed region of the retina for analyzing visual detail and color

frequency theory—an explanation of hearing in terms of hair cell responses that match the frequency of soundwave stimuli

frontal lobe—a brain area involved in movement and higher mental functions such as thinking, planning, and speech

frustration-aggression hypothesis—the idea that frustration leads to aggression

fully functioning personality—a psychologically healthy person who is open, self-trusting, sensitive, and lives in the "here and now"

functional fixedness—the tendency to look at an object according to its typical use or function

functionalism—the school of psychology that studies the adaptive functions of the mind and behavior

gate-control theory—a theory of pain sensation; emphasizes pain signal "gate" mechanisms in the spinal cord

gender identity—the sense of being male or female

general adaptation syndrome—Selye's three-stage model of alarm, resistance, and exhaustion that describes the body's reactions to stress

generalized anxiety disorder—a disorder involving excessive worry about several things

genetics—a branch of biology concerned with heredity

Gestalt laws—principles of perception that describe the visual organization of objects and groups: closure, continuity, similarity, proximity, figure-ground

Gestalt (geh-shtalt) psychology—the school of psychology that studies organized patterns or wholes in mental activity

g-factor—general intelligence; the main component in Spearman's factor theory

giftedness—an IQ score of 130 or higher

group polarization—a phenomenon in which group members' opinions become more extreme after group discussion

hair cells—the sensory receptors for hearing

hallucinogens—psychoactive drugs that cause hallucinations and psychedelic mind alterations

hardiness—traits of commitment, control, and challenge; related to health promotion

health psychology—application of psychology to the understanding and prevention of illness and the promotion of health

hemispheric specialization—the fact that each cerebral hemisphere has specific functions

heritability—the degree to which heredity influences behavior or a trait

heuristic (you-riss-tick)—a rule of thumb

higher-order conditioning—the pairing of a neutral stimulus with a conditioned stimulus so that both elicit the conditioned response

hormones—chemicals that regulate the functions of organs

hostility complex—traits of anger and irritability; associated with heart disease

humanistic psychology—a school of psychology that focuses on individual uniqueness and development

hypnosis—a procedure that alters consciousness and increases openness to suggestions

hypochondriasis (high-poh-konn-dry-uh-sis)—a somatoform disorder involving an excessive fear of having a serious illness

hypothalamus (high-poh-thal-uh-muss)—a forebrain structure involved in physiological control, feeding, aggression, sex, and pleasure

iconic (eye-konn-ik) memory—very brief sensory memory for visual stimuli

id—the part of personality controlled by unconscious instinctual drives and the pleasure principle

identity—a stable sense of self, or self-concept

identity crisis—the struggle to establish a stable identity in adolescence

idiographic (id-ee-oh-graf-ik) approach—Allport's approach to the study of unique trait patterns in individuals

illusion—a false or distorted perception

immune system—bodily mechanisms that identify and eliminate foreign materials

implicit (im-pliss-it) memory—memories that are learned and retrieved without conscious effort

incentive—a stimulus that has a positive or negative value in motivating behavior

incentive theory—the view that motivation is based on the attractiveness, or incentive value, of external stimuli

independent variable—the manipulated variable in an experiment; assumed to be the cause of the dependent variable

individual psychology—Alfred Adler's psychodynamic theory emphasizing social dimensions of personality

industrial-organizational psychology—a kind of applied psychology concerned with human behavior in the workplace

information-processing model—the view of memory as a system with three stages: sensory, short-term, and long-term

insight learning—a type of learning, studied by Köhler, based on perceptual interpretations

insomnia—a sleep disorder involving delay in the start of sleep or problems staying asleep

instinct theory—a view of motivation; traits that increase the chances of survival are passed on to offspring as inherited patterns of behavior

instrumental conditioning—a type of learning in which behavior is directed toward a goal

intelligence—the mental management of one's life in a constructive, purposeful way

intelligence quotient—a method of calculating intelligence: IQ = mental age divided by chronological age, then multiplied by 100

interference theory—the view that forgetting is due to proactive or retroactive interference of memories with each other

interpersonal theory—a psychodynamic theory of personality as a product of interpersonal relationships

James-Lange (Lonn-ga) theory—a model that proposes that interpretations of bodily changes determine emotion

job analysis—a method of evaluating whether workers are doing their jobs as well as they are supposed to

language—an organized system of using symbols to communicate thoughts and feelings

latent learning—learning that is revealed only when an incentive is provided

law of effect—Thorndike's rule that behaviors followed by satisfying consequences are strengthened and those followed by unsatisfying consequences are weakened

learned helplessness—a state in which a person believes he cannot control unpleasant events

learning—a change in behavior as a result of experience

life structures—the underlying patterns or designs of adult life; based primarily on relationships

limbic system—a forebrain region involved in emotions, learning, and memory

linguistic-relativity hypothesis—the notion that language shapes perceptions of reality

locus-of-control—a personality variable that reflects an individual's beliefs about whether events are controlled by internal or external forces

long-term memory (LTM)—the final stage of memory; unconscious storage for an indefinitely long duration

lucid dream—a dream in which the dreamer is aware of and influences the course of dreaming

maintenance rehearsal—rehearsal by repetition of information to be remembered

major depressive disorder—a mood disorder marked by major depressive episodes

marijuana—the *Cannabis* plant containing the drug THC (tetrahydrocannabinol) that causes calming and sensory alteration

maturation—the unfolding of innate biological programs for development

medulla—a hindbrain structure involved in vital functions such as respiration and heart rate and sensory functions such as taste, touch, and hearing

memory—the system of mental abilities for acquiring (encoding), retaining (storage), and accessing (retrieval) information

menarche (men-ark)—a girl's first menstruation

menopause (men-oh-paws)—the stage of development in a woman's life marked by the end of menstruation

mental disorder—abnormal behavior associated with suffering, pain, death, or disability

mental retardation—a condition marked by below-average IQ and deficits in adaptive functioning

mental set—the tendency to approach problems in rigid ways

mid-life crisis—a period of uncharacteristic behaviors and attitudes, indicating the distress of middle adulthood

mnemonic (nee-mon-ik)—a strategy to reorganize the information in memory to improve recall

monocular cues—distance and depth cues that are available from one eye

mood disorder—a mental disorder involving episodes of depression or mania or an alternation of the two

moral reasoning—thinking or judgments about right and wrong

motivated forgetting—unconsciously motivated forgetting of memories that are emotionally disturbing

motivation—the process that activates and directs behavior toward a goal

narcolepsy (narr-koh-lepp-see)—a sleep disorder characterized by sudden attacks of REM sleep

naturalistic observation—a research method involving the study of behavior in natural settings

need for affiliation—the motivation to seek out others, value their company, and care about them

need for power—the motivation to exercise control over events that affect one's life

need hierarchy—Maslow's sequence of needs in which we are motivated to satisfy "lower" (basic) needs before "higher" (growth) needs

need theory—Maslow's theory of personality as a hierarchy of basic needs and growth (self-actualization) needs

needs analysis—an organizational method to determine the need for training

negative correlation—a relationship in which the values of associated variables change in opposite directions

negative reinforcer—a stimulus, that if removed after a response, increases the probability that the response will be repeated

neodissociation (nee-oh-diss-so-see-ay-shun) theory—view that hypnosis causes a trance state of divided consciousness

network model—a theory that describes unconscious problem-solving activity in dreaming

neural impulse—the electrical activity, or firing, of a neuron

neuron (noo-ron)—a cell in the nervous system that is specialized to receive and transmit information

neurotransmitters—chemicals released at the synapse to communicate between neurons

NREM sleep—the four stages of non-rapid-eye-movement sleep characterized by slow brain waves

obedience—submission to a demand made by another person

observational learning—learning by observation and imitation

obsessive-compulsive disorder—an anxiety disorder involving either obsessions or compulsions

occipital lobe (ox-si-pi-tull)—the primary visual area of the brain

operant conditioning—a type of learning in which responses called operants are strengthened or weakened by their consequences

operant theory—Skinner's version of instrumental conditioning in which learning is determined by the consequences of reinforcement and punishment

operational definition—the objective measurement of a variable

opiates—a class of narcotic drugs including opium, morphine, codeine, and heroin

organizational behavior—the motivation, satisfaction, and leadership of workers

panic disorders—anxiety disorders marked by frequent, unexpected panic attacks

paranoid personality disorder—a disorder with maladaptive traits of distrust, suspiciousness, fear, and jealousy

parietal (puh-rye-eh-tull) lobe—a brain area; involved in skin sensations and visual and spatial associations

partial reinforcement schedule—a reinforcement method in which a response is reinforced occasionally

peer pressure—the forces for compliance or conformity from peer group members

perception—the interpretation and organization of stimulus information; based on sensation and cognition

perceptual constancy—the tendency to perceive constant features in an object despite changes in the retinal image of the object

peripheral nervous system—nerves outside of the brain and spinal cord

personality—a stable pattern of behaviors and characteristics that distinguish an individual

personality disorder—a mental disorder characterized by maladaptive, inflexible, and distressing personality traits

personal space—an area surrounding you that you stake as your own

personnel psychology—the branch of industrial-organizational psychology concerned with the selection, placement, and training of employees

phobia disorder—an anxiety disorder involving excessive and unreasonable fears and avoidance of a certain type of object, activity, or situation

physiological motives—motives that stem from bodily needs necessary for survival; hunger, thirst, sex

placebo (plah-see-bow) effect—an effect that causes a manipulation to work because the subjects believe it will work

place theory—a hearing theory that emphasizes the sensitivity of parts of the basilar membrane to different soundwave frequencies

pons—a hindbrain structure involved in vital and sensory functions and facial movements

positive correlation—a relationship in which the values of associated variables change in same direction

positive reinforcer—a stimulus that, if applied after a response, increases the probability that the response will be repeated

posttraumatic stress disorder—a mental disorder identified by anxiety, concentration problems, and reexperiences of the traumatic event

prejudice—a negative attitude toward members of a social group

prenatal stage—the period of development from conception to birth

preoperational stage—stage of cognitive development marked by symbolic thinking, egocentrism, and animism

primary mental abilities—Thurstone's seven intelligence factors

procedural memory—memory for learned responses and action patterns

projective test—a personality test in which subjects interpret ambiguous stimuli

proprioception (proh-pree-oh-sep-shun)—the sense of muscle movement

psychoactive drug—a drug that changes a person's feelings, thoughts, perceptions, or behavior

psychoanalytic (sye-koh-anna-litik) school—the school of psychology that emphasizes unconscious forces in behavior and mind

psychodynamic therapy—a type of treatment pioneered by Freud and Breuer that focuses on the individual's internal conflicts and personality

psychodynamic (sye-koh-die-nam-ik) view—the view that personality results from conflicting mental forces

psychology—the science of behavior and mental processes

psychophysics (sye-koh-fizz-iks)—the study of relationships between physical stimuli and sensations

psychosomatic (sye-koh-so-mat-ik) disorder—a physical symptom or disease caused in part by psychological factors

psychotherapy—the treatment of mental disorders based on psychological principles and methods

puberty—the period of rapid physical and sexual maturation during early adolescence

punisher—a stimulus that decreases the probability that a response will occur

quality circles—groups of employees who get together regularly to deal with work-related issues

reconstructive memory—a view that remembering is affected by schemas, personal beliefs, and inferences

reinforcer—a stimulus that increases the probability that a response will occur

reliability—the element of psychological testing concerned with the consistency of test scores

REM sleep—a sleep stage with rapid eye movements (REM), irregular fast waves, muscle inhibition, and dreaming

restoration theory—the view that sleep renews the brain's physical resources

reticular formation—a brain area for arousal, attention, sleep, and waking

retina—the inner surface of the eye; contains the rod and cone receptors, fovea, periphery, and blind spot

rods—visual receptor cells that respond to brightness and low light intensity

sample—a group of subjects participating in research

schizophrenia—a psychosis involving problems in judgment and reasoning, emotions, perceptions, and behavior

scientific method—the strategy of observation, theory formation, and hypothesis testing

sedatives—psychoactive depressant drugs with a calming or tranquilizing effect

selective attention—the ability to selectively focus on specific stimuli

self-actualization—the tendency to reach your full potential

self-efficacy (eff-uh-kuh-see)—beliefs people have about the effectiveness of their behavior

self-esteem—evaluations and feelings about oneself that influence the sense of personal worth

self-managed work teams—groups of workers who are responsible for assigning jobs to members, solving production problems, and selecting and training new members

self-perception theory—the view that attitudes form and change as a result of how you perceive your own behavior

self-report test—a personality test that asks questions about behavior, attitudes, and traits

self theory—Carl Rogers's theory of personality that included the self-concept and phenomenal field

semantic memory—the memory for factual knowledge based on verbal information

senescence (suh-ness-ens)—late adulthood or old age

sensation—the process of detecting and responding to sensory stimuli

sensory memory—the very brief, but nearly complete, first stage of memory for sensory data

sensory-motor stage—the stage of cognitive development in which thinking is dominated by immediate sensory impressions and bodily movements

sensory receptors—neurons in sensory organs specialized to detect physical stimuli

sexual response cycle—Masters and Johnson's four-stage process of sexual arousal involving excitement, plateau, orgasm, and resolution

shaping—the reinforcement of successive approximations to the correct response

short-term memory (STM)—the active, conscious, working stage of memory, with short duration and limited capacity

signal detection theory—a view of sensation that emphasizes decisions about stimulus signals and background noise

skin senses—the senses that detect temperature, pain, and pressure through touch

sleep apnea—a condition of disrupted or stopped breathing during sleep

sleep cycle—a sequence of mental and physiological changes involving NREM and REM sleep stages

social cognition—thinking about other people and the causes of their behavior

social exchange theory—the view that relationships are maintained by an exchange of reinforcements and costs

social facilitation (fah-sill-i-tay-shun)—improvement in an individual's behavior or performance due to the presence of others

social identity theory—the view that identification with social groups defines identity and behavior

social learning theory—a theory of learning based on the interaction of cognitive and environmental factors

social loafing—a loss of motivation and performance due to the presence of others

social motives—motives shaped by society such as achievement motivation

social psychology—the scientific study of social behavior

social support—the functions performed for a distressed individual by others

sociobiology—the study of the genetic foundations of social behavior according to the principles of evolution

somatoform (soh-matt-oh-form) disorders—mental disorders in which a physical symptom suggests a physical disorder for which no medical basis can be found

spontaneous recovery—the reappearance of an extinguished response without retraining

sports psychology—the application of psychological methods and principles to athletic performance

standardization—the specification of the conditions under which a psychological test is administered, scored, and interpreted

Stanford-Binet Intelligence Scale—an IQ test for people ages 2–adult

stereotypes—general beliefs about a group's characteristics, often reflecting unfavorable attitudes

stimulants—psychoactive drugs that excite or arouse the nervous system

stimulus discrimination—the selective response to a specific stimulus

stimulus generalization—a response to a stimulus that is similar to the conditioned stimulus

stimulus motives—motives in which a person seeks an increase in stimulation

stress—a relationship between a person and the environment that is appraised as threatening to well-being

stress management—techniques designed to reduce the bodily arousal associated with stress

stressor—the stimulus or event that is distressing

structuralism—the first school of psychology; studied the structure of the conscious mind through the method of introspection

structure-of-intellect model—Guilford's theory of intelligence based on 150 factors along three dimensions: contents, operations, and products

substance-related disorder—a mental disorder involving a maladaptive pattern of drug use

suggestibility—a state of openness and responsiveness to hypnotic suggestions

superego—the part of personality that controls moral judgment, conscience, and the ego-ideal

survey—a research method in which data are collected by means of interviews or questionnaires

temperament—inborn style of emotional and behavioral responding

temporal lobe—brain area involved in hearing, language comprehension, visual perception, and emotions

thalamus (thal-uh-muss)—a forebrain structure involved in sensation, movement, emotions, sleep and waking

theory of multiple intelligences—Gardner's theory based on seven distinct types of intelligence: linguistic, musical, logical-mathematical, spatial, bodily-kinesthetic, interpersonal, intrapersonal

thinking—the act of mentally representing information

traits—the stable characteristics of behavior, thinking, and emotion that distinguish individual personality

transformational grammar—a set of rules that determines how one sentence can be transformed into another

triarchic theory (try-ark-ick)—Sternberg's model based on three types of intelligence: componential, experiential, and contextual

trichromatic (try-crow-mat-ik) theory—explanation of color vision in terms of actions of three cone types

Type A behavior pattern—characteristics of competitive striving for achievement, hostility, and time urgency; associated with heart disease

Type B personality—lack of competitiveness, anger, and time urgency; associated with health promotion

type theory—Eysenck's theory of personality types based on three dimensions: extraversion-introversion, neuroticism, and psychoticism

unconditioned response—a reflexive response to an unconditioned stimulus

unconditioned stimulus—a stimulus that naturally elicits a reflexive response

validity—the element of psychological testing concerned with test accuracy

vestibular (ves-tib-you-ler) sense—the sense that controls bodily balance

Wechsler Adult Intelligence Scale–Revised—an IQ test for people 16 and older

wish fulfillment hypothesis—Freud's view that dreams express unconscious wishes, needs, and drives

Yerkes-Dodson law—the rule that states that performance increases as arousal increases up to a certain point; increases in arousal beyond that point result in performance decreases

Name Index

Subject Index

Photo Credits

Chapter 1

Pages v, 4 © Ogust/The Image Works
Pages 11, 12 Archives of the History of American Psychology/University of Akron
Page 21 © 1965 by Stanley Milgram. From the film *Obedience*, distributed by The Pennsylvania State University, PCR

Chapter 2

Page 34 McGill University
Pages vi, 36 Warren Anatomical Museum, Harvard Medical School
Page 39 Courtesy of Caltech

Chapter 3

Page 54 U. S. Navy
Page 59 AP/Wide World Photos

Chapter 4

Pages vii, 76 © Michael Heron/Woodfin Camp & Associates
Page 83 Rush-Presbyterian/St. Luke's Medical Center
Page 85 Brown Brothers
Page 90 © Ira Kirschenbaum/Stock, Boston, Inc.

Chapter 5

Pages vii, 99 Archives of the History of American Psychology/University of Akron
Page 103 Archives of the History of American Psychology/University of Akron
Page 106 © Ken Robert Buck/Stock, Boston, Inc.
Page 108 Archives of the History of American Psychology/University of Akron

Chapter 6

Page 123 THE BETTMANN ARCHIVE
Pages viii, 126 © Ellis Herwig/Stock, Boston, Inc.
Page 132 NASA
Page 139 University of Washington

Chapter 7

Pages viii, 151 Richard Younker
Page 157 *Michael Marsland*/Yale University, Office of Public Affairs

Chapter 8

Page 170 Dr. M. A. Ansary/Science Photo Library/Photo Researchers, Inc.
Page 171 © Michael Dwyer/Stock, Boston, Inc.
Pages ix, 173 © Topham/The Image Works
Page 176 Archives of the History of American Psychology/University of Akron
Page 181 © Myrleen Ferguson Cate/PhotoEdit
Page 189 AP/WIDE WORLD PHOTOS

Chapter 9

Page 194 © James Carroll/Stock, Boston, Inc.
Page 197 Harlow Primate Lab
Pages ix, 209 © 1972 Paul Ekman
Page 210 Courtesy Human Interaction Labortory/Photo by Linda Sue Scott

Chapter 10

Page 220 Archives of the History of American Psychology/University of Akron
Page 223 UPI/BETTMANN
Page 224 Archives of the History of American Psychology/University of Akron
Pages x, 232 © Ken Whitmore/Tony Stone Images

Chapter 11

Page 246 THE BETTMANN ARCHIVE
Page 257 © Will & Deni McIntyre/Photo Researchers, Inc.

Chapter 12

Page 264 AP/WIDE WORLD PHOTOS
Pages xi, 269 AP/WIDE WORLD PHOTOS
Page 271 The Edgar Allan Poe Museum of the Poe Foundation, Inc.
Page 274 National Institute of Mental Health/Laboratory of Psychology and Psychopathology
Page 278 THE BETTMANN ARCHIVE
Page 281 THE BETTMANN ARCHIVE

Chapter 13

Page 294 UPI/BETTMANN
Page 298 Photo by Eric Kroll/Courtesy of Alexandra Milgram
Page 303 © 1990 Burton McNeely
Pages xi, 306 © Elizabeth Crews/The Image Works

Chapter 14

Page 314 AutoAlliance International, Inc.
Page 320 Courtesy of Chrysler Corporation
Page 320 © Renee Lynn/Photo Researchers, Inc.
Page 322 © Elizabeth Crews/The Image Works
Page 326 Boston University Photo Services